D1282933

4.3.78

PITTSBURGH THEOLOGICAL MONOGRAPH SERIES

General Editor
DIKRAN Y. HADIDIAN

10

WORSHIP AND REFORMED THEOLOGY
The Liturgical Lessons of Mercersburg

WORSHIP AND
REFORMED THEOLOGY

The Liturgical Lessons of Mercersburg

by

JACK MARTIN MAXWELL

THE PICKWICK PRESS

PITTSBURGH, PENNSYLVANIA 78 9401 6

Library of Congress Cataloging in Publication Data

Maxwell, Jack Martin, 1939-
    Worship and reformed theology : the liturgical lessons
of Mercersburg.

    (Pittsburgh theological monograph series ; no. 10)
    Bibliography: p.
    Includes index.
    1. Liturgics--Reformed Church--History.
2. Mercersburg theology. I. Title. II. Series.
BX9427.M39   264'.04'2   75-45492
ISBN 0-915138-12-3

To my Mother and Father,

MR. AND MRS. A. V. MAXWELL,

for whom this works represents

the culmination of many hopes and dreams

CONTENTS

FOREWORD

Only half in jest a colleague once asked me, "What good thing can come out of Mercersburg?" His question reflects the relative obscurity which still surrounds this small community nestled in the beautiful hills of southwestern Pennsylvania. Conceivably the community is even more unknown and unnoticed today than it was a century and more ago, when, for twenty years, it gained no little scholarly notoriety in both American and European ecclesiastical circles.

It was Professor James Hastings Nichols who first introduced me to the significance of Mercersburg; and then he, in company with Professors Donald Macleod and Hugh Thompson Kerr, did much to guide my research and then shepherd this volume through the Ph.D. process at Princeton Theological Seminary.

Any litany of thanksgiving would be incomplete without the mention of Dr. Howard G. Hageman, President of New Brunswick Theological Seminary, who not only offered his good counsel and keen insights, but also made available his unpublished lectures on the history of the Dutch Reformed liturgies; and Professor George H. Bricker, Librarian and Dean of the Lancaster Theological Seminary, where most of this research was done, whose life-long love and knowledge of Mercersburg were invaluable. He and his staff, one of whom became my wife, graciously provided all the assistance one could wish. (If nothing else, that is one "good thing" which came "out of Mercersburg".)

The litany would likely end there were it not for this serendipity. Some months ago Professor Robert S. Paul became interested in my research and recommended it to Mr.

Dikran Y. Hadidian, editor of this series. I am grateful to the former for re-awakening my own enthusiasm for this essay, and to the latter for that excellent friendship and patient encouragement which seem to be the special grace of editors.

So, here it is--but not without the sometimes thankless effort and expertise of Kathy Herrin, who typed the manuscript, and Jean W. Hadidian, who proof read it.

All these and others still are remembered with gratitude.

INTRODUCTION

The purpose of this study is to examine the issues which
emerged during the Mercersburg liturgical controversy[1] with a
view toward establishing procedural and theoretical principles
for contemporary liturgical committees in the Reformed tradition. Essentially the latter designation--Reformed--is for
convenience only, since many of the conclusions to be drawn
from an investigation of the Mercersburg liturgical enterprise are pertinent in greater or lesser degrees to other
Protestant traditions generally.

The nature of the Mercersburg liturgical controversy and
the personalities involved in it will receive a fuller treatment in the chapters which follow; however, by way of general
introduction it may be said that the movement which spawned
the controversy centered in the Seminary of the German Reformed
Church, then located in Mercersburg, Pennsylvania. In 1840,
John Williamson Nevin became the Professor of Theology in that
institution; and in 1843, Philip Schaff was elected Professor
of Church History and Biblical Literature. Marshall College
was associated with the Seminary in Mercersburg until 1853,
when it relocated in Lancaster, Pennsylvania, and merged with
Franklin College. In 1851, Nevin resigned his position in the
Seminary and moved to Lancaster. Schaff left both the Semin-
ary and the German Reformed Church to become Professor of
Theological Encyclopaedia and Christian Symbolism in Union
Theological Seminary in 1870. The next year--1871--the German
Reformed Seminary followed Marshall College to Lancaster.

The German Reformed Church changed its name in 1867, and
was known as the Reformed Church in the United States until

1

1934, when it merged with the Evangelical Synod of North America to become the Evangelical and Reformed Church. In 1957, the Evangelical and Reformed Church merged with the Congregational Christian Church to form the United Church of Christ.

To be sure, few today would want to return either to the theological system or the philosophy of history meticulously hammered out on the relatively anonymous anvil of the German Reformed Church in mid-nineteenth century America. In these respects an investigation of Mercersburg is an interesting but principally antiquarian venture. Theological scholarship will always be indebted to Nevin and Schaff, if for no other reason than that through them German thought was first introduced into America. Certainly this alone merits Mercersburg a place in American historical consciousness.

The specific nature of the Mercersburg movement and its significance for nineteenth-century Protestant theology has already been explored. Luther J. Binkley's volume, *The Mercersburg Theology* (Sentinel Printing House, 1953), was the first of several significant studies which have appeared in the past two decades. Chief among these are the works by George W. Richards [*History of the Theological Seminary of the Reformed Church in the United States* (Rudisill & Co., 1952)] and James Hastings Nichols [*Romanticism in American Theology* (The University of Chicago Press, 1961) and *The Mercersburg Theology* (Oxford University Press, 1966)].

No systematic work has been undertaken, however, which centers in the principles and procedures which guided the liturgical committee of the German Reformed Church and by which the Liturgies were introduced to and used by the denomination. Such is the intent of this essay: to examine the issues—doctrinal, procedural, and political—confronting the liturgical committee of the German Reformed Church and the manner by which they were resolved. Both the issues themselves and the manner in which they were resolved yield certain procedural and theoretical principles. These will be found in the final chapter and may serve to guide the work of contemporary Reformed liturgical committees.

In order to accomplish this objective, certain other contextual matters will be detailed. For example, a brief look is taken at the founding of the German Reformed Seminary in Mercersburg, and the essential points of the Mercersburg theology in so far as they pertain to the liturgical problems discussed. Before examining the composition and proceedings of the liturgical committee, the liturgical alternatives available to the denomination are presented. Concluding the historical investigation is an abbreviated look at the *Directory of Worship* and the Peace Movement, again, only in so far as they were influenced by and reflected the procedures and products of the original liturgical committee of the Eastern Synod. The final chapter highlights and summarizes the issues and the liturgical methodology with a view toward establishing procedural and theoretical principles by which contemporary Reformed liturgical committees may benefit from Mercersburg's experience. If the reader is uninterested in the Mercersburg story, but anxious to learn its lessons, he or she should begin with chapter VIII.

Mercersburg is in many respects a paradigm of Reformed liturgical procedures. Whereas a desire for worship reform was evident within the denomination before the Mercersburg movement was an accomplished fact, serious liturgical activity did not begin until the theological "system", as it came to be articulated by Nevin and Schaff, demanded a liturgical expression. The point is that serious theological and historical study preceded the Liturgies produced by the German Reformed

Church and made them imperative. In no sense were these Liturgies created in a vacuum; rather biblical, historical, and sociological principles were carefully articulated before the committee attempted to compose a liturgy.

The committee itself is paradigmatic. While certain individuals—particularly Philip Schaff—were primarily responsible for the Provisional Liturgy and the *Order of Worship*, the Liturgies were nevertheless the product of a committee and reflect that characteristic aspect of Reformed polity. Furthermore, all the advantages and disadvantages of the manner in which a liturgy must make its way through the constitutional processes of Reformed denominational structures and then be introduced to the constituency are clearly played out in the Mercersburg drama. Mercersburg has not a little to tell the contemporary Reformed tradition about such matters as the sort of individual who should be on a liturgical committee, the procedures that the committee should follow, the skills required in leading a liturgy through the maze of polity, and then of introducing it successfully to the people in their local churches. These "lessons" may seem elementary; but Mercersburg offers impressive testimony to the fact that they make a definitive difference in the outcome of any liturgical venture.

The temptation which Mercersburg faced is paradigmatic also—*viz.*, the seductive lure of liturgical romanticism. Can the insights afforded by an examination of the liturgical past be employed without permitting the liturgical present to become an antiquarian exercise in monastic irrelevance? Both the nature of the liturgiologist and the constituency of a liturgical committee will be discussed in this connection.

In two significant respects Mercersburg is not a paradigm. First, the sociological: the German Reformed Church

in the nineteenth century was a small, recently immigrated denomination. The transition from German to English was essentially an accomplished fact by the mid-nineteenth century;
however, there remained a sufficient number of German-speaking
members to necessitate editions of the Liturgies and hymnbooks
in that language. The Liturgies continued to provide services
for the reception of immigrants and forms for use at sea.
Parishes were small and rural; the constituency was predominantly agrarian. Thus, while the sociological circumstances
of the German Reformed Church are certainly dissimilar to contemporary urban living, the principle that a liturgy should
maintain continuity with the past and yet be indigenous is indeed a paradigm.

Second, the theological system developed by Nevin and
Schaff is no longer held in quite the same way today. As
Hugh Thompson Kerr has described it: Mercersburg operated
"on a theological consensus ('Reformed', Heidelberg, etc.) of
sin-mercy-response model which implied man's dependence on a
sovereign God; hence faith and life issues for all 'Mercers-
burgers' reflected *order, harmony, symmetry, consensus,* since
these were (presumably) *revealed* by God, in the Bible and the
created world, through Jesus Christ, via the Holy Spirit, in
the Church and sacraments; and worship was the corporate
demonstration of all these assumptions. *Today* almost none
of these items pertains to current liturgical (or theological)
discussion; not because they have been proved untrue or false,
but because we are interested in other things and the traditional *assumptions* no longer hold."[2] As a "school" Mercersburg did not perpetuate itself, nor did it intend to; yet,
however far contemporary theological interest may have moved
beyond Mercersburg, Nevin and Schaff established and demonstrated the imperative practical and theoretical relationship
between theology and liturgy.

The specific liturgical issues which Mercersburg confronted are as real and often as unresolved today as they were a century ago: the relationship between Word and Sacraments, free and fixed prayer, the universal and the indigenous. These problems are not always unique, and the solutions posed by Mercersburg are frequently more instructive in what is not defensible than in what is sound liturgical procedure. For this reason the essay is sub-titled, "The Liturgical *Lessons* of Mercersburg". Yet, when all is said and done, Mercersburg remains a Reformed liturgical model. The personalities, principles, and procedures that constitute the paradigm are detailed in the pages which follow.

NOTES TO THE INTRODUCTION

1. Approximate dates: 1848–1884.

2. Personal correspondence dated June 23, 1968.

CHAPTER I

The Mercersburg Movement

Between the years 1840 and 1884 an important drama was acted out upon the relatively small stage of the German Reformed Church in America. The spotlight focused primarily upon its Seminary located in Mercersburg, Pennsylvania, and its two leaders, John Williamson Nevin and Philip Schaff. Other personalities made their appearances, however, in roles more or less central to the story; and the scene changed from time to time to include brief glances at Philadelphia, Baltimore, Frederick City, Collegeville, Myerstown, Dayton, London, and Strawberry Ridge.

Within the forty-four years which are to be chronicled in the following chapters, the period of specific interest spans particularly the two decades, 1849-1869. John Henry Augustus Bomberger, a young leader of the denomination, first articulated a series of principles for liturgical revision before the Synod of Norristown in 1849. Twenty years and a bitter controversy later the General Synod of Philadelphia (1869) marked the last serious attempt by those opposed to the Mercersburg liturgies to defeat them. As the drama unfolds the reader will witness a liturgical committee attempting to determine what a Reformed liturgy should be, the tedium of composition, the politics of publishing the Provisional Liturgy of 1857, and the strategy of introducing it to a surprised denomination. Not a few members of the committee found their own liturgical opinions changing through

the years, and the widespread desire for a revision of the
Provisional Liturgy resulted in the *Order of Worship* in 1866.

That the two decades of primary concern may better be
understood, an abbreviated examination of certain contextual
material ought to be made.

Founding of the Seminary

After several false starts, the Seminary of the German
Reformed Church opened its doors in Carlisle, Pennsylvania, in
1825, with Lewis Mayer as its first president and only professor. Relations between Mayer and Dickinson College, whose
facilities he and his students used, were never cordial; so
the Seminary was moved to York in 1829. In 1831 a classical
school was founded under the direction of Frederick Augustus
Rauch; however, it was soon moved from York to Mercersburg
and renamed Marshall College, with Rauch as its first president. Subsequently the Seminary joined the College in Mercersburg, with Mayer still at its head; but after a year of failing health and growing disagreements with Rauch, Mayer resigned in 1839, leaving Rauch in charge of both institutions.

Whereas Rauch and Mayer were of totally different theological stripes, such was not the case with Rauch and his new
colleague, John Williamson Nevin. Nevin arrived in Mercersburg in 1840 and found in Rauch a close personal and intellectual friend. As Richards points out, each man had arrived
at similar conclusions through different means. Nevin was
already "a keen student of the flowering German intellectual
romanticism, finding in it the philosophical confirmation of
his theological conviction, while Rauch, on his part, by
philosophical discipline had arrived at theological triumph"--

Nevin through Schleiermacher and Rauch through Hegel.[1] The
specific degree to which Rauch influenced Nevin intellectually
is debatable. Certainly Nevin was open to anything German and
philosophical in 1840; however, Rauch's death one year after
Nevin's arrival in Mercersburg mitigates against any formative
influence. "Except in the writings of Dr. E. V. Gerhart, it
is difficult to discern the influence of Rauch's thought in
the subsequent theology of the seminary, but his spiritual
vision is markedly present. It was acknowledged by Nevin and
it was represented in the general character of the theology
of the seminary throughout the nineteenth century."[2]

John Williamson Nevin

The career of John Williamson Nevin is integral to the
whole of this thesis, and his development at various stages
will be traced at the appropriate points; however, the main
circumstances of his life and his relationship to the seminary
are in order here. The oldest of nine children, Nevin was
born February 20, 1803, on a farm near Shippensburg, Pennsylvania. His father, John Nevin, was a graduate of Dickinson
College but remained a farmer all his life. The family were
members of the Middle Spring Presbyterian Church, and there
John Williamson was baptized.

His formal education was taken at Union College, Schenec-
tady, New York, originally Dutch Reformed but chartered in
1795 as an inter-denominational institution.[3] Nevin was
rarely certain of his spiritual status, it seems, and his
conversion during a religious revival in his junior year
raised more questions than it answered. If nothing else, however, it did "provide the data of personal experience which he

was to use later in dealing with that subject" [i.e., *The Anxious Bench* and other anti-revivalistic writings].[4]

At eighteen Nevin had obtained his degree, a Phi Beta Kappa key, and a case of "acute dyspepsia, which defied various diets and cures and left him very depressed psychologically".[5] He "retired" to his father's farm and spent the next two years regaining his physical and emotional health. At the end of this time, still feeling uncertain of his piety and his longevity, yet determined to attempt the ministry, he entered Princeton Theological Seminary in 1823 at the age of twenty.

Nevin reached Princeton at a time when that seminary had attained first rank among theological schools. Its two senior professors, Archibald Alexander and Samuel Miller, were in their prime; and their young colleague, Charles Hodge, was just then coming into his own. In spite of the vocational indecision which marked Nevin's five years in Princeton, he was able to say, nevertheless, "I look back upon my days spent at Princeton as, in some respects, the most pleasant part of my life."[6] During his three undergraduate years in this "beleaguered citadel of orthodoxy" Nevin learned his theology from Alexander, whose text was Francis Turretin's Latin *Institutes*, his history from Miller, whose text was Mosheim, and his languages from Hodge.[7] Upon graduation in 1826 Nevin remained to teach Hebrew during the two-year sabbatical of the man who was later to become his chief critic in the Presbyterian Church, Charles Hodge.

Before leaving Princeton in 1828 Nevin was approached by Dr. Herron, president of the board of directors of Western Theological Seminary, then located in Allegheny City, a Pittsburgh suburb. The new seminary was not yet ready, however, and this afforded Nevin another restful interim on the farm.

He was licensed to preach by the Presbytery of Carlisle on
October 2, 1828; and with the exception of periodic preaching in the area, the next fourteen months were spent in "a
general vacation from all regular study".[8] It was not until
December, 1829, that Nevin "crossed the mountains, and joined
Dr. Halsey in the work of organizing the new Western Theological Seminary".[9]

The decade in Pittsburgh provided Nevin time for reflection, especially upon his past education and his present
educational needs. Chief among the several lacuna he con-
fesses is the absence of any sense of history as living,
dynamic process. "First of all, I may say, there was an
utter want of proper *historical* culture in all my thinking
at this time. I had not yet awakened at all to the appre-
hension of what history necessarily is for the life of humanity and the moral world in every view. It was, for me, still a
system only of dead outward facts."[10] Miller and Mosheim left
Nevin "greatly in need of historical emancipation and enlargement".[11]

This lack of historical sensitivity created "a corresponding deficiency in all my theological thinking, as it stood at
this time".[12] His understanding of revelation Nevin describes
as "the old mechanical theory"; and this, in turn, influenced
his Christology. Shorn of his proper historical character,
Nevin's Christ was "made to stand forth *suddenly* among men...
like an abrupt apparition from heaven, in no communication with
the life of the world as it was before".[13] He was not totally
insensitive to the person of Christ; yet he "was not able to
go far enough at all, in this way of seeing in Him the organic
wholeness and fulness of the universal economy of grace".[14]
As will be shown in the pages to follow, Nevin sums up his
theological deficiencies when he writes:

> What I lacked, lies all in the theological
> architecture of the Apostles' Creed. But,
> strange to say, with all my learning I had
> not, even at this time, *learned* the Creed.
> In the whole of my five years at Princeton,
> I do not remember ever to have heard it used
> there as an act of worship. It was, for me,
> a sealed mystery still in large part. I had
> not found the key to its hidden, all-compre-
> hensive and all-glorious sense.[15]

By the end of his Pittsburgh sojourn Nevin had still not
appropriated the Creed as fully as he was to do in the early
Mercersburg years, when it became the norm for all his theology; and in 1840 he still considered himself to be "Low
Church", although his "first glimpse...of what the church
spirit really means came...unexpectedly from looking into a
volume of the Oxford Tracts..."[16] Nevin did discover Neander
before leaving Pittsburgh; however, the full and considerable
implications of this were to remain latent until his move to
Mercersburg. The years, 1830-1840, were important ones because they prepared Nevin for the substantial change his
thinking was to undergo in the twenty years to follow. Perhaps only in retrospect could one predict this theological
transformation, for upon his arrival in Mercersburg he was
still "a conservative Irish evangelical, molded by Princeton
scholasticism, strong for private-judgment biblicism and a
vigorous promoter of various evangelistic and moralistic
causes".[17]

Nevin's social stand on temperance and anti-slavery had
not won him an abundance of friends in Pittsburgh. The
seminary was in desperate financial condition and owed Nevin
a considerable sum in back salary. Its future was seriously
in doubt, and Nevin was clearly available for other ventures
when he was visited by Schneck and Fisher with a call to

become Mayer's successor at Mercersburg. After some months of deliberation and consultation with Alexander and Miller, Nevin accepted the call and moved to Mercersburg in the spring of 1840. The year he spent with Rauch before the latter's death completed Nevin's introduction to German thought--as will be shown in more detail below--and made him a man of whom Philip Schaff, his future colleague, could write: "I think I could not have a better colleague than Dr. Nevin. I feared I might not find sympathy in him for my views of the church; but I discover that he occupies essentially the same ground that I do and confirms me in my position. He is filled with ideas of German theology."[18]

It is small wonder that the students and townsfolk of Mercersburg held a parade on the occasion of Schaff's advent; and John Nevin was likely the happiest of them all, for since Rauch's death he had been in sole charge of the seminary, save for an instructor in Hebrew, and served at the same time as the President of Marshall College.[19]

Philip Schaff

A special meeting of synod was called for January 24, 1843, to elect a German professor as successor to Rauch. The spunk of this small Reformed denomination in shooting for the professorial stars must be admired; however, their success in winning Nevin gave them courage. The decision was to extend a call to F. W. Krummacher of Elberfeld, "pastor of the largest Reformed congregation in Germany, and...one of the most eloquent pulpit orators of the nineteenth century".[20] Benjamin S. Schneck and Theodore L. Hoffeditz were elected to prosecute the call, which they did during the summer of

1843. Krummacher appeared to be favorably disposed and debated
the move for four weeks before declining for reasons of age and
a desire to remain in the pulpit. Schneck and Hoffeditz reported Krummacher's decision to the synod of 1843, but brought
with their report a recommendation that a suitable alternative
would be Philip Schaff, a young professor in the University of
Berlin. He had been highly commended by Neander and Krummacher,
and was straightway elected by synod, "only one vote being cast
against him, which was done out of fear lest some German neology
might through him find an entrance into our Church".[21]

Schaff was born January 1, 1819, near Chur in eastern
Switzerland. At fifteen he entered the academy at Kornthal,
in Württemberg.

> Here, in his first year and amid the pangs of
> homesickness, young Schaf[22] experienced a con-
> version experience of the pietist sort and was
> confirmed by the Lutheran village pastor. He
> now determined to prepare for the ministry,
> relinquishing his previous ambition to be a
> poet. For the rest of his life he was to be
> characterized by the fervor of Württemburg
> pietism and by the heightened eschatological
> expectation especially characteristic of
> Kornthal.[23]

After five years in Kornthal Schaff moved seven miles to
Stuttgart, where he entered the gymnasium. In 1837 he matricu-
lated at the University of Tübingen, center of Hegelianism and
home of Ferdinand Christian Baur. According to Nichols, Baur
was "the first to apply rigorously to the documents of early
Christianity the critical nineteenth-century methods of
general historical and literary analysis. He revolutionized
the study both of the New Testament and of early church history".[24] Tübingen also introduced Schaff to Isaac Dorner,

later claimed by both sides in the Mercersburg liturgical dispute. Dorner had received his education under Hegel and Schleiermacher, and was ideally suited for students like Schaff "who wished to master the new critical and speculative problems without losing their Christian faith".[25]

From Tübingen Schaff went first to Halle, where he lived for a time with Professor F. A. G. Tholuck; then on to the University of Berlin. Here he completed his doctorate and became a licentiate in theology. Undoubtedly the most significant opportunity Berlin afforded Schaff was an association with Neander, the historian of whom Nevin wrote: "How much I owe him in the way of excitement, impulse, suggestion, knowledge, both literary and religious, reaching onward into all my later life, is more than I can pretend to explain; for it is in truth more than I have power to understand."[26]

In the fall of 1843 Philip Schaff accepted a call to become the second professor in a struggling seminary of the German Reformed Church located in Mercersburg, Pennsylvania, and to become the colleague of one whose intellectual route had been radically different from his own, but whose destination was remarkably similar. Schaff was ordained April 12, 1844; then he spent six weeks in England, "meeting personally Pusey and Newman of the high-churchmen and Stanley and Jowett of the broad-churchmen".[27] He first set foot on American soil at the New York port, July 28, 1844. There he was met by B. C. Wolff of Easton, Pennsylvania; and that begins another tale.

New Theory of History

The Anxious Bench

If there were a single omen of the future controversy to emerge from Mercersburg, it was Nevin's pamphlet, *The Anxious Bench*, published in 1843.[28] In Pittsburgh Nevin cast his lot with the old school Presbyterians against the "new-measures" revivalism and its awesome "anxious bench". "For him, as for his Princeton teachers, the greatest danger was theological-- the implication in the whole technique that sinners had the inherent powers of decision and self-conversion or that revivalists could manipulate the Holy Spirit. Such denials of God's free sovereignty in man's redemption were the very hinge of the new-school heresy."[29]

Within two years after his arrival in Mercersburg Nevin was debating the issue of revivals with John Winebrenner in *The Weekly Messenger*. The issue crystalized in the village of Mercersburg itself, when the Reformed congregation there extended a call to the Rev. William Ramsey, a new-measures Presbyterian from Philadelphia and a former classmate of Nevin in Princeton. Ramsey preached fervently in Mercersburg that Sunday morning in 1842, and after the sermon, "believing that he was master of the situation, he invited all who desired the prayers of the Church to present themselves before the altar".[30] The congregation was quite taken with Ramsey and the consistory extended him a call in spite of Nevin's warning that emotionalism led to self-deception. Nevin went even farther and wrote to Ramsey, urging him to accept the call, but pointing out "that if he came to Mercersburg, it would be necessary for him to give up his new-measures and adopt the catechetical system in vogue in the Reformed Church, else they could not work together harmoniously and he might be obliged to stand in his way".[31] Ramsey refused the call and blamed Nevin. The congregation was disturbed and disappointed, but they chose to listen to Nevin. It was a different matter entirely with the students of the Seminary, however, and Nevin answered their opposition to his position in a series of lectures on "new measures". Later, in a desire to make his position clear to the denomination, he developed these lectures into *The Anxious Bench*.

The explicit design of the tract "is to show that the Anxious Bench, and the system to which it belongs, have no claim to be considered either salutary or safe in the service of religion. It is believed, that instead of promoting the cause of true vital godliness, they adapted to hinder its progress."[32] The presumed success of the anxious bench is better attributed to the power of fear than to the power of the Holy Spirit, Nevin argued, and fear can be engendered by the most inadequate and unscrupulous minister. In short, new-measures revivalists are religious "quacks", whose concern with techniques of emotional manipulation must inevitably mean that "preaching will become shallow. The catechism... will be shorn of its honor and force. Education may be considered to some extent necessary for the work of the ministry, but in fact no great care will be felt to have it either thorough or complete."[33]

Nevin's position is summarized by Nichols: "The Kingdom of God was not advanced by such methods [as the anxious bench], but rather by a teaching ministry, by preaching with light and unction, by faithful systematic instruction, by pastoral visitation, church discipline, and zeal for holiness --what Nevin called the 'system of the catechism'."[34] This argument was favorably received by journalistic organs of the

Presbyterian, Dutch Reformed, and Lutheran denominations; but
it drew expected criticism from Methodist papers. More significant, perhaps, is the widespread support Nevin received from
his own denomination, especially from the likes of Berg, J. H.
A. Bomberger, and J. I. Good, who were later to become his
chief critics.

Although *The Anxious Bench* and Nevin's sermon on "Catholic
Unity", delivered before the Triennial Convention of the Dutch
and German Reformed Churches in 1844, were important first
steps in Mercersburg's articulation of the doctrine of the
church, they also prepared the way for Schaff's thesis, *The
Principle of Protestantism as Related to the Present State of
the Church*,[35] and the theory of history it sought to develop.
When the provincial sectarianism of American Protestantism in
the nineteenth century is recalled, one is hardly surprised
that an understanding of the church as "the mother of all her
children, imparting her life to them",[36] rather than as the
mechanically assembled aggregate of individual parts, would
necessitate a fresh approach to ecclesiastical history.

"Catholic Unity"

On August 5, 1844, Philip Schaff and B. C. Wolff departed
New York for Easton, Pennsylvania, then across the Pennsylvania
hills to Harrisburg and the Triennial Convention.[37] Here
Schaff met Nevin and first learned that in him he would find
an intellectual friend. Nevin's sermon, "Catholic Unity",[38]
was based on Ephesians 4:4-6, and was divided into two parts:
"the first treats of the Nature and Constitution of this Holy
Catholic Church, and the second of the Duty of Christians as
it regards the unity, by which it is declared to be thus Cath-

olic, and Holy, and True."[39] Not a little of Nevin's later
theology, especially as regards the Eucharist, is foreshadowed
in this keynote sermon: through the Lord's Supper believers
have a mystical union "with the entire humanity of Christ",
Nevin argued. "Partaking in this way of one and the same
life of Christ, Christians are vitally related and joined together as one great spiritual whole; and this whole is the
Church. The Church, therefore, is His Body, the fullness of
Him that filleth all in all. The union by which it is held
together, through all ages, is organic."[40] As Nichols observes, Nevin's statement that the unity of the visible church
is the "most important interest in the world" was more than a
"pardonable homiletical overemphasis". Rather, "this ecumenical thrust was to be a main feature of the Mercersburg movement".[41]

The Principle of Protestantism

The Synod of Allentown convened October 17, 1844, and
featured a stirring sermon by Joseph F. Berg, retiring president of Synod, distinguished minister of the Race Street congregation in Philadelphia, and full-time antagonist of Roman
Catholicism. Berg's sermon was, in most respects, "a perfect
reflection of current denominational opinion".[42] In brief,
he argued for a strong denominational spirit and a Reformed
self-consciousness that admitted no need of further reformation. After its adjournment in Allentown, Synod moved to
Reading for Schaff's inaugural address, delivered on October
24, 1844. At the conclusion of his long, German lecture entitled *Das Princip des Protestantismus*, "even the most modest
member of the Synod could readily decipher that the glorious

Berg and the untried Schaff were scarcely striking the same themes".[43]

Berg's static orthodoxy, which pictured the doctrines of the Reformation leaping across the centuries from apostolic times and landing untainted in the theological lap of Martin Luther, encountered in Schaff a theory of history as dynamic development, with which it was simply not prepared to deal. Berg sincerely believed that once one admitted any connection between Protestantism and Medieval Catholicism, the entire position of Rome must be conceded.

As untenable as Berg's position was, he vociferously defended it in the pages of his own *Protestant Banner* and in those of the *Weekly Messenger*, official voice of the denomination; thus the first open controversy was underway. After Berg accused the Mercersburg professors of heresy--based on their affirmation of the spiritual real presence--both he and Schaff rushed their pronouncements into print, and the battle consumed four days during the Synod of York in 1845. The professors were vindicated by a decisive vote of forty to three; however, the issue was far from settled.[44] Berg continued the debate with Nevin in the *Weekly Messenger* throughout 1847 and 1848, claiming that Nevin was "on the high road to Rome, because you believe, with Romanists, in divine sacraments and a supernatural church". Nevin retorted with his customary tact that if Berg did not believe in those very things, then he was keeping company with "all Socinians, Rationalists, and Unitarians [who] have no faith whatever in the Holy Catholic Church, as anything better than a mere human institution".[45]

Berg concluded at last that he did not receive the support he felt he deserved from either the denomination or the Philadelphia Classis, thus he resigned his pastorate and

on March 14, 1851, preached his farewell sermon on "Jehovah
Nissi". "The sermon was a bitter attack on the tendencies,
as he conceived them, in the theological views of the Mer-
cersburg professors."[46] A substantial portion of the Race
Street congregation withdrew to Berg's new charge, the Second
Dutch Reformed Church in Philadelphia. Here he remained un-
til 1861, when he became Professor of Didactic and Polemic
Theology in the New Brunswick Seminary of the Dutch Reformed
Church. Nevin shed few tears. In his review of Berg's
"Farewell Words" to the Race Street congregation Nevin
chortled: "The mountain in labor has once more given birth
to a ridiculous mouse."[47]

The Principle of Protestantism, with its lengthy introduction by translator Nevin, along with "Catholic Unity",
made an imposing volume; and four years after its publication
Nevin could claim that no one had yet answered it scientifi-
cally.[48] Even though Schaff's son later claimed that his
father "was never conscious that he had produced anything
original or distinctive",[49] the work was certainly both an
original and distinctive intrusion into the American ecclesiastical scene. It consists of two major parts. In the first,
Schaff seeks to establish the fact that the lineage of the two
central doctrines of Protestantism--the doctrine of the
supreme authority of Scripture and the doctrine of justification by grace through faith--can be traced through the
Middle Ages. Protestantism is thus seen not as an abrupt
revolution, but as a *stage* in a process of historical development. Part II seeks to move beyond the conventional
Protestant principles of the Bible and justification by grace,
since these principles have historically degenerated into the
"diseases" of "rationalism--or one-sided theoretic subjectivism"--and "sectarianism--or one-sided practical subjectivism."

Into the static orthodoxy of Protestantism Schaff injected
"the principle of movement, of progress in the history of the
church; progress, not such as may go beyond the Bible and
Christianity, but such as consists in an *ever-extending
knowledge* of the Bible itself, and an *ever-deepening appropriation* of Christianity as the power of a divine life, which
is destined to make *all* things new."[50] In sum: "The principle of Protestantism, if we may compress the formula, is the
principle of a growing, corporate, biblical tradition."[51]

Puseyism was a reaction to the "diseases" of Protestantism; and while Schaff acknowledges Pusey's appreciation of
tradition and his high doctrine of the church, he argues that
the Oxford Movement is not the answer, as it looks backward
and does not understand the significance of the Reformation.
Rather the remedy is a Protestant or Evangelical Catholicism.
This synthesis was not *Reformation* Protestantism and Roman
Catholicism, for Schaff clearly demonstrated that later
Protestantism, with its subjectivism, doctrinal rationalism,
sectarianism, and political radicalism, would have been
vigorously opposed to the Reformers themselves. "The synthesis
Schaff was urging, consequently, seemed rather to be a syn-
thesis of pseudo-Protestant autonomy and of arbitrary Roman
Catholic heteronomy, and in fact to be very close to the
original intention of the Reformers."[52]

In spite of certain unresolved questions in *The Principle
of Protestantism*, Nichols concludes that "Schaff opened to
American Protestants vast historical perspectives, by which
they might learn to know themselves better and understand
better their relations to other Christians....The principle
of historical development, with all its ambiguities, was cast
as a bridge of understanding across otherwise unbridgeable
chasms to other forms of Christianity."[53] Even more than

this, Schaff opened the doors to the liturgical treasures of early and medieval Christianity, and, as shall be shown in the pages to follow, the liturgies of Mercersburg drew heavily from these ancient storehouses.

Nevin entered the fray in Schaff's defense and wrote numerous articles in the *Mercersburg Review*. Among the more important of these are the series on "Early Christianity"[54] and "Cyprian".[55] As one would imagine, Nevin's argument was decidedly anti-Puritan, historically and theologically, and that brings us directly to a discussion of the Mercersburg theology.

Mercersburg Theology

There is a sense in which Mercersburg theology began in protest against what Richards has called "erroneous doctrines and practices in the American churches from Catholicism to Unitarianism, including Puritanism, Methodism, and Anabaptism".[56] As has been shown above, revivalism and sectarianism received solar-plexus blows from both Nevin and Schaff; and, while their detractors would have one believe that the professors were verging on Romanism, both Rome and Oxford received ample historical and theological criticism from Mercersburg. If protest was its beginning, Mercersburg theology soon moved beyond it to a positive doctrinal position.

The "System"

The theology of Mercersburg is not directly at issue in this essay; yet a description of its leading tenets is in order,

since the project is concerned with the manner in which the
subsequent liturgies of Mercersburg articulated in devotional
language the doctrinal positions previously established. No
one of the contemporary scholars who examine Mercersburg theology in detail has called it a "system"; however, each does
point out that from the central doctrine of the Incarnation,
the remaining emphases fall quite logically and necessarily
into line. Nevin's thought may be characterized as a series
of Chinese boxes; the largest one containing all the others
is the "glorified humanity" of Christ, which "continues to be
the only medium of gracious communication from God to mankind,
and of all real approach of man to God, and fellowship with
him".[57]

> From this theory of the person and work of
> Christ logically followed the conception of
> the *Church* as being the organic continuation
> of the divine-human life of Christ in time
> for the salvation of men; and of the *Holy
> Ghost* as the bearer, through all ages, of
> Christ, the true life, and as the condition
> of the helpless sinner participating in His
> grace; of the *sacraments* as the organs of
> the Church, or means of grace, by which men
> are made partakers of the life of Christ;
> of *regeneration* as the inception of divine
> power of the new life in the act of transi-
> tion from the state of fallen nature to the
> sphere of the new creation; of *conversion*
> as the voluntary act of the conscious sub-
> ject, acknowledging and submitting, in
> contrition of heart, to the authority of
> the spiritual kingdom in which he was
> brought by baptism; of *justification* as
> the act of God by which the believing
> sinner is made righteous in Christ; of
> *worship* as the common act of the congrega-
> tion of believers offering themselves, in
> union with Christ's glorious merits, on
> the altar of the gospel, in sacramental
> acts, in confession, prayer, and praise;

of *hades* as an imperfect state, intermediate
between death and the resurrection; and of
the *resurrection* as the consummation of the
regenerated life in the triumph of the entire
man, soul and body, over sin and all the
powers of darkness.[58] [*Italics mine.*]

Doctrine of the Incarnation

"The organizing principle of Nevin's theology is unmis-
takably the Incarnation."[59] Here alone is redemption to be
found, for only in the glorified humanity of Christ can the
necessary union between God and man take place. Nevin made
much of Paul's discussion of the First and Second Adams, sum-
ming up the whole of history in their respective humanities.
His argument for the organic nature of mankind's relationship
with Adam and Christ drew an argument from Hodge, whose position was that the guilt of Adam and the redemption of Christ
were both imputed legalistically and arbitrarily. The prevailing orthodox view of the crucifixion was substitutionary
and expiatory. Against this Nevin contended that as man is
in and identified with Adam's guilt, so he is in and identified with Christ's perfect life; and this latter identification
results in a "mystical union", "the true and actual formation
of Christ's life into the souls of His people".[60]
So theologically encompassing was Nevin's view of the
Incarnation that he understood the Atonement only in light of
it, and this seeming depreciation brought him not a few critics.
For twenty years and more Nevin attempted to make the relationship between Incarnation and Atonement clear. In commenting
on Taylor Lewis' review of the Mercersburg school, Nevin disagreed vigorously when Lewis ranked the Atonement of greater
importance. "The true order is, the mystery of the Incarnation

first, and then the Atonement...."[61] The April and May, 1868,
issues of the *Weekly Messenger* contain six articles by Nevin
on the "Church Movement". In this series he takes the opportunity afforded by H. J. Rütenik's[62] criticism of *The Order
of Worship* to argue the Incarnation again. He asserts once
more that "the true ground principle of Christianity...is not
Christ's death, but His incarnation; which not only comes before the atonement, but forms the basis also of its universal
possibility and power".[63] In the third article[64] Nevin writes
that those who focus exclusively on Atonement must conclude
that Incarnation was solely for the purpose of the crucifixion
and that had Adam not sinned, there would have been no Incarnation. "But who may not see, that this is at once to sink the
constitution of Christ's person to the character of being *means*
merely for an end not comprehended in His person, an end hold-
ing out of Himself and beyond Himself altogether?" Nevin
readily agrees that there could be no salvation apart from the
death and resurrection of Christ; "but still neither His death
nor His resurrection, formed the original root of this salvation. That lay, first of all, in the constitution of His own
glorious person...."[65] Nevin would not wish to make any
qualitative comparison of the Incarnation and Atonement; he
would simply insist that the latter is *in* the former. Indeed,
the mystical union between God and man, which *is* the Incarnation, is at the same time the "at-one-ment", as Apple was to
write in his description of Mercersburg theology.[66]

Doctrine of the Church

From this position on the Incarnation the step is small
to Mercersburg's understanding of the Church, for the one is

a logical development of the other. "If the central doctrine
of the Mercersburg Theology was Christology, then the most
important corollary of this view was the doctrine of the
Church."[67] In fact, Nichols contends that "it is the high-
church or catholicizing tendency within the framework of
German idealism and historical thought which is the characteristic note of Mercersburg theology".[68] It was primarily
with the church that *The Anxious Bench*, "Catholic Unity", and
The Principle of Protestantism were concerned. "To Nevin it
had become unthinkable to discuss the church as an aggregation
of believers brought together by external means into a pious
sodality. The church, he said emphatically, 'is truly the
mother of all her children. They do not impart life to her,
but she imparts life to them.'"[69]

Nevin gave a new importance to the visible dimension of
the church, but changed the familiar categories from "visible"
and "invisible" and discussed instead the "ideal" and the
"actual" church. These categories better permitted Mercersburg to articulate its understanding of the church as dynamic
rather than static, as germinating and gestating, seeking
ever to reach its full and ideal potential as the visible
Body of Christ. The "actual" church is imperfect and only
a reflection of the "ideal"; yet

> within the actual church, however imperfect
> it may be, the 'hidden force' of the ideal
> church struggles to realize itself. Hence
> if the visible church of history is not
> always perfect, it is always the true
> church; for it is the living body in which
> the ideal church struggles to realize its
> true nature, and its ministries are peren-
> nially valid.[70]

This "eschatological" sense of the church as *becoming* provided the impetus for Mercersburg's "evangelical-catholicity" It represented Schaff's "synthesis"; while for Nevin the "last phase of the Incarnation would be found when the ideal church would become the actual church, the Lord would return, and the saints would be raised in glory to praise him".[71]

The church, understood in its ideal catholicity, is an object of faith; and Nevin could not long discuss the church without arguing the Apostles' Creed as well. The Creed makes the church an objective yet supernatural fact which men are required to affirm as a necessary part of the Christian faith. According to Nevin, the church is the "connecting medium between all that goes before and all that follows after". The grace of Christ in his birth, life, death, resurrection, and ascension "is the same that then discharges its full stream into the bosom of the Church, and that is poured forth from this again in the benefits of redemption, for the remission of sins onward to the life everlasting".[72]

Doctrine of the Sacraments

The Eucharist

As Mercersburg's doctrine of the church is a logical corollary to the doctrine of the Incarnation, so does the doctrine of the sacraments logically emerge from the doctrine of the church. So important are the sacraments that Nichols has observed: "The Mercersburg movement might be called essentially a sacramental, more particularly a Eucharistic revival....Probably this aspect of the Mercersburg position was the most thoroughly worked out and consistently maintained, and in this lay much of its enduring contribution."[73]

The essence of Mercersburg's eucharistic theology is to be found in Nevin's treatise, *The Mystical Presence: A Vindication of the Reformed or Calvinistic Doctrine of the Holy Eucharist*, published in June 1846.[74] The author wastes little space in establishing his position:

> As the Eucharist forms the very heart of the whole Christian worship, so it is clear that the entire question of the church, which all are compelled to acknowledge--the great life problem of the age--centers ultimately in the sacramental question as its inmost heart and core. Our view of the Lord's Supper must ever condition and rule in the end our view of Christ's person and the conception we form of the church. It must influence, at the same time, very materially, our whole system of theology, as well as all our ideas of ecclesiastical history.[75]

Nevin had three primary purposes in writing *The Mystical Presence*: (*i*) to show that American Protestantism had fallen away from Calvin and was quite content with Zwingli's eucharistic theology; (*ii*) to re-establish and re-interpret Calvin's doctrine; (*iii*) and to correct Calvin's "psychology", or his "sursum-corda" mechanics.

A simple statement of Calvin's eucharistic doctrine was sufficient to prove Nevin's contention that American Protestantism had abandoned it. Berg and Hodge, the Dutch and the Lutherans were not a little uneasy at such thoughts as these:

> ...the sacramental doctrine of the primitive Reformed Church stands inseparably connected with the idea of an inward living union between believers and Christ, in virtue of which they are incorporated into his very nature, and made to subsist with him by the power of a common life.

> In full correspondence with this concep-
> tion of the Christian salvation, as a process
> by which the believer is mystically inserted
> more and more into the person of Christ, till
> he becomes thus at last fully transformed into
> his image, it was held that nothing less than
> such a real participation of his living person
> is involved always in the right use of the
> Lord's Supper.[76]

In attempting to correct Calvin's faulty eucharistic
mechanics, whereby the Spirit must transport the believer into
the presence of Christ, Nevin pointed out three sources of
"embarrassment".[77] First, Calvin "does not make a sufficiently
clear distinction between the idea of the organic *law*, which
constitutes the proper identity of a human body, and the
material volume it is found to embrace as exhibited to the
senses". Nevin's point is that communication between the
Body of Christ and the bodies of his people need not necessarily imply "any transition of his flesh as such into their persons". Calvin's second difficulty, according to Nevin, is
that "he fails to insist, with proper freedom and emphasis,
on the absolute *unity* of what we denominate 'person', both
in the case of Christ himself and in the case of his people."
In short, Calvin made too great a distinction between Christ's
flesh and his soul or his divinity. The life of Christ which
is communicated to man is body and soul. Man's new life, thus
produced by union with Christ, is "a continuation in the
strictest sense of Christ's life under the same form". The
third mistake Calvin made is his lack of distinction between
"the individual personal life of Christ, and the same life
in a *generic* view". As the first Adam was both individual
and *generic* man, so is the second Adam. If this distinction
is clearly made, then "there may be a real communication of
Christ's life to his people, without the idea of anything like

a local mixture with his person". In principle and in fact Calvin is correct, Nevin contended; however, the mechanics Calvin suggested, when forced to answer the "how" of the mystical presence of Christ in the Eucharist and his mystical union with believers, were faulty.

Reaction to *The Mystical Presence* was swift within the German Church. As has been described above, Joseph Berg was already convinced, based on *The Principle of Protestantism* and "Catholic Unity", that heresy was rampant in Mercersburg. When the historical rug was pulled out from under him, Berg readily conceded that all the leading Reformers save Zwingli were tainted with transubstantiation anyway. Such a theory as Nevin advocated had certainly never been held in America, and Berg was not about to be a party to its introduction.

In spite of the considerable European support Nevin received from J. H. A. Ebrard, incumbent of Zwingli's chair at Zurich, and Krummacher, leading preacher in Germany, Charles Hodge was finally moved to enter the fray against Nevin. Hodge began his review of *The Mystical Presence* with an intellectual yawn: "We have had Dr. Nevin's work on the 'Mystical Presence' on our table since its publication, some two years ago, but have never finally read it, until within a fortnight."[78] He concluded the review with a sad wag of his orthodox head, allowing only that Nevin's theory, obviously borrowed from Schleiermacher, "is only a specious form of Rationalism", with a "strong affinity for Sabellianism".[79]

Between the yawn and the wag one finds Hodge laboring to show how completely Nevin has lost the historic Reformed beacon, seen as well in Zwingli as in Calvin, and seen clearly only in the Consensus Tigurinus, for there alone was the Reformed position established with no concession to the Lutherans. The element in Nevin's theory which most aroused

Hodge's ire concerns the mystical union with the "glorified
humanity" of Christ. Our union with Christ is real indeed,
Hodge contended, but it is effected by the Holy Spirit and
not through our participation in the "glorified humanity".
Any attempt to assert the latter diminishes the role of the
Holy Spirit in the Trinity.[80] In a lengthy passage brimming
with Princeton orthodoxy Hodge gave a positive statement of
the Reformed doctrine of the Lord's Supper as he understood
it.

> The Lord's supper is a holy ordinance insti-
> tuted by Christ, as a memorial of his death,
> wherein, under the symbols of bread and wine,
> his body as broken for us and his blood as
> shed for the remission of sins, are signified,
> and, by the power of the Holy Ghost, sealed
> and applied to believers; whereby their union
> with Christ and their mutual fellowship are
> set forth and confirmed, their faith strength-
> ened, and their souls nourished unto eternal
> life.

Christ is "really present", according to Hodge, not bodily but
spiritually, not locally but efficaciously. Not his human
life, but his broken body and shed blood are received by faith.
"The union thus signified and effected, between him and them
[the believers] is not a corporeal union, nor a mixture of
substances, but spiritual and mystical, arising from the indwelling of the Spirit."[81]

Nevin recognized Hodge's review to be his most serious
challenge--"the only respectable or tolerable attempt yet made
to set aside the historical representation contained in *The
Mystical Presence*"[82]--and he set out at once to answer his
former professor. For weeks during the spring and summer of

1848 the *Weekly Messenger* creaked under the weight of Nevin's response to Hodge. This otherwise chatty journal bore the burden since no other periodical would dare print a rebuttal to Hodge. Out of this boycott came the *Mercersburg Review*, "which from 1849 onward became the chief outlet of the school".[83] The second volume, 1850, carried Nevin's *Weekly Messenger* series in an article of over one-hundred pages entitled, "The Doctrine of the Reformed Church on the Lord's Supper". In this article Nevin sought again to state the Reformed doctrine; then, in an expanded form, to give it a "historical trial" by tracing it in the major Reformers and the principal Reformed creeds and confessions. Of Nevin's rebuttal Robert Clemmer writes: "This reply, which revealed Nevin's vastly greater mastery of the historical sources, completely silences Hodge and constitutes one of the most brilliant and devastatingly effective pieces of polemical writing in the history of American theological controversy."[84] Nichols puts it simply: "Hodge did not reply. He was beyond his depth and, whether he fully realized it or not, he had been demolished."[85]

Baptism

Although the subject received considerable attention in the denominational press, "the Mercersburg theologians did not produce a comprehensive interpretation of baptism comparable to their Eucharistic theology".[86] Since the essence of Mercersburg's position on baptism can be inferred from the doctrine of the sacraments, already discussed, suffice it to observe here that Nevin stated with no hesitation: "In *baptismal grace*, I firmly believe";[87] yet he was never anxious

to speculate about the means by which this grace is received:
"...we meddle not with it here any further than to assert the
fact of grace objectively present in the sacrament under *some*
form. Allowing this, there is room still for a similar
difference of view in regard to its precise nature; just as
there is room for a similar difference of view in regard to
the specific power of the Lord's Supper."[88] Ten years later
Nevin wrote that baptism is more than a sign; it is an objective transaction

> ...making what it signified to be actually
> at hand for its subjects, and available for
> their use thenceforward, as it had not been
> before....[Yet] we do not find the opinion
> entertained for a moment that it was suffi-
> cient of itself to insure the salvation of
> those who were its subjects. On the con-
> trary, it is everywhere taken for granted,
> that it carried with it no assurance what-
> ever.[89]

Doctrine of the Ministry

For the purposes of this essay, there yet remains one
aspect of Mercersburg theology which invites special treatment:
the doctrine of the ministry. Nichols argues convincingly that
"with the doctrine of the ministry the Mercersburg men broke
most definitely with the Reformers".[90] It is not difficult to
understand Nichols' point if one examines Nevin's sermon, "The
Christian Ministry".[91] This was addressed to the congregation
in Chambersburg in November 1854 on the occasion of Bernard C.
Wolff's installation as Nevin's successor in the chair of theology at Mercersburg. The controversy surrounding Nevin's doctrine of ordination did not develop for a decade, and then it

centered primarily around the liturgies; however, his theory
of the ministry was expressed in Chambersburg on November 29,
1854.[92]

The address was based on Ephesians 4:8-16, and Nevin
began straightway to discuss the "Origin of the Christian
Ministry". The Incarnation, he said, resulted in the gift
of the Holy Spirit, promised at the Ascension and given at
Pentecost. This is not one gift among many, but the "Gift
of gifts".

> This Gift now forms the origin and
> ground of the Christian Church; which by
> its very nature, therefore, is a super-
> natural constitution, a truly real and
> abiding fact in the world, and yet, at the
> same time, a fact not of the world in its
> natural view, but flowing from the resur-
> rection of Christ and belonging to that
> new order of things which has been brought
> to pass by his glorification at the right
> hand of God....[93]

The Christian ministry originates within the context of the
church's commission and is "identified with the institution
of the Church itself".[94]

The "Nature of the Christian Ministry", Nevin's second
point, is, in a word, "supernatural" because it "refers itself
at once to the ascended and glorified Christ".[95] The ministry is not "natural" in any sense, since it "proceeds directly
and altogether from a new and higher order of things brought
to pass by the Spirit of Christ in consequence of his resurrection and ascension".[96] The Church began in the Apostles,
Nevin contended, and extended itself through them to the
world. "They were to stand between Christ and the world, to
be his witnesses, his legates, the representatives of his

authority, the mediators of his grace among men."[97] So,
too, the Christian ministry functions in these capacities as
"the great agency which Christ is pleased to employ for the
edification of his Mystical Body".[98]

The nature of ministerial authority is "downwards and
not upwards, from the few to the many, and not from the many
to the few".[99] To say, as American Protestantism in the nineteenth century certainly would have said, that "the Church is
before the ministry in the order of existence, and in no way
dependent upon it, but complete without it", is, in Nevin's
opinion, "a heresy which at once strikes at the root of all
faith in the supernatural constitution of the Church, and
turns both the apostolical commission and the gift of Pentecost into a solemn farce".[100]

Nevin believed that institutional apostolic succession
was imperative to this understanding of the ministry. Ordination was understood to be "the veritable channel through
which is transmitted mystically, from age to age, the supernatural authority in which this succession consists".[101] On
the one hand, both Nevin and Schaff wished to maintain an un-
broken succession of the ministry through the Roman Church and
the Reformation. "On the other hand, if there *were* any irregularity in the transmission of orders through the Reformation, as Nevin at least suspected there might have been, he
believed that the church as a whole had the reproductive
powers to restore a damaged organ."[102]

The "Design of the Christian Ministry", Nevin's third
point, is described quite simply and scripturally. Christian
Ministry "is the agency through whose intervention in the
Church, Christ is pleased by his Spirit to provide for the
building up of his people in the faith and hope of the gospel
into everlasting life".[103]

In light of the above summary, it is small wonder that
Nichols wrote: "I may be wrong, but it seems to me that
Nevin's views on the ministry are, from an historic Reformed
basis, his widest deviation. On the Lord's Supper, on the
contrary, where most of the fighting focused, I think he was
much more of an orthodox theologian than his opponents."[104]
Nevin had his critics in his own day as well. Isaac Dorner
accused him of making ordination a "third sacrament"; however, since this charge applies more appropriately to the
liturgical discussion, it will be considered in that connection.

Emergence of a Liturgical Articulation

The concluding task of this chapter and the transition
to the chapters which follow is to indicate that Mercersburg
theology naturally expressed itself liturgically. That the
Mercersburg liturgies are "a working out in an art form of
the ideas and faith of the Mercersburg Theology", as Binkley
states,[105] is one of their more distinctive and paradigmatic
characteristics. In Hageman's opinion, "what made the liturgical movement [in Mercersburg] remarkable was not the *Order
of Worship*, despite its high degree of liturgical skill. It
was rather the fact that it was the first liturgy in the
Reformed Church to articulate a theology. Indeed, it was at
Mercersburg that there was worked out, often in the heat of
battle, for the first time in the Reformed churches what could
be called a theology of the liturgy".[106]

For Nevin and Schaff the liturgy was far more than an
aid to decency and order. "It was the sum of other things:
the expression of doctrine, the voice of the catholic church

at worship, the guarantor against arbitrary freedom, the
instrument of the common priesthood, and an art form which
expressed the spirit of communal worship."[107] Yet the practical and personal significance of the liturgy was not over-
looked either. Schaff wrote: "Next to the Word of God, which
stands in unapproachable majesty far above all human creeds
and confessions, Fathers and Reformers, popes and councils,
there are no religious books of greater practical importance
and influence than catechisms, hymn-books, and liturgies...."[108]

It was the theology of Mercersburg, however, which demanded a liturgy. The latter was never a discipline independent of but rather always a consequence of the former. As
Hageman points out, the theology of worship did not prescribe
the specific order of worship, but it did establish certain
principles.[109] For example, the liturgy must be an "altar"
rather than a "pulpit" liturgy, i.e., it must be a corporate
vehicle by which the eucharistic union between Christ and his
people can transpire rather than simply a collection of prayers
and forms for the minister alone. Again, the liturgy must give
rise to a worship which is objective--a genuine encounter between the Church and her living, present Lord--rather than a
worship which indulges, if not exploits, the subjective emo-
tions of the individual.

By the Baltimore Synod of 1852 Schaff had worked out the
specific liturgical implications of the Mercersburg theology.
These principles will be evaluated in detail in the following
chapter. Concluding the present discussion is a summary of
Nevin's apologia for the *Order of Worship* which capsules both
the Mercersburg theology in general and the theology of worship
in particular. He characterized the Mercersburg theology in
three ways: first, it is Christological--i.e., the Person of
Christ is the head "from which the whole body is joined and

knit together". Second, Mercersburg theology "moves in the
bosom of the Apostles' Creed"--i.e., it is systematic and
dynamic. "Starting in the great fact of the Incarnation,
and following its movement, our theology has finally the third
general character of being objective and historical...."
Persons must indeed be brought to experience the power of the
Incarnation, but their salvation is not in the experience or
in the faith; rather in the Object of faith. The historical
nature of this "Object" "is nothing more nor less than the
idea of the holy catholic Church as we have it in the Creed."

> Such a churchly theology, we feel at
> once, can never be otherwise than sacramental.
> Where the idea of the Church has come to make
> itself felt in the way now described, as in-
> volving the conjunction of the supernatural
> and the natural continuously in one and the
> same abiding economy of grace, its sacraments
> cannot possibly be regarded as outward signs
> only of what they represent. They become,
> for faith, seals also of the actual realities
> themselves which they exhibit....In the end,
> also, unquestionably, the sacramental feeling
> here cannot fail to show itself a liturgical
> feeling.
> A theology which is truly Christocentric
> must follow the Creed, must be objective,
> must be historical; with this, must be
> churchly; and, with this again, must be sacra-
> mental and liturgical.[110]

NOTES TO CHAPTER 1

1. G. W. Richards, *History of the Theological Seminary of the Reformed Church in the United States* (Lancaster, Pa.: Rudisill & Co., Inc., 1952), pp. 544-545.

2. *Ibid.*

3. J. H. Nichols, *Romanticism in American Theology*, [Hereinafter referred to as *Romanticism*], (Chicago: The University of Chicago Press, 1961), pp. 9ff.

4. Richards, *op. cit.*, p. 546.

5. Nichols, *op. cit.*, p. 14.

6. J. W. Nevin, *My Own Life: The Earlier Years* (Lancaster, Pa.: Papers of the Eastern Chapter of the Historical Society of the Evangelical and Reformed Church, No. 1, 1964), p. 20. This is a reprint of the series of articles Nevin wrote for the *Weekly Messenger* from March 2 to June 22, 1870.

7. Nichols, *op. cit.*, p. 16.

8. Nevin, *op. cit.*, p. 30.

9. *Ibid.*, p. 38.

10. *Ibid.*, p. 40.

11. *Ibid.*, p. 47.

12. *Ibid.*, p. 48.

13. *Ibid.*, p. 57.

14. *Ibid.*, p. 65.

15. *Ibid.*

16. *Ibid.*, p. 57.

17. *Ibid.*, p. 65.

18.   Quoted in David S. Schaff, *The Life of Philip Schaff* (New York: Charles Scribner's Sons, 1897), p. 103.

19.   Joseph H. Dubbs, *The Reformed Church in Pennsylvania* (Lancaster, Pa.:   The New Era Printing Co., 1902), p. 303.

20.   James I. Good, *History of the Reformed Church in the U.S. in the Nineteenth Century* (New York: The Board of Publication of the Reformed Church in America, 1911), p. 204.

21.   *Ibid.*, p. 206.

22.   Philip Schaf changed the spelling of his name to Schaff in 1847.

23.   Nichols, *op. cit.*, p. 65.

24.   *Ibid.*

25.   *Ibid.*, p. 66.

26.   Nevin, *op. cit.*, p. 139.

27.   Good, *op. cit.*, p. 209.

28.   Nevin, John W., *The Anxious Bench* (Chambersburg, Pa.:   Office of the *Weekly Messenger*, 1843).   A second and expanded edition was published in 1844.   References are to the first edition.

29.   Nichols, *op. cit.*, p. 53.

30.   Theodore Appel, *Recollections of College Life at Marshall College, Mercersburg, Pennsylvania from 1839-1845* (Reading, Pa.:   Daniel Miller, Printer and Publisher, 1886), p. 317.

31.   *Ibid.*, p. 319.

32.   Nevin, *The Anxious Bench*, p. 7.

33.   *Ibid.*, p. 26.

34.   Nichols, *Romanticism*, p. 57.

35.   Philip Schaff, *The Principle of Protestantism as Related to the Present State of the Church*, trans. with an Introduction by John W. Nevin (Chambersburg, Pa.:   Publication Office

of the German Reformed Church, 1845). Reprinted in the Lancaster Series on the Mercersburg Theology, Vol. I, ed. with an Introduction by Bard Thompson and George H. Bricker (Philadelphia: United Church Press, [1964]). All references will be to the latter edition.

36. Nichols, *Romanticism*, pp. 59-60.

37. D. Schaff, *op. cit.*, p. 92.

38. John W. Nevin, "Catholic Unity," printed as an Appendix to Philip Schaff, *The Principle of Protestantism* (Chambersburg, Pa.: Publication Office of the German Reformed Church, 1845), pp. 191-215.

39. Theodore Appel, *The Life and Work of John Williamson Nevin* (Philadelphia: Reformed Church Publishing House, 1889), p. 218.

40. Nevin, "Catholic Unity," quoted in *Ibid.*, p. 219.

41. Nichols, *Romanticism*, p. 60.

42. Bard Thompson and George Bricker, "Editors' Preface," Philip Schaff, *The Principle of Protestantism*, p. 8.

43. *Ibid.*, p. 7.

44. *Ibid.*, p. 16.

45. *Weekly Messenger*, (Hereinafter referred to as *WM.*), August 4, 1847.

46. Charles E. Schaeffer, *History of the Classis of Philadelphia of the Reformed Church in the United States* (Philadelphia: published by the Classis of Philadelphia, 1944), p. 68.

47. John W. Nevin, "Dr. Berg's Last Words," *Mercersburg Review*, (Hereinafter referred to as *MR.*), IV (1852), p. 283.

48. John W. Nevin, "True and False Protestantism," *MR*, I (1849), p. 85.

49. David Schaff, *op. cit.*, p. 107.

50. Philip Schaff, *The Principle of Protestantism*, p. 201.

51. Nichols, *Romanticism*, p. 135.

52. *Ibid.*, p. 138.

53. *Ibid.*, p. 139.

54. John W. Nevin, "Early Christianity," *MR*, III (1851), pp. 461-489, 513-562; IV (1852), pp. 1-54.

55. John W. Nevin, "Cyprian," *MR*, IV (1852), pp. 259-277, 335-387, 417-452, 513-563.

56. George W. Richards, "The Mercersburg Theology--Its Purpose and Principles," *Church History*, XX, 3 (1951), p. 43.

57. *Ibid.*, pp. 46-47.

58. *Ibid.*, p. 47.

59. Nichols, *Romanticism*, p. 140.

60. John W. Nevin, "The New Creation in Christ," *MR*, II (1850), p. 6. Quoted in Nichols, *Romanticism*, p. 143.

61. John W. Nevin, "The Apostles' Creed," *MR*, I (1849), p. 343.

62. Rütenik was editor of *Reformirte Wächter*.

63. *WM*, April 8, 1868.

64. *WM*, April 22, 1868.

65. *WM*, April 29, 1868.

66. Thomas G. Apple, "The Internal History of the Seminary," *MR*, XXIII (1876), p. 73.

67. Luther J. Binkley, *The Mercersburg Theology* (Manheim, Pa.: The Sentinel Printing House, 1953), p. 109.

68. James H. Nichols, ed., *The Mercersburg Theology* (New York: Oxford University Press, 1966), p. 11.

69. Nevin, *The Anxious Bench* (2nd ed., 1884), pp. 128-129, quoted in Bard Thompson, "The Catechism and the Mercersburg Theology," *Essays on the Heidelberg Catechism* (Philadelphia: United Church Press, [1963]), pp. 62-63.

70. Thompson, "The Catechism and the Mercersburg Theology," p. 63.

71. Nichols, *Romanticism*, p. 158.

72. John W. Nevin, "Thoughts on the Church," *MR*, X (1858), p. 193.

73. Nichols, *Romanticism*, p. 84.

74. John W. Nevin, *The Mystical Presence: A Vindication of the Reformed or Calvinistic Doctrine of the Holy Eucharist* (Philadelphia: J. B. Lippincott & Co., 1846). Reprinted in the Lancaster Series on the Mercersburg Theology, Vol. IV, ed. with an Introduction by Bard Thompson and George H. Bricker (Philadelphia: United Church Press [1966]). All references will be to the latter edition.

75. *Ibid.*, p. 23.

76. *Ibid.*, p. 31.

77. *Ibid.*, pp. 151-160.

78. Charles Hodge, Review of *The Mystical Presence*, by John W. Nevin, in *Biblical Repertory and Princeton Review*, XX (1848), p. 227.

79. *Ibid.*, pp. 275-276.

80. *Ibid.*, p. 255.

81. *Ibid.*, pp. 258-259.

82. John W. Nevin, "Doctrine of the Reformed Church on the Lord's Supper," *MR*, II (1850), p. 422.

83. Nichols, *The Mercersburg Theology*, p. 246.

84. Robert Clemmer, "The Present Significance of the Mercersburg Theology," *Bulletin of the Theological Seminary of the Evangelical and Reformed Church*, XXI (1950), p. 19.

85. Nichols, *Romanticism*, p. 89.

86. Nichols, *Romanticism*, p. 235.

87. *WM*, August 11, 1847.

88. John W. Nevin, Review of Noel's "Essay on Christian Baptism," *MR*, II (1850), p. 265.

89. John W. Nevin, "The Old Doctrine of Baptism," *MR*, XII (1860), pp. 196, 202-203.

90. Nichols, *Romanticism*, p. 259.

91. John W. Nevin, "The Christian Ministry," *MR*, VII (1855), pp. 68-93. Reprinted in James H. Nichols, ed., *The Mercersburg Theology*. References are to the latter edition.

92. Charles E. Schaeffer, *A Repairer of the Breach: the Memoirs of Bernard C. Wolff* (Lancaster, Pa.: The Historical Society of the Evangelical and Reformed Church, 1949), p. 69.

93. Nevin, "The Christian Ministry," p. 353.

94. *Ibid.*, p. 354.

95. *Ibid.*, p. 355.

96. *Ibid.*, p. 356.

97. *Ibid.*, p. 359.

98 *Ibid.*

99. *Ibid.*

100. *Ibid.*, p. 360.

101. *Ibid.*, p. 361.

102. Nichols, *Romanticism*, p. 267.

103. Nichols, *The Mercersburg Theology*, p. 365.

104. Letter, James H. Nichols to Miss Elizabeth Clarke Kieffer, December 16, 1959, Library of the Evangelical and Reformed Historical Society, Philip Schaff Library, Lancaster Theological Seminary, Lancaster, Pa.

105. Binkley, *op. cit.*, p. 109.

106. Howard Hageman, *Pulpit and Table* (Richmond: John Knox Press, 1962), p. 92.

48

107. Thompson, "The Catechism and the Mercersburg Theology," p. 72.

108. Philip Schaff, "The New Liturgy," *MR*, X (1858), p. 199.

109. Hageman, *op. cit.*, pp. 95-96.

110. John W. Nevin, "The Theology of the New Liturgy," *MR*, XIV (1867), pp. 28-44.

CHAPTER II

Liturgical Lineage of the German Reformed Church

The service begins, according to A. R. Kremer in his description of an often repeated Sunday evening in an American
Protestant parish, with the preliminary exercises: a devotional hymn, reading of Scripture, prayer, and perhaps another hymn.
These exercises were designed both to prepare the people for
the noted evangelist and to heighten their anticipation of his
arrival. "As the last lines of the hymn are reached, the
great man leaps upon the platform, scans his audience, looks
pleased, steps to the front, and reads his text." Where had
he been during the "preliminaries"? Sequestered in a room
behind the platform, "gathering himself up, getting in mental
trim, keeping himself fresh for the evening's effort, and
letting the small fry (the D.D.'s and other clergy) attend
to the hymns and prayers". The evangelist's absence before
the sermon created the impression that "the devotional part
of the service is more ornamental than useful, a sort of
fringe or red tape to the sermon...." The sermon itself, as
Kremer characterizes it, often contained much of value; however, the usual pattern of the discourse "was a harangue
against faith in Church ordinances". For example: "Why, if
I believed that people were saved by baptism [A straw man,
of course, since few of his high church brethren would ever
make such a claim.], you wouldn't catch me going over the
country preaching. I would go through the streets with a
bucket of water and douse every sinner I could meet, whether
he wished it or not...."[1]

If worship in the Reformed tradition is liturgical, as the Mercersburg professors insisted and sought to document, what happened between the sixteenth and the nineteenth centuries which made services such as the one described above the order of the day? No one knew precisely what had occurred in Reformed worship until the romantic movements in England, Scotland, and America again introduced the Protestant tradition to its liturgical heritage. As the result primarily of the Oxford Movement, the Church Service Society, and the Mercersburg Movement Reformed churches in Europe and America discovered that there was a substantial difference between worship in the sixteenth century and that inspired by the Puritans and subsequently the revivalists in the nineteenth century. Some members of the German Reformed Church in America remembered that once the Palatinate Liturgy had played some role in their denomination's history, but only after a lengthy search could a copy of it—and only a partial edition at that—be located.

The lineage of Reformed worship can be traced with even greater accuracy today than it was during the mid-nineteenth century, and certainly with less heated emotion. So conflicting was the historical testimony proffered by the opposing factions during the Mercersburg debate that clergy and laity alike simply did not know whom or what to believe. Most of the facts were available after the research done by Schaff and Ebrard, yet the conclusions were so conflicting that the issue remained clouded for many in the German Reformed Church.

So, then, how did the Reformed tradition move from the liturgies of Calvin and Zwingli, Knox and à Lasco to the revivalism Kremer describes?

As Nichols has shown,[2] the Reformers were basically quite conservative in their liturgical reform. There was no serious attempt made to return to a New Testament liturgical pattern; rather the second-century wedding of Synaxis and Anaphora was maintained. With few exceptions, Protestant liturgical reform in the sixteenth century was more theological than structural. Preaching was restored to its rightful place in worship; congregational participation, imperative from the Protestant point of view, was facilitated through the use of the vernacular and the introduction of hymns; an attempt was made, more or less successfully, to restore the centrality of the Eucharist; and the concept of sacrifice was changed from propitiation to an oblation of praise and thanksgiving.

The two liturgical patterns open to sixteenth century Protestants, Lutheran and Reformed alike, were both derived from medieval models. "One option was to translate and reform the Mass, whether a sung Mass or a 'low' spoken Mass. The other was to take over the forms of services in the vernacular that had been developed in the Middle Ages, at least in southern Germany and Switzerland, the order for preaching services, and the order for administering Communion to the laity."[3] These two services could be used separately or together. If the latter, then the practical effect of the combination was much the same as that obtained from using a translation of the Mass.

It is generally known that Calvin and Bucer chose a translation of the Mass and a retention of its basic liturgical structure. The fascinating manner in which Bucer "taught" liturgies to Calvin, and then the influence which both had on Cranmer's *Book of Common Prayer* and Knox's "Form of Prayers" is documented by Nichols, Thompson, and others. Zwingli's liturgical option and its subsequent influence on the German,

Dutch, and Hungarian Reformed traditions is a story not so
well known. Johan Surgant, the Basel professor and pastor,
introduced Zwingli to the medieval preaching service. Its
emphasis on preaching (easily acceptable in the Roman tradition since it was no more than an optional addendum to the
Mass) suited Zwingli's "low" doctrine of the Eucharist, and,
with a minor change or two in the sequence, he "took over the
form entire".[4]

Clearly Zwingli had--or developed--different theological
reasons for using the medieval Prone than Surgant had in introducing it in Basel. Surgant intended a liturgical reform
which would "revive biblical preaching and congregational worship"; Zwingli, on the other hand, arrived at an understanding
of worship in which the sermon was "the solemn center...to
which everything else referred--from the first plea for the
presence of the Spirit who 'opens the Word', to the last act
of Confession, made in the knowledge of human misery and
divine mercy which only the Word affords".[5] The Zurich Liturgy of 1525 is simple and austere. It begins with a prayer for
illumination, beseeching God to "open His holy and eternal
Word to us poor men"; then follows a prayer for Christian
rulers and for those "persecuted and oppressed" for the sake
of the Word, the Lord's Prayer, the Hail Mary, Scripture and
sermon, necrology, thanksgiving for the dead, general confession, and prayer for forgiveness.[6]

The Dutch, Hungarian, and Palatinate German liturgies
are closer in structure to the Basel-Zurich pattern than to
the Strassburg "shape"; however, the "doctrine is similar to
that of the services of the Mass type. Mere 'memorialism'
had been laid aside even in Zurich since 1549".[7] Since the
Palatinate Liturgy is the liturgical parent of the German Reformed Church in America, its history is noted here in some
detail.

The Palatinate Liturgy

John à Lasco, Polish nobleman and Erasmian Catholic, declined a bishopric and joined the Reformed Church in 1538. After the defeat of the Protestants by Charles V, à Lasco left his pastorate at Emden on the Dutch border of western Germany and joined the flood of Continental refugees who sought sanctuary in England. The abandoned Church of the Austin Friars in London was available to the Reformed refugees, and à Lasco became their "bishop". He drew up a plan of government and a liturgy for the congregation, organized in 1550 as the "Church of the Strangers". *Forma ac Ratio* was not printed until after the Strangers became refugees again upon Mary's accession in 1553. The Latin version of à Lasco's liturgy, printed in 1555 in Frankfort, was subsequently to shape the Dutch liturgy and to influence the Palatinate Church Order of 1563.

"The Lord's Day order for the *Forma ac Ratio* was a typical preaching order. All proceeded from the pulpit, in contrast to the Strassburg and Anglican Mass orders."[8] In contrast to Zurich, however, the Communion order was used monthly, always preceded by the service of preparation. The latter, with the Lord's Day afternoon service featuring a systematic exposition of the catechism, was a distinctive emphasis of à Lasco's liturgical scheme. This strong, almost urgent insistence upon examination and preparation for the Eucharist was its own testimony that à Lasco considered Communion to be significantly more than a memorial.

In his effort to bring some measure of peace among the contending Protestant parties in the Palatinate, Frederick the Pious appointed Ursinus and Olevianus to draft a new confession, and with Tremellius, to draw up a liturgy.[9]

The Heidelberg Catechism and the Palatinate Church Order were ready in 1563, the latter deriving directly from the *Forma ac Ratio*. A more detailed examination of the Palatinate Liturgy will be made subsequently in this chapter. Let it simply be said here that the Palatinate Liturgy was a preaching order which found its liturgical focus in the sermon. Preaching in the mornings was expository and done "in course"--the pattern established by Zwingli; in the afternoons the catechetical service featured specified questions from the Heidelberg Catechism, designed largely with this procedure in mind. As Nichols points out, the result of preaching through the Catechism "had some of the utility of a church year lectionary, in that the full cycle of Christian affirmations was set before preacher and congregation systematically each year".[10]   The Palatinate Liturgy also followed à Lasco's pattern of monthly preparations for and celebrations of the Eucharist--a discovery which was to shock the German Reformed brethren in America three centuries later.

The Palatinate Liturgy and its liturgical cousin, the Netherlands Liturgy, established by the Synod of Dort in 1619, made their way to America in the seventeenth century. In the years to follow both liturgies were virtually lost to the memory of American Reformed congregations, primarily because of their apparent irrelevance to an increasingly English speaking constituency, the desperate shortage of clergy, and, even more significantly, the influence of Puritanism and revivalism.

Puritanism and Revivalistic Evangelicalism

While it is important to remember that Puritanism was
not originally anti-liturgical (witness Baxter's Savoy Liturgy in 1661), the fact remains that ill-treatment by the Church
of England and the gradual influence of Separatist notions of
the church meant "the virtually complete reaction of British
and American Reformed Church in the 18th century against all
forms in worship. They dropped liturgical prayers, the Creed,
the Ten Commandments, the Gloria Patri, even the Lord's Prayer,
and sometimes even the reading of Scripture."[11] Such a service was once held at the Race Street Reformed Church in Philadelphia.

> So fearful was the congregation at times
> lest the high church or liturgical tenden-
> cies should creep into their worship that
> they often discussed the advisability of re-
> peating together the Lord's Prayer and the
> Apostles' Creed. Indeed the sentiment on
> occasions was so strongly against all forms
> of formalism that there were periods when
> the congregation had absolutely no part in
> the service except the singing of hymns.[12]

Revivalistic evangelicalism, the very death of historical sacramental and liturgical worship, made its entry into
the Reformed tradition through the sacramental door, ironi-
cally enough. Whereas some of the Puritans--Wesley, for
example--increased the frequency of celebrating the Eucharist,
the overall effect of Puritanism was a reduction in the number of celebrations. In spite of these annual or perhaps
semi-annual occasions, the Puritans did retain a "high" doctrine of the spiritual real presence in the sacramental action.
They surrounded the celebrations with lengthy "sacramental

seasons" of four-day duration, during which times hundreds, often thousands, would prepare themselves to receive Communion. Since a number of the "un-converted" would attend these meetings, which doubtless had all the attractions of a major social gathering, the preaching gradually shifted its emphasis from the sacramental to a concern to save the "lost", and thus the revivalistic camp meeting.

Revivalism understood the Church to be "an assemblage of religiously inclined neighbors",[13] rather than the People of the Word, as Calvin had argued. With this fundamental change came the erosion of much that was characteristic of the classical Reformation tradition: the "focus on Word and Sacraments in the historic church as the loci and media of salvation",[14] for example. The "means of grace" became the conversion experience itself with its attendant public confession of sin and profession of faith. Objectivity in worship yielded to the maudlin sentimentality of revivalistic hymns, and the "liturgy" lost its historic sense of a corporate oblation in response to God's gift in Jesus Christ. The purpose of worship was conversion, and the "liturgy" became an instrument used by clergy and choir to precipitate the sort of emotional crisis which would guarantee conversion.

The German Reformed Church

The mid-nineteenth century witnessed a reaction against revivalism in the form of romanticism. Nevin's quick response to revivalism, in *The Anxious Bench*, did much to prevent its widespread influence in his denomination; thus the typical service of worship in the German Reformed Church prior to the *Provisional Liturgy* in 1857 was nearer that described by E. V.

Gerhart than the description with which this chapter began.

> The prevailing custom, so far as we can
> now ascertain, embraced the following par-
> ticulars. The minister, having taken his
> place at the altar, began by saying, as the
> congregation arose: In the name of the
> Father, and the Son, and the Holy Ghost.
> Amen. Then he announced two or three stan-
> zas of a hymn; afterwards, he offered a
> free prayer at the altar, concluding with
> the Lord's Prayer; or, as was more common-
> ly the case, retired from the altar while
> the last stanza was sung; or, omitting
> this, he passed immediately without sing-
> ing to the sermon, the people, according
> to a general custom, rising when the text
> was read. The form of concluding worship
> after the sermon, differed very little
> from that which obtains generally at the
> present time. From this order, there
> were some unimportant variations. The
> Lord's Prayer was sometimes connected
> with the prayer succeeding the sermon.
> The first prayer may have been offered
> by some ministers from the Liturgy; but
> this was the exception to the rule.
> Liturgical prayers were commonly confined
> to the administration of Baptism and the
> Lord's Supper, to the rite of confirmation,
> the solemnization of marriage, and other
> special offices; but there is no evidence
> that these special offices were adminis-
> tered without using the Liturgy, as was
> so frequently the case twenty and thirty
> years ago. In the administration of these
> offices, the Liturgy was always used.[15]

Although the Palatinate Liturgy was never published in
America before Bomberger's English translation in 1850, it was
used more extensively than any other liturgy, according to
Philip Schaff.[16] As will be shown in more detail in the following chapter, the liturgy of the Dutch Reformed Church was based

partially on the Palatinate Liturgy.[17] From 1767, the New
York edition of the English translation of Dathenus' Netherlands Liturgy was appended to Dutch Reformed hymnbooks;
therefore Palatinate-like forms were available. Demarest
indicates that while the New York edition amended the
Netherlands Liturgy in certain particulars, it remained unchanged so far as the forms made imperative by the constitution (Baptism, Eucharist, Ordination, Excommunication and
Restoration) were concerned.[18] Many German ministers used
adaptations from the liturgies with which they were familiar
in the several sections of Germany, Switzerland, and Holland.
Still others used portions of the *Book of Common Prayer* or
compiled their own forms, while the majority of German Reformed clergy were completely "free" in their Lord's Day
worship. In so far as the occasional services were concerned, "ministers generally used manuscript collections of
uncertain origin, which, in many instances, they had committed to memory".[19]

The liturgical diversity of German Reformed worship in
the eighteenth and early nineteenth centuries is no indication of the seriousness with which the act itself was taken.
As shall be shown below, the informality of certain parishion-
ers and the sacerdotalism of clergy and choir did receive some
critical attention in the mid-nineteenth century; however,
the high doctrine of German Reformed worship was clearly established in the Constitution of 1748, adopted by the Second
Coetus. It was prescribed that Communion should be administered twice a year. Only that person who had "evidence of a
godly life, or proper testimonials from another Reformed congregation" was admitted. All members of the congregation were
to attend the preparatory service. The adult members were
admonished to instruct the young "in Reformed worship" and to

"see to it that they give faithful attention to the hearing
of the Word of God" in order that they "may also be admitted
to the Holy Communion". The minister was instructed by the
Constitution as follows:

> It shall be the office and duty of the
> minister to preach the pure doctrine of the
> Reformed Church according to the Word of God,
> and to administer the holy seals of the
> Covenant at their appointed time and place;
> always to adhere to the confession of faith
> of the Reformed churches and to the Heidel-
> berg Catechism; to explain the same regular-
> ly and consecutively; to hold catechetical
> instruction, etc. He shall give special
> attention to church discipline and correct
> practice, together with those who have the
> oversight of the congregation....[20]

In the same year--1748--Boehm and Schlatter, the "founding fathers", had a serious disagreement over which order of
worship was proper.[21] Schlatter was using the Order of St.
Gall and argued that everyone should have the freedom to prescribe his own order. Boehm desired some general standardiza-
tion around the Palatinate Liturgy. According to Richards,
Boehm's view prevailed; however, the number of Palatinate
Church Orders available was so small that it had little use,
if, indeed, any general authority among those ministers who
preferred other forms. One such form, privately compiled and
printed, was published in Germantown, Pennsylvania, in 1798
and was known as the "Germantown Manual". It contains no
services for the regular Lord's Day; rather it provides forms
for baptism, the preparatory service, marriage, excommunication, restoration of the disciplined, ordination of ministers,
elders, and deacons. The first four forms are taken verbatim
from the Palatinate Liturgy, while the remainder of the "Manual"

is borrowed from the Northern Rhine Reformed Liturgy.[22] The
"Germantown Manual" was a pulpit-liturgy, prepared for the
minister's personal use. Although it was not widely circulated, it is an indication that the German Reformed Church in
America was not indisposed to liturgical forms *per se*.

A similar manual of forms known as the "Weisz Liturgy"
was commissioned by the Synod of Ohio in 1827 and published
the following year. Like the "Germantown Manual", the Weisz
Liturgy provided no liturgical forms for the regular Lord's
Day services. Rather it contained only the offices of baptism, the preparatory service, Communion, marriage, the ordination of ministers, and the installation of a consistory.
"Strangely enough it contains a form for the installation of
trustees as well as elders and deacons, an office never recognized in our Church."[23] The Weisz Liturgy was based largely
on the Palatinate Liturgy; and, although it had some measure
of denominational sanction, it was neither widely circulated
nor used.

As theoretically disposed as German Reformed clergy may
have been to liturgical forms, the worship over which they
presided in the mid-nineteenth century was sacerdotal and,
in some quarters, quite informal. In 1853 a correspondent
chastised those who "have their spittons [*sic*] arranged
through their pews, so that they could intersperse their
devotion with a bit of carnal enjoyment, with seeming impor-
tunity".[24] A month later the same correspondent wrote again,
complaining about the dearth of congregational singing. The
choir completely dominates the service and the people do not
even know what is being sung. In a telling comparison he
wrote: "The sale of indulgences in the Romish Church is a
practice regarded by Protestants with unmitigated abhorrence,
but the habit of depending upon others to praise God for us

in the sanctuary involves precisely the same principle. It is
an effort to make an unwarranted transfer of personal duty,
which accords as little with reason as it does with revelation."[25]   Two years later, as the denomination expectantly
awaited the results of Schaff's "blue-ribbon" committee,
another correspondent described the prevailing conditions in
worship even more pointedly. "The minister does the preaching
and praying,...the choir is drilled to a fiddle-de-dee music,
and does the singing; and the people are the listening specta-
tors, and receive credit if only they perform *that* part in a
wakeful and silent way....The preacher takes the Bible to himself, the choir takes the hymnbooks, and liturgy we have none."
If the minister fails, the service fails. "For the benefit of
the congregation, then, and the elevation of the ministry as
an order, or institution, give us a Liturgy."[26]

Early Liturgical Stirrings

Mercersburg finally produced that Liturgy in 1857; however, as B. C. Wolff pointed out, the earliest liturgical
stirrings in the German Reformed Church began before some of
the Mercersburg professors were born.[27]   On May 3, 1820, at
the first meeting of the Maryland Classis, it was agreed that
it "be recommended to Synod to improve our Church Liturgy, and
at the same time to translate it into English and to promote
its printing".[28]   Synod responded favorably and appointed a
committee consisting of Hendel, Hinsch, Helffenstein, Rahauser,
and Becker, *unsere Kirchen Agende zu verbessern*. "This was
the first direct step towards a new liturgy, under the auspices
of Synod."[29]

In 1821 the committee reported "no progress", primarily because the difficulties in travel had prevented a meeting. Helffenstein reported in 1822 that the committee "proposed to retain the old liturgy--probably the Palatinate Liturgy--with some improvements, and a Committee, consisting of Messrs. Wack, Helffenstein, and Ven der Sloot, was appointed to make them".[30] The intentions of the Synod were made quite clear in 1823 when, after Helffenstein again reported "no progress", it "expressed its disapprobation of the dilatory course of the Committee".[31] Helffenstein proposed a specimen liturgy in 1824 and another committee was appointed by Synod to examine it; however, "this was the last that was heard of the improved liturgy for several years. This committee, in all probability, never met"--again because of the difficulty and expense of travel.[32]

After a decade the question of a liturgy once again came before Synod, this time through an overture by Susquehanna Classis in 1834. A committee was appointed consisting of Mayer, Rauch, Hoffeditz, Fries, and Geiger. The bulk of work fell to Mayer, whose health, physically and emotionally, was not good during this period. He did submit a liturgy in 1837 to the Synod of Sunbury, which sent it to the Classes for adjudication, and the next year, 1840, Synod pronounced its adoption, and allowed its use.[33] This came to be known as the Mayer Liturgy.

Although this Liturgy will be evaluated in more detail in the following chapter, it may be said that it was an extremely didactic book of forms for occasional services, which never required a second printing. In 1847 the Classis of East Pennsylvania openly expressed its dissatisfaction with the Mayer Liturgy and requested that...

'the old Liturgy [i.e., the Palatinate Liturgy] should be reprinted, or a new one prepared more

congenial to the spirit of the Heidelberg
Catechism'. The whole subject 'of the revision of the Liturgy so as to secure one
which is adapted to the wants of the whole
Church, and the general use of which can be
enforced', was referred to the consideration
of the several Classes, and at the next Synod
at Hagerstown [1848], it appeared that all
the Classes, with the exception of North
Carolina, had expressed themselves in their
minutes in favor of a new Liturgy.[34]

Norristown Proposals

The Hagerstown Synod appointed a committee to study the
proposal, and this action marks the beginning of the Mercersburg liturgical movement. The committee, chaired by J. H. A.
Bomberger and consisting of Daniel Zacharias, J. F. Mesick,
George Besore, and William Cameron (the latter two being
elders), reported to the Synod of Norristown in 1849, "earnestly advocating the propriety and importance of Liturgies in
general, and urging the necessity of a new Liturgy as called
forth by the wants of the Church".[35] In the preface to its
specific proposals to the Synod the committee sought to establish the biblical imperative to worship God. Christ urged
his disciples to preach the Word; however, there is nothing
which would indicate that this preaching was to supercede the
"acts and duties of ancient worship". The external forms of
worship changed under the "new dispensation", but the "spirit
and principle" of the "old dispensation" were retained.

And now to aid them in their worship, and
to secure the desired uniformity and edification in their devotions, the earliest Church
organizations of whose history any authentic
traditions have reached us--at once availed

themselves of set forms of devotional hymns
and prayers, which were in part transferred
from the Jewish Church, and in part framed
expressly for the latter, by those to whom
their superintendence was committed. And
these acts of devotion, their singing and
praying, and reading of the Scriptures,
constituted an important public worship.
*This again was by divine appointment, and
under apostolical sanction.*[36]

This *pure* worship of the early church was perverted beyond
description during the thirteenth, fourteenth, and fifteenth
centuries, the preface continues. The Reformation brought
many changes; "but amidst all these the thought of abrogating
all forms of Church worship was never once cherished". Rather,
the forms were changed and liturgies suitable to the German
Reformed and Lutheran Churches of Germany were devised, and
the use of these liturgies has been characteristic of both
traditions since that time.

Because the specific proposals made by the committee took
on added significance as the history of the liturgical controversy progressed, they are quoted here in full.

1.   That the use of Liturgical forms of church
worship, as recognized by our forefathers, has
the clear sanction of the practice and peculiar
genius of the original protestant Churches.

2.   That there is nothing in the present circumstances of our Church in this country to
call for or justify a total departure from
this ancient and long-established usage.

3.   That the Liturgy now authorized and
partially used by the Church [the Mayer
Liturgy] is inadequate to our wants, inasmuch
as apart from other deficiencies which may be
found in it, it makes *no provision for ordinary occasions of public worship.*

4. That whilst the older Liturgies of the
Church, and especially that of the Palatinate,
are of such a character as to commend the
greater portions of them for adoption, there
is still need of various modifications in
order to adapt them fully to our wants and
circumstances.

5. That the present would be as favorable a
time for making the requisite provision in
the case, as any which may be anticipated in
the future.

6. That Synod, therefore, proceed to make
such arrangements as it may in its wisdom
think best for the securing of this object.[37]

To have attended this and the several subsequent meetings of
Synod would have been a delight--especially for one a century
later who intended to analyze the liturgical dispute. Beginning
with Norristown and continuing for the next thirty years the
German Reformed Church was engaged in a liturgical discussion
which often produced more heat than light; nevertheless, one
in which fundamental questions concerning worship were debated
as they had not been debated before in the Reformed tradition.

The heat, if not the light, began in Norristown; for as
inoffensive as these proposals may seem today--or even when
compared with the more detailed and far-reaching proposals
made three years later in Baltimore--they provoked a lengthy
debate in the Synod. The editor of the *Weekly Messenger*
attempted to reconstruct the sessions on the liturgy for his
readers;[38] and while he relied on his memory and notes for this
abbreviated account, one can still appreciate something of the
exchanges between these volatile Germans.

Bomberger made the committee report, and immediately the
other members of the committee objected, both because of
personal disagreements with the proposals and because the

committee had never met. These were, in fact, Bomberger's
proposals and not those of the committee. The Chairman explained that travel was too difficult and interest too little
to justify a meeting. For purposes of discussion the report
was received, however, and the debate on the several proposals
begun seriatim.

The first proposal--that the use of liturgical forms was
sanctioned by the Protestant churches--was not in serious
doubt. Rather than liturgy or no liturgy, the question was:
What kind of liturgy should it be? Bomberger argued that all
knew the German Reformed Church had been unfaithful to the
Reformation [actually, all did not know it]. All he now asked
was that the Church "go back, and by no means beyond, the
spirit of the Reformed Church at the Reformation". There are
three views on the liturgy, he said: rigid adherence to form;
a service which is completely free; and "a liturgical service,
leaving sufficient room, however, for the exercise of free
prayer...." It is with the last that he desired to cast his
liturgical lot.

The second proposal--being in effect an amplification of
the first--was not debated. Proposal three--stating the in-
adequacy of the Mayer Liturgy and the desirability of a liturgy which would make "provision for [the] ordinary occasions of
public worship--did draw expected disagreement. Douglas of
Maryland Classis said that prayers from the book would split
the Church. Mann of Philadelphia Classis insisted that it
would do no such thing. Bomberger again came to the defense,
repeating the historical precedent for the use of liturgies.
Preaching has, to a large extent, monopolized the public worship of God. This was clearly not so with the early Christians, who centered their worship in prayer and praise.
"Preaching the Word, cannot be too highly prized--but Prayer

and Praise are first and foremost, inasmuch as the former only derives its efficacy and power, when blessed from on High in answer to Prayer." The German Reformed Church is preaching-centered in contrast to the plain fact that historically the devotions of the people are of the greatest importance. In no sense did Bomberger wish to depreciate preaching; yet, he insisted, "let us realize also, that the eloquence of the preacher...is as sounding brass apart from the fervent, believing prayers, and cheerful praises of humble and devoted Christians".

Ingold of the North Carolina Classis said that all this suggested that God did not hear anything but proper prayers.

Berg replied that it suggested no such thing. The question is not which is acceptable to God, but "which is most unto the edification of the Church".

Naille of Montgomery Classis asked if, when he prayed in the words of another man, it was not the other man who prayed.

Berg replied: "No--unless you wish to apply the same reasoning to a hymn."

Welker of the North Carolina Classis informed the Synod that the churches of the South would not tolerate liturgical uniformity. [He must have known whereof he spoke, for his Classis subsequently seceded from the Synod, objecting to the whole of the Mercersburg movement.]

Bernard C. Wolff, an important member of the liturgical committee in the years to come, and Nevin's successor in the Seminary, spoke in favor of a "fuller Liturgy" as a doctrinal safeguard against heretical preaching.

The statement of a Mr. Sechler of Zion's Classis summarized and concluded the discussion of the third proposal. He said that the liturgical desires of the German Reformed Church revealed nothing new; rather something quite old, for "she has

always been a *liturgical* Church, if you please. The only
difficulty with us is, that we have, like other and younger
branches of the Reformed family, to a considerable extent
cut loose from the ancient landmarks. We have been tinkering
at the good old Liturgy, until at last we got hold of *Didactic
forms*. Instead of going back to the Reformation landmarks,
we got up something of our own [the Mayer Liturgy], bran-new
[*sic*], and we find out now, that it satisfies neither our
hearts nor our heads. We *want* nothing *new*; we want something
that is improved by experience and age. In other words, we
wish to take up what we should never have cast out."

Nevin had apparently remained silent throughout the preceding debate. When the fourth proposal was taken up--the
importance of adapting the historic Reformed liturgies to the
needs and wants of the American Church--he spoke, indicating
his surprise at the "conservatism" of the earlier discussion.
"We should take the Bible and the History of the Church before
us as our guide, and in the light thus afforded us, we should
go forward, without regard to anything else." There were two
questions facing the Synod, Nevin said: "What was theoretically
right?" and "What was expedient?" Clearly he felt that the
Synod should take the course which was theoretically correct,
if, indeed, any course were to be taken at all. The wisdom
of the latter was not certain, as Nevin indicated in his concluding remarks: "I have no personal interest in this matter.
Unless the Church, as such, feels the need of it, we had better
do without it."

Schaff evidently felt the need, and he spoke at length in
favor of the committee's resolutions. Because of the distinctive nature and needs of the American Church, its liturgy
should be the copy of no other. He particularly emphasized
the need for aid in family worship, as well as the assistance

which could be given to the prayers in the sanctuary, for the latter "were not generally such as could be called *prayers by the congregation*. The idea of most persons is, that the *minister alone* prays--it is not regarded by the bulk of even Christian hearers, as an act of the Church. And in the nature of the case it cannot be." By contrast, Schaff argued, a prayer which is known beforehand can be an honest prayer of the congregation.

The notion that the liturgy would be a barrier to free prayer was also repudiated by Schaff. Free and fixed prayer must never exclude each other in the Reformed tradition. If the liturgy were simply to be a "*crutch* to lean upon, then a thousand times better do without, than to use it with such motives and in such a spirit".

The statements of the Mercersburg professors, added to the affirmative positions of such men as Bomberger, Berg, and Wolff, carried the day, and it was resolved that a committee be appointed to report to the next Synod "a Plan or Schedule of a Liturgy....It is expected, therefore, that this Committee will thoroughly examine the various Liturgies of the Reformed Churches and other works published on this subject in later times, and specify as far as this may be done, the particular forms that are believed to be needed, and furnish specimens also such as may be called for in the circumstances of the Church in this country."

In the debate at Norristown positions were taken and arguments advanced which, in retrospect, give one a preview of much that was to come during the thirty-years' liturgical war. For example:

1. Bomberger was later accused of vacillating in his position on the *Provisional Liturgy*, and in a sense he did; however, he in fact never moved far from his liturgical line

articulated in 1849. He wanted a liturgy, but not one which would in any way ante-date the Reformation. He definitely wanted a liturgical service, yet one which would leave room for free prayer.

2. Optional forms for the occasional services were no serious problem; however, any attempt to standardize the regular Lord's Day service was unacceptable to a substantial number of ministers in the Synod. Since their only references for a Lord's Day service were the Mass and the *Book of Common Prayer*, both of which were offensive, it is little wonder that the idea frightened them.

3. The extent to which German Reformed worship had become didactic at the expense of the devotional was underscored at Norristown. Bomberger's plea for the return of "prayer and praise" appears to have been an eloquent one.

4. It was none other than the venerable Berg who answered two of the oft-repeated objections to the use of a liturgy. His reply to Ingold's statement that a liturgy implied that God only listened to "proper prayers" established one of the strong positive arguments for the use of a liturgy--*viz.*, that it serves to edify the church. In the years to come the advocates of the liturgy returned occasionally to this argument--especially in their defense of the Church Year--however, they never seemed fully to appreciate the strength of their position.

5. Berg also made the classic reply to the fear that if one prayed in the words of another man, then it was the other man who prayed. If one held this position, then Berg insisted that the same logic be applied to the singing of hymns.

6. Wolff's remark highlights still another positive argument for the use of a liturgy: it can be a doctrinal safeguard against heretical preaching. This was undoubtedly in the minds

of those who framed the two liturgies of the German Reformed
Church, although it was never articulated to its full effect.

7. Sechler's statement did establish a position often
debated during the next three decades. He insisted that the
American church had left its liturgical moorings. The committee's proposals called the church to no new worship; rather
to a form of worship as old as the Reformation. Until the
translation of the Palatinate Liturgy appeared the following
year, however, this argument could not be appreciated either.
That it subsequently proved to be true still did not impress
the older generation of German Reformed ministers, as will be
shown.

8. Nevin's remarks are especially interesting, for they
reveal his growing pessimism with the denomination, which
would culminate in his resignation from the Seminary in 1851.
Throughout the liturgical controversy Nevin resisted attempts
to tinker with what he believed to be "theoretically right"
in order to make it politically "expedient"--a position he
articulated at Norristown. He did not believe that the church
was ready for a liturgy which was "theoretically right", and
in this he was correct.

9. Certain of Schaff's liturgical interests and emphases
appear in abbreviated form at Norristown. He insisted that
any new liturgy should be distinctly American, "the copy of
no other". At Norristown Schaff also established the argument
that the liturgy should be both ecumenical and indigenous.
His emphasis on the importance of prayers for family worship,
and his belief that free and fixed prayer should never exclude each other influenced the Provisional Liturgy in ways
which shall be shown subsequently.

In compliance with the Synod's resolution, a committee
was appointed by the President, J. Rebaugh. It consisted of

John W. Nevin, chairman, Philip Schaff, Elias Heiner, Bernard
C. Wolff, John H. A. Bomberger, Henry Harbaugh, Joseph F.
Berg, and elders William Heyser, J. C. Bucher, Caspar Schaeffer, and George C. Welker.[40] During the following year B. C.
Wolff translated the introduction to Ebrard's *Reformirtes
Kirchenbuch* and Bomberger translated portions of a 1684 edition of the Palatinate Liturgy, both of which appeared in the
Mercersburg Review for 1850; however, the committee had no
meetings. Although no member of the committee pressed the
issue, apparently, the fact that the committee did not meet
is further evidence of Nevin's reticence to proceed. His report to the Synod of 1850 makes that clear.

> The committee appointed to commence the
> preparation of a new Liturgy, respectfully
> reported, that after such attention as they
> have been able to give to the subject, and in
> view of the general posture of the Church at
> the present time, they have not considered it
> expedient as yet to go forward with the work.
> Should it be felt necessary on the part of
> Synod to bring out at once a new formulary for
> public use, it is believed that the *most ad-
> visable course for the present would be to
> give a translation simply of the old liturgy
> of the Palatinate; although the Committee are
> by no means of the mind, that this would be
> the best ultimate form in which to provide
> for the great interest here in question.* Al-
> together, however, it is felt that the other
> question of vital moment now before the Church,
> need first to be settled, in order that it may
> become important really to bestow any full and
> final care on this question of a new Liturgy.[41]
> [Italics mine]

What these "other questions of vital moment now before the
Church" were is not entirely clear. Schaff believed them to
be three[42]: first, the debate concerning the removal of the

College and Seminary from Mercersburg to Lancaster was lengthy and lively and of some consequence. Second, the theological discussion of the church-question had not yet been resolved. According to Schaff, Nevin's Norristown remarks had been emphatic in linking liturgical worship with the idea of the church as the body of Christ. Nevin was pessimistic about the willingness or the ability of Protestantism to understand itself as the body of Christ and to act on the consequence of that understanding. His own depression was so deep and debilitating that it became the third "question of vital moment now before the Church" which must be resolved before further liturgical progress could be made. In retrospect Schaff concluded that "the delay of action on the side of the liturgy committee was altogether judicious and wise under the circumstances. The work itself only gained by it in the end."[43] The greatest gain made by the delay was Nevin's resignation as chairman of the committee in 1851. His "dizziness", as Good characterized his mood at the time, was clearly in the way of even a revision of the Palatinate Liturgy. He did, however, remain a member of the committee, now under the chairmanship of Schaff.

When the Synod of 1851 adjourned, no one could possibly have known that the German Reformed Church was but one short year away from adopting a series of liturgical proposals which would precipitate a bitter and protracted debate. These proposals, made by Schaff during the Baltimore Synod in 1852, the manner in which they guided the work of the liturgical committee, and the two liturgies which resulted are the primary subjects which are to be examined in the remainder of this essay.

NOTES TO CHAPTER II

1. A. R. Kremer, *A Biographical Sketch of John William-son Nevin* (Reading, Pa.: Daniel Miller, 1890), pp. 58-63.

2. James Hastings Nichols, *Corporate Worship in the Reformed Tradition* (Philadelphia: Westminster Press, 1968), p. 12.

3. *Ibid.*, p. 53.

4. *Ibid.*, p. 71.

5. Bard Thompson, ed., *Liturgies of the Western Church* (Cleveland: The World Publishing Company, [1961]), pp. 143-144.

6. *Ibid.*, pp. 147-148.

7. Nichols, *Corporate Worship*, p. 75.

8. *Ibid.*, p. 76.

9. *Ibid.*, p. 78.

10. *Ibid.*, p. 79.

11. James Hastings Nichols, "The Liturgical Tradition of the Reformed Churches," *Theology Today*, XI (July, 1954), 214.

12. J. H. A. Bomberger, J. I. Good, et al., *The Reverend H. A. Bomberger, Centenary Volume* (Philadelphia: Publication and Sunday School Board of the Reformed Church in the United States, 1917), p. 99.

13. Julius Melton, *Presbyterian Worship in America: Changing Patterns Since 1787* (Richmond: John Knox Press, 1967), p. 51.

14. Nichols, *Corporate Worship*, p. 112.

15. E. V. Gerhart, "The German Reformed Church in America: Faith--Government--Worship," *MR*, XIV (1867), pp. 272-273.

16.   Philip Schaff, "The New Liturgy," p. 204.

17.   Nichols, *Romanticism*, p. 286.

18.   David D. Demarest, *The Reformed Church in America* (New York: Board of Publication of the Reformed Church in America, 1889), p. 146.

19.   Dubbs, *op. cit.*, p. 269.

20.   H. M. J. Klein, *The History of the Eastern Synod of the Reformed Church in the United States* (Lancaster, Pa.: Published by the Eastern Synod, 1943), pp. 41-43.

21.   Richards, *History of the Theological Seminary*, p. 333.

22.   *Ibid.*

23.   Good, *op. cit.*, p. 169.

24.   *WM*, March 30, 1853.

25.   *WM*, April 20, 1853.

26.   *WM*, February 28, 1855.

27.   *WM*, January 30, 1867.

28.   Guy P. Bready, *History of Maryland Classis* (n. p.: Privately published and copywritten, 1938), p. 26.

29.   B. C. Wolff, *WM*, January 30, 1867.

30.   *Ibid.*, *WM*, February 6, 1867.

31.   *Ibid.*

32.   *Ibid.*

33.   *Ibid.*

34.   Philip Schaff, "The New Liturgy," p. 207.

35.   *Acts and Proceedings of the [Eastern] Synod of the German Reformed Church* (1866), p. 95.

36.   *Acts and Proceedings of the Eastern Synod* (1849), quoted in Philip Schaff, "The New Liturgy," p. 210.

37. *Ibid.*, pp. 211-212.

38. *WM*, November 7, 1849.

39. *WM*, October 24, 1849.

40. *Acts and Proceedings of the Eastern Synod* (1866), p. 95.

41. *Acts and Proceedings of the Eastern Synod* (1850), quoted in Philip Schaff, "The New Liturgy," p. 214.

42. Philip Schaff, "The New Liturgy," p. 214.

43. *Ibid.*, p. 215.

CHAPTER III

Liturgical Alternatives

Before discussing the important report Schaff made to the
Synod of 1852, at which time the liturgical die was firmly
cast, it will be informative to examine the several possible
directions open to the liturgical committee. There was little
desire in the denomination to retain the Mayer liturgy; thus a
closer look at it will reveal primarily the direction in which
the committee definitely did not wish to go. The Palatinate
Liturgy is examined since it is the "parent" liturgy of the
denomination, and since it was posed by some as a temporary
measure, by others as the liturgical goal. The Dutch Reformed
Church, a sister denomination, published a new provisional
liturgy in 1857. It is basically an adaptation of the Palatinate Liturgy, and the result of a liturgical procedure advocated by many within the German Reformed Church. The Presbyterian Church was half a century behind the German Reformed
Church in denominational liturgical action. Private compilations were the Presbyterian liturgical "way" during the latter
part of the nineteenth century, and this possibility needs to
be examined. Whereas each of the following Liturgies will be
surveyed generally, only the more significant forms--especially
those for the regular Lord's Day, the Lord's Supper, and Ordin-
ation--will be detailed.

The Mayer Liturgy[1]

Marriage

The first service offered in the Mayer Liturgy is a Form of Marriage, consisting of five parts: a lengthy, biblical statement concerning the origin of woman and her relationship to man; a biblical statement specifying the duties of each in regard to the other; a single question of intent addressed to each (There is no exchange of vows.); the declaration of marriage; and a prayer of supplication for the couple.

Ordination

The second form is the Ordination of a Minister to the Gospel. It begins with an Invocation; then proceeds to an Address to the Ordinand, setting forth the doctrine of the ministry. The Christian minister is an "ambassador for Christ, in an embassy of mercy and of reconciliation between heaven and earth". He is set apart by the apostolic act of the laying on of hands. "This rite is not a mere ceremony"; rather, if the ordinand's heart is "right" in the sight of the Lord, then the laying on of hands is "both a recognition of his authority, as a minister of the gospel, and a symbolic assurance given him from above, that his consecration of himself is accepted, and the Lord's Spirit shall be with him".

The minister is "constituted a bishop or overseer, in the church". It is his "duty to preach the gospel in its purity, as it is contained in the holy Scripture". He must be a minister of the gospel everywhere and at all times, always aware that his purpose is that of the gospel: "to save sinners".

There are four Ordination Questions in the Liturgy:

1. Do you receive *holy Scripture* 'as the record of the revelation of God, and as the sufficient and only rule of faith and life?'

2. Do you receive the *Heidelberg Catechism* 'as substantially the system of Christian doctrine taught in the holy Scripture?'

3. Do you sincerely believe that 'you are called of God to this ministry...?'

4. 'Do you receive the constitution of our Church, and promise to yield obedience to it in all your ministerial conduct?'

The ordinand, after giving satisfactory answer to the above questions, kneels for the Laying on of Hands and the Consecration Prayer. According to this prayer he is "appointed ...to the ministry of reconciliation, to proclaim [Christ's] gospel, to administer the sealing *ordinances* of his Church, to exercise Christian discipline therein...." Following the Consecration Prayer the ordinand receives the right hand of fellowship and the Apostolic Benediction.

The Charge to the newly ordained minister may be original; however, there is one provided. It is lengthy and didactic, urging the brother to learn from and follow the example of Christ in all things. From this Charge it is clear that Mayer believed the minister should walk taller than ordinary men, for he was to be an example before them, "exhibiting a purer life, a more perfect resignation, a holier devotion, and a more diffusive benevolence than others". He must discipline his flock, yet not "lord it over them"; he must not permit the "applause of men" to influence either his preaching or his conduct; his own house must be kept in order at all times; and he must constantly seek to improve his talent.

Unless the Installation is to follow, the service of
Ordination concludes with a Prayer of Supplication for the
newly ordained minister. Save for a few didactic lines such
as, "Thou hast heard the answer he has made to our interroga-
tory", this prayer has a devotional quality uncharacteristic
of the service as a whole.

The ministry as set forth in Mayer's service of Ordination, while it could never be open to the charge of being a
"third sacrament", is nevertheless high and exalted. There
is, however, no sense in which the minister's authority is derived from the church; rather his authority is in his calling,
proof of which is to be seen in his exemplary conduct. Johnson
argues that the "exemplary image" of the ministry is a Protestant misconception which developed through a combination of
the Puritan ethos and the American frontier. The fallacy is
not that the minister should lead a moral life, but that
"either the personal spiritual experience of the ordained
minister, or the moral pattern of his life is of *first* importance to the ministry of the Church".[2]

The service of Ordination devotes a great deal of attention to the minister's preaching: he must "preach the gospel
in its purity, as it is contained in the holy Scripture"; his
preaching must be "pure, sincere, drawn from the warmth of a
believing heart"; his preaching must never be influenced by
the "applause of men, or the desire of gain"; he must constantly work to improve his preaching. By contrast, the
Liturgy simply states that one of the reasons for which he is
ordained is "to administer the sealing *ordinances* of [Christ's]
church"; he is to "baptize believers in the gospel, and their
infant children, as commanded by [Christ]", and to "administer
the Lord's Supper with a seriousness and love like [Christ's]".
[Italics mine] Undoubtedly this imbalance reflects more than

the fact that a minister celebrates less often than he preaches; for, though the Mayer Liturgy would certainly expect the celebrations of the sacraments to be solemn occasions, it nevertheless articulates a Zwinglian theology of the Eucharist. This will be shown in more detail in the discussion of the "Administration of the Lord's Supper".

Installation of a Minister

These same emphases on exemplary conduct and preaching are carried into the lengthy Charge with which the Installation of a Minister begins. In the paragraph dealing with the minister's exercise of discipline the Liturgy states: "The Church is an institution of God for the production of holiness among the children of men. It is designed to recover man from the ruin of his fallen state, to bring him back to God, and to form anew in him that resemblance to the Deity in his moral character which is lost by the fall." The church is the agency through which the heathen is converted and the backslider reclaimed; the primary instrument through which both of these goals are accomplished is preaching.

Baptism of Infants

The Form of Infant Baptism consists of a lengthy address to the parents or sponsors; two questions concerning the parents' acceptance of the "gospel of Jesus Christ, as it is contained in the Holy Scriptures" and their professed desire to "dedicate this child to the service of God"; the act of Baptism using the Trinitarian formula; a second, lengthy charge

to the parents; and a prayer of supplication. The most obvious feature of this service is the conspicuous absence of
any statement that the action is an objective sacrament. In
fact, the word, "sacrament", never appears; rather the term,
"ordinance", is used consistently throughout. The parents
have presented their child "for the purpose of dedicating it
to the service of God in baptism, as *an infant member* of his
church". Baptism is "the *rite of initiation* into the Christian Church, and is therefore to be conferred on all *who are
entitled to be received* as members into its communion...."
[Italics mine] The authority to baptize children of believing
parents "is derived from the fact that they, as well as their
parents, are included in the covenant and church of God".

If the author of this Liturgy and the committee which
revised it held any trace of historic Reformed sacramental
theology, the words of the Liturgy do not convey it. Baptism
"represents to us the promise of salvation"; it "denotes that,
as sinners, we are unclean". The parents, far more than the
child, are the center of attention; and the several statements
concerning their responsibility for the child culminate in a
distasteful threat, which is more indicative of superstition
than Christian theology: "If this child should grow up in
ignorance and sin by your neglect, it is most likely that it
will perish in ignorance and sin; but the guilt of its per-
dition will be upon you; and it will be fearful indeed for
you to appear before God, if you be stained with its blood."

Baptism of Adults

Two features in the Baptism of an Adult deserve comment.
First, the rubrics make it clear that Baptism is an *occasional*

service which need not necessarily be performed within the context of corporate worship: "It is not necessary that all the ordinary ceremonies of public worship be performed, or that a sermon should be preached: it is requisite only that the meeting be religious, and of sufficient publicity to make the baptism a public profession of faith in Christ."

Second, the word "sacrament" is used for the first and only time in either service of Baptism. The statement is classic Zwinglianism:

> Sacraments possess no power in themselves to confer grace by the mere use of them. All their efficiency is derived from faith in the recipient. The preaching of the word is designed as a means, both to produce faith in the heart, and to nourish it when produced; but the sacraments, as sealing ordinances, are intended only to confirm a previously existing faith, and therefore can be of use only to those who already believe.

The service of Confirmation is not distinctive. It consists of address to the congregation[3] and to the candidates, the confirmation questions and blessing, followed by a prayer of dedication. The rubrics direct that the service "shall always take place before the communion".

Lord's Supper

The structure of the Administration of the Lord's Supper is as follows:

    I.   Sermon: "short, not exceeding half an hour's length".

    II. Words of Institution.

    III. Address based on the Words of Institution: This

address seeks, first, to set forth the doctrine of the Lord's
Supper. The memorial aspect of Communion is stressed, re-
minding the congregation that Jesus instituted the Lord's
Supper because "*an absent friend is easily forgotten*". [Ital-
ics mine] To recall "what Jesus is [and] what he has done for
us" the address proceeds through a detailed rehearsal of the
events of holy week.

In the "holy ordinance", then, the breaking of the bread
and the pouring of the wine "*represent*" Christ's crucifixion
and death--"the propitiation for our sins".

The "manner in which we may profitably come to the Lord's
Table demands our most serious attention". There follows a
positive rather than a negative "fencing"--i.e., the address
specifies those who may come (the humble and repentant) rather
than those who may not.

This statement is followed by the prayer of consecration,
containing elements of confession, thanksgiving, and supplication. There is a form of epiclesis which invokes God's blessing "on the emblems of thy broken body and shed blood before
us", and beseeches his presence "in the solemn exercise in
which we are engaged". In keeping with the theme of an
"absent friend", the verbs in the "anamnesis" are all in the
past tense: "to refresh our hearts with the remembrance of
Jesus Christ; the remembrance of what he was and of what he
has done and suffered for us".

IV. Hymn.

V. Fraction and Distribution: The minister is to
"break the bread to each communicant, and having poured out
the wine, he shall give the cup to the first and let it pass
from one to the other until all shall have received it". Three
means of receiving the elements are provided: the congregation
may "take their places standing around the table or the altar",

or they may sit "around a table provided for the purpose", or, if the congregation is large, the elders may serve them in their pews. That the words of distribution may not become monotonous, the Liturgy provides eight pages of scriptural forms for the bread and the wine.

    VI.   103rd Psalm may be read.

    VII.   Hymn or Admonition: The celebration concludes with either a hymn or admonition, or both, "as time and circumstances may require".

The several inescapable features of this Liturgy are: a funereal stress on propitiatory atonement and the consequent absence of joy; virtually no congregational participation; no affirmation of faith through one of the historic creeds; and what has been characterized as a "doctrine of the real absence". The extent to which the Mayer Liturgy carries "the real absence" may be typical of Zwinglianism, as it came to be expressed historically; but one may certainly assume that Zwingli himself would have been offended by such a statement as "an absent friend is easily forgotten". It must be said again, however, that as much as the Mayer eucharistic theology may be inconsistent with that expressed in the confessions and catechisms of the sixteenth century, the Liturgy gives every indication that the celebrations were taken seriously and conducted in a manner befitting the occasion.

Following the Lord's Supper the Liturgy provides forms for the Installation of Elders and Deacons, Constituting of a Church, the Laying of a Cornerstone, Dedication of a Church, and the Burial of the Dead. These forms will not be treated in detail.

Everyone commenting on the Liturgy agrees that it was far too dull and didactic;[4] however, not everyone draws similar conclusions from the Liturgy's poor reception. B. C. Wolff insisted that one reason for Mayer's failure to be widely used was that it did not "provide an order of worship for the sanctuary. It was a book of forms made up of *agenda*—of acts to be performed by the minister; while the *legenda* parts of the service, in which the people should take part were wanting."[5] Good objected to this argument, claiming that "the official adoption of such a liturgy [i.e., one without a form for the Lord's Day service] clearly shows that our church was accustomed to have the free service on the Lord's Day".[6] This position slightly twists the facts; for whereas Mayer's adoption may indicate the practice of the church at the time, it did not indicate the desire of the denomination. That desire for a Lord's Day service is clearly evidenced in Bomberger's Norristown proposals:

> 3. That the Liturgy now authorized and partially used by the Church [the Mayer Liturgy], is inadequate to our wants, inasmuch as apart from other deficiencies which may be found in it, *it makes no provision for ordinary occasions of public worship.*

The extent to which Good uses his sources to his own advantage is illustrated in his account that the desire of Synod to reduce the length of Mayer's forms is proof that the church wanted fewer forms rather than a fuller and more complete liturgy, as Mercersburg argued. He quotes a portion of a correspondent's article in the *Weekly Messenger*, June 2, 1841, to support his position. The correspondent does indeed want the Mayer Liturgy abbreviated even more than the revision committee was willing to do; however, his reason for desiring this abbreviation is the oppressive "didactive method". Good stops short of this telling sentence: "It [the Mayer Liturgy] seems to be rather full of argument, reasoning, etc., for such a work."

Nevin concluded that the Mayer Liturgy never received a second printing,[7] primarily because it was but "the continuation of a mode or manner of worship, which it was felt the life of the Church had outgrown, so as to need now a different style of worship altogether".[8] Rauch had apparently criticized the Mayer Liturgy's "external, mechanical character". In this context, according to Nevin, Rauch made his observation on the nature of a liturgy--an observation Nevin was never to forget: "A Liturgy...should be of one cast, a single creation, ruled throughout by the presence of one central ideal; in this respect like a poem, or other true work of art."[9]

The Mayer Liturgy failed for four principal reasons. First, it was so didactic and argumentative--James I. Good notwithstanding--that even nineteenth-century doctrine-loving Germans found it unacceptable. Second, it did not reflect the denomination's growing desire for a regular Lord's Day service (granting, certainly, that few in the denomination desired an *obligatory* Lord's Day service). The third reason was political: the Liturgy was prepared almost exclusively by Lewis Mayer himself, yet the attempt was made to present it as the work of a committee. As shall be evident throughout this study, one of the profoundest lessons contemporary liturgical committees can learn from Mercersburg is the extent to which politics and personalities influence not only the content but also the reception of a liturgy. Good is uncertain of the reasons in every case, but he is likely correct in his hunch that those who did not hold Mayer himself in the highest esteem--especially the Helffenstein clan--were not particularly pleased with his Liturgy.

A fourth reason for the Liturgy's cool reception is a constitutional one. Church polity and the liturgy will receive extensive treatment when evaluating both the Provisional Liturgy and the *Order of Worship*; however, the same problem arose with the Mayer Liturgy. The Liturgy was presented to the Synod in 1837. It was submitted to a revision committee, then sent to the Classes. The majority of the Classes approved the Liturgy and it was adopted by the Synod of 1838; yet another revision committee was appointed *after it had already been adopted*. The revised edition was sent to the Classes once more; however, they could only pass on the revisions and not the Liturgy itself, since it had already been adopted. The result was that in its final form the Mayer Liturgy was adopted by a minority (only four) of the Classes.[10]

The best benediction which could be pronounced on this abortive experience is to join Bomberger[11] and Theodore Appel,[12] both of whom claim that if nothing else, the Mayer Liturgy was a learning experience which may have paved the way for a better understanding of what future form the denomination's worship ought to take.

The Palatinate Liturgy

The general history of the Palatinate Liturgy has been presented in the previous chapter. It now remains to examine in some detail the design of the Palatinate Church Order and several of its liturgical forms, the better to understand the German Reformed liturgical heritage and to become better acquainted with one of the resources for the Provisional Liturgy. The liturgical committee reflected the denomination's wishes in proposing and producing a liturgy distinct from the

Palatinate; however, that the Palatinate was before the committee throughout its deliberations is certain. As shall be shown in the pages to follow, many of the liturgical principles which produced the design of the Palatinate Liturgy are also to be found in the Provisional Liturgy; however, the "parent" influenced the *details* of the "child" at only a few points.

Two English translations of portions of the Palatinate Liturgy have been published: Bomberger's translation, which appeared in the *Mercersburg Review* throughout 1850 and 1851, was based on an incomplete edition initially published in 1684 and reprinted in 1763. He translated as much of the entire Church Order as remained in the tattered copy in Father Pomp's library. A more recent translation has been provided by Bard Thompson.[13] The forms for the Lord's Day, Preparation for Communion, and Communion were translated from the original edition of the Palatinate Church Order.[14]

Four sections constitute the Palatinate Church Order: "Of Doctrine", setting forth various regulations for the sermon; "Of Public Prayer", providing the Lord's Day service and special prayers for use after a sermon on the Catechism, for a fast day, Christmas, New Year's, Good Friday, Easter, Ascension, Whitsunday, and a morning and an evening prayer; "Of the Administration of the Holy Sacraments", being forms for Baptism, Preparation for Communion, and Communion, and a statement concerning Christian discipline; "Of Other Church Customs and Services", which specifies the festival days to be celebrated,[15] the clerical dress to be worn,[16] and forms for Marriage, Visitation of the Sick, Communion to the Sick, Visitation of Prisoners, the Burial Service, Baptism of Jews and Ana-baptists, and Confirmation. Of the several forms provided, the Lord's Day service, Preparation for Communion, and the Administration of the Lord's Supper will be examined in detail.

Lord's Day

The Lord's Day service begins with a blessing ("Grace, peace, and mercy...") and a psalm, followed by a general confession. This prayer of confession is an adaptation of Bucer's confession,[17] also adopted by Calvin, with a paragraph analogous to Calvin's Collect for Illumination. The first corporate recitation of the Lord's Prayer precedes the sermon, which is followed by a second corporate confession, more specific than verbatim from the Würtemburg Liturgy of 1536.[18] An absolution and proclamation of judgment is again followed by the Lord's Prayer, which precedes the prayers of Thanksgiving, Supplication, and Intercession. The Lord's Prayer, or a lengthy paraphrase (typical of Calvinistic liturgies), is repeated for a third time; and the service concludes with a Psalm and the Aaronic Benediction.

Several features of the Lord's Day service must have been surprising to American Germans in the nineteenth century. There was, for example, no place for free prayer. This was typical of sixteenth century Reformed liturgies, of course, and Harbaugh (and others) argued that free prayer came into Reformed worship through the "fanatic" Jean de Labadie in the seventeenth century.[19] Although Labadie did popularize free prayer in the Lord's Day worship at Geneva, where the informal worship he conducted in the homes was gradually transferred to the Lord's Day, the practice had already existed upon his arrival in Middleburg.[20]

A second surprise was the extent of corporate participation in the Lord's Day liturgy. Congregations accustomed only to singing hymns and, perhaps, repeating the Lord's Prayer were shocked to find that their ancestors regularly repeated the Lord's Prayer at least twice and joined in a corporate prayer of confession each Lord's Day. Furthermore, a corporate rendering of the Apostles' Creed was a part of each celebration of the Eucharist.

The strong and unmistakable absolution in the Palatinate Liturgy must have surprised and disturbed still others. Not a little of the controversy which followed the publication of the *Order of Worship* in 1866 concerned the absolution in that Liturgy; however, as will be shown, that absolution appears to have been modeled after the Palatinate Liturgy.

A fourth surprise in the Palatinate Liturgy was surely the prayers prescribed for the eight festival days. Evidently there was no general acknowledgment of any festival days in nineteenth century German Reformed worship until the Provisional Liturgy in 1857. According to Appel, Schaff introduced the first Good Friday service ever held in Mercersburg.[21]

Preparatory Service

The rubrics differ slightly (but significantly) in the 1684 edition used by Bomberger and in the 1563 edition used by Bard Thompson. In the former it is stated that communion "shall be administered in the larger towns at least once in two months, in other places four times each year, viz.: on Christmas, Easterday, Whitsuntide, and on the first Sabbath in September. Yet as the edification, custom, or want of the Church may require it, it is proper to administer it more frequently." The 1563 edition prescribes a more frequent celebration: "at least once a month in the towns, once every two months in the villages, and on Easter, Pentecost, and Christmas in both places". The rubric goes on to prescribe the manner in which, after the sermon, both the adults and those children about to receive their first Communions are to be further instructed.

This instruction comes in the form of lengthy questions, to which the congregation is to respond, "We do". The first question summarizes the structure of the Heidelberg Catechism [sin, redemption, gratitude], and presents Christ's summary of the Law, and calls the people to a confession of their sin. The second question consists of a summary of the Gospel [essentially that God in Christ accomplished for us what we could not accomplish for ourselves--the forgiveness of sin] and a statement concerning the efficacy of the Holy Supper: "Do you also believe that by means of His Holy Supper...and through the action of the Holy Spirit in your heart, Christ now again confirms to each among you this redemption He once promised and granted to you in Holy Baptism...?" The benefits of Christ accrue to the believer by analogy--i.e., as surely as the bread is eaten and the wine drunk, so "the Lord Christ Himself feeds and nourishes your hungry and contrite heart and weary soul with His crucified body and shed blood unto eternal life"; therefore "the passion and death of Christ is as certainly your own, as if you had suffered in your own body all that the Lord endured in His blessed body on your behalf". The statement concludes on the eschatalogical note that Christ instituted the Eucharist "for the sake of this comfort" and "in remembrance of Him" "until He shall come in the clouds to deliver us wholly...." To the question, "Is this your faith?" the congregation responds, "It is."

The third question calls the congregation to renounce "all envy, hatred and bitterness", and to forgive their neighbors. "All who now find this in their hearts should not doubt that they already possess the forgiveness of their sins.... Wherefore, let each one who heartily desires this say: Amen." The Lord's Prayer and the benediction conclude the service.

Of particular note in this service is the objective view of the Eucharist and the dynamic presence of the living Christ which is anticipated in the celebration. Here there is no "absent friend...easily forgotten"; rather a victorious Christ who calls his people to share in his triumph. Another feature of this service is the congregational responses. The extent of the responses was to be much greater in the Provisional Liturgy and the *Order of Worship*; however, the precedent for them in German Reformed worship was established in the Palatinate Liturgy.

Lord's Supper

The Communion service follows that prescribed for the regular Lord's Day; however, before the final psalm, the "Minister of the Word shall read out the following exhortation --clearly, forcefully, and earnestly--by the Table at which the Supper is to be celebrated". This is a lengthy address consisting of three parts: first, the Pauline *Words of Institution*, establishing the warrant for the celebration. Second, the congregation is directed to *examine themselves*, again using the structure of the Catechism: sin, redemption, and gratitude. This section includes a "negative" fencing, warning "all to abstain from the Lord's Table who know themselves to be afflicted with the following sins...." Third, "let us now consider to what end the Lord hath instituted His Supper for us, namely that we do this in remembrance of him". The anamnesis centers on the crucifixion and the atonement. The Words of Institution are repeated; then this affirmation: Christ's death has taken away our sin "and hath obtained for us the life-giving Spirit: that through the same Spirit...we might have true communion

with Him, and be made partakers of all His benefits, of
eternal life, righteousness, and glory". This communion
with Christ results, finally in communion with one another
"in true brotherly love".

The Consecration Prayer is relatively brief. It consists of a supplication-epiclesis, beseeching God "to act
upon our hearts by Thy Holy Spirit in this Supper...that
through the power of the Holy Spirit our weary and contrite
hearts may be fed and quickened by His true body and blood,
yea of Him who is true God and man, the only bread of heaven".
The first part of this prayer is an adaptation of the next-
to-last paragraph of Calvin's Great Prayer.[22] Following
this prayer in the Palatinate Liturgy is the Lord's Prayer,
the Creed, and the "shadowy" Sursum Corda, typical of the
liturgies of Farel, Calvin, Knox, and à Lasco.[23]

After the Administration and Distribution of the elements
(during which there may either be singing or the reading of
John 14-18 and Isaiah 53), the Post-Communion Thanksgiving
consists of verses from Psalm 103, Romans 8, and Romans 5,
"each one saying in his heart"--i.e., the congregation
silently repeating the words after the minister. An option
may be a prayer, provided in the Liturgy. The Aaronic Benediction concludes the service.

A rubric concerning excommunication follows the liturgy
of the Lord's Supper and makes the relationship between discipline and the Eucharist quite clear. The verbal "fencing"
was to have practical consequences in the lives of the people;
for excommunication must be exercised both to protect an unworthy recipient from the Eucharist and to protect the Eucharist from profanation by the unworthy. Care is exercised to
insure that the authority for excommunication be vested not
in the minister alone, but "in the entire Christian congrega-

tion, to which the minister, as well as the humblest member of the church are subject". Several "honorable and god-fearing men shall be appointed from the congregation". It is their duty to exhort ("once, twice, or three times, according to circumstances") the sinner to amend his ways. If he does not respond to these exhortations, he is to be "separated from the Christian congregation by the denial of the holy sacraments", until he promises and gives proof of amendment.

The above description should give substance to Nichols' observation that "while in structure they [the German, Dutch, and Hungarian liturgies] are closer to the liturgies of Basel and Zurich than to those of Strassburg or Scotland, the doctrine is similar to that of the services of the Mass type".[24] In the Palatinate Liturgy one finds a wedding of the medieval preaching order and the form for administering communion to the laity. This wedding creates a liturgical structure which is slightly cumbersome and difficult to rationalize; yet it does restore the relationship between Word and Sacraments, a restoration attempted by all the major Reformers in the sixteenth century, save Zwingli. The Palatines were somewhat more successful than Calvin was in increasing the frequency of Communion: "at least once a month in the towns".

There can be no doubt that the Palatinate Liturgy articulates a doctrine of the Eucharist defensible by Calvin's standards: the strong emphasis on preparation for communion, the benefits of Christ which accrue to the believer by faith, the care with which discipline is exercised, the statement that through the Holy Spirit we have "true communion" with Christ and are "made partakers of all His benefits, of eternal life, righteousness, and glory", the Sursum-corda mechanics by which the believer's heart and faith are lifted into heaven, there to be "fed and nourished with His body and

blood, as truly as we receive the holy bread and cup in remembrance of Him"--these are all themes established by Calvin
and reiterated in the Heidelberg Catechism. The repetition of
the Creed set the Eucharistic action within the context of
historical Christianity; the participation of the congregation
made the Eucharist a corporate oblation of praise and thanksgiving.

Although the Palatinate Liturgy does have some "heavy,
stiff, didactic features" which mean a certain "deficiency in
liturgical glow and devotional warmth",[25] it is nevertheless
rooted in sound doctrine and vitally related to a system of
polity.[26] Bomberger's translation came at a judicious time
and a rediscovered Palatinate Liturgy did much to prepare the
way for the Provisional Liturgy in 1857.

Liturgies of the Reformed Protestant Dutch Church in North America

The worship of the Dutch Reformed Church in America combines "the advantages of both form and freedom", according to
Demarest.[27] Such was the case, in theory at least, by the end
of the nineteenth century; however, this return to the sixteenth century Reformed attempt to balance freedom and form
came only as the result of a liturgical movement which, in
certain particulars, paralleled that of Mercersburg.

Throughout the Colonial Period the Dutch and German Reformed Churches had close and cordial relations, as could be
expected among denominational siblings. It was, after all,
the Amsterdam Classis which financed the German venture in
America. In the late eighteenth century a merger would hardly
have been surprising; however, "after the [American] Revolution,

the [Dutch] Reformed Church decided to set up housekeeping for itself and to do it in the English language".[28] The German Reformed Church was not yet prepared to make such a move officially; therefore "little more than language kept the two Churches apart".[29] In 1844 the Dutch and German Churches met for the first of several Triennial Conventions, designed to provide an opportunity for discussions on matters of mutual concern and conceivably to pave the way for a merger. Whatever success this early venture in ecumenicity might have had, however, the coming of Nevin and Schaff to Mercersberg precluded; for the Dutch were among the first to recoil at Mercersburg's "Romanizing tendencies". "Catholic Unity", *The Principle of Protestantism,* and *Mystical Union* were enough to fill the pages of the Dutch *Christian Intelligencer* with invective against Nevin and Schaff. When the German Synod of 1851 refused to receive Nevin's resignation from the Seminary, the Dutch delegates reported to their denomination that Nevin's *writings* had been endorsed. This was likely not the case at all; rather the Synod's action more nearly represented simply a refusal to repudiate Nevin personally. The German Synod of 1852 did accept Nevin's resignation, upon which he insisted, but did not reject his theology. Failure to do so led the Dutch Synod to cease ecclesiastical relations with its German cousin in 1853.

Although Hageman would not have the division too sharply drawn--call it a separation rather than a divorce, because "there was in the Dutch Church a strong undercurrent of sympathy with the German Church"[30]--the pages of the *Christian Intelligencer* testify to the extent of Dutch hostility toward Mercersburg Theology. One example of this lost love should suffice. Henry Harbaugh was one of the German Reformed delegates to the Dutch Synod in June, 1853. In his remarks he said, "We consider ourselves persecuted and slandered by the secular and religious journals." Elbert S. Porter, editor of the *Christian Intelligencer*, replied in this fashion:

> As to the general tendency of the Mercersburg
> Theology, there can be no doubt. A clergyman
> was once asked by a lady whether she might
> not wear all the finery and ornaments of
> worldly people, since these were mere exter-
> nals and showed nothing of the state of the
> heart. 'Why, madam,' he answered with much
> gravity, 'When I see the fox's tail sticking
> out of the hole, I generally conclude that
> the fox himself is there.' Just so the doc-
> trines, the language, the spirit, the whole
> tenor of the Mercersburg writings indicate
> a state of mind far removed from genuine
> Protestantism. So various parties, without
> collusion, without intercourse, yet possessed
> of at least an ordinary measure of under-
> standing, deliberately and repeatedly de-
> clare. And we submit that in doing so, they
> neither slander nor persecute.[31]

The fact that the Dutch refused to send delegates to the German Reformed Synod did not disturb Nevin so much as the manner in which he felt the Dutch to be purposely arousing dissent within the German Reformed Church. He charged that the *Christian Intelligencer* "has granted the free use of its columns to any disaffected minister, or layman, of the German Reformed Church, who could be induced to make them the channel of his spleen or pride; besides encouraging every scribbler at home to write what trash he pleased in the same vein and for the same general purpose".[32] So far as Nevin was concerned, the Dutch Reformed Church was unchurchly, unsacramental, and unliturgical. It had forgotten the Creed in its worship and simply had no better wit than to assume that when Mercersburg made the Creed central to its theology, it was Romanizing.

Different positions on the Creed inevitably led to different
doctrines of the Church: for the one [Mercersburg, of course]
the Church is historical, holy, and catholic; for the other
[the "Low Dutch Church"] Christianity has become "a religion
of sects, the product of private judgment and private will".[33]
A different understanding of the church thus yields different
interpretations of the ministry and the sacraments; and a
difference regarding the sacraments means a difference in
matters liturgical. Nevin observes that the liturgical matter
has not yet become an issue between the Germans and the Dutch,
but it will; and when the Provisional Liturgy is completed,
the real line between churchliness and Puritanism will be
drawn once and for all.[34]

This forecast was a true one, but the Dutch were already
moving toward a liturgy of their own. The Synod of 1853
appointed a committee to study liturgical revision; and thus
began twenty years and more during which the Dutch Reformed
Church witnessed a succession of liturgies. Hageman attri-
butes the Dutch move at this time to four factors: a feeling
on the part of Dutch leaders that they had better produce a
revision of their own before they had to face "the finished
product of their German cousins which was bound to be influential in some Dutch circles and equally bound, in view
of its sponsors, to be pestilential in its theology"; "seep-
age" of Dutch Reformed ministers and laymen into the Episcopal
Church was considerable; the "Gothic age" had influenced not
a few in the Dutch Church; and, finally, "by 1853 men were
tired in the Reformed Church...of liturgical chaos".[35]

What did the committee of 1853 have to revise? As has
been indicated in the previous chapter, the Netherlands was
to align itself liturgically with the Palatinate pattern of
worship. Peter Datheen [also Dathenus] provided a liturgy

for the Dutch and French refugees in Frakenthal, "using elements from the French liturgy that Calvin had prepared for
his congregation at Strasbourg, the order of service that à
Lasco had used in London, and the new liturgy that had been
prepared in 1563 for the Church in the Palatinate".[36] The
first Synod met outside the Netherlands in the Palatinate
city of Wezel in 1568. Datheen's translations of the Psalms
and the Heidelberg Catechism were adopted. Six years later
in 1574, the Netherlands Synod adopted Datheen's liturgy, en-
joined the observance of the major Christian festivals, and
prohibited free prayer in the Sunday Service.[37]

Additional forms such as the "Consolation of the Sick
and Dying" were gradually added to Datheen's liturgy, and, in
1619 the Synod of Dort prescribed a "Compendium of the Christian Religion" and the form for the administration of Baptism
to adults. The Liturgy was translated into English for the
Scottish and English refugees in Holland; and, as was noted
in the previous chapter, "in 1767, three years after Rev. Dr.
Laidlie had begun to officiate in English in the church of
New York, an amended edition of this translation was published
by the Consistory of that church, which, so far as the forms
made imperative by the constitution are concerned, has remained unchanged".[38]

The *Constitution of the Reformed Dutch Church in the
United States of America* specifically states the balance between freedom and form which the denomination wished to maintain:

> Firmly believing, that the gifts of the Holy
> Spirit for the edification of Zion in every
> age, are promised and bestowed, the Reformed
> Dutch Church judges it sufficient to shew in
> a few specimens the general tenor and manner

in which public worship is performed, and
leaves it to the piety and gifts of her
ministers to conduct the ordinary solem-
nities of the sanctuary, in a manner they
judge most acceptable to God, and most
edifying to his people.[39]

Concerning the Lord's Supper the Constitution prescribes this:
"Every Church shall observe such a mode in *administering* the
Lord's Supper as shall be judged most conducive to edification;
provided, however, that the external ceremonies prescribed in
the word of God, be not altered, and that all superstition be
avoided."[40] The Lord's Supper is to be celebrated "once every
two months, if the same shall be convenient; and it will be
expedient where the circumstances of the church admit, that
it be administered at Easter, Whitsuntide, and Christmas".[41]
As Nichols points out, among American Reformed churches there
was a general resistance to recognizing festivals such as
Christmas and Easter. "The Continental Reformed churches had
always observed these, but the Scottish and Puritan rejection
of them prevailed generally in America."[42] There is no evidence that the festivals prescribed by custom and constitution
in the Netherlands ever enjoyed a general, liturgical observance in the Dutch Reformed Church in America.

The Liturgy of 1767

The Liturgy with which the Dutch Reformed Church began
its English language "housekeeping" in America[43] prescribes
a prayer before the sermon, to consist of confession ("We all
are, by original sin, unclean in Thy sight and children of
wrath, conceived in sin and brought forth in iniquity"), a

plea for pardon, an intercession for the preacher, and the Lord's Prayer. Following the sermon is an even longer prayer of confession and a general intercession for the world, the church, the president, and those in authority, the persecuted, those chastized by God, and the Lord's Prayer a second time.

Significant differences are to be observed between the Dutch and Palatinate Lord's Day services. The Palatinate prescribes a *corporate* confession and ministerial absolution following the sermon; and the general prayer after the absolution consists of thanksgiving, supplication, and intercession. The Lord's Prayer or a paraphrase, a psalm and benediction then conclude the worship. In short, the Palatinate has some semblance of a liturgy *per se*, whereas the Dutch Liturgy consists simply of prayers "for the opening and closing of the sermon". Curiously, none of the several liturgical revisions approved by the Dutch during the nineteenth century restored the confession and absolution.

Certain of the same differences between the two Lord's Day services are also to be found in the respective orders of Baptism. Although the doctrine articulated is similar and both services are quite didactic, the Palatinate Liturgy does provide for congregational participation in the Lord's Prayer and Creed. The absence of the latter in the Dutch Liturgy is a significant deviation from the Reformed tradition--indeed the Christian liturgical tradition--and, as has already been noted, it drew severe criticism from Nevin.

Another surprising absence from the Dutch Liturgy of 1767 is a separate service of Preparation for Communion. As shall be shown below, the 1873 revision suggested in a footnote that the opening portion of the Eucharistic order could be used "at the usual service, preparatory to the Communion"; however, a separate service was not provided as in the Palatinate. This

is perhaps the more surprising since the Administration of
the Lord's Supper in the Dutch Liturgy is a verbatim rendering of that in the Palatinate.

Liturgical Revision

Hageman believes the Dutch liturgical interest to have
been revived in 1835 by George Washington Bethune. The prevailing state of liturgical affairs, according to a committee
appointed by the Synod in 1847, was chaotic. "Not only were
the prayers in the liturgy ignored, but even the sacred didactic passages themselves were being tempered to suit individual
tastes."[44]

There was sufficient interest in some measure of liturgical revision for the Synod of 1853 to appoint a committee for
that purpose. The Synod gave the committee only this single
directive: "That no alterations shall be made in the doctrinal
sentiments contained in the forms now in use in the Church."[45]
That the demand for liturgical revision was not unanimous,
however, can be seen in the vote recorded on the motion just
to establish the committee: sixty ayes and twenty-four nays.

Seven regular meetings of the committee were held in New
York, and a detailed set of alterations was presented to the
Synod in 1854. There was no intention to make the worship of
the denomination any more liturgical "than it has been from
the beginning, or to fetter the exercise of individual gifts
in conducting religious worship, any further than is already
done by the Constitution".[46] Instead the committee sought to
correct certain language in the Liturgy, abbreviate forms that
were too long, and provide new forms "as appeared to be required by the wants of the Church". Specifically this meant:

(1) Revision of certain prayers and the introduction of 'a full series for the morning
service of the sanctuary....'

(2) The sacraments were substantially unchanged. The Baptism orders were slightly
abbreviated and the prayer of thanksgiving
in the rite for Infants modified. So, too,
was the Lord's Supper form abridged.

(3) Changes in phraseology but nothing more
were proposed for the Office of Church Discipline; no change in "Of Comforting the Sick".

(4) New Offices were prepared for Marriage,
the Dedication of a Church, and the Burial
Service.

(5) The 'System for the Yearly Reading of
the Bible' was 'transferred from the old
Dutch Bibles, to which it had been attached
nearly a century ago by the Synod of Dort'.

The committee was unanimous in recommending the above modifications, "with, at the same time, a full allowance to any
minister or church to use the old forms, if they so prefer".
These proposals were apparently not extensive enough; therefore the Synod resolved unanimously to refer the issue to the
committee for further revision and report to the Synod of 1855.

Revision of 1855

This report was presented the following year in a form
considerably more forceful and less apologetic. "We can not
forget, and we would not if we could, that we are strictly and
truly a *Liturgical* Church."[47] A brief historical summary of
the Dutch liturgical lineage was presented[48] along with an admission that a substantial number of ministers are either

averse or indifferent to the use of a liturgy. In hopes of
offering a liturgy which would correct that aversion and indifference the committee undertook further modification and
abridgement, as directed by the Synod. Again the committee
report was presented unanimously. It was resolved "that 250
copies of the Liturgy, as proposed to be revised, be printed
for the use of the Synod at its adjourned session in October
next, and that they be distributed among the members of the
same".

The "Prefatory Note" in the 1855 revision[49] makes it quite
clear that none of the forms is obligatory save those for administering the sacraments. Changes in the sacramental forms
are slight and inconsequential in any event; the fundamental
change came in the new forms and in the greatly emended Lord's
Day service. Since the more complete edition of the Liturgy
which appeared in 1857 makes no significant changes in the
forms contained in the 1855 edition, no special note will be
taken of the latter.[50]

At its special meeting in October, 1855, Synod referred
the entire matter to the committee for further deliberation.
The report of 1856 indicated that the committee held fourteen
meetings during the course of its three-year existence, and
now believes that its work reflects the "understood wishes of
the Church...." Not "one jot or tittle of the doctrines contained in any of the offices of the old Liturgy" was altered;
rather the committee

> endeavored simply to amend the phraseology
> of the old forms, where they were manifestly
> in need of correction, to expunge in some in-
> stances, and especially from a few of the
> prayers, sentences which had become inappro-
> priate or obsolete, to re-cast into a more
> readable form passages which, by their great

length, severely tasked the vocal organs,
and to abridge where abridgement was
necessary, in order to avoid tedious repe-
titions.[51]

To accomplish this task the committee "examined other Liturgies...weighed words and phrases...touched and retouched, again
and again, passages, both in the old and new forms, in order to
secure a full Liturgical style, free from rhetorical pretension
but severely simple in the utterance of evangelical truth".[52]
Various sections of the Liturgy were assigned to sub-committees
and their work was in turn examined and corrected by the committee as a whole.

In presenting its revision the committee acknowledged
that the "new" Liturgy would not immediately bring about uniformity of worship within the denomination; yet some measure
of uniformity was expected to come through the inclusion of
new forms for the occasional services and a general improve-
ment of the language in the sacramental forms. Such a basic
uniformity the committee presumed to be the desire of the
church as reflected in the initial call for liturgical revision

Certain amendments in the sacramental forms were voted by
Synod--among them that in printing the Creed, the phrase "he
descended into hell" be enclosed in brackets[53]--and it was resolved that these forms be sent to the Classes for action.
The remainder of the Liturgy was to await further consideration by the Synod in 1857.

Revision of 1857

The Synod of 1857 reflected the extent of denominational
indifference to the entire liturgical enterprise: only

thirteen of thirty Classes reported, five approving the sacramental forms and eight rejecting them. On this basis Synod resolved to

> ...approve the portions of the Revised
> Liturgy of 1856, not yet acted upon, so
> far as to authorize the Board of Publica-
> tion to issue the same in a separate
> volume, and also to allow Ministers and
> Consistories who may choose to do so, to
> use them--it being understood that this
> is a provisional arrangement, to continue
> until the stereotype plates from which
> the Liturgy is now printed are worn out,
> when the whole subject shall be finally
> determined.[54]

Lord's Day. -- Among the forms which were revised, the most radical change came in the Lord's Day service. From a service which provided little more than a prayer before and after the sermon, the committee recommended the following:[55]

> *Invocation:* 'Send down upon us plentifully
> of thy Holy Spirit, to the end that we, not-
> withstanding our manifold sins, our weakness
> and folly, may worship thee in the beauty of
> holiness....'
>
> *Salutation:* 'Grace, mercy, and peace....'
>
> *The Reading of the Law*, after which 'may be
> chanted a brief prayer taken out of Scripture'.
>
> *Reading of the Scriptures:* both Old and New
> Testaments.
>
> *Prayer Before Sermon:*
>   Adoration.
>   Thanksgiving for creation, providence,
>   redemption in Christ sealed by the
>   Holy Spirit, the means of grace
>   (Word, sacraments, ministry, worship).

      Confession and plea for forgiveness and
          redemption.
      Intercession for the preacher, congrega-
          tion and officers of the congrega-
          tion.
      General intercession for the church,
          America, the president and all in
          authority, the sorrowful, prisoners,
          the sick, young children, those who
          are tempted, the bereaved, the widow,
          those absent from their homes, the
          impenitent and ungodly.

Prayer After Sermon: [brief: one short para-
      graph] For the blessing of the Word and
          its effectiveness in the lives of the
          hearers.

The Lord's Prayer

Benediction
      Aaronic or Apostolic.

Hageman's analysis of the Lord's Day service in "the
first liturgical book that the Reformed Church in America had
ever possessed" is helpful.[56] Several surprising additions
are to be noted, beginning with the opening Invocation. This
sort of prayer "would have struck our Reformed ancestors as
slightly blasphemous since God had promised to be present and
it was on the basis of that promise that they assembled". It
made its way into the 1857 edition, Hageman surmises, through
the Anglican door. So, too, does the *Book of Common Prayer*
seem to have influenced the chant and the Old and New Testament lessons. The most Anglican feature of the Lord's Day
service is the reversal of the order of the prayers. Classic
Reformed liturgies preceded ne sermon only with prayers of
confession and for illumination; the longer prayer of thanksgiving and intercession followed the sermon. Not so in Morning Prayer, which was originally a daily office with no sermon

at all, and to which a sermon was added at the end; "thus quite by accident the principle prayers of thanksgiving and intercession came before the sermon". Still another result of Morning Prayer is the separation of Scripture and sermon for the first time in the 1857 revision. Yet for all its obvious influence, the *Book of Common Prayer* did not succeed in restoring the confession and absolution.

Bucer Litany. -- The third form provided in the provisional Liturgy is a Litany which, according to a footnote, is a "literal translation from the Reformer Bucer's 'Reformation of Doctrine and Worship'." Bucer's version is a modified form of the historic Litany which appears in the *Book of Common Prayer*. This writer has been unable to determine the source of the modification and is suspicious that it may be spurious. In any event it does not differ sufficiently from that form in the *Book of Common Prayer* to justify a separate liturgical existence, and Bucer's name was likely used on the assumption that it would be a more acceptable source than the *Book of Common Prayer*.

Lectionary. -- Another distinctive feature of the 1857 proposals is the "Order for the Reading of Scripture in Public Worship". Although it is not based on the Church Year, this lectionary is continuous, providing Old and New Testament lessons, morning and evening, for fifty-three Sundays. The arrangement for the Old Testament readings is as follows:

Genesis: seventeen Sundays
Exodus: eight Sundays
Deuteronomy: five Sundays
Joshua: three Sundays
Judges: one Sunday
Ruth: one Sunday

```
1 Samuel:  four Sundays
2 Samuel:  two Sundays
1 Kings:  six Sundays
2 Kings:  two Sundays
2 Chronicles:  one Sunday
Job:  two Sundays
```

The New Testament lessons are designed to cover the life of Christ chronologically, and readings are provided in the following proportions:

```
Matthew:  eighteen Sundays      [not consecu-
Luke:    twelve Sundays          tive as are
John:    twenty-two Sundays      the Old Testa-
Acts:    one Sunday              ment readings]
```

All of the New Testament lessons prescribed for evening worship are taken from the Epistles. Together morning and evening lessons are taken from every book of the New Testament except Mark, 1 and 2 Timothy, Titus, Philemon, 2 Peter, 2 and 3 John, and Jude. The Old Testament evening lessons are from the Prophets, Isaiah being prescribed for thirty-three of the fifty-three Sundays.

With slight modifications the Prayers for Special Occasions retain those provided in the 1767 Liturgy. The following are added, however: prayers for Rain, Fair Weather, Peace, in the time of Pestilence, for those Absent from Home; and thanksgivings for Rain, Fair Weather, Harvest, Deliverance from Pestilence, a Safe Return Home.

Sacraments. -- The sacramental orders remain essentially unchanged in the 1857 revision. There appeared to be no serious desire to modify them substantially; however, had there been that desire, the committee rightly supposed that

anything more than stylistic changes would not have been received by the denomination. The 1857 edition returned to the
Words of Distribution as found in the Palatinate Liturgy, rescinding the change made in the 1855 proposal.

Ordination. -- The forms for Church Discipline and
Ordination also remained unchanged, again because of no
apparent desire to change them and the realization that any
significant revision would require an amendment to the Constitution. A new service for the Installation of a Pastor appeared
in 1857 and the form for the Dedication of a Church, which initially appeared in 1855, was retained.

Reception of the 1857 Revision. -- Two major problems
mitigated against widespread acceptance of the provisional
liturgy of 1857. The first was the denomination's seeming indifference to the whole liturgical enterprise, seen in the refusal of the Classes to consider the matter. As reported to
the Synod of 1858, "only seven of the Classes...are in favor
of any revision, and of these only five go beyond a change in
one sentence. It is evident, therefore, that the great majority of the Classes are either so indifferent that they have
taken no action, or have expressed their opposition to any revision."[57] The Synod resolved, therefore, to rescind its permission to use the sacramental forms and those for Church
Discipline and Ordination,[58] and simply to leave the matter
at that. "That" meant essentially nowhere.

The lack of liturgical interest is reflected as well in
the absence of correspondence regarding the matter in the
Christian Intelligencer. Scattered letters of a general
nature appeared in 1854. One of these is from a visitor to
Charleston, South Carolina, where he worshiped with the

Hugenots. The experience impressed him so much that he presented a copy of the Hugenot liturgy to the Dutch liturgical committee.[59] A series of articles of dubious historical accuracy appeared under the pseudonym, "Caesariensis", from January through June of 1854; however, these represented the desires of but one man and aroused little interest.

Four interesting and perceptive articles appeared during 1855. The first was apparently inspired by Baird's *Eutaxia*,[60] for the author rejoices in the Dutch liturgical heritage and points out the advantages of denominational uniformity, clearly seen by comparison with the "irregularity" of American Presbyterian worship.[61] A second correspondent simply suggests that the liturgical revision currently underway could be a step toward Christian unity if the committee would make use of forms from other liturgies.[62]

J. B. Steele, a Dutch Reformed minister, wrote a lengthy denunciation of liturgical revision in October, 1855.[63] He claims to use the 1789 Liturgy without modification and argues that any provisional services proposed by the Synod could not insure uniformity since they have no force of constitutional law. Steele was answered in the next issue of the *Intelligencer* by one who "has never heard the office of baptism used, but once, without the omission of a considerable portion of it, and never heard the whole communion service read, but once, and that by a Presbyterian clergyman".[64]

Steele's observation concerning the constitutional authority for provisional forms underscores the second serious problem encountered by the Synod. The sacramental rites and those for ordination and discipline were prescribed by the Constitution, and, presumably, two-thirds of the Classes must vote to amend that Constitution if so much as a word was changed. In fact, the Classis of New York pushed the matter

a step further in debating the 1873 liturgical revision. The
entire Liturgy is a part of the Constitution and new forms
can be added only by amendment. This meant rescission of
permission to use the provisional forms granted by the Synod
of 1874. The issue was sent to the Classes in 1876, but less
than half reported. Not until 1878 did such forms as the
Installation of Ministers, Laying of a Corner Stone, Dedication of a Church, and Burial of the Dead receive constitutional authority.

Nichols has suggested that the Dutch Liturgy as revised in 1857 "seemed in many ways a fulfillment of Bomberger's Norristown proposals for the German Reformed
Church".[65] In many ways it was, and for this reason the
Dutch revision represented a genuine alternative for the
German Reformed liturgical committee. The essence of Norristown was a liturgy which took the sixteenth century as its
boundary and norm; yet a liturgy which went beyond either the
Mayer Liturgy or the Palatinate Liturgy in seeking a contemporary, indigenous relevance and devotional quality. The sixteenth century norm, as implied by the Norristown proposals,
likely meant a liturgy which provided forms--complete forms--
but which permitted free prayer, minimal responses, and which
was not binding in the Anglican manner. According to Bomberger: "...until at least 1852 [i.e., until the Synod of
Baltimore], the main thought and desire [of the denomination]
seem to have been, to reproduce our old Palatinate Liturgy,
with such modifications in language, in the construction of
sentences, and similar matters of no vital importance, affect-
ing no Scriptural or ecclesiastical principle, as would serve
to render the book more available and more edifying."[66] It
should be noted that, whereas this statement by Bomberger
could essentially pass as a description of the Dutch Liturgy

of 1857 (insofar as the sacraments are concerned), it represents Bomberger's later and somewhat modified position. A
more detailed analysis of Bomberger's liturgical position
and influence is yet to come; however, let it be said here
that he would likely have gone beyond the Dutch in revising
the sacramental forms and retained more of the Palatinate in
the Lord's Day service.

The Dutch Liturgy of 1857 is the product of a committee
appointed by Synod. Because this committee was only partially
revising an existing liturgy rather than writing a new one
altogether, its activity was small by comparison with the
German Reformed liturgical committee. So, too, was the Dutch
context considerably different. The product of its committee
was not the result of a self-conscious theological movement
which demanded liturgical expression. Rather the Dutch Church
became aware of its liturgical heritage, as did other denominations, through the romantic movement in the nineteenth century. As one Dutch minister put it in 1855: "The fact is
that our Church, although theoretically a Church with a
Liturgy, is in practice little removed from those Churches
which eschew one....[The Dutch Reformed Church] has become
so assimilated to the Presbyterian and Congregational Churches
around her that but for her name few would be able to determine which was which...."[67] This question--Who are we vis-à-
vis the Presbyterians?--did much to maintain interest in
liturgical matters and partially motivated the revision of
1873.

Hageman sees considerably more widespread liturgical
interest in the denomination at large than does this writer.
Doubtless there were a number of "Gothic" ministers who desired fairly extensive liturgical revision, and still others
who felt that if the Dutch Church was not going to merge with

the Presbyterians, then she should evidence a liturgical
difference; however, the sluggish action of the Classes and
the lack of interest to be seen in the *Christian Intelligencer* would appear to be a reliable barometer of grass roots
opinion.

No doubt Hageman is correct in assessing the influence
of the 1857 edition; for, even though it was never approved
by Synod, it was in circulation within the denomination, in-
spiring an apparent rash of liturgical experimentation. One
such example is a rather substantial prayer book which appeared
anonymously in 1866. According to the preface, the "manual"
was prepared "at the request of the Consistory of the Church
of which the compiler is Minister, and is issued by them for
the use of the Congregation".[68] The sacramental and constitutional forms remain unchanged, and the Lord's Day service is
but slightly altered. A new "Order of Scripture Reading" is
provided, designed "to bring a larger portion [of Scripture]
into profitable use". While the readings are concentrated in
certain books, the table of readings is not *lectio continua*
in the classic Reformed sense. In fact, no scheme is apparent.
Special readings are provided for the Lord's Supper, Baptism,
Good Friday, Easter, Pentecost, Thanksgiving, and Christmas.
Both the Marriage and Burial forms have been changed, and a
more extensive section of chants and ancient hymns is provided.

Although it moves beyond the scope of immediate interest,
a brief word concerning the provisional liturgy of 1873 is in
order. Eventually adopted by the Synod in 1882, this revision
closely follows the format of the 1857 edition, perpetuating
its unfortunate characteristics such as the separation of
Scripture and sermon, and becoming further indebted to the

Book of Common Prayer. "With exceptions so minor as to be
negligible", the lectionary in the 1873 Liturgy is taken from
the German Reformed Church's *Order of Worship* published in
1866.[69] This is the first evidence of direct borrowing among
the two committees, and there is still another. Hidden away
in the section of "Prayers for Special Occasions" is a Eucharistic Prayer—the first such to appear in Dutch service books.
According to Hageman's analysis, this prayer is a composite
from the *Book of Common Prayer*, the liturgy of the Catholic
and Apostolic Church, and the *Euchologion*. (A more detailed
examination of this trans-Atlantic borrowing will be made in
Chapter VII.) It is, in short, "nothing less than a beauti-
fully traditional canon of the Mass...somebody's attempt to
put Reformed liturgy into the mainstream of catholic liturgical tradition".[70]

In the nineteenth-century Dutch liturgical activity,
then, one finds a committee moving cautiously to up-date a
Liturgy inherited from another culture and circumstance, top-
heavy with doctrine, of blessed memory, yet generally neglect-
ed. To the extent that the Dutch Liturgies did fulfill the
implications of the Norristown proposals—i.e., retaining the
sixteenth century as the liturgical and doctrinal norm, and
maintaining essentially the American Reformed pattern of a
pulpit manual, a "lectionary" which amounted to a variation
on *lectio continua*, acknowledging only the chief Christian
festivals—the liturgical committee of the German Reformed
Church could find a liturgical alternative in their denominational neighbors.

The Presbyterian "Way"

Because of a general aversion to liturgies--the result primarily of severe persecution by the Church of England and the influence of Separatist liturgical ideas--American Presbyterianism in the seventeenth century evidenced a wide latitude in worship. The frontier conditions and a shortage of trained clergy increased the degree of tolerance even further. When the "Great Awakening" and its judgment of worship in terms of its psychological effectiveness is added to an already loose liturgical situation, the understatement in Melton's observation can be better appreciated: "Presbyterians entered the national era [after 1786] with no firm tradition of a recognized and controlling standard to order effectively the denomination's worship."[71]

Proposal of 1787

In 1787 a committee of John Rodgers, Alexander MacWhorter, and Alexander Miller produced a draft of the revised Directory for Worship. "The revision committee aimed at promoting worship which gave *worthy homage to God*; but it was also concerned that services *impress the worshiper* and call forth from him sincere devotion."[72] Essentially the committee proposed a pre-Puritan Reformed liturgy, in which the suggested order of worship was as follows:

> Prayer of adoration, invocation, and
>   preparation
> Reading of Scripture
> Singing of praise
> Long prayer of adoration, confession,
>   thanksgiving, supplication and
>   intercession, followed by Lord's Prayer

> Sermon
> (Lord's Supper, when celebrated)
> Prayer
> Singing of a psalm
> Offering
> Blessing[73]

The report of the committee was defeated by the Synod and virtually no other denominational action is recorded prior to the twentieth century.

Nineteenth-Century Developments

During the nineteenth century--the period of immediate concern--there was considerable liturgical activity within Presbyterianiam, but none of it official. The Old School-New School split in 1837 reflected two different positions regarding worship. "Uppermost in the mind of a New School Presbyterian leader of worship was evangelistic effectiveness. An Old School minister was more sensitive to the scripturality and decorum of his services."[74]

Charles Baird

Romanticism did not leave American Presbyterians unaffected; however, of all the members of the Reformed family they had the greater aversion to a liturgy. Only after Charles Baird provided Presbyterians with a new awareness of their liturgical heritage could some experimentation begin without embarrassment. In view of the extensive historical documentation Baird offered, one could hardly argue with his

conclusions: "first, That the principles of Presbyterianism
in no wise conflict with the discretionary use of written
forms; and secondly, That the practice of Presbyterian churches
abundantly warrants the adoption and the use of such forms."[75]
Baird sensed the growing interest among members of the Reformed
family in matters liturgical; however, he held little hope for
American Presbyterianism. He urged a return to the following
as a liturgical minimum: use of the Lord's Prayer, Decalogue,
and Apostles' Creed; "the regular and continuous reading of
Holy Scripture, at every religious service, and in sufficient
portions"; and "a more strict adherence to the prescribed
order of the Directory of Worship....Without supplying the
need of a liturgy, it was designed to prevent irregularity,
and to secure uniformity in the performance of public prayer.
The rigid observance of that order, is incumbent upon every
minister who officiates in the Presbyterian Church."[76] Baird
then went on to describe his liturgical "dream":

> In addition to these measures [the three noted
> above], there are others which we hope to see
> ultimately prevail. We look for the time
> when our congregations shall take part in the
> public prayers of the Church, by an audible
> *Amen*, at the close of each prayer; and by
> the recital of the Lord's Prayer and the
> Creed, after the minister. We hope, also, to
> see the want of a formulary of Public Prayer
> and the administration of ordinances supplied,
> by a compilation of the best forms of devo-
> tion which have been used in our Church and
> in other Churches; furnishing sufficient
> variety for voluntary selection. This should
> not be the work of a single individual, nor
> can it be well accomplished within a short
> term of years. The endeavors of all who are
> favorable to such a production, should be
> combined; and the general wants of our
> clergy should be consulted. And while we

> have little expectation that such a formulary,
> however perfect, will ever be adopted as a
> standard of the Church, we see not why at
> some future period it may not be recognized
> and sanctioned as a lawful aid to those who
> may desire its use.[77]

Charles Hodge

Charles Hodge did not wait two years to review *Eutaxia*; and, likely to the surprise and dismay of some, he supported Baird's proposals. After repeating the well-rehearsed arguments against an obligatory liturgy, Hodge snuggled into the "wide and safe middle ground" between the *Book of Common Prayer* and complete freedom, calling for

> ...the optional use of a liturgy, or form
> of public service, having the sanction of
> the Church. If such a book were compiled
> from the liturgies of Calvin, Knox, and of
> the Reformed Churches, containing appropri-
> ate prayers for ordinary public worship, for
> special occasions, as for times of sickness,
> declension, or public calamity, with forms
> for the administration of baptism, of the
> Lord's Supper, for funerals and for marriage,
> we are bold to say that it would in our
> judgment be a very great blessing. We say
> such a book might be *compiled*; we do not
> believe it could possibly be written.[78]

Such a work would have these advantages, according to Hodge: "it would be a great assistance to those who are not specially favoured with the gift of prayer"; it would preserve the "unity and harmony" of the sacraments; and it would provide much desired guidance for funerals and weddings.[79] Apparently fearing that his position might be misconstrued, Hodge con-

cluded his review with this sentence: "Let it be remembered
that we have not advocated the introduction of a liturgy,
but simply the preparation of a book which may be used as
the occasion calls for it."[80]

Baird took Hodge's earlier hint and attempted such a
compilation in 1857.[81] Schaff took considerable note of this
volume and welcomed it, even though he was critical at several
points. In the first place, the prayers were too didactic.
Second, Schaff objected to "a simply optional or discretionary
liturgy", believing that "a liturgy, like the catechism, the
constitution, and the hymn book, should have the sanction of
ecclesiastical authority...." Third, Baird did not base his
work on the Christian Year, and this, too, is imperative
according to Schaff.[82]

St. Peter's

The role of laymen in Presbyterian liturgical activity is
an interesting one. Levi A. Ward made St. Peter's Church,
Rochester, New York, a liturgical laboratory for nearly fifty
years. The liturgy used in this Romanesque building was compiled principally by layman Ward, with assistance from the
succession of young ministers who served the congregation. A
year and a half after the organization of the congregation the
first *Church-Book* was published.[83] It received a favorable
review in the *Weekly Messenger*, October 24, 1855; and, although it was not nearly as complete a liturgy as the German
Reformed Church was subsequently to produce, one can be certain that the German committee examined it carefully.

Melton concludes that "although St. Peter's service was
responsive in nature, it is not clear to what extent liturgical

prayer replaced extempore prayer".[84]   A letter from a member
of the Church to the *Weekly Messenger* indicates that in 1855
at least, there was no liturgical prayer *per se*. He describes
the worship as follows:

> The minister wears a gown and bands. The
> congregation chants Psalms and other sen-
> tences of Scripture. Behind the pulpit are
> tables with the 10 commandments, Lord's
> Prayer, and Creed, which are used in the
> service....The people repeat Amen as di-
> rected by the O. T. and 1 Corinthians 14:16.
> ...All the prayers in our service are free.
> We have no liturgy [which he defines as
> written prayers]. We have simply an order
> of worship varying somewhat from that
> commonly in use in our Church. We claim
> the *right* to use a full liturgy, written
> prayers and all, if we choose; it is not
> against any of the laws of our Church,
> neither is it without high Presbyterian
> precedent; but we prefer free prayer.
> Probably the very best form of service
> would include both written and extempo-
> raneous prayer. In the preparation of
> our service, the leading idea has been
> *to have the people* unite in it.[85]

The liturgical significance of St. Peter's did not extend beyond the 1870's; however, membership at St. Peter's
peaked at five hundred in the early 1900's and the congregation was dissolved in 1923, "but not before it had made a
significant witness in behalf of better worship for Presbyterians".[86]

One who may be aware of developments in Presbyterian
worship in the latter half of the nineteenth century will
miss such names as Shields, Comegys, Archibald Alexander
Hodge, van Dyke, and Benson in the abbreviated survey above;
however, their activity came after the publication of the

Provisional Ligurgy in 1857 and, therefore, could not legiti-
mately be considered as posing a liturgical alternative for
the German Reformed committee. The Presbyterian story will be
resumed in Chapter VII, since it more nearly parallels the
publication of the German Reformed Church's *Directory of Worship* in 1884.

In Baird and Charles Hodge one can see the Presbyterian
liturgical "way" in the making--that "wide and safe middle
ground", to quote Hodge again, between an obligatory liturgy,
such as the *Book of Common Prayer*, and the sheer liturgical
chaos of complete freedom. Both Baird and Hodge were interested in establishing a minimum degree of uniformity in Presbyterian worship; and, while Baird would likely have gone
further than Hodge in making that minimum a requirement,
neither gave evidence of desiring an obligatory *peoples'*
prayer book. So, too, there was no hint that liturgical
"formularies" should dip any deeper into the liturgical well
than the sixteenth century. Schaff's rejection of Baird's
Book of Prayer in 1857 is the German Reformed answer to the
Presbyterian "Way"; for in the Baltimore proposals, adopted
by the German Reformed Synod in 1852, Schaff's committee set
a course away from a didactic, discretionary, pulpit manual,
and produced instead a peoples' prayer book which found its
focus in the Eucharist. With those proposals and the committee which produced the Provisional Liturgy the following
chapter is concerned.

NOTES TO CHAPTER III

1. *Liturgy for the Use of the Congregations of the German Reformed Church in the United States of North America* (Chambersburg, Pa.: Printed at the Publication Office of the German Reformed Church, 1841).

2. Robert Clyde Johnson, ed., *The Church and Its Changing Ministry* (Philadelphia: Office of the General Assembly of the United Presbyterian Church in the United States of America, [1961]), p. 36.

3. This is the first notice taken of the congregation. No words are addressed to them in either the Baptism of Infants or Adults.

4. The one exception is James I. Good, who argues, incomprehensibly: "The cause generally assigned [for the failure of Mayer's reception] is that it was too doctrinal in its form and was argumentative rather than devotional. The liturgy was so simple in its forms that it did not have the Apostles' Creed in it, which was considered its crowning sin by the Nevinites." Good, *op. cit.*, p. 175.

5. *WM*, February 2, 1867.

6. Good, *op. cit.*, p. 175.

7. There is no information as to the number of copies originally printed; however, the fact that this was the first Liturgy sanctioned by the German Reformed Church in America and the fact, too, that it was issued in both German and English should have insured it a certain measure of success.

8. John W. Nevin, *Vindication of the Revised Liturgy* (Philadelphia: Jas. B. Rodgers, 1867), pp. 8-9.

9. *Ibid.*

10. Good, *op. cit.*, p. 174.

11. J. H. A. Bomberger, *The Revised Liturgy: A History and Criticism of the Ritualistic Movement in the German Reformed Church* (Philadelphia: Jas. B. Rodgers, 1867), p. 17.

12. Appel, *The Life and Work of John Williamson Nevin*, p. 481.

13. Bard Thompson, trans., "The Palatinate Liturgy," *Theology and Life*, VI (Spring, 1963), 49-67.

14. Wilhelm Niesel, ed., *Bekenntnisschriften und Kirchenordnungen*, Evangelischer Verlag A. G. Zollikon-Zurich (1938), 195-205.

15. These are Christmas with the day following, New Year's Day, Easter with the day following, Ascension Day, and Whitsunday with the day following.

16. That is "genteel and plain apparel".

17. Thompson, *Liturgies of the Western Church*, p. 168.

18. Thompson, *Theology and Life, op. cit.*, note 7, p. 55.

19. *Tercentenary Monument in Commemoration of the Three Hundredth Anniversary of the Heidelberg Catechism* (Chambersburg, Pa.: M. Kieffer & Co., 1863), pp. 281-282.

20. Nichols, *Corporate Worship*, pp. 115-116.

21. Appel, *Reflections of College Life*, p. 167.

22. Thompson, *Liturgies of the Western Church*, p. 202.

23. Thompson, *Theology and Life, op. cit.*, note 7, p. 55.

24. Nichols, *Corporate Worship*, p. 75.

25. *Tercentenary Monument*, p. 238.

26. Franklin D. Slifer, "The Traditions of Worship in the Evangelical and Reformed Church" (unpublished paper in the Archives of the Lancaster Theological Seminary, 1950).

27. David D. Demarest, *op. cit.*, p. 142.

28. Howard G. Hageman, Unpublished lectures on the history of the liturgy of the Reformed Church in America, II, p. 3. (Hereinafter referred to as "Lectures".)

29. *Ibid.*, p. 10.

30. *Ibid.*

31. *Christian Intelligencer*, June 16, 1853.

32. John W. Nevin, "The Dutch Crusade," *MR*, VI (1854), p. 74.

33. *Ibid.*, pp. 92-93.

34. *Ibid.*, p. 97.

35. Hageman, "Lectures," II, pp. 9-13.

36. Howard G. Hageman, *Lily Among the Thorns* (Teaneck, N. J.: The Half Moon Press, 1961), p. 42.

37. *Ibid.*, p. 52.

38. Demarest, *op. cit.*, pp. 146-147.

39. *Constitution of the Reformed Dutch Church in the United States of America* (New York: Wm. Durell, 1793), pp. v-vi.

40. *Ibid.*, Article LXII.

41. *Ibid.*, Article LXIII.

42. Nichols, *Mercersburg Theology*, p. 262.

43. *The Psalms of David, with the Ten Commandments, Creed, Lord's Prayer, etc. in Metre. Also, the Catechism, Confession of Faith, Liturgy, etc.* Translated from the Dutch. For the Use of the Reformed Protestant Dutch Church of the City of New York (New York: Printed by James Parker, 1767).

44. Hageman, "Lectures," II, p. 8.

45. *Acts and Proceedings of the General Synod of the Reformed Protestant Dutch Church in North America* (New York: Printed for the Synod, by John A. Gray), June, 1853, p. 357. (Hereinafter referred to as Dutch: *Acts and Proceedings*.)

46. *Ibid.*, June, 1854, p. 452.

47. *Ibid.*, June, 1855, pp. 576-580.

48. The Dutch became considerably more aware of their liturgical history with the publication of Baird's *Eutaxia* in 1855.

49. *Liturgy of the Reformed Dutch Church in North America* (New York: John A. Gray, Printer & Stereotyper, 1855).

50. The most substantial difference between the 1855 and 1857 editions is that the latter contains all the forms, whereas the former abbreviates those from the 1767 edition which were unchanged by the committee. In the 1855 edition the words of fraction and distribution were changed to include that portion of the Words of Institution appropriate to the bread and the wine. The 1857 edition returned to the words prescribed in the Palatinate Liturgy. It should be noted that the Lord's Day service first appeared in 1855 and was unchanged in 1857.

51. Dutch: *Acts and Proceedings*, June, 1856, p. 92.

52. *Ibid.*, p. 93.

53. This provoked an article in the *Christian Intelligencer* [April 23, 1857]. Either leave the phrase in or take it out, the correspondent argued. Brackets solve nothing.

54. Dutch: *Acts and Proceedings*, June, 1857, pp. 193-194.

55. *Liturgy of the Reformed Protestant Dutch Church in North America* (New York: Board of Publication of the Reformed Protestant Dutch Church [1857]).

56. Hageman, "Lectures," II, pp. 15-18.

57. Dutch: *Acts and Proceedings*, June, 1858, p. 330.

58. Such action on the latter two forms had already been taken at the special session of Synod in October, 1857.

59. *Christian Intelligencer*, June 1, 1854.

60. C. W. Baird, *Eutaxia, or the Presbyterian Liturgies: Historical Sketches* (New York: N. W. Dodd, Publisher, 1855).

61. *Christian Intelligencer*, May 3, 1855.

62. *Ibid.*

63. *Ibid.*, October 18, 1855.

64. *Ibid.*, October 25, 1855.

65. Nichols, *Romanticism*, p. 291.

66. *WM*, March 12, 1862.

67. *Christian Intelligencer*, October 25, 1855.

68. *Church Book: Containing the Sacramental Offices of the Reformed Dutch Church; Together with Other Offices for Christian Service* (New York: Chas. Scribner & Co., 1866).

69. Hageman, "Lectures," III, p. 12.

70. *Ibid.*, pp. 6-11.

71. Melton, *op. cit.*, p. 17.

72. *Ibid.*, p. 20.

73. *Ibid.*, pp. 21-22.

74. *Ibid.*, p. 29.

75. Baird, *op. cit.*, p. 5.

76. *Ibid.*, pp. 256-259.

77. *Ibid.*, p. 260.

78. Charles Hodge, Review of *Eutaxia, Biblical Repertory and Princeton Review*, XXVII (1855), p. 460.

79. *Ibid.*, pp. 461-464.

80. *Ibid.*, p. 467.

81. Charles Baird, *A Book of Public Prayer Compiled from the Authorized Formularies of Worship of the Presbyterian Church as Prepared by the Reformers Calvin, Knox, Bucer, and Others; with Supplementary Forms* (New York: Charles Scribner, 1857).

82.   Philip Schaff, Review of Baird's *Presbyterian Liturgies, MR*, VIII (1857), pp. 324-326.

83.   *Church Book of St. Peter's Church, Rochester* (Rochester: Lee, Mann, & Co., 1855).

84.   Melton, *op. cit.*, p. 96.

85.   *WM*, December 12, 1855.

86.   Melton, *op. cit.*, p. 97.

CHAPTER IV

The Provisional Liturgy: Development

The Baltimore Proposals

After the parenthesis in Chapter III, a return is now made to the German Reformed Synod which met in Baltimore in 1852. During the summer of 1852 the committee members engaged in serious liturgical labors for the first time during their appointment. Their task as given them at Norristown was to "propose a general plan and [present] a few specimen of liturgical forms". At this early date certain patterns began to take shape in the procedures of the liturgical committee. Where possible, groups of members living in general proximity formed something of a subcommittee, and were assigned specific tasks which they would then present to the whole committee for review. The Mercersburg members--consisting of Nevin, Schaff, and Thomas C. Porter--met weekly, likely to shape the general design of the liturgy. Other members were given specific forms to prepare. The "general plan", as reported to the Synod of Baltimore, is as follows:

    I.   The Regular Service on the Lord's Day
    II. The Festival Seasons, especially
           Christmas, Easter, Pentecost,
           and Trinity Sunday
    III. Prayers for Miscellaneous Occasions
    IV. The Administration of Infant and
           Adult Baptism
    V.   The Order of Confirmation
    VI. The Holy Communion

The evolution of the table of contents is an interesting indicator of the committee's liturgical priorities, and the several forms in which it appeared will be examined in greater detail in Chapter V. It can be seen at once, however, that from the start the committee intended a complete prayer book. Specimen forms for the regular Lord's Day (four forms), infant baptism, adult baptism, and marriage were presented to the Synod. These forms were designed to illustrate in some measure the seven principles which the committee suggested should guide their future liturgical labors. First:

> The liturgical worship of the Primitive Church, as far as it can be ascertained from the Holy Scriptures, the oldest ecclesiastical writings, and the liturgies of the Greek and Latin Churches of the third and fourth centuries, ought to be made, as much as possible, the general *basis* of the proposed Liturgy; the more so, as they are in fact also the source from which the best portions of the various liturgies of the six-

teenth century were derived, such as the
forms of confession and absolution, the
litanies, the creeds, the Te Deum, the
Gloria in Excelsis, the collects, the
doxologies, etc. For the merit of the
Reformation in the department of worship,
if we except hymnology, which has been
very materially enriched, especially by
the evangelical churches of Germany,
does not so much consist in producing
new forms of devotion, as in transfer-
ring those handed down from former ages
into the vernacular tongues, in purify-
ing them from certain additions, in re-
ducing them to greater simplicity, and
in subordinating them to the preaching
of the Gospel, as the central part of
Protestant worship.[2]

The first principle is perhaps the most profound in its
implications, for it opens up the early history of the Christian Church and makes it available, if not *normative*, for
contemporary liturgical composition. Norristown was not
specifically clear on the question as to which century or
period should be liturgically normative, simply because it
never entered anyone's mind in 1849 that the committee would
seriously consider anything prior to the sixteenth century.
Nevin was less than convincing when he attempted to argue
that Baltimore was *merely* an amplification of Norristown;
however, he is more persuasive in his reasons why the sixteenth century cannot provide a liturgical paradigm for the
nineteenth century. "The position occupied by the Churches
of the Reformation was not in general favorable to the production of good liturgies. Attention was too much taken up
with other interests; there was too little knowledge of
liturgical antiquities; the subject was given up too much
to mere particular fancy and taste, without any regard to
necessary principles and laws."[3]

Schaff and Nevin constantly argued that the sixteenth century was a great century for doctrine, but not for the development of liturgy. Preaching was restored to its rightful place in worship; however, with that came a didacticism undesirable in the nineteenth century. Even though Calvin and Bucer attempted to design a liturgy which climaxed in the Eucharist, though absent most of the time, they succeeded only in theory. According to Nevin, the German Reformed Liturgy was to adopt the sacramental principle of the ancient church, and with that came an appropriation of the forms to facilitate the principle. Note should be taken of the fact that the "liturgies of the Greek and Latin Churches of the *third and fourth* centuries" were to be the primary reference point, rather than the worship of the New Testament church. Scripture was understood to be a source--historical and devotional--but not the norm of worship. This meant simply that the two part structure of Word and Eucharist, fused after the canonical period, was accepted as liturgical fact.

In this intention to be ecumenical and catholic in its liturgy, the committee nevertheless made it quite clear that:

> Among the later liturgies special reference
> ought to be had to the old Palatinate and
> other Reformed liturgies of the sixteenth
> century.[4] [This is the second Baltimore
> proposal.]

Here the peculiar insights of the Reformation are acknowledged, as is the distinctive contribution made by the Palatinate-German wing of the Reformation; however, the sixteenth century is pointedly made a secondary liturgical reference.

From the third century in the first principle, the committee moved to the sixteenth in the second, then to the nineteenth in the third:

> Neither the ancient Catholic nor the Reformed
> liturgies, however, ought to be copied slavish-
> ly, but reproduced rather in a free evangelical
> spirit and adapted to the peculiar wants of our
> age and denomination; inasmuch as these Litur-
> gies themselves exhibit to us a considerable
> variety with essential unity, and as every age
> of the Church has the promise of the Spirit
> and a peculiar mission to fulfill. For the
> same reason, new forms may be prepared also,
> where it may seem desirable, but in keeping
> always with the devotional spirit of the Church
> in her purest days.[5]

In short, the liturgy must be indigenous both to the denomination and to the geography. Schaff's dynamic view of history
and revelation is clear in this principle. The liturgy is,
as it were, a tent rather than a tabernacle--i.e., its form
and emphasis must change with time and circumstance. There
were distinct advantages, according to Schaff and Nevin, in
maintaining many of the historic forms of the ancient church.
The Decalogue, Lord's Prayer, Magnificat, Te Deum, etc. could
not be excelled for their devotional quality and their ability
to lend continuity and context to the church's worship; however, the excellence of these ancient forms did not preclude
new forms peculiar to the present age and place of the church.

In the fourth principle the theory of adaptability and
indigenization is to be seen again.

> Those portions of the Liturgy which are
> most frequently used, as the regular ser-
> vice on the Lord's Day, and the celebration
> of the Lord's Supper, should embrace several
> forms, some shorter, some larger, some with
> and without responses, with the view to
> avoid monotony, and to adapt them the more
> readily to the condition and wants of our
> various ministers and congregations which
> are evidently not prepared for an entire
> uniformity.[6]

There is a sense in which this principle is more strategic
and practical than theoretical. As it was eventually published, the Provisional Liturgy did contain the internal
options described above; however, they were all removed in
the subsequent *Order of Worship*. Even though the retention
of them in the *Order of Worship* would have been strategically
wise, Nevin seemed bent on what ought to be rather than what
would "sell".

> The language and style ought to be throughout
> scriptural as much as possible; that is,
> simple, sublime, and devotional, such as we
> find in the Psalms especially, and in the
> Lord's Prayer. The doctrinal tone, which
> predominates too much in most of the Calvin-
> istic Liturgies, ought to be used only with-
> in certain limits.[7]

In the fifth principle the committee established the devotional mood as their goal. This is an interesting and potentially difficult task in view of the fact that the liturgy is
to be "a working out in an art form of the ideas and faith of
the Mercersburg Theology".[8] Schaff believed that it was
possible to be both theologically sound and inspirational.
His success will be evaluated when the liturgy is examined.

> The addition of a Family Liturgy, including
> twelve or more prayers, seems to be very
> desirable, not only on account of its inde-
> pendent value, but especially also because
> it would facilitate the introduction of
> the Liturgy amongst our laity, and thus
> promote its right use in the Church. For,
> in the opinion of your committee, a Litur-
> gy will never be sufficiently appreciated
> by the congregations, if it is confined to
> the hands of the minister. Like the Bible,

> the Catechism, and the Hymn Book, it ought
> to be the common property and manual of
> every member of the Church. The laymen
> will take a far deeper interest in the
> devotional exercises, if they can follow
> the minister by their book, and respond
> at least with an audible Amen at the end
> of each prayer.[9]

Here one finds one of the more distinctive characteristics
of the Provisional Liturgy: it is to be a *peoples' prayer
book*, rather than a pulpit manual of forms. To some this may
have seemed to be the first step in Mercersburg's "Romanizing"
tendencies; however, as Nichols has shown, a peoples' prayer
book is a Protestant, not a Catholic idea: "All were to understand and participate in the service, which meant that, if
possible, every literate layperson should possess and use a
service book. These same manuals would serve for private and
family devotions as well as for Lord's Day worship, each en-
riching and deepening the other. The conception of a book of
'common' paryer was a specifically Protestant idea."[10]

Amidst the implied theory one also finds an awareness of
very practical strategy at work in this principle--*viz.*, if
the people had the liturgy in their homes and used it in their
family devotions, they should be more inclined to know and use
it in their Lord's Day worship. Schaff's insistence that the
people should know the prayers of the minister before they
can be expected to pronounce their "Amen" reflects an awareness of 1 Corinthians 14:16: "...If you bless with the spirit,
how can anyone in the position of an outsider say the 'Amen'
to your thanksgiving when he does not know what you are saying?"

In the seventh principle one finds another distinctive
characteristic of the Reformed tradition, and an issue around

which much of the Mercersburg liturgical controversy polarized: the relationship between free and fixed prayer.

> Finally, a liturgy ought not to interfere
> with the proper use of extemporaneous
> prayer, either in public or in private,
> but rather to regulate and promote it.
> Sufficient room should be left for its
> exercise in connection with the Sunday
> afternoon and evening services, as well
> as in weekly Bible lectures, social
> prayer meetings, catechetical exercises,
> and on special occasions.[11]

Calvin, it will be remembered, provided for certain variation
in the prayers, and permitted free prayer at only two points
in his liturgy;[12] and he even provided models for these. "But
Calvin did not consider it wise to leave too much to the dis-
cretion of each individual minister."[13] The seventh principle
reflects this same reticence regarding free prayer, relegating
it to occasions other than the sacraments, ordinances, and
regular Lord's Day worship.

It is surprising that more discussion was not aroused at
Baltimore by these proposals. The reasons for the Synod's
adoption of this plan to produce a liturgy "which will be a
bond of union both with the ancient Catholic Church and the
Reformation, and yet be the product of the religious life of
our denomination in its present state"[14] must be three: first,
there were undoubtedly a number of ministers and elders who
simply didn't follow these principles out to their logical
liturgical conclusions. Who could believe, for example, that
the committee would actually produce a liturgy with no free
prayer? Second, there were doubtless others present who were
sufficiently desirous of a new liturgy that they concluded to
wait and see just what the committee would produce. Finally,

the number of those who saw and approved the direction in
which the committee intended to move was likely not small.
Nevin and Schaff were a teaching team for eight years and,
at this juncture, had more disciples than detractors.

Whatever the reasons, the Synod of Baltimore permitted
the scope of Norristown to be decidedly enlarged--by fifteen
centuries. Perhaps even Nevin and Schaff were not aware of
the full implications of their proposals, as Richards suggests;[15] however, this writer is inclined to think that
Schaff, if not Nevin, knew precisely where they would lead.
Richards is quite correct in this observation: "The Baltimore principles are clearly in harmony with Schaff's and
Nevin's conception of Church History, the idea of development and the continuity of the one holy Catholic Church
through the centuries, yet always subject to the Holy Scriptures."[16] In short, the judicial doors were now open wide
and Mercersburg was given the opportunity to articulate its
theology liturgically.

Composition and Character of the Liturgy Committee

Of the years, 1852-1855, Nevin writes: "The more the
Committee read and studied, and talked together, on the subject, the more they found that it was no small thing to make
a Liturgy; and could only smile at the easy credulity with
which it had imagined at the first, that such a work might be
carried through in the course of a single year."[17] Who were
the members of the liturgical committee and what did each
bring to his task?[18]

John Williamson Nevin

Of Nevin's brief chairmanship of the liturgical committee--from 1849-1852--and his dyspeptic approach to the activity of the committee in the years following 1852, little more need be said. As has been seen in Nevin's remarks at Norristown, he knew what he felt ought to be, yet he despaired that it could either be produced by the committee or accepted by the denomination. "Before Nevin there seemed to hover some notion of a cosmic liturgy, with which a worshiping congregation might be attuned."[19] He never forgot Rauch's remark that a liturgy should be a "work of art".

> The conception of a liturgical service is
> closely allied to the conception of a work
> of art, in its true sense; as indeed all
> art comes finally to its highest sense in
> the idea of worship. But now it lies in
> the very nature of every true work of art,
> that it must have its end and meaning in
> itself, and not in something beyond. It
> is not, like a mechanical fabric, an in-
> strument merely for some different pur-
> pose. To ask in relation to it: What
> is the *use* of it? is to wrong its nature,
> and expose our own want of culture at the
> same time. So we say of a true liturgical
> service; its meaning and value are in it-
> self, and in this form open of course only
> to the presence of a sound liturgical
> taste; whereas the moment we begin to
> think of it as an outward help simply
> to something else, we overturn the whole
> conception, and substitute in place of
> it something of a different nature alto-
> gether.[20]

In defending his resignation from the chairmanship Nevin wrote this: "I had not led the way at all in the movement; my heart

was not in it with any special zeal; I was concerned with it
only in obedience to the appointment of Synod; other interests
appeared to me at the time to be of more serious account; and
I had no faith in our being able to bring the work to any
ultimate success."[21]

In spite of his pessimism, Nevin did remain on the committee. Under Schaff's leadership "I tried to do my share
of service, and spent hours in what was found to be a generally tedious and irksome task. The work involved necessarily,
liturgical studies; and these brought with them a growing
liturgical culture, which required an enlargement of the
range, within which it was proposed, originally, to confine
the course of the movement."[22]

As late as 1855 Nevin's heart was still "not in it with
any special zeal". He wrote to Schaff regarding the portions
of the liturgy he had been assigned:

> I will try to furnish the family prayers you
> request for the Liturgy. But I must de-
> cline the task of the other services you
> mention. I have no helps here at hand, no
> access to the ancient Liturgies. [Nevin
> was writing from retirement in Lancaster.]
> This is one difficulty. But what is worse,
> I have no heart, no faith, no proper courage
> for any such work. A *leitourgia* (communion
> service) in the old sense demands a sort of
> faith in the 'real presence', which I am
> afraid goes beyond all that is possible to
> engraft on Protestantism, even in our German
> Reformed version of it. And without this,
> I feel that it is for me at least a species
> of mockery to pretend to the use of the like
> words and forms. I cannot bear the sense of
> unrealness which comes over me when I think
> of manufacturing on any such plan for public
> use a form of worship, into which our faith
> is not allowed to breathe the same mysteri-
> ous soul.[23]

By June, 1856, Nevin appears to evidence a greater interest in the activities of the committee:

> We are by no means prepared to call a meeting
> of the Liturgy Committee any time soon. The
> business is too serious to be done in a
> hurry. It cannot be carried through before
> Synod [in October]. I have been giving it
> as much attention as I could since you were
> here, meeting very often with Harbaugh.
> The other two brethren [composing the "Lan-
> caster group"], Gerhart and Porter, have
> not been able to help us much so far; but
> hope to be with us more hereafter.[24]

In March, 1857, he wrote to Schaff again, requesting that the meeting of the committee be postponed from April to July, in order to permit him to complete his work. "My affairs are such for the next two weeks that I shall not be able to bestow any proper attention on what was placed in my hands; not having found time and opportunity as yet to fulfil my task, and not wishing to pass it off in a merely superficial and hasty way."[25] Nevin's enthusiasm was gradually returning, and it was he who prepared the report of the committee to the Synod of 1857, an abstract of which is the "Advertisement" in the Provisional Liturgy.[26] The minutes of the final session of the committee find Nevin pronouncing the benediction:

> The meeting was then [following remarks by
> Chairman Schaff] closed with prayer--Dr.
> Nevin leading in a fervent address to the
> Throne of the Heavenly Grace--and the sing-
> ing of the 1st Doxology in our Hymn Book.
> LAUS DEO!!![27]

Undoubtedly the members of the committee deferred to Nevin at many points; however, the evidence that the elder statesman

moved from virtual indifference in 1851 to a marked measure
of enthusiasm in 1857 is convincing. It reveals not a little
to find that he attended ninety-one of the one hundred two
sessions of the committee--only two fewer than the chairman.[28]

Philip Schaff

Schaff's spiritual and ecclesiastical background fitted
him well for the task now at hand, for he was able to bring
to his German liturgical assignment a wealth of experience
gleaned from the protracted debate and extensive historical
research occasioned by the Prussian King's attempt to force
his Liturgy upon the United Church in the early 1820's. Four
years after King Wilhelm III effected the Reformed-Lutheran
union in 1817 (the tercentenary of Luther's "Ninety-Five
Theses") he introduced a new Liturgy, not only making it
obligatory but forbidding any criticism of it either in synod
or in print.[29]

Brilioth observes that the Prussian Agenda of 1821
represented a revival of Lutheran worship "in its richer
form". In addition to a fuller, more historic liturgical
pattern, the Agenda reestablished the Eucharist as central
to all worship and ordered that it be celebrated at the chief
Sunday service.[30] In outline, the Agenda prescribed the
following for the Lord's Day:

       Solemn Declaration
       Confession of Sin
       Prayer of Forgiveness
       Kyrie Eleison
       Gloria in Excelsis
       Versicle
       Collect for the Day

```
Epistle and Gospel for the Day
Creed
Preface and Sanctus  (Even when there was
    no celebration of the Eucharist.)
Lord's Prayer
Sermon
Benediction  (If there was no celebration.)[31]
```

According to Nichols, the King's Agenda was "largely ritua-listic antiquarianism. The sermon was to be shorter and free prayer eliminated. Congregational participation similarly would be replaced by professional choral performances."[32]

There was immediate resistance to these courtly liturgi-cal "reforms". Not only did the Reformed wing of the United Church object to the added ceremony; perhaps even more its voice was raised in opposition to the King's arbitrary methods of enforcing the Agenda, and subsequently, to the Erastian principle of the union itself.[33] The "Old Lutherans", on the other hand--particularly in the areas of north and east Germany, where there were virtually no Reformed--could see little reason for the Union. After several attempts to leave the United Church, they were permitted to emigrate to America in 1840, forming the Buffalo, Ohio, and Missouri Synods.

As was noted in Chapter I, the young Philip Schaff experienced a conversion experience "of the pietist sort" and was confirmed by a Lutheran village pastor. Some years later, as a student in Berlin, Schaff again was greatly in-fluenced by Lutherans--this time by representatives of the Prussian High Orthodoxy: Hengstenberg, Ludwig von Gerlach, and Loehe.[34] The latter--Wilhelm Loehe--was a leading figure in the confessional and churchly revival of the 1830's, and was "the chief agent in reviving ancient liturgical tra-ditions, including private confession and unction for the sick".[35]

Fresh from his experiences with this Lutheran-oriented, but nevertheless ecumenical Christianity, it is small wonder that Schaff evidenced his particular liturgical orientation. In America, however, the young professor first encountered an entrenched anti-liturgical bias, the rigidity of which he may well have underestimated. Perhaps this may explain Schaff's optimism in presenting the Baltimore proposals--largely reflecting his own mind and theory rather than any reasoned consensus of the committee. On the other hand, Nevin's first-hand acquaintance with the American liturgical scene is no small reason for his pessimistic approach to the ambitious nature of the German Reformed liturgical enterprise.

In addition to his ecclesiastical and academic background, Schaff also brought considerable personal gifts to bear upon his liturgical endeavours. He was a poet of some accomplishment; he knew well the hymns and other devotional treasures of the church catholic; he clearly possessed the tact, knowledge, and maturity, unexpected in one so young,[36] but requisite for the strong leadership demanded in such a task; and "he possessed the gift of compilation, of using the resources of other men and other ages and of bringing them together into the unity of a new and living organism".[37] If Schaff's liturgical genius is to be located in a single ability, it is his gift of compilation. Every committee which hopes to produce a liturgy that is Catholic, Reformed, and contemporary must have one such member; and in the case of the German Reformed Church, that member was its chairman.

Bernard C. Wolff

Bernard C. Wolff [1794-1870] was made a member of the liturgical committee in 1849 and remained a member through the publication of the *Order of Worship* in 1866, attending only thirty-four of the initial one hundred two sessions. He entered the Seminary at Mercersburg at the age of thirty-seven, a well-to-do layman from Martinsburg, Virginia [now West Virginia]. His wife was the granddaughter of William Heyser, an elder-member of the liturgical committee during its work on the Provisional Liturgy. Wolff's daughter, Sue Barton, married Theodore Appel, a Mercersburg intimate and brother of Thomas G. Apple, who became a member of the liturgical committee in 1864.

Throughout his career--which included pastorates in Easton and Baltimore before he followed Nevin as Professor of Didactic and Practical Theology in 1854--Wolff was characterized as a mediator. David Schaff wrote of him: "While Dr. Wolff had given his support to the Mercersburg professors in their time of stress and arraignment, he was averse to controversy and had sought to act the part of a mediator in the church. His election [as Nevin's successor] was a wise choice, calculated to establish confidence in all circles."[38] According to Wolff's biographer, his membership on the liturgical committee "had a stabilizing influence. He was a mediationist, and the church at large had implicit confidence in his orthodoxy. His irenic spirit was deeply felt by all who had a part in the formation of the new Liturgy."[39]

John Henry Augustus Bomberger

In many ways John H. A. Bomberger [1817-1890] is the most fascinating member of the committee. He is certainly the man who most determined the course of the liturgical movement within the German Reformed Church; however, the details of that tale are best told later.

Bomberger graduated from Mercersburg in 1838. He then held pastorates in Lewistown (1838-40), Waynesboro (1840-45), Easton (1845-54), and Race Street, Philadelphia (1854-1869). He founded Ursinus College in 1869 and became its first president, continuing in that capacity until his death in 1890. To his work on the Provisional Liturgy Bomberger brought a bounding enthusiasm, no mean poetic ability, and a talent for editorial work. As has been indicated above, it was Bomberger who first articulated at Norristown the direction in which the German Reformed liturgical activity should go. He approved the Baltimore Proposals in 1852, and was a faithful contributor to all the work of the committee, as will be shown in more detail below.

Henry Harbaugh

Henry Harbaugh [1817-1867] was one of the more active members of the liturgical committee, serving as its only secretary. Many of the sessions were held in Harbaugh's study in Lancaster, where he was minister of the First Reformed Church from 1850-1860. Before his decade in Lancaster Harbaugh served a congregation in Lewisburg from 1843-50; after it he spent three peaceful years at St. John's Reformed

Church in Lebanon. In 1863 Harbaugh was elected Wolff's
successor in the Seminary. There he died in 1867.

Although Harbaugh had his difficulties with Bomberger
during the '60's, and his problems with the Lancaster congregation during the '50's (primarily because of his unyielding
stand on temperance and the liturgy), he was, nevertheless,
a popular minister whose company was welcomed by his teachers,
Nevin and Schaff. His sense of humor, his poetic ability,[40]
and his passion for the liturgy, were most remembered by the
German Reformed Church. In eulogizing Harbaugh, Schaff wrote:

> He took a leading part in the Liturgical
> Committee from the beginning to the close
> of their labors. He kept the records of
> the Committee. The Confirmation Service,
> the Burial Service, and most of the Family
> Prayers are mainly the production of his
> pen. The difference of opinion which now
> prevails in the Church, concerning the
> new Liturgy, will, of course, affect the
> estimate put upon his services in this
> connection. Nor is it time yet to judge
> finally of a movement still in progress.
> But all must admit the sincerity of
> motive, and the earnestness and devoted-
> ness of spirit, as well as the vigor of
> intellect, which he showed on every occa-
> sion, and which breathes in all his numer-
> ous publications. He was thoroughly
> American German Reformed in all his sym-
> pathies, but with a truly Catholic spirit.[41]

Nichols' treatment of Harbaugh is incomplete and thereby
unjust in its implications. He deals only with two articles
entitled "Christian Cultus: Its Nature, History, and Relations,
with special reference to the German Reformed Church", published
by Harbaugh in 1854 and 1855.[42] If only these articles are considered, Nichols' conclusions are just:

> [Harbaugh's] essays are historically in-
> accurate and theologically confused....
> His general conception was evidently closer
> to Bomberger's proposals of 1849 than to
> Schaff's of 1852. He oriented himself en-
> tirely to Reformation precedents with no
> concern for the ancient catholic forms....
> Since Harbaugh was personally a strong
> supporter of the Mercersburg professors,
> it is striking that he shared so few of
> their leading ideas.[43]

One simply cannot leave the evaluation of Harbaugh at
that, as Nichols does. Rather than not sharing Mercersburg's
"leading ideas", it would be nearer the truth to say that in
1854 and early 1855, Harbaugh, Bomberger, Wolff, nor anyone
else fully understood the liturgical implications of those
ideas. Serious work on the liturgy did not begin until
March 13, 1856, and Harbaugh's liturgical education cannot
be dated prior to that time. His address to the Tercentenary
Convention in 1863 reflects considerable maturity in the area
of liturgics.

Beyond this, it must be said that Harbaugh's greatest
contribution to the Mercersburg liturgical enterprise, excepting his work as secretary of the committee, was not as a
liturgiologist but as a popularizer. He immediately recognized the educational value of the liturgy and the Christian
Year, and was one of the few German Reformed pastors who
succeeded in instituting substantial portions of both in his
congregations. The means he employed in his attempts to introduce the liturgy will be discussed in more detail below;
however, let it be underscored here that Harbaugh is not a
little responsible for whatever success the Mercersburg liturgical movement did have.

Elias Heiner

Heiner was a respected pastor of the First German Reformed Church in Baltimore from 1835 until his death in 1863, and a member of the liturgical committee from 1849. He was conservative and "low church", as can be seen in this statement: "Personally, individual piety is to be preferred to any outward connection with the church whatever....There are thousands in the world who belong to Christ, and yet have no outward or formal connection with his visible church."[44] Heiner was sick much of the time during the last ten years of his life and attended only twenty-six sessions of the liturgical committee: the Lancaster meeting from August 25-September 3, 1857.

There is no evidence prior to the publication of the Provisional Liturgy that Heiner had any serious objections to the work. He was assigned certain forms to prepare, although none of them was eventually used.[45] He wrote to Schaff on November 27, 1857, that he was "indeed much pleased with the book". Apparently Heiner had pressed for a service for prisoners and one for use at sea, and the fact that neither was included distressed him. "What will my half dozen or more sea captains say to this omission?...I would cheerfully go to the expense of printing one of the services that were accepted, and of having it inserted in the next edition, if it could be done."[46] Heiner's death in 1863 precluded any influence he might have had on the second phase (1862-69) of the liturgical controversy.

Daniel Zacharias

Daniel Zacharias [d. 1873] was appointed to the liturgical committee chaired by Bomberger in 1848, and he remained
an active member through the revision of 1866. In spite of
the burden of a parish in Frederick City, Maryland, he managed
to attend forty-one sessions on the Provisional Liturgy and
twenty of the revision sessions. As late as 1853, Zacharias
was openly hostile to Mercersburg, for at the Synod of Philadelphia he brought charges against S. R. Fisher, editor of
the *Weekly Messenger*, "for refusing to publish articles
against the Mercersburg theology".[47] These charges reflect
Zacharias's own feeling more than his sense of journalistic
objectivity, and his resounding defeat by the Synod left him
scarred for some years to come.

Within the liturgical committee minutes there is no
evidence to indicate that Zacharias was anything but cooperative. Why and when he changed his position cannot be determined, but the following letter from Harbaugh to Lewis H.
Steiner in 1862 is informative:

> I have deeply sympathized with Dr. Zacharias
> in his illness. I can't tell you how seri-
> ously I was affected by that item in your
> letter. Dr. Z has always been a favorite of
> mine. I loved his geniality--his deep
> [Christian?] Churchliness. I knew that his
> heart was growing warmer on the Liturgy
> project year by year. He always knew what
> the book meant, which cannot be said of
> some others on the Liturgical Committee.[48]

Zacharias hosted a three-day meeting of the revision committee
in Frederick City in August, 1865; and his election as president

of the important General Synod of 1866 was considered by
Good as a victory for the "Nevinites".

Thomas Conrad Porter

Porter [1822-1901] was added to the liturgical committee
when Nevin resigned as chairman in 1851; and he continued to
serve it faithfully through 1866, attending eighty-three
sessions on the Provisional Liturgy and forty-five of the
revision sessions. Porter's father was a life-long elder in
the Presbyterian Church, and he sent his son to Lafayette
College and then to Princeton Theological Seminary, from
which he was graduated in 1843. After briefly serving parishes in Monticello, Georgia, Philadelphia, and Reading, Porter
became Professor of Chemistry, Botany, and Zoology, first in
Marshall College, and then in the merged Franklin and Marshall.
In 1866, he became Professor of Botany, Zoology, and Geology
at his alma mater, Lafayette, and was concurrently pastor of
the Third Reformed Church of Easton from 1877 to 1884.

Porter's scientific bent is deceptive, for he was an
extremely sensitive and cultured man whose avocation fitted
him well for duties on a liturgical committee: "In the field
of English literature few men of our times are so deeply read.
He may be said to have been familiar with all the English
classics. The poets were his special delight."[49] He did
extensive translating in both the literary and liturgical
fields,[50] and frequently published essays of literary criticism. Hymnology was still another of his many interests,
and it was Porter who was given the responsibility of preparing two hundred suitable hymns for the Provisional Liturgy.
(The story of that presentation is better told in another
place.)

The point is that Porter's talents and interests well
suited him for his job as editor of the *Order of Worship*--
if, indeed, the hunch of Miss Elizabeth Clarke Kieffer is
correct:

> There must have been a hand...to give unity
> of style to all this [i.e., the *Order of
> Worship*], and I do not believe it was Har-
> baugh's. I should be more inclined to sus-
> pect that here again T. C. Porter who,
> while not himself a creative genius, had a
> distinct facility in altering the work of
> others, and may have given the final polish-
> ing to the brilliant mosaic which was final-
> ly brought to press in 1866.[51]

That hunch will be evaluated in Chapter VI.

E. V. Gerhart

In E. V. Gerhart one encounters a leopard which definitely
changed its spots. As the President of Heidelberg College and
Professor of Theology in its associated Seminary, he wrote this
"confidential" letter to Bomberger in 1852:

> In my opinion Dr. Schaff and Dr. Nevin,
> particularly, are no longer true Protes-
> tants....Indeed, if I could believe all
> Dr. Nevin's and Dr. Schaff's teachings--
> should I yield passively to their in-
> fluence, I would become a Romanist or an
> infidel. Hence I would not send a son
> or brother to Mercersburg....To my mind
> the time has come when *you* and others
> should take up the pen against these
> Romish innovations, and in favor of the
> *Reformed* character of the Reformed Church
> and of the Heidelberg Catechism.[52]

But Gerhart did not know either his own mind or the mind of Mercersburg. He was elected to the presidency of Franklin and Marshall College in 1854; and "It was thought," writes Good, "that Gerhart might harmonize the East again, but after he became president he went over fully into the Mercersburg camp".[53] In fact, it was Gerhart who produced the only formal treatment of Mercersburg Theology in 1891,[54] and it is generally conceded that with his death the force, but not the influence, of Mercersburg Theology came to an end.

Gerhart was made a member of the liturgical committee in 1855, presumably to represent the interests of the Western Synod, which had also engaged in liturgical discussions. He took an active role, attending sixty-three sessions on the Provisional Liturgy and all but one session which dealt with revision.

Samuel R. Fisher

Perhaps it is to be expected that the editor of the denomination's journalistic voice would be a controversial figure. In any event, Samuel R. Fisher [d. 1881] was just that; and, although he attended only two of the possible one hundred fifty seven sessions of the liturgical committee, he had as much influence on the destiny of the denomination's liturgies as any man. Fisher's influence will be examined more carefully in the discussion of the introduction and reception of the liturgies; however, it may be stated here that the Mercersburg liturgical controversy proved the infinite value of a good working relationship between any liturgy committee and its denomination's press.

Fisher apparently adopted a "wait and see" approach to the Mercersburg controversy during the 1840's and early 1850's; however, in Zacharias' abortive charge against him in 1853, there is likely the truth that, if anything, Fisher was slightly pro-Mercersburg. He was appointed to the liturgy committee in 1852, primarily to see the work through the press, once it was ready for publication. Even though he attended no meetings during the committee's work on the Provisional Liturgy, he did submit manuscripts of three prayers: "in time of affliction and distress", and a morning and evening prayer.[55] The accompanying letter to Schaff indicates that as of June 26, 1856, Fisher was very much in agreement with what he knew of the committee's proceedings. As shall be shown in Chapter VI, however, an incident occurred which did much to determine the course of the liturgical controversy.

Thomas G. Apple

There is little to be said about Thomas G. Apple. He was appointed to the liturgical committee to replace Elias Heiner in 1864. Only twelve of the revision sessions record his attendance; yet he wrote the report of the committee to the Eastern Synod in 1866 and to the General Synod in 1869. From 1871-1898 he was Professor of Church History and New Testament Exegesis in the Seminary.

Apple was a second-generation Mercersburg advocate, whose name is always to be found with those of Nevin, Schaff, Harbaugh, and Gerhart; yet he seems to have offended no one seriously. J. I. Good, whose hostility toward all that resembles Mercersburg has been previously noted, has this to say of him:

"Professor T. G. Apple was the clearest of all the theologians
of the Mercersburg School in his statements of their views,
and in the peace and liturgical commissions he was the fair-
est and broadest-minded of the Mercersburg leaders. He represented the later Mercersburg rather than the earlier Mercersburg of Nevin, Gans, etc."[56]

William Heyser, George Schaefer, and George Welker

Of three of the five laymen whose names appear on the
liturgical committee's roster there is nothing of importance
to be said. Schaefer is a complete unknown. William Heyser,
a prominent lawyer in Chambersburg and a member of the committe
from 1849, attended none of the meetings. It was he, however,
who argued that the church had a moral obligation to honor the
ten year contract between the liturgical committee and Lindsay
& Blakiston. This argument did much to disuade the Synod of
1862 from initiating revision at that time. George C. Welker
appears in the records of the liturgical committee only once.
He wrote to Schaff on January 5, 1856,[57] explaining that he
could not attend the meeting of the committee because of sick-
ness in his family. He goes on to urge Schaff to make the
liturgy "permanent" rather than "provisional", since the
latter "will be an obstacle to its general introduction".

John Rodenmayer

Equally little of a personal nature is known about
Elder John Rodenmayer, made a member of the committee in 1852.

He was a member of Third Reformed Church in Baltimore and sang in its choir. His pastor, J. S. Foulk, championed the liturgical cause and did much to promote the Provisional Liturgy and the *Order of Worship* in the pages of the denominational press. Rodenmayer was a faithful member of the liturgical committee, attending thirty sessions on the Provisional Liturgy and fifteen on the *Order of Worship*, always requesting permission to be excused on the other occasions.

Lewis H. Steiner

Perhaps the most notable layman in the German Reformed Church during the Mercersburg period was the Baltimore physician, Lewis H. Steiner. He was a confidant of all the Mercersburg men and the recipient and *preserver* of a substantial correspondence with each of them. For many years Steiner served as a trustee of Franklin and Marshall College, and eventually became an important member of the United States Sanitary Commission. Steiner was appointed to the liturgical committee in 1864, and attended every revision session except one, serving as its secretary pro tem in Harbaugh's absence. One of Steiner's many interests was hymnology, and in 1859 he published *Cantate Domino*.[58] An examination of this volume will be found in Chapter VI.

To summarize: from 1849 to 1866 the liturgical committee consisted of nineteen different men. Excepting the five elders who played no active role in the committee's work, and Joseph F. Berg, who left the denomination in 1852, nine of the remaining thirteen were committed advocates of the Mercersburg

Theology: Schaff, Nevin, Wolff, Harbaugh, Porter, Gerhart, Fisher (after 1862), Apple, and Steiner. Zacharias, Fisher, and Rodenmayer appear to have been more in than out of the Mercersburg camp. Heiner was cooperative, as was Bomberger, during work on the Provisional Liturgy. The committee operated from 1855 to 1866 with a ratio of ten clergymen to four elders; and, as has been noted, only two elders contributed anything to the work.

A remarkable number of the clergymen on the committee had poetic ability: Schaff, Bomberger, Harbaugh, and Porter. If the liturgy is an art form in any sense of the word, then a committee would be fortunate to have such a quartet of poets numbered among its members.

Meetings and Procedures of the Committee

In preparing the Provisional Liturgy, the liturgical committee sat for five formal meetings between March 13, 1856, and October 21, 1857. Harbaugh misnumbered two sessions[59] during the first meeting; thus the minutes total 102 sessions, when the accurate count is 104. If each session lasted three hours, the committee spent a total of 1740 man-hours, the equivalent of 72 1/2 twenty-four hour days, in formal meeting. Were one to add the unnumbered hours spent privately by each individual member, the meetings of sub-committees, and the days of Synod debate, the result would be an awesome testimonial to the staggering amount of time and energy which was consumed in producing the Provisional Liturgy. These formal meetings and the procedures of the committee, in so far as they can be reliably ascertained, are detailed below.

Prior to the first meeting of the committee in 1856, information concerning the committee's informal activity is ketchy. Schaff became chairman in October, 1851; and the irst sign of liturgical life is found in this open letter rom Schaff to the denomination dated February 7, 1852, inicating that he and the committee are now ready to begin ork on the liturgy. He requests that committee members nd ministers generally

> ...furnish me with any advice and contributions within their reach, which may be of direct or indirect benefit to this important object. I have thus far found the task far more difficult than I anticipated....Besides the formulas for all the public services of the Church, usually provided for by a full and regular liturgy, it is the intention of the chairman...to embody a family liturgy, or a collection of suitable prayers for domestic worship in the work....[60]

Of particular interest in this first statement by Schaff s his early admission of the difficulty in the task before im. In the three months following his appointment, the chairan apparently discovered what was soon to become apparent to he other committee members: this was no easy task. Seven ears and one Liturgy later Schaff was to write to Eli Keller, member of the committee to prepare a German translation of he Provisional Liturgy: "Your committee will have a hard oad to travel. I would not again go through the trouble I ad as chairman for seven years for any sum of money. But he members of your committee are fresh and new and can stand t."[61]

The extent of the denomination's response to Schaff's equest for "advice and contributions" cannot be judged accurately. As shall be documented below, a number of contributions were made by ministers not on the committee; however, most of these were received during 1856-57. It is more likely that Schaff arbitrarily requested certain members of the committee to prepare the forms that were presented to the Synod in 1852, while he, Nevin, and Porter worked on the general design of the Liturgy and, perhaps blocked out the four Lord's Day Services. There is no indication who might have prepared the marriage service. None of the forms from 1852 are extant, and there is no evidence that they are the same as the forms printed in the *Mercersburg Review*, 1854-1855. An undated manuscript of a marriage service prepared by Heiner has been preserved, and it is possible that he was given that assignment in 1852.

Bomberger was assigned the Eucharist and Confirmation services to be prepared during the summer of 1852. Considering the description of his work in a letter to Schaff,[62] it is clear that they are the forms published in the *Mercersburg Review*.[63] Subsequently Bomberger prepared forms for Baptism, based largely on the Palatinate Liturgy; however, these were never published.

During 1853, Schaff directed the work of the committee, assigning services to be prepared, suggesting volumes for the members to study, but calling no meetings. He had sole responsibility for the Seminary during this year and liturgical endeavors necessarily were secondary. On November 21, 1853, he wrote the committee, informing them that Wolff was to be chairman *pro tem* during his sabbatical, and urging them

> ...not to suffer this absence to cause any
> delay in the completion and publication of
> the proposed specimen-liturgy. All I may
> contribute yet towards it, can be added and

printed afterwards with the consent of the
Committee. For I expect and sincerely hope,
that the work, after it is once fairly
before the Church for examination and trial,
will not finally be adopted for *several
years* to come. There is now evidently a
growing liturgical movement going on in
various branches of Protestantism both in
Germany and England, as well as in America,
which will no doubt lead ultimately to
most important results, and I think we will
be better prepared in a few years than now,
to adopt such a book of public and private
devotion, as will come up to the proper
idea of divine worship and meet all our
wants. But, in the meantime, we need a
specimen liturgy, not only as a basis for
the one, which will ultimately be adopted;
but also for present use....I would also
respectfully ask those members of the Committee who cannot procure Renaudot's
Liturgiae Orientales or similar rare and
costly collections, to put themselves in
possession, if possible, of Bunsen's late
work on *Hippolytus and his age*, which, I
understand, will shortly be republished
in this country. The fourth volume of it
contains the eucharistic services of the
Primitive Church, which ought to be, by
all means, consulted, together with the
liturgical works of the sixteenth century.[64]

It would seem from this statement that Schaff was not antici-
pating a liturgy as complete as that eventually published in
1857; however, from the beginning he wanted a *provisional*
liturgy and nothing more. He maintained his insistence upon
the provisional nature, resisting early attempts of the Synod
either to adopt or revise it before a decade of experimental
use by the denomination; however, Schaff's year in Europe and
England may well have changed his thinking somewhat on the
nature and extent of a provisional liturgy. The influence of

Schaff's sabbatical on the Liturgy of 1857 will be examined
in greater detail below.

In 1854, the *Mercersburg Review* contained several specimen liturgical forms, most of them but way stations enroute
to the completed Liturgy of 1857: Baptism of Infant and Adult,
Marriage, Laying of a Cornerstone, four forms for the Lord's
Day, Confirmation, Preparation for Communion, and Communion.
In every case except the forms for the fourth Lord's Day service, Marriage and the Laying of a Cornerstone, significant
change and revision occurred during the next three years.
Other forms, such as those for Baptism and Communion, were
set aside entirely and new ones prepared.

Schaff returned physically refreshed and anxious to be
about his liturgical chores. In another open letter to the
committee he requested that the members finish their assignments and either send them to him or publish them in the July
and October numbers of the *Mercersburg Review*.

> It is expected and desired that each member,
> besides his contribution to the public forms,
> should furnish about seven morning and even-
> ing prayers of one or two pages each for the
> domestic liturgy to be incorporated in the
> collection.
> It is proposed to hold a final confer-
> ence of the Committee immediately before the
> next annual meeting of the Synod at Chambers-
> burg, and to have the Specimen Liturgy ready
> for the action of this body, in reference to
> its publication for the Church's inspection
> and experimental use.[65]

Here, too, the sort of liturgy which Schaff describes seems
inconsistent with that which was finally to appear in 1857.
The "conferences" held by the committee during each meeting

f Synod led Schaff to believe in May, 1855, that a "Specimen
iturgy" could be published before October, 1855. In October
e was still optimistic, supposing that the work could be
ompleted before the meeting of the Classes in May, 1856; yet
he difficulty of the task and the committee's own sense of
nsufficiency made Schaff once more urge a delay of any final
ction by the Synod. The intention remained simply "to fur-
ish, according to the best of their ability, a *provisional*
iturgy, including a sufficient variety of forms, for *examin-
tion* and *optional* use, until the Church be fully prepared by
ractical experience, to bring it into such a shape and form,
s will best suit the wants of our ministers and congregations,
nd make it, under the blessing of God, a rich fountain of
ound piety and fervent devotion for many generations to
ome".[66] Synod accepted the report, directed the committee
o prepare "a solemn reception service for emigrants", and
educed the quorum of the committee to five.

Schaff apparently realized that more than annual meetings
f the committee were now required, and on February 27, 1856,
he *Weekly Messenger* summoned the members to their first
ormal meeting to begin on March 13 in Lancaster. In the
ecture room of St. Paul's Reformed Church Henry Harbaugh
as appointed secretary of the committee, and the official
ecord of its activities began. These meetings consisted of
ore than simply debating the use of this form or that; rather
hey were occasions also when "liturgical lore was explored
rom the original sources. The German liturgies and forms
ere translated and revised, and all the literature and
istory of the Church as it pertained to the subject was
amiliarized and presented by the various members. Drafts
f prayers were submitted, freely criticized, altered, re-
ritten, and finally adopted."[67]

March 13-26, 1856

The first meeting, March 13-26, 1856, consisted of thirty-one sessions. According to an agenda penciled on the final page of a manuscript of the Provisional Liturgy written in Schaff's hand, the order of business was to be the "order of the book"; however, in following the minutes one must remember that the "order of the book" changed somewhat from the plan presented in 1852. Discussion on the "Catholic" or "Primitive Forms" and the Festival Prayers consumed the first fifteen sessions. Little by way of detailed information is included in the minutes. Most entries read like this: "Took up the 2nd Good Friday prayer and passed it." One is left to fill in the blanks concerning who said and did what. Occasionally the position of a particular individual is noted--e.g., Zacharias had to return home during the ninth session and before doing so he voiced his disapproval of including collects in the liturgy. Apparently he was not persuasive, for during the fifteenth session "it was unanimously passed to embody collects in the liturgy. ..."

Issues, prayers, forms and procedures were all presented to the members; they discussed the matter, and voted when they were ready. Rarely is the distribution of a vote recorded. When a form proved particularly difficult or time-consuming for the whole committee, sub-committees of one or more members were appointed to study the matter and report. Here is one example: "The collect to follow the reading of the Commandments was referred to Revds. Harbaugh and Porter, to report tomorrow morning."[68]

Revision of the regular service for the Lord's Day began during the fifteenth session. A copy of the forms as they

appeared in the *Mercersburg Review* was on hand, and the emendations, excisions, and marginal notations testify that the
four forms were "examined and corrected...sentence by sentence".

The committee returned to the Festival Prayers and the
Primitive Forms, taking a final vote on the order in which
they would appear. The final entries of each meeting are
generally helpful, as they record the work assigned individuals or groups for the intervening periods. Before the next
meeting Harbaugh was to confer with both M. Kieffer and "some
publishing house in Phild. in regard to the publication of
the Liturgy in a manner most advantageous". The Mercersburg
group was given the "family Liturgy", while "the rest of the
forms were placed in the hands of the Lancaster members".
All other forms--those prepared by committee members and
those received from ministers at large--were read, debated,
and "laid aside" as they did not possess "sufficient merits
to be considered". The extant manuscripts in the archives
of the committee witness to these procedures: "accepted",
"laid aside", "laid over", "not needed at present" are the
customary entries.

January 2-9, 1857

The second meeting of the committee was held in Lancaster
from January 2-9, 1857, and consisted of nineteen sessions,
most of them in Harbaugh's study at the First Reformed Church.
Several of the opening sessions were spent in selecting the
Scripture verses for the section entitled "Christian Worship".
The first decision to change the plan of the Liturgy as it was
presented in 1852 came during the tenth session:

> It was decided that the collects and
> scripture lessons form the second
> division of the Liturgy. Because they
> fix at once the ecclesiastical year,
> and also contain special collects which
> partake of the nature of elements. De-
> cided to give it the title 'The Church
> Year'--with a subtitle, 'Scripture
> lessons and collects'.

At the same session a curious decision was made which makes
the Provisional Liturgy quite distinctive and untraditional:
"Decided that the Gospel be first, then the Epistle, and the
Collect last." No other prayer book contains this reversal
of the customary Epistle-Gospel arrangement. Slifer's explanation is that "the Gospel is read first because it contains
the historical portion".[69]

The intention of the committee regarding the four forms
for the Lord's Day is revealed at this meeting. "The conclusion was that the first form be the regular morning service; and the other three for optional use in the afternoon
and evening." Two observations should be made regarding this
decision: first, the form prescribed as the "regular" Lord's
Day service is the highly responsive one. Second, Bomberger
was not present during the session which made the decision
regarding the first form--a fact the implications of which
will be clear as the plot thickens. All four forms were presented, and any one of them could be used as the "regular"
morning worship, of course; however, so far as Schaff, Nevin,
Porter, and Harbaugh--not a quorum in any event, had anyone
wished to challenge their "conclusion"--were concerned, it
was the first form which should be used on the Lord's Day.

The Mercersburg "division" was directed to prepare a
second series of Scripture readings for the lectionary;

Harbaugh and Porter were to prepare a selection of 150 possible hymns to be submitted to the committee; a general discussion was held regarding the forms for Baptism, Confirmation, Marriage, and Communion; and the committee adjourned after it had "reviewed what had been passed over and assigned to different hands the unfinished part".

April 20-25, 1857

On April 20, 1857, the committee convened in Harbaugh's study for its third formal meeting, this one to extend for but five days and nine sessions. Eight of these sessions were primarily concerned with the second series of Scripture readings presented by Schaff. Each of them was discussed, revised, and approved. Harbaugh was directed to "make a table of the first series of scripture readings; and both readings, or tables of readings, are to precede the collects and printed readings, as the beginning of the chapter on the Church Year".

Matters regarding the printing of the liturgy were discussed; however, these will be detailed in a separate section below. The ninth session was concerned primarily with "fixing the order of the Provisional Liturgy", different, as will be shown subsequently, from the plan of 1852 and from that which was eventually published in 1857. Adjournment came with the following resolution:

> That all the unfinished chapters of the
> Liturgy according to the table of contents
> adopted, be entrusted to a subcommittee
> consisting of Rev. Harbaugh, Gerhart,
> Porter, and Bomberger, with full discre-
> tionary powers for final revision before

the next meeting of the Committee in
August, so that nothing be left for
the action of the Committee except the
Communion Service, the Ordination and
Installation Services, and the Hymn-
book.

August 25-September 3, 1857

The committee met for a fourth time in Lancaster from
August 25 to September 3, 1857: twenty-three sessions.
According to the minutes of the previous meeting and the
notice which appeared in the *Weekly Messenger* on August 18,
1857, it was hoped that this would be the final meeting;
however, such was not to be the case. Several of the occasional services were first on the agenda: Confirmation,
Burial, Visitation of the Sick, and Public Reception of
Immigrants. The committee then "took up the Preparatory
Office of the Lord's Supper", and the detailed manner in
which the members worked can be seen in this entry: "The
title was fixed: 'The Service of Preparation for the Holy
Communion'. The use of the commandments adopted. The use
[as] proposed of the Litany was adopted. Singing was then
adopted as proposed, before the sermon. Singing again after
the sermon adopted. Finished the service to the prayer...."
The same careful procedure was followed in the committee's deliberation on the Eucharist: "Fixed the order,
and corrected the language of the rubrics. Took up the
Address (after deciding that it be introduced) to the communicants sentence by sentence. Corrected and adopted it
as amended. Also reviewed the Confession and following
blessing by the minister--and adopted." The form for the

Eucharist was again taken up the following morning, and both the seriousness of the occasion and the weariness of the committee can be read in this entry: "Discussed the offertory prayer [from 8:30 A.M.] til 1/4 before 11 o'clock; when it was adopted. The discussions were deeply earnest and solemn; and the vote was taken under a strong sense of the solemnity involved in the point." The Eucharistic order was completed during the next session.

Confirmation, Visitation of the Sick, Marriage, Communion of the Sick, and the Burial service were then discussed again. With no details given the Ordination services were debated and adopted, as was the Excommunication service, which had been prepared by Gerhart.

An interesting non-liturgical incident occurred at this session. That he may "possess and preserve the likenesses of all the members of the Liturgy Committee now present" [Schaff, Gerhart, Porter, Nevin, Heiner, and Zacharias], Harbaugh asked the members "as a personal favor...to sit in a group for an ambrotype". It was resolved "that this request be granted, provided that no public use be made of the fact or of the picture". Apparently the finished product revealed Porter with his eyes shut, and Steiner made some remark to him about it. Porter replied that Steiner's remark was entirely just, and that he and Nevin had objected to the picture in the first place, but Harbaugh prevailed.[70]

The title of the Provisional Liturgy came about in this fashion on the evening of September 2, 1857:

> The committee having been invited to take
> tea with Father Bausman, walked out after
> five o'clock. After tea, in the twilight
> of the evening, an informal meeting was
> held before the house where the committee

had been engaged in friendly social conversation, and the question as to the Title
was discussed. Each one was asked by the
chairman to give a Title. Such as the
following were given:

    Dr. Nevin: An Order of Christian
Worship: Prepared by the direction and
for the use of the German Reformed Church
in the United States of America.

    Prof. Porter: Liturgy: or Order of
Christian Worship, Prepared etc....

    H. Harbaugh: Liturgy: or Order of
Christian Worship, etc....

    The rest of the committee agreed
with one or the other of these substantially. Without a vote the committee
pretty generally came to a final decision
in favor of the following Title:

A

Liturgy

or

Order

of

Christian Worship, Prepared, etc....

    It was agreed that the committee meet
tomorrow morning at 8 o'clock. The committee
returned home between 8 and 9 o'clock in the
evening. It was a lovely evening, and the
committee seemed much refreshed and pleased
with the walk, kind hospitality of Father
Bausman, and the fraternal communion enjoyed
in the visit during the evening.

    It was quite apparent to the committee that yet another
meeting was necessary before its work could be completed;
therefore the assignments before adjournment were extensive.
Porter and Heiner were to examine the Consecration of a Church
and Burial Ground; Zacharias and Heiner had responsibility for
the Visitation of Prisoners; Excommunication was reserved for
the "Committee of the Whole"; Harbaugh took the Burial form
and the Family Prayers; Schaff was assigned the Guide to Pri-

vate Devotion; and Porter was in charge of the Hymns and Psalms. After adjournment, Gerhart, Porter, and Harbaugh remained in discussion, and there follows this curious and unofficial entry in the minute book: "The members of the committee remaining by a letter requested him [Dr. Nevin] to prepare a regular Lord's Day Service which they may lay before the general committee at the next meeting; feeling as they do that what we have is not equal to the other parts of the Liturgy." Apparently Nevin did not do as they asked, for there is no record of any further discussion of the Lord's Day service.

October 13-21, 1857

The final meeting of the committee was held from October 13 to 21, 1857, the twenty sessions convening in the "Old Consistory room of the 1st German Reformed Church in Philadelphia". Bomberger was pastor of this congregation and secretary *pro tem* of the committee in Harbaugh's absence. Most of this meeting was taken up with reading and revising proof and preparing the remaining services for the printer. It was concluded, unwisely according to Heiner, to omit the "occasional services"—Service at Sea and Visitation of Prisoners—in order to have room for the Family Prayers and 104 of the 200 hymns Porter had prepared.

The final session has in part been described above. By contract with Synod the committee was to receive fifty copies of the Liturgy, and they were disposed of as follows: one copy each to Fisher, Heyser, Schaeffer, and Welker—i.e., the four members who had taken no part in the proceedings of the committee; one copy each to the seminaries in Mercersburg

and Tiffin, and to Franklin and Marshall and Heidelberg
Colleges; one copy each to St. Paul's Reformed Church in
Lancaster and First Reformed Church in Philadelphia, the
two churches in which the committee had met; and the balance
of forty copies to be divided equally among the remaining
members of the committee. After remarks by Schaff and
various members of the committee, Nevin closed the session
with prayer and the committee rose to sing the Doxology.
In Schaff's words:

> The members will not easily forget the
> old fashioned round walnut table in the
> consistory room of St. Paul's church at
> Lancaster, and the similar table in the
> equally comfortable consistory room of
> the Race street church in Philadelphia.
> ...There the Committee sat many a day
> praying, writing, consulting together,
> criticising, examining and pondering
> over Bibles, Concordances, Liturgies,
> old and new, from the Clementine down
> to the Irvingite....They applied the
> pruning knife very freely to their own
> productions and laid aside whole piles
> of manuscript. Human nature, unaided
> by divine grace, would hardly have sub-
> mitted to such an unceremonious process.
> But the book, I am sure, is only the
> better for it. Almost every sentence
> and word were rigidly examined and
> measured. Sometimes interesting theo-
> logical discussions would spring up
> and relieve the mind of the wearisome
> minute verbal criticism. The whole
> was a capital training school, and if
> the committee could have recommenced
> their labors where they stopped, with
> the experience they had acquired, they
> would probably make a much better book
> than the one now published. Several
> forms prepared with considerable care,
> as prayers at sea, could not be finally

> acted upon, partly from want of time,
> partly from want of room, the agreement
> with the publishers limiting the book
> to 400 pages.[71]

Schaff's personal benediction tells it all: "I regret no time and labor bestowed upon the work, although I am free to confess, that I would never have consented to act as chairman, could I have foreseen the amount of trouble, anxiety and vexation which it involved."[72]

Nevin made the committee's "final report" to the Synod in 1857, before the printing of the Liturgy was completed; therefore, the members of Synod did not have copies before them. The work could have been completed in shorter time, had a mere compilation of prayers been desired; however, "it was felt from the beginning, that the true idea of a Liturgy involved a great deal more than this...." The committee matured with the work, according to Nevin, and what satisfied the members in the beginning "proved wholly unsatisfactory afterwards to themselves...." As the result of the committee's diligence, "the new Liturgy is not a mere compilation, or outward putting together of heterogeneous parts. It has a true life of its own, such as gives harmony to it as a whole...."

There is no desire on the part of the committee "to force the Liturgy upon the Church, without such general inward and free consent to its use....It must go forth among the churches simply as an *experiment*", each congregation determining its own liturgical desires. For this reason, "the Liturgy must work its own way [without "ecclesiastical sanction"] quietly and silently, into general use; or else pass away at last without any authority whatever, as a provision for which after all there has been no real demand in the reigning life of the Reformed Church". It was Nevin, more than the committee, who wrote the last sentence: "...It is not too much to say, that if the present Liturgy should prove inadequate..., no other is ever likely to be formed that will be attended with any better effect."[73]

Publication of the Provisional Liturgy

The Provisional Liturgy was finally available late in November, 1857. Since certain of the details of its publication may have influenced its reception, as has been suggested above, a brief examination of those details is in order. On March 26, 1856, the committee requested Harbaugh to consult both M. Kieffer and Company and "some publishing house in Philadelphia in regard to the publication of the Liturgy in a manner most advantageous". He wrote a letter of inquiry to Lindsay and Blakiston in Philadelphia on April 7, and received a reply from the firm on May 19, 1856. The terms of printing the liturgy were as follows:

> I should be willing to pay to the committee
> 10 cents per copy for all copies sold. Also
> to give them fifty copies of the first
> edition of the work. If the retail price
> of the work was one dollar per copy, our
> price to the bookseller would be seventy-
> five cents, being a discount of 20 per-
> cent, the usual discount to the trade.
> When the work was required by Ministers of
> the Church we would make a discount of 33
> per-cent selling them the book at 67
> cents....[74]

If, on the other hand, the committee wanted "an inferior

edition", one could be produced for about seventy-five cents; but it was not recommended.

Fisher was not heard from until April 21, 1857. Harbaugh apparently wrote him asking for the cost of the "proposed book", and Fisher replied, rather indignantly, that he could not estimate the cost until more details were received—such as "the kind of type to be used, the size of the page, the quality of the paper, the number of copies,...the style of binding...." Fisher resented the suggestion that M. Kieffer and Company agree to rebate the committee, in the fashion that Lindsay and Blakiston agreed to, since "Synod, by existing contract shared equally with the firm in all the profits of their publication operations, in view of which fact and by virtue of the contract referred to, the Synod is also under obligation to give its patronage to the firm".

Synod had such an agreement with M. Kieffer and Company and, in light of that fact, the committee acted quite precipitously in directing Harbaugh to reply to Fisher "giving the reasons why the committee cannot comply with the conditions furnished us in relation to the publication". It was further resolved that "the committee entrusted with the printing of that portion of the Liturgy now ready [Porter, Harbaugh, and Bomberger] be authorized to make such a contract with Lindsay and Blakiston in regard to the publication of the Liturgy, as they may regard most in accordance with the views of the general committee".

Lindsay and Blakiston responded quickly. May 1, 1857, Bomberger sent Harbaugh and Porter the first specimen pages of the Liturgy and the articles of contract. The latter is not extant; however, Bomberger is in agreement with it save for the right of the committee to insist "on the publication

of a smaller [i.e., abbreviated] edition when it seems desirable, and of fixing the price wholesale and retail".
Bomberger is quite aware of Fisher's fury and concludes
his letter with this telling suggestion: "And how would
it be to effect an arrangement with Chambersburg [M. Kieffer
and Company], for having the Establishment there nominally
recognized as co-publisher? *It might have an assuaging influence.*" [Italics mine.]

The editorial symbols which fill the margins of the
page proofs testify to Bomberger's diligence and ability as
an editor; and, while several members of the committee did
their share of reading proof, it was Bomberger who assumed
the task of shepherding the Liturgy through the press. He
was, after all, the only member of the committee in Philadelphia. The procedure seems to have been for Bomberger to
read the page proofs and make his suggested corrections;
then, when possible, refer the proofs to the author of the
service for his approval. Mr. William O'Neill was Bomberger's contact at Lindsay and Blakiston, and the evidence
suggests that these men spent unnumbered hours in preparing
the Liturgy for the press.

On November 17, 1857, Bomberger wrote Schaff that due
to a printing error the publication would be delayed a few
days. The cost of corrections in printing the Liturgy
amounted to $104.91--lower by $50.00 than he had feared.[75]
By December 1, 1857, the *Weekly Messenger* was able to
announce that the Provisional Liturgy was available at the
following prices:

>   Roan: $1.00;
>   Embossed marble edges: $1.25;
>   Embossed gilt: $1.50;
>   Imitation Turkey gilt: $2.00;

Turkey morocco gilt: $3.00;
Antique Turkey gilt: $3.00.

In the January, 1858, issue of the *Mercersburg Review*
Schaff proudly announced that "the first edition of a
thousand copies was already sold (mostly to outsiders, it
seems) within three weeks after its issue from the press".[76]
According to Linn Harbaugh, the third edition was "called
for almost in the same year of its publication".[77]

At the Synod of 1858, Fisher made an issue of the
liturgy committee's decision in regard to M. Kieffer and
Company. The result was a partial clarification of the contractual relationship between the Synod and the Printing
Establishment; however, no new action was taken in 1858.
In reporting the deliberations of Synod, Schaff's reasoning
is better understood. He simply argued that the Synod, "in
furnishing [M. Kieffer and Company] a new and profitable
book, and thus increasing the productive capital of the
firm, is...entitled to a legal percentage, as much as any
other author for his own work, or as the members of the firm
themselves are justly entitled to the annual interest accru-
ing from their pecuniary investment in the establishment...."[78]
If this was his only reason for choosing another publisher,
the hindsight of history would indicate that political dis-
cretion may have been the wiser course than literary principle. As has been argued above, Fisher's displeasure was incurred at a time when the fledgling Provisional Liturgy needed
an influential journalistic friend. Even though Schaff came
to the defense of the Liturgy during the years of bitter debate which followed its publication, he was clearly more interested in principles than in politics: "For my own part, I
feel almost indifferent as to the result [of the Provisional

Liturgy in winning its way within the denomination], leaving
it altogether in the hands of that merciful Providence which
has thus far guided the German Reformed Church in this
country."[79]

NOTES TO CHAPTER IV

1. *Wm*, November 3, 1852.

2. *Ibid.*

3. John W. Nevin, *The Liturgical Question with
Reference to the Provisional Liturgy of the German Reformed
Church: A Report by the Liturgical Committee* (Philadelphia:
Lindsay & Blakiston, 1862), p. 40.

4. *WM*, November 3, 1852.

5. *Ibid.*

6. *Ibid.*

7. *Ibid*

8. Binkley, *op. cit.*, p. 109.

9. *WM*, November 3, 1852.

10. Nichols, *Corporate Worship*, p. 54.

11. *WM*, November 3, 1852.

12. Prayer for Illumination before the Scripture and the
prayer after the sermon.

13. Nichols, *Corporate Worship*, p. 41.

14. *WM*, November 3, 1852.

15. Richards, *History of the Theological Seminary*, p. 338.

16. *Ibid.*

17. Nevin, *Vindication of the Revised Liturgy*, p. 21.

18. All of the significant members of the liturgical
committee from 1849 to 1866 are discussed in the pages to
follow. In dealing with certain men—Apple and Steiner, for

example--and in giving the number of meetings concerned with the *Order of Worship* each attended, strict chronology is not followed; however, a general survey of the entire committee is in order at this juncture.

19.   Nichols, *Romanticism*, pp. 293-294.

20.   *WM*, March 29, 1848.

21.   Nevin, *Vindication of the Revised Liturgy*, p. 15.

22.   *Ibid.*, p. 17.

23.   Letter, John W. Nevin to Philip Schaff, December 3, 1855, Library of the Evangelical and Reformed Historical Society, Philip Schaff Library, Lancaster Theological Seminary, Lancaster, Pa. (Hereinafter referred to as E & R Historical Society.)

24.   Letter, Nevin to Schaff, June 6, 1856, E & R Historical Society.

25.   Letter, Nevin to Schaff, March 28, 1857, E & R Historical Society.

26.   Minutes of the Liturgical Committee, 19th session, October 21, 1857. (Hereinafter referred to as PL Minutes.)

27.   PL Minutes, 20th session, October 21, 1857.

28.   Appendix I.

29.   James Hastings Nichols, *History of Christianity* (New York: The Ronald Press Company, 1956), p. 154.

30.   Yngve Brilioth, *Eucharistic Faith and Practice: Evangelical and Catholic* (London: Society for Promoting Christian Knowledge, 1930), p. 146.

31.   Scott F. Brenner, *A Handbook on Worship* (Philadelphia: The Heidelberg Press, 1941), p. 34.

32.   Nichols, *History of Christianity*, p. 154.

33.   John T. McNeill, *The History and Character of Calvinism* (New York: Oxford University Press, 1962), p. 386.

34. Klaus Penzel, *Church History and the Ecumenical Quest. A Study of the German Background and Thought of Philip Schaff* (unpublished Th.D. dissertation, Union Theological Seminary in the City of New York, 1962), p. 102.

35. Nichols, *History of Christianity*, p. 156.

36. Schaff was thirty-two when he became chairman of the committee.

37. Scott F. Brenner, "Philip Schaff the Liturgist," *Christendom*, XI (Autumn, 1946), p. 456.

38. David Schaff, *op. cit.*, p. 198.

39. Schaeffer, *A Repairer of the Breach*, p. 50.

40. Among Harbaugh's many poems is the hymn, "Jesus, I Live to Thee".

41. *WM*, January 22, 1868.

42. *MR*, VI (1854), pp. 573-600; VII (1855), pp. 116-135.

43. Nichols, *Romanticism*, pp. 299-300.

44. *WM*, October 15, 1845, quoted in Nichols, *Romanticism*, p. 153.

45. MSS of a marriage service and several general prayers are in the E & R Historical Society.

46. E & R Historical Society.

47. Good, *op. cit.*, p. 307.

48. Letter, Harbaugh to Steiner, December 9, 1862, E & R Historical Society.

49. Samuel A. Martin, ed., *Thomas Conrad Porter, Essays, Verses, Translations* (Chambersburg, Pa.: Henderson and Mong, n.d.), p. 18.

50. Porter's translation of Calvin's Order of Baptism appeared in *MR*, XI (1859).

51. Elizabeth Clarke Kieffer, *Henry Harbaugh, Pennsylvania Dutchman, 1817-1867* (Norristown, Pa.: Norristown Herald, Inc., 1945), p. 223. [This is vol. LI, *The Pennsylvania German Society, Proceedings and Addresses, 1945.*] In private conversations with Miss Kieffer she reiterated that her conclusion in regard to Porter was purely an intelligent hunch, based on her knowledge of the literary styles of both Harbaugh and Porter.

52. J. H. A. Bomberger, J. I. Good, *et al.*, *The Reverend John H. A. Bomberger*, Letter from Gerhart to J. H. A. Bomberger, October 14, 1852, pp. 180-184.

53. Good, *op. cit.*, p. 297.

54. E. V. Gerhart, *Institutes of the Christian Religion* (2 vols.; New York, 1891, 1894).

55. E & R Historical Society.

56. Good, *op. cit.*, p. 599.

57. The date represents the customary first of the year confusion, for the context clearly implies 1857.

58. Lewis H. Steiner and Henry Schwing, *Contate Domino: A Collection of Chants, Hymns and Tunes, Adapted to Church Service* (Boston: Oliver Ditson & Co., 1859).

59. A "session" consisted of a morning, afternoon, or evening meeting, and generally lasted three hours.

60. *WM*, March 3, 1852.

61. David Schaff, *op. cit.*, pp. 202-203.

62. Letter, J. H. A. Bomberger to Philip Schaff, August 25, 1852, E & R Historical Society.

63. VI (1854), pp. 554-572.

64. *WM*, November 30, 1853.

65. *WM*, May 23, 1855.

66. *WM*, October 31, 1855.

67. Linn Harbaugh, *Life of the Rev. Henry Harbaugh, D.D.* (Philadelphia: Reformed Church Publication Board, 1900), p. 243.

68. PL Minutes, March 19, 1856.

69. Morris D. Slifer, "The Liturgical Tradition of the Reformed Church in the U.S.A." *Studia Liturgica*, I (1962), p. 236.

70. Letter, Thomas C. Porter to Lewis H. Steiner, October 26, 1857, E & R Historical Society.

71. Schaff, "The New Liturgy," pp. 222-223.

72. *Ibid.*, p. 227.

73. *Acts and Proceedings of the Eastern Synod*, October, 1857, quoted in Schaff, "The New Liturgy," pp. 224-225.

74. Letter, Lindsay & Blakiston to Henry Harbaugh, E & R Historical Society.

75. E & R Historical Society.

76. *MR*, X (1858), p. 165.

77. Linn Harbaugh, *op. cit.*, p. 244.

78. Philip Schaff, "The Synod at Frederick," *MR*, XI (1859), p. 45.

79. Schaff, "The New Liturgy," pp. 226-227.

CHAPTER V

The Provisional Liturgy:
Structure, Sources, and Analysis

General Structure and Design

To provide a general context for a detailed examination
of the Provisional Liturgy the general structure and design
of the book is first considered. The types of services to
include and the arrangement of them within the book were
apparently matters of some significance to Schaff, and the
seven extant versions of the table of contents testify to a
constant flux in the order. The seven tables can be dated
with reasonable accuracy by comparing the number and arrangement of the forms with the minutes of the liturgical committee.

Table of Contents

Number one is the original plan for the Liturgy presented
to the Synod of Baltimore in 1852.[1] All of the forms are in
the first table which appear in the final one, with these exceptions: the Visitation of Prisoners was deleted and forms
added for Excommunication and Restoration, Consecration of a
Burial Ground, and Reception of Immigrants.

Number two: The second table reflects a certain sophistication and consolidation in the order of forms. It could not
have existed prior to March 18, 1856, for on that date the

committee determined to include Collects. Occasional Prayers and the Service at Sea make their first appearance.

Number three: This table appears in the minutes of the liturgy committee and represents the committee's thinking at the conclusion of the January, 1857, meeting. Forms for Excommunication and Restoration are found for the first time.

Number four: This table is a part of the committee minutes for April 24, 1857. It is both curious and important. All of the forms thus far introduced are retained with one exception: due to an apparent oversight the Confirmation Service was omitted; however, it reappeared in the next table. Forms for the Consecration of a Burial Ground and for the Reception of Immigrants are added, the latter by direction of the Synod in 1855. The most significant change in the order of the forms is found in this April edition. Previous versions listed the sacraments sequentially--i.e., Baptism, Confirmation, and Communion; but the fourth table places the Holy Communion after the Festival Prayers, which immediately follow the Lord's Day service. Surely this reflects the committee's desire to underscore the centrality of the Eucharist.

Numbers five and six: The fifth table appears to be Schaff's working copy for the final meeting in October, 1857. All of the forms previously listed were retained until the final meeting, and the cuts which were made during the last few sessions of the committee are to be seen in the fifth and sixth tables. The Visitation of Prisoners, Occasional Prayers, and Service at Sea were deleted, primarily in an effort to keep the volume within the designated four-hundred pages.

Number seven: The final version of the table is that which is printed in the Provisional Liturgy.

An examination of the Canticles, Prayers, and Hymns reveals the same evolution in both number and arrangement. The plan of 1852 reflects Schaff's insistence that worship revolve around the Christian Year; however, at first only a lectionary was proposed, along with the Festival Prayers. Collects and a separate section of Primitive Forms appear in the second table. One also finds the lectionary moving from the last "chapter" in 1852 to the second "chapter" in 1856. The reason must have been that the lectionary and the Christian Year upon which it was constructed was thereby better shown to provide the context for all the forms.

In the third table (January, 1857) a new section of Scripture verses is added: "Christian Worship". Seven selections (symbolic of perfection) were chosen to represent the "Introduction" to the volume. Other verses were gradually added to form a catena of Scripture appropriate to Confession and Absolution, Profession of Faith, Reading of Holy Scripture, Preaching, Prayer, Praise, the Holy Sacraments, and Benedictions.

The Synod of 1856 gave the committee this direction:

> ...to prepare and publish in one volume
> with their proposed Provisional Liturgy a
> new and critical selection of about one
> hundred and fifty standard Psalms and Hymns
> for public worship, including good trans-
> lations of the best Latin, and especially
> German hymns, which are so intimately
> interwoven with the history and piety of
> our mother Church in Europe, and which
> should be secured as far as possible for
> the devotional use of our English as well
> as our German congregations.[2]

The committee debated this direction on January 9, 1857, and such a section appears in the fourth table (April, 1857). The

Baltimore proposals did not specify that Psalms and Hymns
be printed in the Liturgy; however, the final principle
strongly implied it. From the beginning, Schaff insisted
that the Liturgy must be a peoples' book, owned and used by
them; thus he urged that a selection of Psalms and Hymns be
printed, and he persistently resisted attempts by Heiner to
reduce the Family Prayers and the Guide to Private Devotion
in order to retain Visitation of Prisoners and the Service
at Sea. The addition of Psalms and Hymns meant the necessity
of an Appendix, which together added sixty-eight pages to an
already expanding volume.[3]

The end result of sifting forms and debating priorities
produced the most extensive prayer book ever issued by an
American Reformed denomination. Its only close competitor
is the Huguenot Liturgy, which contains many more Canticles
and occasional prayers, but only slightly more than half as
many specific services.

Hymnbook

Two further considerations by way of describing the
general characteristics of the Provisional Liturgy may be
made here, before the sources for the specific services are
examined: first, the hymnbook; second, the lectionary.

According to Nichols, Schaff "brought himself up to
date on the current efforts to restore classical hymns for
modern use" while in Germany in 1854.[4] It was quite natural,
then, for the Synod to make him chairman of the committee
appointed in 1855 to prepare a German hymnbook. Schaff did
not want the chairmanship; however, "It is true, I have
always felt an interest in Hymnology. I was acquainted too

with the leading Hymnologists in Germany."[5] *Deutsches Gesang-buch* was published privately by Schaff in 1859.[6] The follow-ing year Porter's translation of Schaff's article on "German Hymnology" appeared in the *Mercersburg Review*. Schaff argued his familiar theme--that the hymn has a powerful and formative influence on the individual--and then went on to write: "The church-hymn is one of the most powerful means for promoting the *unity* of the faith and the *communion* of saints."[7] The principles Schaff employed in the selection of hymns are listed: only "classical hymns, derived from all ages and divisions of the Church" should be used; the original text is to be preferred where feasible; "the arrangement should... blend the order of the Apostles' Creed and the evangelical Church Year together"; where possible, the chronological order of history--Israel through the Reformation to the present--is desirable; "in a work designed for *America*, good translations from English authors like Watts, Wesley, Cowper, and Newton are altogether in place"; and the inclu-sion of critical and explanatory notes are helpful in the larger editions. Hymns to be avoided are those which exhibit "offensive dogmatism, subjective caprice or mediocrity in contents and form, prosaic dullness, weak sentimentalism and trifling, artificial phraseology, a dry, didactic tone and similar effects...."[8]

When it was discovered, during the final session of the liturgical committee, that the 150 or more hymns prepared by Porter, must be seriously reduced, the result was likely as painful to Schaff as it was to Porter. "The narrow limits allowed for these [the hymns] caused painful perplexity, as many of the best hymns had to be cut out, in order to secure some variety under each head. The conclusion of this work was referred to a sub-committee of those members of the Committee who might remain over to-morrow."[9]

The result of the sub-committee's work disturbed Porter. In a letter to Steiner he wrote:

> At a late meeting in Philadelphia I reported (having been appointed to prepare it) a selection of some 200 hymns, on which I had bestowed the greatest care and labor. It was a work of love and well done. Discussion insued and I had made up my mind to withdraw it. This they would not permit, and after I had left (for I was obliged to leave) its fair proportions were sadly marred.[10]

At first Porter supposed Schaff to have been the one who made the cuts; however, he learned differently, as is seen in another letter to Steiner. "In Harrisburg I met Dr. Schaff on his return home from Huntingdon....He told me what I was glad to hear, that he had no hand in mangling my collection of hymns. Drs. Bomberger and Zacharias did the mischief."[11]

The outcome of Bomberger's and Zacharias' "mischief" "did not in all respects correspond to the assignment" given the committee by Synod.[12] As is shown by the Index of Authors,[13] nearly half of the 104 hymns are from Watts (43) and Doddridge (9). It would be interesting to examine the complete list as it was originally proposed by Porter, however, it is not extant. Of "good translations of the best Latin, and especially German hymns, which are so intimately interwoven with the history and piety of our mother Church in Europe", there are only token offerings. The arrangement does comply with one of Schaff's hymnological principles: the Apostles' Creed. As outlined in the Provisional Liturgy, the subjects are: God the Father, God the Son, God the Holy

Spirit, the Holy Trinity, the Church, the Means of Grace
(the Lord's Day, the Word of God, Prayer, Baptism, Confirmation, the Lord's Supper, Ordination), Christian Experience
(Penitence, Faith, etc.), the Last Things, and Times and
Seasons.

Even though the precise selection of the hymns did not
entirely fulfill the Synod's direction nor satisfy the
liturgy committee, the hymnbook and Liturgy bound together
did provide the denomination with a peoples' liturgy. As has
been stated above, this marked a return to Reformation precedent and did fulfill the final liturgical principle adopted
by the Synod of Baltimore.

Lectionary

The arrangement of the hymns around the seasons of the
Church Year suggests the second general observation to be made
regarding the general design of the Provisional Liturgy--*viz.*,
the lectionary. Nevin simply could not conceive of a liturgy
which was not "built" around the Christian Year. "Looking
at the matter historically, it is easy enough to see that the
use of a liturgy and a regard for Christian festivals move
always hand in hand together. We have no example of the one
in any age without the other."[14] Schaff's Baltimore plan
underscored this imperative. The lectionary is implied in
the first two principles--that "the Greek and Latin Churches
of the third and fourth centuries, ought to be made, as much
as possible, the general *basis* of the proposed Liturgy" and
that "special reference ought to be had to the old Palatinate
and other Reformed liturgies of the sixteenth centuries".
The liturgies from both periods were structured around the

Christian Year, of course; and J. S. Foulk, the Baltimore
minister who did much to instruct the denomination in the
devotional value of the lectionary through a series of fifty-
six articles in the *Weekly Messenger*,[15] took some delight in
answering "A Minister's" charge that the Church Year was an
evil invention of the Pope in the sixth century.[16]

Nevin first sought to develop a theology of the Christian Year in an article in 1856. "Religion in the form of
nature, and religion in the form of history come here [in
the Christian Year] to a perfect understanding and agreement.
The constitution of the world is sanctified, by being taken
up into the constitution of grace."[17] He was still arguing
his point in 1862: nothing "is more undeniably true than
that there is an inward connection, in some way, between the
sense for the sacramental in worship, and what may be termed
a sense for church festivals, and the idea of a church
year...."[18]

Assuming that the Christian Year was to be followed at
all--and there was never any serious consideration given to
the Presbyterian refusal to acknowledge any Christian festi-
vals--two alternatives were open to the liturgical committee.
Luther retained and Cranmer maintained the *lectio selecta*
system which provided readings and collects for every Lord's
Day. The historic Christian seasons determined the entire
secular calendar. Zwingli and Calvin, on the other hand,
followed the *lectio continua* pattern of continuous exposition,
interrupted only for brief celebrations of the major Christian
festivals. Such was the pattern of the Netherlands and
Palatinate Liturgies; and, in a modified form, the pattern
proposed by the liturgical committee of the Dutch Reformed
Church in America.

Although it does not appear that the German Reformed liturgical committee seriously debated the alternatives, this interesting rubric in Schaff's hand[19] was written in the margin of one manuscript copy of the Provisional Liturgy: "For the other services on Sundays and during the week [i.e., other than the regular Lord's Day], it is recommended that entire books of the Bible, especially of the New Testament, be read in order." Apparently Schaff considered the merits of *lectio continua*; however the rubric did not appear in the printed edition of the Provisional Liturgy. Instead the Luther-Cranmer pattern was followed and a lectionary was provided based on four major seasons: *Christmas* (First in Advent through Sixth after Epiphany), *Easter* (Septuagesima through Third after Easter), *Pentecost* (Fourth after Easter through Whitmonday), and *Church* (Trinity and the Twenty-seven Sundays following).

As it appears in the Provisional Liturgy, the lectionary consists of two "series": Old and New. The "Old Series" is taken almost entirely from the lectionaries of the Catholic Apostolic Church Liturgy[20] and the *Book of Common Prayer*. Only six lessons in this series are new to the Provisional Liturgy:

> Sixth after Epiphany (Gospel),
> Palm Sunday (Gospel),
> Fifteenth after Trinity (Epistle),
> Twenty-sixth after Trinity (Epistle),
> Twenty-seventh after Trinity (Gospel
>   and Epistle).

Only six Old Testament readings appear in either series of the lectionary.

Old Series: Ash Wednesday (Joel 2:12-18),
New Series: Pentecost (Joel 2:28-32),
Circumcision (Psalm 90),
Epiphany (Isaiah 60:1-15),
Ash Wednesday (Psalm 51),
Easter (Isaiah 53).

According to the minutes of the liturgical committee,[21] the "New Series" was prepared by Schaff, and Harbaugh arranged the readings in tables for publication. A complete analysis of the sources of the lectionary will be found in Appendix III.

The collects provide an interesting example of the liturgical methodology of Schaff and his committee. During the first meeting of the liturgical committee the collects were put "into the hands of Dr. Schaff to make a selection".[22] Sometime between then and June, 1856, Schaff prepared a lengthy document containing his suggestions for the arrangement of the lessons and collects. In the extant portion of this manuscript Schaff listed the lessons from the "Old Series" and adopted or adapted the collect from the *Book of Common Prayer*. He then gave the lesson from the "New Series" and wrote a collect appropriate to it. The collects for the fourth through the twenty-fifth Sundays after Trinity in this manuscript are in printed form on pages Schaff cut out of a *Book of Common Prayer*.

The liturgy committee minutes do not record the change in assignment; however, the Lancaster Division--Nevin, Harbaugh, Porter, and Gerhart--was given the final responsibility for preparing the collects. Schaff sent his suggestions to Nevin, who replied that he was using Schaff's work as "a directory in preparing a system of collects...." Then this:

I have been giving it as much attention as I could since you were here, meeting very

often with Harbaugh. The other two
brethren, Gerhart and Porter, have not
been able to help us much so far; but
hope to be with us more hereafter. All
Harbaugh and myself have been able to
do yet, has been to form a system of
collects. This proved a pretty hard
task; more so than I expected. The
greater part of them (including all
after Trinity and many before) had to
be original--more full than the Episcopal and more true to the reigning idea
of the Lessons--in the case of which
it seemed not safe to vary from the old
order.[23]

Seven months later, January 6, 1857, the "Lancaster Division"
presented the collects to the full committee for examination.

The sixty-nine collects can be considered in three
divisions: first, those borrowed directly from the *Book of
Common Prayer* and the Catholic Apostolic Liturgy, of which
there are eleven:

First in Advent (two collects),
First after Epiphany
Septagesima,
Ash Wednesday,
Second in Lent,
Easter Eve,
Easter Day,
Sunday after Ascension,
Whitmonday,
First after Trinity.

Second, the committee adapted fourteen collects, again from
either the *Book of Common Prayer* or the Catholic Apostolic
Liturgy:

Second and Third in Advent,
Christmas Day,

> St. John's Day,
> The Innocents' Day,
> Circumcision--New Years',
> Epiphany,
> Third, Fifth, and Sixth after Epiphany,
> Quinquagesima,
> First, Third, and Sixth (Palm Sunday)
>   in Lent.

Third, forty-four original collects were prepared by the Lancaster Division--i.e., by Nevin and Harbaugh primarily:

> Fourth in Advent,
> St. Stephen's Day,
> Sunday after Christmas,
> Second and Fourth after Epiphany,
> Sexagesima,
> Fourth and Fifth in Lent,
> Good Friday,
> Easter Monday,
> First, Second, Third, Fourth, and Fifth
>   after Easter,
> Ascension,
> Pentecost,
> Trinity,
> Second through the Twenty-seventh
>   after Trinity.

The prayers adapted by the committee may involve the change of only one word, as in the case of the collect for Quinquagesima: "the very bond of peace" is rendered the "very bond of *perfection*"; or, as in the case of the Third Sunday in Lent, more extensive changes are made:

> *Book of Common Prayer:* We beseech thee,
> Almighty God, look upon the hearty desires
> of thy humble servants, and stretch forth
> the right hand of thy Majesty, to be our
> defence against all our enemies; through
> Jesus Christ our Lord. Amen.

Provisional Liturgy: Almighty God, who
hast been the hope and confidence of Thy
people in all ages; mercifully regard, we
beseech Thee, the prayer with which we cry
unto Thee out of the depths, and stretch
forth the right hand of Thy majesty for
our salvation and defence: through Jesus
Christ our Lord.   Amen.

By way of summary, then, it may be observed that the Provisional Liturgy is, in its basic design and orientation, "a
bond of union both with the ancient Catholic Church and the
Reformation, and yet...the product of the religious life of
[the German Reformed Church in America] in its present state".
The Church Year and the Apostles' Creed provide the ancient
liturgical superstructure for a peoples' liturgy and hymnbook.
Scripture is the norm throughout: verses being provided which
call the people to worship, and verses for the individual to
consider "whilst washing and dressing".   There are, on the one
hand, the great canticles and corporate prayers prescribed for
the festival seasons; while on the other hand, there are the
humble prayers suggested for the family altar:

Visit, O Lord, with Thy grace this house
and family. Drive far from us all snares
of the enemy. Let Thy holy angels have
charge over us to preserve us in peace;
and let Thy blessing be upon us forever,
through Jesus Christ our Lord.

The Preface to the first edition of the Provisional Liturgy,
probably written by Schaff, describes the Liturgy this way:

The work herewith offered to the Christian
public is designed as a directory and help
to public and private worship; and is the

result of several years' earnest and prayer-
ful labor. This labor, however, was not devoted to the composition of original forms,
so much as to the digesting and reproduction
of evangelical forms and services already at
hand, both ancient and modern, with such
modifications in the mode of expression and
other minor details, as a change of time and
circumstance, seemed, to a conservative judgment, to demand. Whilst the book, therefore,
it is believed, will be found redolent of the
sweetest liturgical devotions of earlier
times, it will also be found savory of the
freshness of an original production. The
spirit which predominated in its preparation,
was that of filial regard for everything
good and true in past ages, joined to the
spirit of genuine Christian liberty. But in
all cases in which older forms are used, the
original Greek or Latin sources were consulted and followed.

As stated in the advertisement, this
Liturgy has been prepared with primary
reference to the Reformed Church in this
country. At the same time, a mere glance
at its contents will show that the book is
wholly free from anything strictly denominational. Even the name of the Church under
whose auspices it is published, occurs only
on the title-page and in the advertisement;
no other denominational allusions are found
except in the few forms in which the doctrinal standard of the Reformed Church, the
Heidelberg Catechism, had to be named. In
this view, therefore, the new Liturgy
commends itself to general favor and use.
Any Christian clergyman, not hostile to all
such forms, will find it offering to his
hand helps of which he may most profitably
avail himself. And in Christian families
it is calculated to serve as a book of
social and private devotion, suited to all
the ordinary seasons and services of the
Christian year.[24]

Between the call to worship and the final, personal benediction
to be uttered at midnight one finds twenty-one services of the
church, and it is the sources of these services that provide
the next consideration.

Summary of Sources

Liturgies

It is not surprising that other liturgies provided the
first and most profitable source for the committee in con-
structing the Provisional Liturgy. Were it possible--which
likely it is not--one could write a substantial essay, simply
tracing all the borrowed liturgical strains to be found in
each of the services. Such an endeavor will be attempted
with only three orders in the Provisional Liturgy: the
first Lord's Day service, the Eucharist, and Ordination of
Ministers; however, the following list of liturgies or collections is instructive. It represents every parenthetical
entry made in the margins of the several extant manuscripts
of the Provisional Liturgy, and the various liturgies translated or discussed by Porter, Harbaugh, and others in the
historical articles which flooded the *Weekly Messenger* and
the *Mercersburg Review* during the years of the controversy.
The list is certainly not exhaustive; yet it does give one
some notion of the extent of the committee's resources:

> St. James,
> St. Mark,
> Gelasian,
> Leonine,
> English Occasional Service and Diarium
> Pastorale,

Ebrard's Reformed Kirchen Buch,
Luther Agenda von 1785,
Kirchen Buch Noch der Agenda fur
    Evangelische Kirchen,
Daniel's Codex Liturgicus, vol. iii,
Renaudot, Liturgiae Orientales,
Bunsen, Hippolytus and His Age,
Ex Libro Thomas Hughes,
Liturgy of Neuschatel,
Book of Worship, Leo Juda, 1523,
Swiss Liturgy,
Hessian Agenda, 1748,
Prussian Agenda,
Schauffhausen Liturgy of 1592, 1672,
Bern, 1581,
St. Gall, 1738,
Biel, 1752,
Basel, 1707, 1752, 1826,
Geneva, 1543,
Liturgy of Zurich, 1529, 1535, 1563,
    1581, 1612, 1675,
Palatinate Liturgy
Book of Common Prayer,
Liturgy of the Catholic Apostolic
    Church.

From this partial enumeration of the committee's liturgical resources it is readily apparent that the aid and guidance
of both the early church and the Reformation was sought, as
Schaff intended. Viewing the numerous liturgies from the
Reformed churches of the sixteenth, seventeenth, and eighteenth
centuries, it may seem somewhat surprising that the critics of
the Provisional Liturgy were so disturbed by its "Romanizing
tendencies"; however, it must be remembered that most of the
Reformed liturgies consulted by the committee were structurally
of the preaching-service variety described by Nichols (above).
As has been pointed out, the Reformed preaching orders shared
a common theology with those of the Mass type; but the denomination was unaware of this. Furthermore, what greeted the
German Reformed Church in the Provisional Liturgy was certainly

more "catholic" than anything short of the *Book of Common Prayer* itself--and for good reason. As was suggested in the course of the brief discussion of Schaff's liturgical background, he knew and preferred the Lutheran-type Prussian Agenda of 1821. Its closest English equivalents at the time were the *Book of Common Prayer* and the Catholic Apostolic Liturgy; thus they became the primary liturgical resources for the basic design and the major services of the Provisional Liturgy.

For a prayer book which was as generally influential on the Reformed worship of the nineteenth century as scholars are now concluding it was, little definitive analysis has been done on the Catholic Apostolic Liturgy. The beginning of the Catholic Apostolic Church and something of its development are chronicled principally in the historical treatments by Edward Miller[25] and P. E. Shaw.[26] Edward Irving, Chamlers' assistant in Glasgow for three years (1819-1822), then minister of the Caledonian Church in London, was the enigmatic preacher whose fiery sermons began a movement which was to culminate in the Catholic Apostolic Church.

In 1826 the wealthy and influential Henry Drummond summoned a group of fifty men--mostly clergy and laity of the Church of England--to his country estate at Albury, West Surrey, "to consider by earnest study and discussion all that was prophesied in the Scriptures on the Second Coming of our Lord".[27] During the decade to follow it was the financial support of Drummond and the liturgical skills of John Bate Cardale which succeeded in establishing the Catholic Apostolic Church. Irving fell on evil times with the Presbytery of London, and enjoyed only a brief period of influence in the new church before he died.

It was revealed to the band at Albury that the Second Coming would not occur until there was a period of spiritual preparation in the church. It was Christ's purpose to restore the ministry of the apostles, "and twelve men were designated as such by the Spirit speaking through prophets. The first [Cardale] was so designated in 1832; but it was not until 1835 that the number was completed, and in a solemn service they were separated to their work as an apostolic college."[28] Of the twelve apostles, eight were Church of England, three were Church of Scotland, and one was an Independent.

As the denominational connections of the apostles would indicate, two distinct schools of liturgical thought came into a forced relationship in the Catholic Apostolic Church: the Presbyterian and Non-Conformist, with their repugnance to written or prescribed forms of prayer, and the members of the Church of England, whose "habits and instincts were all in favour of fixed forms of prayer".[29] The latter influence predominated as the cultus evolved in several editions throughout the remainder of the nineteenth century. In 1838, the apostles issued a lithographed liturgy of the Eucharist which was sent to all the churches. The first printed edition of a fuller liturgy, prepared and used by the apostles in their chapel at Albury, appeared in 1842. According to Shaw, a revised edition was published in 1847 and another in 1850.[30] Extreme unction and the distinctive "Sealing" service were added in 1847, as were a manual of rubrics and services for Christmas, Easter, and Pentecost. In 1850 reservation of the elements was practiced. Candles were used on the altar and incense was permitted in 1852, and holy water was used in 1868.

Without attempting in any way to detail further the history or the theology of the Catholic Apostolic Church, it is

important to note that the Eucharist was central to all the
worship and work of the church. "Transubstantiation was
denied but the Real Presence was conceived as localized in
the consecrated elements...."[31]

> ...send down Thy Holy Spirit upon our
> sacrifice before Thee, and make this
> bread and this wine to be the most
> precious body and blood of Christ, our
> Saviour, given for remission of sins
> and for eternal life. And grant unto
> us so to eat His flesh and drink His
> blood, that our sinful bodies may be
> made clean by His body, and our souls
> be washed in His most precious blood;
> and that we may evermore dwell in Him
> and He in us.[32]

Worship in the large cathedral church in Gordon Square, London
(completed on Christmas Eve, 1853), was rich in symbolism and
combined a fascinating blend of liturgical formality and evangelical spontaneity. A worshiper in Gordon Square wrote this
in the *Episcopal Recorder*: "While one of the Priests was reading the first lesson in a very calm manner, I was startled by
hearing him begin to vociferate as loudly as he could, some
incoherent remarks of his own, keeping at the same time his
eyes set upon the book. I afterward learned that this was
regarded as the movement of the Spirit of God."[35] Another
worshiper in 1854--*Philip Schaff*--described his experience in
a letter to his wife:

> Sunday I spent the greater part of the day
> with the Irvingites. In the morning I found
> their beautiful Gothic church in Gordon
> Square, the first of the seven churches in
> London, thronged with devout worshippers.
> The Lord's Supper was administered with

> great solemnity, an imposing ceremonial,
> many hundreds communing. They observed
> the best of order, passing up one aisle,
> then kneeling and passing down the other
> aisle. The liturgy is very beautiful.
> I dined with the angel of the church, Mr.
> Heath, meeting his large and amiable
> family, and have seldom been in a house-
> hold so adorned with Christian graces.
> Then at four I attended the service
> designated for the congregation and at
> seven the service of the evangelists
> for outsiders. *The service this morn-*
> *ing, I believe, was the most beautiful*
> *and perfect liturgical service I have*
> *yet attended:* even more so than the
> one in St. George's....[34] [Italics
> mine.]

Such an encounter with "the most beautiful and perfect
liturgical service I have yet attended", coming as it did
while the liturgical work of the German Reformed Church was
in progress, could hardly have been other than influential.
Hageman is correct in assuming that Schaff's visit to Gordon
Square was no mere chance. Nevin had been in correspondence
with the leading American Catholic Apostolic convert, William
Watson Andrews, so Schaff was obviously aware of the movement.
It is also possible that he had already seen a copy of the
Liturgy, as an edition was published in New York in 1851.[35]
As Hageman observes, "we *can* safely assume that Schaff returned to Mercersburg with a copy of the Catholic and Apostolic liturgy in his luggage";[36] however, it is difficult to
know precisely which edition he used in his work on the Provisional Liturgy. Because the 1851 edition is the likeliest
possibility, it is the one used in the detailed examination
of the Provisional Liturgy to follow below.[37]

As might be expected from the constituency of the twelve
apostles, the Catholic Apostolic Liturgy borrows heavily from

the *Book of Common Prayer*, as will be evident in the comparison with the Provisional Liturgy below; however, as Nichols has shown, Cardale--the liturgical architect among the apostles --ranged far beyond the Church of England Liturgy to reveal

> ...a rather impressive level of liturgical scholarship, especially in Greek and patristic materials. Cardale exploited the classical liturgical studies of the seventeenth-century Roman Catholic pioneers, e.g., the Dominican Goar's Greek texts from *Euchologion* (1667), the *Thesaurus sacrorum rituum* of the Barnabite Bartholomeus Gavantus, in Merati's eighteenth-century edition (1736-1738), and Cardinal Bona's *Rerum liturgicarum libri duo* (1671), the first comprehensive history of the Mass. For Western texts and usages, especially Gallican, he had the four volumes of the Maurist Dom Martène, *De antiquis ecclesiae ritibus editio secunda* (1735-1738). These and other similar works put at his disposal a wealth of historical material unknown to the Reformers or the Counter-Reformation. Cardale handled it with considerable independence, nerved no doubt by his sense of Apostolic responsibility, shaping a service book with coherence and character.[38]

One can thus better understand Schaff's enthusiasm, "for the Catholic Apostolic Liturgy embodied the evangelical catholic principles of [his] liturgical report [to the Synod of Baltimore] more fully than any other Reformed liturgy of the period. The Catholic Apostolic order then became through Schaff the stabilizing influence in the shaping of the Mercersburg communion service."[39] This claim will be documented in the section to follow.

Heidelberg Catechism

The Heidelberg Catechism was more a theological influence
than a liturgical source. The constitution of 1828 required
theological professors to use the Catechism exclusively in
their teaching; however, in light of its Calvinistic-Melanch-
thonian sacramental doctrine, one wonders just how much of the
Heidelberg Catechism was actually taught. The Mayer Liturgy
required subscription to the Catechism for ordination; yet the
same Liturgy talks of "an absent friend easily forgotten".
Nevin did much to re-incarnate the Catechism in the life of
the German Reformed Church. Throughout 1840-42 he published
a series of twenty-nine articles on the Catechism. Subsequently he published a book on the Catechism in 1847,[40] and
between this volume and *The Mystical Presence* (1846) Nevin
made his point that the lineage of the German Reformed Church
was neither Puritan nor Zwinglian, but was rather to be traced
to Calvin and Melanchthon. He apparently had a hearing in
the denomination, for the Synod of 1847 "received a request
for either a reprinting of the Palatinate Liturgy or the
drafting of another 'in the spirit of our catechism'."[41]

The spirit of the Catechism—its irenic catholicity, its
doctrine of the Real Presence, and its devotional, pastoral
mood—is evident throughout the Provisional Liturgy; while
the ordination forms for a minister and for elders and deacons
require the ordinand "to receive the doctrines of the Heidelberg Catechism as flowing from the Bible, and answering to
the proper sense of the ancient Christian Creeds".

Individuals

The process of delineating the individuals responsible
for the various services and prayers in the Provisional
Liturgy is tedious and can be done with certainty only to
the extent that the liturgical committee minutes, diaries,
letters, and signed manuscripts identify the responsible
parties. In some instances authors can be determined by
calligraphy. As indicated in the note above, when an identification is made on that basis, it is so specified.

Schaff issued a general invitation for ministers in the
denomination to submit forms. Some perhaps responded volun-
tarily; however, all the extant manuscripts submitted by
ministers not on the committee were specifically requested
by Schaff. The nine non-members and the manuscripts they
submitted are as follows:

Samuel Helffenstein, Sr., one of the denomination's
patriarchs and subsequently described by Bomberger as opposed
to the Provisional Liturgy,[42] submitted two original prayers
for one in trouble or distress. In the accompanying correspondence to Schaff, dated December 6, 1855, he included a
prayer in time of affliction, composed by his son, *Samuel
Helffenstein, Jr.* None of these prayers was used in the Provisional Liturgy.

Moses Kieffer, Gerhart's successor in the College and
Seminary in Tiffin, Ohio, sent a form for Visitation and
Communion of the Sick and morning and evening prayers for
the family, all of which were marked "Superseceded" [*sic*]
by some member of the committee. In his letter to Schaff he
asked to be excused from preparing the form for Laying of a
Cornerstone.

A. R. Kremer, minister in Carlisle from 1845-1869, and biographer of Nevin, submitted a morning and evening prayer. Neither is dated and both are marked, "Laid Aside".

Herman Rust, professor of church history at Heidelberg College, sent his contributions to Schaff on December 25, 1855: Burial of a Child and Burial of Communicant Members. There is no indication as to the disposition of these prayers; however, neither was used in the Provisional Liturgy.

Benjamin S. Schneck, one of the German Reformed commissioners who summoned Nevin from Pittsburg to Mercersburg, and associated with Fisher in the Printing Establishment at Chambersburg, sent several contributions on January 6, 1856. He acknowledged the Palatinate Liturgy and the *Book of Common Prayer* as sources for his Visitation and Communion of the Sick, and his prayer in times of public calamity is "after the liturgy of Zurich, 1581". In addition to these forms Schneck sent a service for Burial at Sea, which was apparently original. None was used.

George Williard, subsequently to become a member of the liturgy committee of the Western Synod and a critic of the Provisional Liturgy submitted morning and evening prayers for the family. Neither was used.

David Winters, an influential minister in Dayton, Ohio, submitted an evening prayer on October 30, 1855. This prayer was not used by the committee.

George Wolff is not identifiable. He could have been either one of B. C. Wolff's sons, who became a Roman Catholic after his father's death; or G. D. Wolff, a clergyman in the Eastern Synod. Whoever he was, he submitted two forms for the marriage service on March 11, 1856. One is unmarked while the other indicates the committee's initial acceptance; however, neither was eventually used by the committee. In addition to these services there is an undated "Form for Administration of the Lord's Supper" which bears the signature "Geo. Wolff". It relies heavily on the Palatinate Liturgy and was considered, perhaps, by the committee, but it was not used.

Four of these nine ministers were from the Western Synod at the time they submitted their correspondence. This indicates only that the Western church was not initially opposed to the preparation of a liturgy; however, that the Western Synod soon became vigorously opposed to the Provisional Liturgy and the *Order of Worship* will be shown in the next chapter. Another interesting observation to be drawn from the above is that, with the exception of Wolff's Eucharistic order, none of the major liturgical forms were solicited from ministers not members of the committee. Except for the Laying of a Cornerstone, Marriage, and Visitation and Communion of the Sick, all the contributions were family prayers.

Still another important notation to be made from an examination of the above manuscripts is that not one of them was used. The Provisional Liturgy is entirely and exclusively a composition and compilation by members of the liturgical committee. As revealed by the committee minutes and in private correspondence between the members, the following responsibilities can be determined.

Advertisement: an abstract of Nevin's report to the Synod of 1857, approved by the committee on October 21, 1857.

Calendar for the Principal Festival Days for a Period of Ten Years: This table is mentioned briefly in the liturgical committee minutes on October 21, 1857. It may have been prepared by Harbaugh, who was responsible for establishing the lectionary in tables, or by Schaff.

Table of Contents: As has been indicated above, the Table of Contents underwent extensive evolution. It was approved by the committee at its various stages; however, the last two editions of it are in Schaff's hand, and he clearly guided the committee's thinking as to the arrangement of the forms.

Christian Worship: The contents of this section have already been discussed. It was apparently the combined work of the committee as a whole. The arrangement of these selections on the page can be attributed to Bomberger and an unidentified proof-reader, who suggested the arrangement to Schaff. The latter apparently agreed and Bomberger made the changes in the margins of the page proofs.

Primitive Forms: These "catholic forms" were completed by the committee on March 13, 1856. The title of the section was determined on March 18 and the order established on March 26, 1856. Procedure on the *Litany* is revealing: on March 18 the "committee took up the subject of the Litany. Different forms were taken by different members, and from them all the committee constructed a Litany."

The Church Year: The lectionary has been discussed above.

Scripture Lessons and Collects: As noted above, the collects were orginally put into the hands of Schaff "to make a selection". He reported his work to Nevin, and the latter, along with Harbaugh, prepared the collects.

The Regular Service on the Lord's Day: Extant manuscripts indicate that Schaff prepared the first and second Lord's Day forms, at least, and it may be safely assumed that the third and fourth are his also. The services appeared originally as part of the Specimen Liturgy presented to the Synod of 1852. The committee "took up" the several forms on

March 19, 20, 21, and 24, 1856. The agenda for the January, 1857, meeting indicates that the Regular Service on the Lord's Day is "not quite finished (a confession is to be prepared). Committed to Dr. Schaff; and Dr. Nevin is to prepare a new confession and absolution for the regular service." On January 6, 1857, the order of the regular Sabbath service was "reviewed and fixed"; and on January 7, 1857, it was decided that the first form should be the regular morning service, while the other three forms were to be provided for optional use in afternoon and evening services. Porter's Invocations for the first and second Lord's Day forms were discussed and adopted April 23, 1857, on which date the committee also corrected and adopted the Confession for the first form. This marks the end of any reference to the Lord's Day service in the committee minutes, save for the tantalizing entry referred to above, at which time Nevin was unofficially asked to prepare a new Lord's Day service. Since it does not appear in the minutes again, it can be assumed that nothing came of this *ad hoc* request.

Prayers for the Festival Seasons: The authorship of these several prayers is difficult to determine. In certain cases the decision rests on a conclusion concerning the penmanship--and even if that is correct, it is no guarantee that the prayer is original.

Advent: The minutes indicate that this prayer was assigned to Porter, then to the Lancaster sub-committee. Its eventual resolution is not recorded.

Christmas: The Christmas prayers were discussed by the committee on March 14, 1856. A copy of the first prayer, definitely in Schaff's hand, is extant; however, there is no indication as to the author of the second prayer.

New Year: A copy of the first prayer indicates Schaff's authorship. The second prayer was referred by the committee to Harbaugh and Zacharias. The extant copy is in Harbaugh's hand.

Good Friday: This prayer was discussed on March 15, 1856. The copy is in Schaff's hand. The second prayer appears to have been written by Harbaugh.

Easter Day: A notation indicating "unfinished business" inserted between the March, 1856, and January, 1857, meetings indicates that Nevin was assigned an Easter prayer. If he complied with the request, then his is the first of the two prayers. The second appears in Harbaugh's hand.

Ascension Day: According to the minutes for March 17, 1856, the first Ascension prayer, "being a translation from Ebrard's *Kirchenbuch* was corrected and adopted". There is no indication as to the member assigned to prepare either of the Ascension prayers.

Whitsunday: Harbaugh was asked to prepare a Whitsunday prayer, according to the notation referred to above. The first of the prayers is extant and indicates that it was "compiled from various sources". There is no copy of the second prayer.

Trinity: The minutes prior to the January, 1857, meeting indicate that Nevin was assigned one of the Trinity prayers. On April 24, 1857, a "prayer for Trinity Sunday presented by H. Harbaugh as per appointment was read and referred to the sub-committee in Lancaster".

To summarize, according to the assignments made by the committee, corroborated by the penmanship in certain cases, Schaff, Nevin, Harbaugh, and Porter were primarily responsible for preparing most if not all of the Festival prayers and canticles.

Preparation for the Holy Communion: The minutes record the session during which the Preparation form was discussed-- August 27, 1857--but there is no information as to the author. Harbaugh's diary indicates that he did some work on the Preparatory Service on January 16, 1857;[43] however, in his eulogy of Harbaugh[44] Schaff did not mention this service. It will be argued below that the same man prepared both the Preparation service and the Eucharist--and that man was Schaff.

The Holy Communion: On January 8, 1857, "three endevors [sic] were presented, read, and the general principles discussed; then laid on the table for the present". Of the three forms one was likely Schaff's, another Bomberger's, and the third was possibly that which carries George Wolff's signature. According to the agenda for the January meeting, the three forms were "committed to Dr. Nevin to examine and report on them". There is no further indication of Nevin's considerations; however, it would be no speculation to assume that he would prefer Schaff's work to that of either Bomberger or Wolff. The committee returned to its consideration of Communion on August 27 and 28, 1857, discussing the service line by line and finally adopting it as a whole. Whatever the committee's choices--and a letter from Bomberger to Schaff and an order for the Eucharist in Schaff's hand confirm that at least these two men prepared forms--it will be shown in the following section that Schaff was the architect of the Eucharist in the Provisional Liturgy.

Holy Baptism: Baptism of Infants: There is little evidence in personal correspondence or in the committee minutes concerning the authorship of the Baptism forms. They were first discussed on March 25, 1856. On January 7,

1857, "the three Baptismal forms were re-read, corrected, and finally adopted". The title was fixed as "Holy Baptism". On August 28, 1857, the rubrics for Baptism were adopted. Bomberger wrote a Form for the Administration of Baptism to Infants, which was modeled closely after the Palatinate Liturgy; however, this form was "Laid on the Table". It was not used in either the Specimen Liturgy, which appeared in the *Mercersburg Review* or the final version of the Provisional Liturgy. The question of authorship is conclusively resolved, however, in a manuscript of the Baptism orders in Schaff's hand. These are they which appear in the Specimen Liturgy and were eventually published in the Provisional Liturgy. The familiar style and extensive dependence upon the *Book of Common Prayer* and the Catholic Apostolic Liturgy would confirm Schaff's authorship, were his delicate calligraphy not sufficient proof.

Baptism of Adults: It is interesting to observe in connection with this form that even though Schaff wrote it, Bomberger made two substantial changes in it when reading the page proofs, and there is no indication that he either sought or received Schaff's approval. The blessing or "confirmation" following the act of Baptism originally read: "Defend, O Lord, Thy servant with Thy heavenly grace...." Bomberger changed it to read: "The very God of peace sanctify you wholly...." The final lengthy, Biblical charge to the newly baptized was added by Bomberger.

Confirmation: This service first came to the committee's attention on August 25, 1857. On August 27, it was "committed to Dr. Zacharias to report on it", and on August 28, it was referred to Harbaugh and Zacharias. Apparently this is Harbaugh's service, for he was requested to prepare an "introductory address embodying the Scripture authority" prior to the January, 1857, meeting; and in his eulogy Schaff attributed the service to Harbaugh.[45]

Marriage: There are four manuscripts of marriage services in the E & R Historical Society, two of which bear the signature of George Wolff and one that of Elias Heiner; however, none was used in the Provisional Liturgy. The minutes reveal an interesting process in regard to this form. Apparently the committee initially intended to include two Marriage services—a shorter "family marriage", and a "Church Service". The former was examined and corrected on January 8 and 9, 1857. Then on August 28, 1857, there is this curious entry: "Took up the Marriage Service. They were committed to Professor Porter *to make two out of the three and report*". [Italics mine.] The January agenda indicated that Porter had already been given the responsibility for preparing a Marriage Service; therefore, it is defensible to conclude that the one form which appears in the Provisional Liturgy is essentially his work.

The Visitation and Communion of the Sick: These two services, incorporated under one rubric, are essentially the work of Harbaugh, according to Schaff's statement in the *Weekly Messenger*;[46] however, Nevin and Porter each had a hand in the review and revision. Harbaugh's diary entry for April 16, 1857, indicates that he was working on the two services, which he presented to the committee on August 29, 1857. The Visitation of the Sick was "committed to Dr. Nevin till Monday morning". He reported it on August 31, and it was adopted. Communion of the Sick "was recommitted to H. Harbaugh for abridgment" during the following session.

Porter also became involved in the Visitation Service and on September 1, 1857, he "reported the abridgment of the prayer for a sick person not prepared to die, which was accepted and amended and adopted". At the same session, Harbaugh's abridgment of the Communion of the Sick was discussed and adopted.

Ordination and Installation: The Ordination service will be examined in detail in the section to follow; however, it may be said here that it was the work of Nevin. The January agenda assigns him the "Ordinations etc. and Instalation [*sic*] etc." These services were reported on September 1, 1857, and adopted in a portion of only two sessions. It is interesting that services of such length and importance would consume less of the committee's time than the Marriage form, for example. Was the committee not anxious to challenge *the Professor*?

Excommunication and Restoration: The only name to be associated with these forms is E. V. Gerhart. The January agenda assigns them to him, and he first reported to the committee on September 2, 1857. Several sessions were consumed in examining the forms, and they were not approved finally until the last meeting of the committee in October, 1857.

Laying of a Cornerstone: The January agenda assigned this form and the *Consecration of a Church* to Porter and Harbaugh; however, the minutes for September 3, 1857, record a change in assignment: Heiner replaced Harbaugh. The Laying of a Cornerstone was reported on October 15, 1857. Apparently two forms had been prepared, for "the shorter form was received and, after consideration, recommitted to be reported in the morning". "In the morning" the service was "reported and taken up--and after some emendations, adopted". In correcting the page proofs Bomberger reconstructed the rubric directing the minister to read the inscription on the stone. The Consecration of a Church was also approved on October 15.

Consecration of a Burial-Ground: The minutes of September 3, 1857, assign this form to Porter and Heiner. It was reported and adopted on October 16, 1857.

Public Reception of Immigrants: There are no extant manuscripts of this service and the minutes give it short shrift: it was corrected and adopted on August 26, 1857. The only other mention of the form is in Harbaugh's diary. On August 22, 1857, he made this entry: "Prepared a service for the reception of Emigrants [*sic*] for the new Liturgy today; and also corrected some other parts of it." There is no reason for Harbaugh to have prepared such a service had he not been requested to do so, and the dates--August 22 and August 26--lead this writer to believe that he is the author.

Burial of the Dead: It appears to have been general knowledge that this was Harbaugh's service. The minutes do not indicate that it was ever assigned to a sub-committee, although the full committee did examine the service on January 5 and August 31, 1857. It was "left with" Harbaugh on September 3, 1857, and finally adopted on October 16. Linn Harbaugh quotes Apple's account of his father's funeral, which was conducted in Mercersburg by Nevin, Apple and Gerhart: "'The liturgical service was among the last works which he [Harbaugh] gave to the church, the office for burial being mainly his own contribution.'"[47]

Family Prayers: On March 26, 1856, the family forms were placed in the hands of the Mercersburg sub-committee, which presented a report on January 3, 1857. Nothing more was reported prior to September 3, when the "Family Prayers were left with H. Harbaugh". Harbaugh could not attend the final meeting of the committee "on account of family affairs";[48] however, he sent his "part of the last distribution of work down with Dr. Schaff". On October 19, the

committee adopted the first series of Family Prayers, and
occupied the following day in selecting, correcting, and
adopting the second series. Harbaugh's responsibility was
more than editorial, as Schaff indicated that "most of the
Family Prayers" were written by him;[49] however, manuscripts
are extant in Schaff's and Bomberger's hands. In the first
series Harbaugh definitely compiled or composed the prayers
for Sunday evening, Monday morning and evening, Tuesday
morning and evening, and Wednesday morning. No further
manuscripts are extant. In the second series Schaff compiled or composed prayers for Sunday morning and evening,
and Monday morning and evening. The prayer for Wednesday
morning, the Litany for Wednesday evening (which was discussed by the committee on March 19, 1856), and the prayer
for Saturday morning are in Bomberger's familiar script.

Guide to Private Devotion: This was definitely Schaff's
work, and he insisted that it remain in the Liturgy even at
the price of excluding the Service at Sea and Visitation of
Prisoners. The committee placed this series of Scripture
selections and collects in Schaff's hands on September 3,
1857. On October 18, Schaff's work was "revised, corrected,
and adopted".

A Selection of Hymns, for Public and Private Worship:
The original selection was Porter's work, as has been described above; and, according to Schaff, Bomberger and
Zacharias made the final selection after the last meeting
of the committee. It is reasonable to assume, then, that
Bomberger also was responsible for the "Index of Subjects"
and the "Table of First Lines".

To summarize the above, one finds that all active
members of the committee except Wolff and Rodenmayer were
given specific assignments which were eventually published

in the Provisional Liturgy. There is no indication that Wolff submitted any forms; and, although he attended thirty-four sessions, his specific responsibilities remain a mystery. Rodenmayer submitted a series of prayers for the Occasional Services, which were to be included in the Liturgy until it became apparent at the final meeting that space would not permit. As delineated above, the individual responsibilities were as follows:

Schaff: the Lectionary, the Regular Lord's Day Service, Festival Prayers, Preparation for Communion, Communion, Baptism, Family Prayers, and Guide to Private Devotion.

Nevin: Advertisement, Collects, the Regular Lord's Day Service, Festival Prayers, Communion, Visitation and Communion of the Sick, Ordination and Installation of Ministers, Elders, and Deacons.

Harbaugh: Table of the Lectionary, Collects, Festival Prayers, Confirmation, Visitation and Communion of the Sick, Public Reception of Immigrants, Burial of the Dead, Family Prayers.

Bomberger: Calendar of Festival Prayers, Family Prayers, selection of the Hymns and Tables, and most of the responsibility for reading proof and seeing the Liturgy through the printer.

Porter: Festival Prayers, Marriage, Visitation and Communion of the Sick, Laying of a Cornerstone, Consecration of a Church, Consecration of a Burial Ground, Hymns. It should be noted that Porter prepared the Visitation of Prisoners, which was dropped at the last meeting of the committee.

Gerhart: Excommunication and Restoration.

Heiner: Laying of a Cornerstone, Consecration of a Church, Consecration of a Burial Ground. Heiner prepared the Service at Sea, which was eliminated at the last meeting.

Zacharias: Reported on Confirmation and assisted Bomberger in the final selection of hymns.

The *Committee as a Whole*, certainly under the direction of Schaff, determined the Title, the Table of Contents, Christian Worship, and the Primitive Forms. Every member of the committee, noted above, shared to some degree in the reading of proof. Several sessions were devoted entirely to this task; then Bomberger had the final responsibility. As has been noted, the arrangement of several of the forms on the page, and the rubrics of certain services are his responsibility also.

Theological and Liturgical Examination of Forms

The Lord's Day

"The Regular Service on the Lord's Day" is definitely the work of Philip Schaff. Although this discussion will be restricted to the first form, since it was specified as the regular morning service by the committee, it should be noted that Schaff is also responsibile for at least the second, if not the third and fourth forms, designated for afternoon and occasional use. Two manuscripts in Schaff's hand include the first two forms; and, in each case, the manuscript is incomplete, leading one to assume Schaff's authorship for the third and fourth forms as well. The four services are decreasingly "liturgical", as the following orders indicate:

First Form:

    [Anthem by choir]
    Invocation [at the altar]

Confession of Sin
    Call to Confession
    Corporate Prayer of Confession
    Declaration of the Remission of Sins
      First Form
      Second Form
    The Peace
Apostles' Creed
    Response
Praise [Psalm, Te Deum, Gloria in Excelsis]
Scripture Lessons and Collect
    Gospel
    Epistle
    Collect
    Gloria Patri [responsive]
General Petition
    Thanksgiving (creation, redemption, sanctification)
      and Supplication
    Prayers for the Church, the Nation, all Sorts and
      Conditions of Men
    The Lord's Prayer
Hymn [during which the minister enters the pulpit]
Sermon [Ordinarily not to exceed forty minutes. It
    may follow the order of the lectionary, the Chris-
    tian Year, the Bible, or the Catechism.]
Prayer [This may be free.]
Collection
Hymn
Benediction [Mosaic or Apostolic].

Second Form:

    Invocation
    Hymn
    Scripture
    General Petition
      Confession and Prayer for Forgiveness
      Prayers for the Church, the Nation, and all Sorts
        and Conditions of Men
    Hymn
    Sermon
    Free Prayer, or Apostles' Creed and Lord's Prayer, or
      Thanksgiving [The Thanksgiving supplied is the
      General Thanksgiving from the *Book of Common Prayer*,
      followed by the Collect attributed to St. Chrysostom.]
    Hymn
    Benediction.

The Second Form is a generally abbreviated version of the
First Form, except the Intercession is placed before the
Sermon. The congregational "Amen" is retained; however,
there is no corporate confession, no versicles and responses.

Third Form:

> Invocation
> General Petition [One long prayer with no "Amen"]
>> General Confession [Amended from the *Book of
>> Common Prayer*]
>> General Supplication
>> Prayers for the Church, the Nation, and all
>> Sorts and Conditions of Men
>> The Lord's Prayer.

Fourth Form:

> One unbroken prayer of:
>> General Thanksgiving
>> Supplication
>> Church
>> Intercession
>> The Lord's Prayer.

The two manuscripts referred to above show the evolution
of the First Form in detail. Schaff wrote out the entire service, complete with rubrics and marginal notations. The edited
version of this manuscript is printed in the *Mercersburg Review*
as a part of the Specimen Liturgy which the committee presented
to the Synod in 1852. The second manuscript consists of these
pages from the *Mercersburg Review* attached to larger sheets,
and contains Schaff's revision, the result of which is to be
found in the Provisional Liturgy.

In the light of the objectivity which Schaff sought to
obtain in worship, his original rubric for the opening of the
Lord's Day service is interesting:

> The most appropriate commencement of the
> service is the Singing of a short *Anthem*
> or *one* verse of a *hymn* by the Choir to
> excite devotional feelings and the spirit
> of worship. During the singing of the
> Anthem the minister shall enter before the
> altar or the reading desk, and, after a
> few moments of silent devotion, pronounce
> one or more of the following sentences of
> Scripture....

The manuscript then goes directly into the Call to Confession
and the corporate prayer of Confession, following the order
of the Catholic Apostolic Liturgy and the *Book of Common
Prayer*. Schaff's confession and absolution is an adaptation
of that found in the Palatinate Liturgy. This is the only
portion of the Regular Lord's Day service which the committee
changed. Porter was directed to write an Invocation, which is
a compilation of the two alternate forms provided in the
Specimen Liturgy, and Nevin prepared a new Call to Confession
and Confession. Both are free renderings of the *Book of
Common Prayer*.

The first Absolution is Schaff's version of that found
in the Palatinate Liturgy, as the marginal notation in his
original manuscript acknowledges, while the second form provided is his adaptation of that found in both the *Book of
Common Prayer* and the Catholic Apostolic Liturgy. The Pax
does not appear in the Specimen Liturgy and was added prior
to the publication of the Provisional Liturgy. Following the
Creed the Specimen Liturgy called for the Salutation and Sursum Corda; however, Schaff changed this to a responsive "Lord,
we believe", "Praise ye the Lord". The congregation then
joins the choir in a sung or chanted response of praise. As
in the *Book of Common Prayer* the Gloria Patri is said responsively, although the Minor Doxology does not follow the
lesson as in the Anglican Liturgy.

The General Petition in the Lord's Day service is, with
minor exceptions, Schaff's own prayer, appearing first in
his hand-written manuscript, composed during the summer of
1852, and thoroughly revised and abbreviated for the publication of the Specimen Liturgy and subsequently the Provisional Liturgy. The opening thanksgiving is modeled after
the ancient Eucharistic prayers, praising God for creation,
redemption, and sanctification. In addition to the Sanctus,
the prayer includes Scriptural references to 1 Peter 2:9,
Luke 1:75, and Romans 5:5. The prayer for the church is
also original with Schaff, and used words and phrases from
Matthew 5:13-14, 2 Peter 3:18, Ephesians 4:3, Psalm 2:8,
and Philippians 2:10-11. Schaff adapted the opening sentence
in his prayer for the nation from the corresponding prayers
in the *Book of Common Prayer* and the Catholic Apostolic
Liturgy; however, the remainder of the prayer is original,
as is the final prayer for all sorts and conditions of men.

The minister ascends the pulpit during the hymn before
the sermon. Regarding the latter, Schaff's original rubric
is interesting:

> The text may be taken from the Gospel or
> the Epistle for the day, or may be selected
> by the minister from any portion of the
> canonical Scriptures. It is always ad-
> visable however, to observe a certain
> system and to follow either the order of
> the Christian year, or of the Bible, or
> of the Catechism, that the people may get
> a full knowledge of all the leading facts
> and doctrines of the Gospel salvation.
> The average length of the sermon should be
> from twenty five to forty minutes.

The reason for the "system" was omitted in the final edition
of the rubric, as was the suggestion that the sermon not excee

twenty-five minutes. Forty minutes was likely shock enough
to some of the brethren, let alone twenty-five. The rubric
providing for free prayer after the sermon is in Schaff's
original manuscript, and is the only opportunity so provided
in the first form. He does provide a post-preaching prayer
which, like the ones which precede it, is original and an
abbreviated form of that which appears in the Specimen Liturgy.

The "collection" comes at the appropriate place for an
ante-communion order of worship; however, Mercersburg made
little of the ancient offering and chose to follow the general structure of Anglican Morning Prayer rather than return to
the Bucer-Calvin pattern. Preaching concludes the service,
for all practical purposes, as in the Prone tradition; however, one could hardly say that the regular Lord's Day service is preaching centered. Until the hymn before the sermon,
the altar is the focus of the service, and "primitive" liturgical forms make this worship devotional throughout. Scriptural language and references predominate. In addition to
those in the General Petition, noted above, this writer has
found the following: Psalm 121:1; Psalm 36:9; Psalm 16:11;
James 1:17; Romans 8:34; Matthew 18:20; Psalm 26; Psalm 96;
1 John 3:8-9; Luke 15:21; Psalm 51:10; Romans 12:1; Luke
1:74-75; Ezekiel 33:11; John 3:16; Romans 6:4; 1 John 2:2.
This thorough-going Biblical character of the Lord's Day
service is one of its most distinctive characteristics.

Another feature is the dialogical nature of the service.
Schaff believed that if worship was to be the people's offering, they must have a part in it--i.e., that the worship must
be responsive. There are eleven opportunities for the people
to respond with the "Amen"; on three occasions the Liturgy
calls for a versicle/response; and four opportunities are

provided for congregational singing or chanting. As shall be
shown in the section to follow, the responsive nature of the
Provisional Liturgy raised the greatest hue and cry against
it within the denomination.

Aside from the opening chant by the choir and the invocation, which Hageman believes to have originated with revivalism (as noted above), the Lord's Day service is objective
throughout. The prayers are straightforward and Biblical in
their language and historic in their pattern. The Apostles'
Creed and the Christian Year--whether through the lectionary
or the Catechism--keep the sermon from becoming subjective
and esoteric.

In the Absolution one detects a high doctrine of the
ministry--although a doctrine no higher than that found in
the Palatinate Liturgy. This aspect of the Provisional Liturgy will be examined in more detail when the Ordination service is discussed below.

To summarize: the Baltimore proposals called for a
Lord's Day service which would "embrace several forms, some
shorter some longer, some with and without responses, with
the view to avoid monotony, and to adapt them the more readily
to the condition and wants of our various ministers and congregations which are evidently not prepared for an entire uniformity". That bill was exactly filled. "The language and
style ought to be throughout scriptural as much as possible;
that is, simple, sublime, and devotional, such as we find in
the Psalms especially, and in the Lord's Prayer." That
specification was also fulfilled in the judgment of this
writer. And so, too, was the final proposal made at Baltimore: "...a liturgy ought not to interfere with the proper
use of extemporaneous prayer, either in public or in private,
but rather to regulate and promote it. Sufficient room should

be left for its exercise in connection with the Sunday afternoon and evening services, as well as in weekly Bible lectures,
social prayer meetings, catechetical exercises, and on special
occasions." The first Lord's Day form was to be the regular
and regulative one, providing the structure and pattern for
all the worship of the church, stated and occasional. Such
was the intention of the committee in 1857; such was not the
willingness of most of the denomination after 1857, as shall
be shown in the pages to follow.

The Eucharist

As is evident in a structural comparison of the Provisional
Liturgy with the Catholic Apostolic Liturgy and the *Book of
Common Prayer*,[50] Schaff followed both *generally*; yet in certain
particulars he was as original in design as he was in the
prayers themselves. These comparisons and contrasts will be
highlighted in the discussion to follow.

The opening rubric[51] does not indicate the frequency of
celebration; however, it does specify that the Eucharist is
not merely an addendum to the preaching service. As in the
Lord's Day service, the "liturgical place" is the "altar",
from which the minister pronounces the *opening declaration*:
"In the name of the Father, and of the Son, and of the Holy
Ghost." The people respond here, and on eighteen other specified occasions, with the "Amen". Thus the service begins on
a note of objectivity and high purpose.

The *collect* is a paradigm of Schaff's synthesizing
technique, being a compilation of the Catholic Apostolic
prayer of access and the *Book of Common Prayer*'s collect for

purity; in turn the one deriving in substance from the Syrian
Jacobite Liturgy and the other from the Sarum.

In the *Scripture sentences* of the Provisional Liturgy,
unparalleled in either the Catholic Apostolic Liturgy or the
Book of Common Prayer, Schaff further sets the tone of the
service and provides a Biblical warrant for all the action to
follow.

The *Gloria in Excelsis* (*Te Deum, Canticle,* or *Hymn*),
follows the historic pattern, broken by Cranmer and restored
in the Catholic Apostolic Liturgy. Shaw suggests a rationale:
the mood of the Gloria is partly penitence and humiliation;
whereas the conclusion of the service should be praise and rejoicing.[52] In the Catholic Apostolic Liturgy the Gloria is
the "Little Entrance", after the Eastern fashion. Schaff's
rubric specified that the congregation stand and join the
choir in this musical response.

Comment has been made above concerning the sequence of
the lessons: *Gospel,* then *Epistle.* So, too, have the *Collects*
and *Festival Prayers* been discussed. The sequence in the
Catholic Apostolic Liturgy is Collect, Epistle, Festival
"Anthem", and Gospel. *Gloria tibi* and *Laus tibi* are not used
in the Provisional Liturgy as they are in both the Catholic
Apostolic Liturgy and the *Book of Common Prayer*.

The *Sermon* or *Homily* (the latter term reflecting the
Catholic Apostolic Liturgy) immediately follows the lessons
in both the Catholic Apostolic Liturgy and the Provisional
Liturgy, thus restoring the separation imposed by Cranmer.
Schaff's concern for brevity at this juncture has a precedent
in the Palatinate Liturgy and the Mayer Liturgy. Instead of
a sermon the Provisional Liturgy provides for "a fit lesson of
moderate length, taken from the Holy Gospels, on the history

of Christ's Passion and Death". Such is also the specified
theme of the sermon in the Palatinate rubric. The place of
preaching in Mercersburg liturgical theology will be assessed
in Chapter VII; however, let it be noted here that Schaff
apparently saw no difference--at least on this occasion--be-
tween the read and the proclaimed Word of God.

Following ancient practice (and that of the Catholic
Apostolic Liturgy but not the *Book of Common Prayer*), the
people stand to say or sing the *Nicene Creed*--point of transition from the Liturgy of the Word to the Liturgy of the Upper
Room. The rubric directs that "on the occasion of the last
Communion in the Church Year, use shall be made in the same
way of the *Athanasian Creed*". A similar practice is prescribed for Christmas, Easter, Pentecost, and All Saints' by
the Catholic Apostolic Liturgy.

The lengthy rubric regarding the *Offerings of the people*
is a combination of Schaff and the *Book of Common Prayer*. In
his original manuscript Schaff attached a page from the *Book
of Common Prayer* and then made his changes in the margins.
Much of Schaff's theology of worship is reflected in this
direction: the minister places the vessel containing the
offerings upon the "altar, in token of its proper meaning,
as an oblation presented to God".

The *Exhortation* is common to all sixteenth century Reformed liturgies in both the traditions of Calvin and Zwingli.
Seldomridge suggests that its original intention was to in-
duce the people to receive communion--as they had not been
accustomed to doing--and also to urge self-examination.[53]
The latter is certainly the dominant motif in the Palatinate
Liturgy. Schaff's Exhortation is entirely his own. Traces
of the Palatinate Liturgy, the *Book of Common Prayer*, and
the Prussian Agenda are to be detected; however, with the

exception of a phrase or two, the words are Schaff's. Three
direct Scriptural references are included: 1 Corinthians
5:7-8; Romans 12:1; Colossians 1:12-14. Even here Schaff's
freedom to improvise can be seen in the phrase he adds to
Romans 12:1: "Present *yourselves on the altar of the Gospel,
in union with His glorious merits*, a living sacrifice...."
The dominical nature and purpose of the action is set forth,
the Reformed doctrine of the Eucharist articulated ("We have
to do here, in a mystery, not with the shadows and types
only of heavenly things, but with the very realities themselves of that true spiritual world in which Christ, now
risen from the dead, continually lives and reigns."), and
self-examination called for briefly and without tedium or
didacticism. The point is clearly made but not labored
that in this "more than in any other service it is fit that
[the peoples'] adoration should be joined with sacred reverence and awe".

Schaff followed the *Book of Common Prayer*'s sequence of
Exhortation, Confession, Assurance rather than either the
Calvinistic pattern which opens with Confession, or the
Zwinglian pattern which prescribes Confession following
the sermon. In this instance, as in so many others, Schaff
synthesized the prayers from the Catholic Apostolic Liturgy
and the *Book of Common Prayer*, and added his own personal
touch--in this case Isaiah 64:6. The prayer is not corporate; however, the people are to kneel and respond with the
"Amen".

The *Assurance* is interesting: it is all Scriptural and
amounts to the "comfortable words" in the *Book of Common
Prayer*. It is neither a priestly prayer for pardon, like
that which precedes the "comfortable words", nor a strong
proclamation of forgiveness, like that in either the Palatin-

te Liturgy or the Preparatory Service of the Provisional
Liturgy. Perhaps Schaff saw such a close relationship be-
ween the Preparatory Service and the Communion that a
epetition was unnecessary. In any event, he constructed
he Assurance in the Eucharist entirely around Ephesians
:17-23 and 3:20-21.

Following the Eastern custom and as prescribed by the
atholic Apostolic Liturgy the congregation stands for the
onsecration Prayer. It begins after the fashion of St.
ames and the Catholic Apostolic Liturgy: *Salutation,*
ursum Corda, Gratia Agamus, Vere Dignum. In his first
anuscript Schaff adopted the Preface from St. James, as
his marginal notation suggests: "This Preface is taken
rom St. James' Liturgy. But perhaps the Preface in the
rvingite Liturgy p. 18-20 may be found preferable." Sub-
equently Schaff discarded the St. James Preface *per se*
nd modeled the entire prayer after the Catholic Apostolic
iturgy; however, Brenner's remark about the Eucharistic
iturgy as a whole is especially applicable to the Conse-
ration Prayer: "It is as though Schaff seated himself at
n organ with the score of the Catholic Apostolic Liturgy
efore him and began to improvise. The improvisation is
chaff's, and it is an organic structure of great power
nd beauty."[54] The reason for Brenner's observation can
e seen by examining this prayer in the Appendix. Schaff
ollowed the historic structure of thanksgiving for creation,
rovidence, redemption, incarnation (using phrases from the
icene Creed), the Holy Ghost, the church and the means of
race, the hope of everlasting life, the second coming; and
hen adoration leading into *Sanctus, Hosanna,* and *Benedic-
us qui venit*. The *Words of Institution* and the fraction
nd elevation are not directly a part of the prayer itself,

yet they come within it and follow Calvin and the Palatinate
pattern of à Lasco.

The *Epiclesis* follows the Eastern pattern generally;
however, the prayer itself is entirely original. In the
briefest possible form it sets forth the essence of Mercersburg's eucharistic doctrine:

> Almighty God, our heavenly Father, send
> down, we beseech Thee, the powerful bene-
> diction of Thy Holy Spirit upon these ele-
> ments of bread and wine, that being set
> apart now from a common to a sacred and
> mystical use, they may exhibit and repre-
> sent to us with true effect the Body and
> Blood of Thy Son, Jesus Christ; so that
> in the use of them we may be made, through
> the power of the Holy Ghost, to partake
> really and truly of His blessed life,
> whereby only we can be saved from death,
> and raised to immortality at the last day.

Calvin's Sursum-corda dynamic has been corrected; it is
through the activity of the Holy Ghost that we participate in
a *mystical union* with the living, present Christ.

In the *Oblation-Anamnesis*--a composite throughout of the
corresponding prayers in the *Book of Common Prayer* and the
Catholic Apostolic Liturgy--the sense of union with Christ
is continued. No "absent friend" here; rather a living Lord
in whose sacrifice is our only hope, and through whose total
and perfect self-oblation our own unworthy sacrifice of praise
is made. Of this prayer Brenner writes:

> The memorial act in the liturgy is not in
> memory of a departed friend who must be
> recalled to mind...but it is a memorial
> before God the Father; that is to say, it
> is the basis of the petitions which we
> direct to God....We present to our heavenly

> Father the memorial of Christ and his cross,
> his resurrection, his ascension, his coming
> again in glory, and we add to this memorial
> oblation the poor sacrifice of our own sin-
> ful lives and cast ourselves upon the mercy
> of God.[55]

The Reformed tradition generally has never completely settled the question concerning the "moment of consecration", and Schaff's changing liturgical ideas reflect the uncertainty in his own mind. In the only complete draft of the Eucharist in Schaff's hand, the Narrative of the Institution appears twice: once to begin the Exhortation (This was dropped in the final version.), and a second time within the Eucharistic prayer itself, at the time of the fraction and elevation. That Schaff considered this to be the "moment of consecration" is apparent, for in the center of the page, following the Sanctus and preceding the Narrative is the title: "The Consecration".

Brenner's analysis of Schaff's quandry and its eventual resolution is accurate. Schaff came to see that the consecration is an act of God in response to the church's prayer to "bless and sanctify"; therefore he rewrote "the entire Eucharistic Prayer as the prayer of consecration and took his stand on the side of the positive and truly Catholic tradition".[56] From Salutation through Oblation this prayer is a tightly-knit structural unit, acknowledging the Real Presence of Christ in the *whole sacramental action*--quite consistent with the emphasis in Calvin's Eucharistic theology. The Narrative of Institution--or more accurately put, the dominical command--is the warrant for the church's action; however, no single element of the Consecration is set apart as the "moment".

The *Intercessions* are greatly dependent upon those in the Catholic Apostolic Liturgy--more so than the direct borrowing would indicate. Only the prayer for those "called to suffer heavy affliction" is entirely original. In the position of the Intercessions Schaff followed the Eastern tradition, adopted also by the Catholic Apostolic Liturgy, but not by the *Book of Common Prayer*. Traditionally the *Lord's Prayer* is the summation of all the church's prayers. The *Benedictions* and the *Pax* follow the order of the Catholic Apostolic Liturgy.

In the rubric prescribing the circumstances of the reception of the elements and in the *Words of Distribution* the Provisional Liturgy reflects the Palatinate Liturgy. The Words of Distribution are variable, however. It is permissible to "repeat the Words of Institution in full relating to each part", or to use other "suitable sentences" from Scripture, or "full silence at times may be better than any words". Each "Company of Communicants" is dismissed with a benediction adapted from the *Book of Common Prayer*.

The *post-communion* prayer may be free--the only such opportunity afforded by the Provisional Liturgy; or use may be made of the prayer provided. It is apparent that Schaff used the precise wording of this prayer from the *Book of Common Prayer*, with one original phrase and one taken from the Palatinate Liturgy; however, it is equally obvious that he recognized the similarity of this prayer to those in the liturgies of the Bucer-Calvin tradition.

The *Benediction* is a paraphrase of Philippians 4:7, the old Episcopal blessing at Confirmation,[57] used both in the *Book of Common Prayer* and the Catholic Apostolic Liturgy. Generally the Reformed liturgies of the sixteenth century used the Aaronic Benediction; however, with both the

Book of Common Prayer and the Catholic Apostolic Liturgy before him, it is not surprising that Schaff used the "Peace of
God".

By way of general evaluation it can be said that Schaff's
Baltimore proposals were not quickly written for the occasion
and then promptly forgotten; rather they were followed to the
letter. Through the several liturgical collections available
to him, Schaff had "the liturgies of the Greek and Latin
Churches of the third and fourth centuries" readily at hand.
Furthermore, in the Catholic Apostolic Liturgy and the *Book
of Common Prayer* he had two superior examples of Protestant
liturgies which relied far more upon those ancient liturgies
than anything produced in the sixteenth century Reformed
liturgical family; yet Schaff must also have been aware of
the extent to which Bucer, Calvin, and Knox influenced the
Book of Common Prayer.[58] Special note was taken of the "old
Palatinate and other Reformed liturgies of the sixteenth century"; however, in relying primarily upon the *Book of Common
Prayer* and the Catholic Apostolic Liturgy Schaff presided
over the construction of a Liturgy which focused entirely
upon the Eucharist rather than the sermon.

The copy of the Provisional Liturgy in the appendix is
colorful testimony to the third Baltimore proposal:

> Neither the ancient Catholic nor the Re-
> formed liturgies, however, ought to be
> copied slavishly, but reproduced rather
> in a free evangelical spirit and adapted
> to the peculiar wants of our age and de-
> nomination; inasmuch as these Liturgies
> themselves exhibit to us a considerable
> variety with essential unity, and as
> every age of the Church has the promise
> of the Spirit and a peculiar mission to
> fulfil.

Armed with Scripture, a sizable array of historic liturgies, and a sensitive, poetic spirit, Philip Schaff composed his own work, borrowing, adapting, and freely creating fresh forms which would articulate Reformed theology as Mercersburg understood it, yet which would also forge a devotional bond between a small band of nineteenth century German immigrants in an American Commonwealth and the saints of the ages. Nevin summarizes the theology of the Eucharistic liturgy in this way:

> [The Liturgy] gives us the true Reformed view of Christ's presence in the Lord's Supper, in a form answering at the same time to the faith and worship of the Primitive Church. It teaches, that the Lord's Supper is more than an outward sign, and more than a mere calling to mind of our Saviour's death as something past and gone. It teaches, that the value of Christ's sacrifice never dies, but is perennially continued in the power of His life. It teaches, that the outward side of the sacrament is mystically bound by the Holy Ghost to its inward invisible side; not fancifully, but really and truly; so that the undying power of Christ's life and sacrifice are there, in the transaction, for all who take part in it with faith. It teaches that it is our duty to appropriate this grace, and to bring it before God (the 'memorial of the blessed sacrifice of His Son'), as the only ground of our trust and confidence in His presence. All this the Liturgy teaches.[59]

And, it may be added, all this the Liturgy accomplishes in a style that is "simple, sublime, and devotional".

Ordination of Ministers[60]

Although Nevin was responsible for both services of
Ordination and Installation, this discussion will be restricted to the Ordination of Ministers. It clearly reveals Nevin's liturgical methodology as well as his theology
of the ministry.

Two manuscripts of the Ordination service in Nevin's
hand are extant.[61] The first is a complete draft of an
Ordination of Ministers, which relies heavily upon the Mayer
liturgy in its exhortation to the ordinand and in the ordination questions. The second manuscript is only partially
complete; however, it is obviously Nevin's final draft, for
it corresponds in every detail with the printed version to
be found in the Provisional Liturgy.

Liturgically Nevin's work is a "compilation", as he
wrote across the top of the first draft; and he was as
successful in using his sources as was Schaff in using his.
In this case those sources were Scripture, the Catholic
Apostolic Liturgy, the *Book of Common Prayer*, and the Mayer
liturgy. As will be demonstrated below, one could defensibly
list Nevin's sermon, "The Christian Ministry", as a liturgical source, since it provides several of the phrases in the
opening address.

Collect: Half of the initial rubric is taken from the
Catholic Apostolic Liturgy; and, excepting the first word,
the collect is entirely from that source.

Address to the Congregation: The ordinand's name is
"distinctly announced" and he presents himself "before the
altar" for the two addresses to follow. First, the congregation is given "an opportunity to express their voice" in the
matter and to show "any just cause or impediment, because of

which [the ordinand] ought not be ordained to the Christian
Ministry...." As shown in the copy of this address to be
found in Appendix VI, several phrases evidence direct
borrowing from the Catholic Apostolic Liturgy; however,
the latter is but an expanded version of the *Book of Common
Prayer*.[62] Nevin followed the phraseology of the former
and the brevity of the latter. The role of the congregation is acknowledged in this "opportunity to express their
voice"; however, as the service is soon to make plain, it
is but a negative "opportunity", since "the office is of
divine origin and of truly supernatural character and force;
flowing directly from the Lord Jesus Christ Himself...."

Address to the Ordinand: The rubric and first paragraph of this address are taken almost entirely from the
Catholic Apostolic Liturgy. Direct borrowing from the
Catholic Apostolic Liturgy is not found again, however,
before the address has passed its mid-point--and then in
only one sentence.

The second paragraph is perhaps the heart of the entire
service, so far as Nevin's doctrine of the ministry is concerned; and it is entirely unique to him:

> The office is of divine origin and of
> truly supernatural character and force;
> flowing directly from the Lord Jesus
> Christ Himself, as the fruit of His
> resurrection and triumphant ascension
> into heaven, and being designated by
> Him to carry forward the purposes of
> His grace upon the earth, in the salva-
> tion of men by the Church, to the end
> of time.

Simply put, that is the thesis and summary of Nevin's sermon,
"The Christian Ministry", delivered on the occasion of Wolff's

installation, and discussed in chapter one. It will be recalled that its three points are the origin, nature, and design of the ministry. In light of the above paragraph these
spot quotations from the sermon are revealing.

> And what we need first and chiefly to fix
> in our minds...is the *supernatural* charac-
> ter [of the ministry]. This lies in what
> we have now seen to be the source from
> which it springs. It refers itself at
> once to the ascended and glorified Christ.[63]

> The peculiarity of the office is that it
> does not originate in any way out of the
> order of this world naturally, but proceeds
> directly and altogether from a new and
> higher order of things brought to pass by
> the Spirit of Christ in consequence of his
> *resurrection and ascension.*[64]

> The terms of [the Apostolic commission]
> are such as of themselves plainly to show
> that the Church was to be considered as
> starting in the Apostles, and extending
> itself out from them in the way of im-
> plicit submission to their embassy and
> proclamation. They were to stand between
> Christ and the world, to be his witnesses,
> his legates, the representatives of his
> authority, the *mediators of his grace*
> among men.[65]

> ...the Church is viewed as being to Christ
> in the world of grace, what the body is to
> the head in the natural world. It is the
> form in which he reveals his presence among
> men through the Spirit, and the organ by
> which he carries into effect the *purposes
> of his grace.*[66]

Two lengthy quotations from Matthew 28:18-20 and Ephesians
4:8-16 are peculiar to the Provisional Liturgy, and are texts
around which Nevin based his arguments in "The Christian

Ministry". These quotations are followed by a lengthy paragraph setting forth the case for apostolic succession, dear to the heart of both Nevin and Schaff, as indicated in the first chapter. Interestingly, with the exception of the word, "investiture", the entire paragraph is based on the Mayer Liturgy.

The next paragraph, establishing the purposes of the ministry--or its "design", to use Nevin's term--is a composite of material original to Nevin, Scripture, and one borrowed sentence from the Catholic Apostolic Liturgy. In short, the "Ministers of Christ are set in the world to be at once the representatives of His authority and the ambassadors of His grace". Their business is to preach, baptize, administer the sacraments, hold up the people of God in priestly intercession, and to exercise the power of the keys.

The final two paragraphs are a more direct and personal appeal to the ordinand to "pray earnestly, through the mediation of our only Saviour Jesus Christ, for the heavenly assistance of the Holy Ghost...." The model in this case is the *Book of Common Prayer*.

Ordination Questions: The liturgical sources for the five questions are the Catholic Apostolic Liturgy and the Mayer Liturgy. Only the second question--demanding allegiance to the persons of the Trinity, the Church, "one true Baptism", and "the system of Faith set forth in the three Creeds..."-- is not found in some form in the Mayer Liturgy. With a slight rearrangement of the wording the question comes entirely from the Catholic Apostolic Liturgy. Although the Mayer Liturgy questions the calling of the ordinand, the wording Nevin used in question four is from the Catholic Apostolic Liturgy. Here, too, Nevin's doctrine of ordination is to be seen clearly: "...do you desire and expect to

eceive, through the laying on of our hands, the gift and
race of the Holy Ghost, which shall enable you to fulfil
his heavenly commission and trust?" And so, too, in the
inal question: "Do you acknowledge the rightful authority
f this Church, from which you are now to receive ordination,
s *being a true part in the succession of the Church Catho-
ic*...?" Nevin meant "universal" in the use of "Catholic";
owever, he clearly meant more--an historic succession and
ontinuity of ministry from the Roman Church through the
eformation to the German Reformed Church in America.

The Ordination: The words of ordination are taken
lmost entirely from the Mayer Liturgy, as are two of the
hree forms by which the newly ordained minister is extended
he *right hand of fellowship.*

Intercession for the Newly Ordained Minister: The call
o prayer is taken verbatim from the Catholic Apostolic Litur-
y, while the prayer itself is a curious mixture of the *Book
f Common Prayer,* Scripture, and Nevin. The overall model
eems to be the Mayer Liturgy; however, there is no direct
orrowing. A *Hymn* and the *Benediction* conclude the service.

The ordination controversy came late in the liturgical
ispute and centered around the *Order of Worship* rather than
he Provisional Liturgy; however, the service in both litur-
ies is essentially the same. Bomberger became increasingly
isturbed by the high-church, priestly character of the minis-
ry articulated by the liturgies. He recognized, and Nevin
eadily admitted, that at the point of ordination and the
inistry the liturgies were more Anglican than Reformed.
orner expressed a similar opinion, and went on to say:
Ordination is openly designated by Nevin as a sacrament."[67]

Did Nevin consider ordination to be a sacrament? What
oes the Liturgy indicate? Taking the language of the

Liturgy in its strict and formal sense, the answer is that
ordination is a sacrament: "actual investiture", "sacramental seal", "do you desire and expect to receive, through
the laying on of our hands, the gift of the Holy Ghost?",
"send down, we beseech Thee, the anointing of the Holy Ghost
upon the head of this Thy servant". Yet, as Gerhart was
quick to point out, by a sacrament Protestants mean that
which confers saving grace. In this sense ordination is
not a sacrament, for "it rather only increases the obligation to fidelity for him upon whom it is conferred".[68] The
Liturgy does beseech God to grant the ordinand a special
merit of grace, the better that he may be able to fulfill
the responsibilities of the office; however, throughout the
service the focus is on the *Office*, and Nevin cannot stress
too strongly that "the office is of divine origin and of
truly supernatural character and force...." The office-
holder is ultimately no nearer heaven after his "actual investiture" than he was before it; rather he is one who is
functionally--not organically--set apart to be the representative of Christ's authority and the ambassador of his
grace.

Nichols observes that Nevin's position in "The Christian Ministry" is ambiguous in its implications, and so it
is. So, too, does a certain ambiguity persist in the ordination ritual; however, there it becomes clearer that ordination does not confer grace or promise forgiveness in the
same sense of Baptism and the Eucharist. Instead the ordinand is clothed with an office, the power and authority of
which derive directly from Christ. This is safely Reformed.
The means by which the office is derived from Christ--
apostolic succession--does indeed place Nevin squarely in
the Anglican camp. Undoubtedly the means influence the end

in any endeavor; yet the services of ordination in the Provisional Liturgy and the *Order of Worship* articulate a high, lofty, and defensibly Reformed doctrine of the office of ministry. The absolution in the Preparatory Service and that one to be found in the Restoration of the excommunicated ("And now, in the name and by the authority of Christ and this Church, I announce to you the pardon of your sins; I release you from the bond of the excommunication which you have incurred...") are no "higher" or more sacerdotal than this from Calvin's Liturgy: "Therefore...in the name and by the authority of our Lord Jesus Christ, I excommunicate all idolaters, blasphemers...."[69] In each case the proclamations are made by an office-bearer carrying "forward the purposes of His grace upon the earth, in the salvation of men by the Church, to the end of time".

It now remains to consider the constitutional implications of the Provisional Liturgy, to evaluate the methods by which it was introduced to the denomination, and to assess the extent of its use in the churches; however, since all of these factors contributed to a revision of the Provisional Liturgy and the publication of the *Order of Worship* in 1866, they are discussed in the chapter to follow.

NOTES TO CHAPTER V

1. See pp. 131-132 above.

2. *Acts and Proceedings of the Eastern Synod*, October, 1856.

3. The total number of pages was 408.

4. Nichols, *Romanticism*, p. 301.

5. *WM*, December 8, 1858.

6. Philip Schaff, *Deutsches Gesangbuch* (Philadelphia: Lindsay und Blakiston, 1859).

7. Philip Schaff, "German Hymnology," trans. by T. C. Porter, *MR*, XII (1860), p. 229.

8. *Ibid.*, pp. 248-250.

9. PL Minutes, October 21, 1857.

10. October 26, 1857, E & R Historical Society.

11. March 15, 1858, E & R Historical Society.

12. Nichols, *Romanticism*, p. 302.

13. Appendix II.

14. *WM*, August 31, 1859.

15. From December 22, 1858 to October 17, 1860.

16. *WM*, March 28, 1860.

17. John W. Nevin, "The Church Year," *MR*, VIII (1856), pp. 474-475.

18. Nevin, *The Liturgical Question*, p. 30.

19. A number of judgments concerning authorship of services, prayers, etc. will be made in the following pages based on this writer's familiarity with the penmanship of several members of the committee. Where there is any doubt, it will be so indicated. As anyone will know who has extensively examined the papers of the liturgical committee and the volumes of personal correspondence extant in the E & R Historical Society, such calligraphic assessments can be made with defensible accuracy.

20. In the following section the Liturgy of the Catholic Apostolic Church will be discussed at some length; however, let it be stated here that both Liturgy and lectionary (especially the latter) depend heavily upon the *Book of Common Prayer*.

21. PL Minutes, April 21, 1857.

22. PL Minutes, March 25, 1856.

23. Letter, John W. Nevin to Philip Schaff, June 6, 1856, E & R Historical Society.

24. Philip Schaff, Review of *A Liturgy: or Order of Christian Worship, MR*, (1858), p. 165.

25. Edward Miller, *The History and Doctrines of Irvingism* (2 vols.; London: C. Kegan Paul & Co., 1878).

26. P. E. Shaw, *The Catholic Apostolic Church* (Morningside Heights: King's Crown Press, 1946).

27. H. C. Whitley, *Blinded Eagle* (Chicago: Alec R. Allenson, Inc., 1955), pp. 22-23.

28. *New Schaff-Herzog Encyclopedia of Religious Knowledge*, ed. by Samuel Macauley Jackson (12 vols.; New York: Funk & Wagnalls Company, 1908), p. 458.

29. Miller, vol. 1, *op. cit.*, p. 221.

30. Shaw, *op. cit.*, p. 106.

31. Nichols, *Corporate Worship*, p. 157.

32. *The Order for the Daily Services of the Church and for Administration of the Sacraments as the Same are to be Conducted at Albury* (London: Moyes and Barcley, n. d.), pp. 73-74.

33. Reprinted in the *WM*, November 8, 1854.

34. David Schaff, *op. cit.*, p. 178.

35. *The Liturgy and Other Divine Offices of the Church* (New York: J. R. M'Gown, 1851).

36. Hageman, *Pulpit and Table*, p. 89.

37. The British Museum lists ten different editions of the Catholic Apostolic Liturgy from 1843-1854 inclusive. In the Philip Schaff Library at the Lancaster Theological Seminary there is only one edition, published in London in 1880. This same edition is to be found in the Library of Union Theological Seminary in New York. Speer Library at Princeton Theological Seminary has one undated edition, which this writer believes to have been issued prior to 1847. It does not contain any of the additions to the liturgy made in 1847, all of which appear in the 1851 edition; the latter is to be found in St. Mark's Library at General Theological Seminary in New York. A careful comparison of the three editions-- "Speer", 1851, and 1880--reveals an evolution in the number, arrangement, and liturgical complexity of the various services; however, *no fundamental difference* in the phrasing or sequence of the major prayers of either Morning Prayer or the Eucharist. Since this is so, it may be assumed that the 1853 and 1854 editions, noted in the British Museum Catalogue, represent only the same evolution in liturgical super-structure with no basic change in the prayers. A remarkable internal correspondence is to be found between the edition in Speer Library--probably the first edition of 1842--and the London edition of 1880.

38. Nichols, *Corporate Worship*, p. 157.

39. Nichols, *Romanticism*, p. 301.

40. John W. Nevin, *The History and Genius of the Heidelberg Catechism* (Chambersburg: Publication Office of the German Reformed Church, 1847).

41. Nichols, *Romanticism*, p. 287.

42. *WM*, March 17, 1858; February 9, 1859.

43. Henry Harbaugh, *The Diary of Rev. Henry Harbaugh, D.D.*, typescript copied from the original manuscript, E & R Historical Society.

44. *WM*, January 22, 1868.

45. *Ibid.*

46. *Ibid.*

47. Linn Harbaugh, *op. cit.*, pp. 292-294.

48. Harbaugh, Diary, October 13, 1857.

49. *WM*, January 22, 1868.

50. See Appendix IV.

51. A reproduction of "The Holy Communion" will be found in Appendix V. It has been color-coded to show the sources of the various parts, as these have been determined through a comparison with the other liturgies Schaff primarily used. A solid line indicates that all the words are found in the same prayer and in the same sequence in the respective liturgy. A broken line indicates adaptation; while a slash (/) indicates an omission.

52. Shaw, *op. cit.*, p. 203.

53. Amos L. Seldomridge, "A Study of the Office of Holy Communion from the Provisional Liturgy" (unpublished paper, Lancaster Theological Seminary, 1947).

54. Brenner, "Philip Schaff the Liturgist," p. 450.

55. *Ibid.*, p. 453.

56. *Ibid.*, p. 452.

57. Massey Hamilton Shepherd, Jr., *The Oxford American Prayer Book Commentary* (New York: Oxford University Press, [1950]), p. 84.

58. While it is not within the scope of this essay, one could nevertheless argue that the *Book of Common Prayer*--both structurally (Bucer and Calvin) and theologically (Zwingli)--is Reformed by sixteenth century standards; thus any fundamental contrast between the *Book of Common Prayer* and sixteenth century Reformed liturgies must not be too sharply drawn.

59. Nevin, *Vindication*, pp. 92-93.

248

60. See Appendix VI.

61. E & R Historical Society.

62. The Anglican Ordinal, in turn, originated with Bucer.

63. Nevin, "The Christian Ministry," p. 355.

64. *Ibid.*, p. 356.

65. *Ibid.*, p. 359.

66. *Ibid.*, p. 364.

67. J. A. Dorner, "The Liturgical Conflict in the Reformed Church of North America with Special Reference to Fundamental Evangelical Doctrines," *The Reformed Church Monthly*, I (1868), p. 356.

68. *WM*, September 11, 1867.

69. Thompson, *Liturgies*, pp. 205-206.

CHAPTER VI

The Order of Worship, 1866

Results of the Provisional Liturgy

Polity Considerations

Two major questions regarding the Provisional Liturgy
were immediately raised, and the denomination's inability to
answer either of them satisfactorily gave rise to the *Order
of Worship* in 1866. The first of these questions concerns
the constitutionality of a *provisional* liturgy. In 1841,
the Synod approved the Mayer Liturgy; and, while it was not
incorporated directly into the Constitution, it did conform
to the Constitution in such particulars as the questions to
be posed at Baptism, Confirmation, and Ordination. The cor-
relation between the Mayer Liturgy and the Constitution can
be seen in this provision:

> Persons possessing the requisite qualifi-
> cations, shall upon application be admitted
> to the communion of the Church by the rite
> of confirmation according to the mode pre-
> scribed in the [Mayer] Liturgy adopted by
> Synod, answering in the affirmative to the
> interrogatories proposed in the baptism of
> adults.[1]

While the Provisional Liturgy followed the Mayer Liturgy
at constitutional points such as the above, changes were made,
and, theoretically, those changes had to be approved by the

Synod before they could be used in worship. Still another
point of discussion concerned the article prescribing the
order for the regular Lord's Day:

> The public worship of the sanctuary shall
> consist in invocation, singing, prayer,
> reading the word, preaching a sermon or
> delivering a lecture and pronouncing the
> Benediction.[2]

Did this preclude the addition of anything else in the worship? And did it mean that the sequence of events could not
be changed? At least one correspondent in the *Weekly Messenger* thought so, and argued that the Provisional Liturgy could
only be used for family devotions until the Constitution was
changed by Synod and the Classes.[3]

This constitutional problem plagued the liturgical discussion until the publication of the *Directory for Worship*
in 1884. Still another article in the Constitution which
was debated specified:

> No selection of Psalms or Hymns shall be
> used in public worship in the German Re-
> formed Churches, except such as has been
> approved and recommended by the Synod.[4]

Those primarily in the Western section of the denomination
who insisted that the Western Liturgy (issued in 1869) and
the *Order of Worship* be sent to the Classes for adoption
argued that the above article prohibited provisional use of
liturgies. The East, on the other hand, maintained that the
article pertained only to hymn books. In short, the question
was never resolved, and it will be discussed more fully in
the final chapter of this essay.

The question of the Provisional Liturgy's constitution-
lity, while not the major factor in the success with which
t was received by the denomination, nevertheless influenced
hat reception and affected the sales of the Book as well.
lder George Welker sensed this problem: "I am in favor of
aking the Liturgy of a permanent character and form. I
on't like the term 'provisional' to be used; it looks for-
ard to be superseded by another. This in my opinion is
bjectionable in every respect. It will be an obstacle to
ts general introduction."[5] Nevin, too, saw the result of
he Liturgy's provisional character, and stated that "the
ery fact of its being an experiment, stood in the way of
ny general serious effort to bring it into use".[6] Many of
he laymen were simply not anxious to purchase a copy of a
iturgy, the very title of which indicated that it would be
eplaced.

rocedure of Introduction

How, then, should the Liturgy be introduced into the
ongregations? This is the second question.

> It is a matter of much satisfaction, we may
> be allowed to add, that no attempt is to be
> made to force the Liturgy upon the Church,
> without such general inward and free con-
> sent to its use. The Synod has ordered it
> to be prepared and published only for pro-
> visional use, and is not expected of course
> to take any action upon it one way or the
> other at the present time. *It must go
> forth among the churches simply as an ex-
> periment*. Every congregation is left to
> settle the question for itself, how far
> it will accept the new book, or whether

it will be accepted and used at all. This
is, in the judgment of the committee, just
as it ought to be. They would be sorry,
indeed, to have the Liturgy introduced,
in any quarter, sooner or farther than
there may be a disposition among the
people to make it welcome, as a help to
them, and not a hindrance in their public
worship. In this way, *the Liturgy asks
no ecclesiastical sanction in its favor.
It is enough that the Synod has sanctioned
the principle of worship in such form, and
that the new book is submitted to the
churches by its direction and order.*
Whether it shall satisfy their judgment,
and be taken into their full confidence
and trust, remains yet to be seen. Years
may be required to settle this question;
and the interest involved in it is so
vast, that no one should object to have
years allowed for the purpose. As the
case now stands, *the Liturgy must work
its own way, quietly and silently, into
general use; or else pass away at last
without any authority whatever, as a
provision for which after all there has
been no real demand in the reigning life
of the Reformed Church.*[7] [Italics mine.]

The Synod complied with the committee's request and--*without
examining the final version*, it must be remembered--approved
the Provisional Liturgy for use by the congregations. After
the publication of the Liturgy this action was regretted by
some. One delegate wrote this: "Had I known...what was the
character of the Liturgy in respect to its new features of
worship, I should have favored a different disposition of the
subject, and I have no doubt many others would have done the
same."[8] No doubt this sentiment was shared by several delegates to the Allentown Synod (1857); however, it must also be
said that had they examined the specimen forms published two
years earlier and recalled the Baltimore principles, the

ature of the Provisional Liturgy should not have been hard
o guess. While the sacramental forms were thoroughly changed,
he Lord's Day service in the specimen forms is sufficiently
like the final version printed in the Provisional Liturgy that
more than a general idea of the volume could have been obtained.

As early as 1849, Nevin insisted that a liturgy could
never be forced on the church: "The Church can never be
hurried into a Liturgy, without her own consent; her own full,
free and hearty consent...."[9] That position was maintained
throughout the following thirty-years' debate, and reiterated
time and again when the anti-Mercersburg faction pointed out
the occasions on which the Liturgy was forced in a particular
congregation. There were undoubtedly such occasions, although
likely not as many as those opposed to the Provisional Liturgy
were anxious to have the denomination believe. The First Reformed Church in Lancaster is a typical case in point and was
the most thoroughly aired of all the congregational contro-
versies. Harbaugh attempted gradually to introduce the Provisional Liturgy into the worship of that congregation during
his final three years there (1857-60), and met with some
success in spite of stiff opposition. In 1868, the Consistory of the church passed a resolution forbidding the use of
the *Order of Worship*, which was used fully by A. H. Kremer,
then minister. The resolution was appealed to the Classis,
which sustained the appeal. Gerhart was chairman of the committee to write the opinion:

> By sustaining the appeal, Classis decides
> that a Consistory has no authority to
> direct the public worship of the sanctuary.
> This authority belongs to the ordained
> minister of the Word. The Consistory has
> no right to command a pastor to introduce
> the use of a Liturgy, or to dispense with

> the use of it—no right to command, or
> forbid, extemporaneous prayer....As the
> case now stands, no one has jurisdiction
> but the pastor; neither the spiritual
> Council [composed exclusively of elders],
> nor the Consistory, nor the Classis, nor
> yet the District Synod.[10]

Although this opinion did not directly contradict the Constitution, one wonders whether it fulfilled the *spirit* of that document; however, the case was not appealed. The position of Classis was simply that so long as General Synod had approved the provisional use of a liturgy, the consistory could neither command or refuse its use.

Several schemes were proposed by which the Liturgy might come into use in the congregations. Of those advocating a gradual introduction accompanied by liturgical education throughout the congregation, J. S. Foulk, minister of the Third Reformed Church in Baltimore, was the most articulate. In a lengthy and perceptive article he investigated the question: "Can the new Liturgy be used in our Churches?"[11] "Yes!" was his unhesitating answer; however, he argued against a hurried or complete introduction at once, for the contrast between the Provisional Liturgy and the unliturgical worship which predominated throughout the denomination was simply too great. Rather the minister must be prudent, though not timid and fearful. "It is mainly against the reading of prayers at *every* service that the opposition is directed"; therefore Foulk recommended that the minister so familiarize himself with the collects of the Liturgy that they become his own. Meanwhile he should use many of the other features of the Provisional Liturgy which do not cause offense—for example, the lectionary and the Christian Year. Then may come the canticles. If the choir will not sing them, then the minister should read them. Since they are composed of "inspired language, where is the congregation that would oppose this?" Foulk never served on the liturgical committee (although one of his elders--John Rodenmayer--did); yet he did as much as any man to popularize the Liturgy and encourage its use. He wrote a series of thirty-nine articles of a historical and devotional nature on the Church Year, and championed liturgical worship in every meeting of the Synod.

Another correspondent in the *Weekly Messenger* argued that the surest way to introduce the Provisional Liturgy was to distribute it among the families and encourage them to use it in their devotional periods. "Let it [the Liturgy] be first introduced to families as a devotional book, and it will then eventually find its way into the worship of the Church."[12] And yet another correspondent said simply: "In my humble opinion, I think, all that our ministers have to do, is to introduce it into their Churches, and to use it on all occasions, and the people will be satisfied. I myself have tried it, and have found it to be so."[13]

Harbaugh and Steiner sought to facilitate the Provisional Liturgy's way into the denomination's worship through education and music. Steiner immediately saw that proper use of the Provisional Liturgy would require musical settings for the several hymns and canticles it recommended; therefore he wrote certain members of the liturgical committee proposing such a volume. Bomberger, Porter, and Harbaugh were enthusiastic and free in their advice to Steiner concerning the selection of hymns.[14] The volume was published in 1859, co-authored by Henry Schwing, a Baltimore professor who edited the music.[15] Bomberger's response is particularly interesting. In a letter to Steiner he informed him that his choir director liked *Cantate Domino* and wanted it introduced into

the choir at Race Street. "Of the other parts of the book
I can of course speak for myself. And although I am probably
not quite as Liturgical as some of my esteemed Brethren, I
am glad to see music for the several services of our Liturgy,
so that when it is desirable to sing them, there will be no
lack of good music for them."[16]

In the Preface to *Cantate Domino* Steiner indicates that
"the first portion of the book was prepared with special
reference to the needs of the Liturgy, published for the use
of the German Reformed Church; but the Chants and Sentences
will be found available by all religious bodies, who may desire to employ the chant-style of music...." It would be
difficult to estimate how widely *Cantate Domino* was used;
however, it is safe to assume that wherever the Liturgy was
introduced, the musical settings provided by Steiner and
Schwing were likely used.

Harbaugh was immediately aware of the educational significance of music for both young and old, especially the young;
and he sought to popularize the Liturgy through the Sunday
School. His first such effort was *The Golden Censer*.[17] In
the Preface Harbaugh argues that as familiarity does not
breed contempt for hymns, neither does it breed contempt for
liturgical prayers. So, too, "as we can read and sing hymns
devoutly, though they have been prepared for us in the same
way [as a liturgy has], so we can use prayers prepared for us
by the highest inspiration of devout and holy men." Then
follow ten "parts" or chapters containing devotional exercises
in preparation for Confirmation, for public worship, private
devotional forms for morning and evening, in times of sick-
ness, etc., concluding with an order of Scripture readings
arranged according to the Church Year. Elizabeth Clarke
Kieffer writes that *The Golden Censer* was the best seller of

all Harbaugh's works because pastors gave it to catechumen
at confirmation. "Written at the time that its author was
deeply engaged in the activities of the Liturgical Committee, the little book was frankly intended as another
method of indoctrinating the young in the chief principles
of Mercersburg theology and preparing them for worship in a
liturgical Church."[18]

On April 11, 1861, Harbaugh was hard at work on a second
volume designated for the Sunday School.[19] It was published
later that year as *Hymns and Chants*.[20] The work is arranged
so that each Sunday has a designated Psalm, Gospel and
Epistle, and Collect, in addition to several appropriate
hymns. There are also three services provided (one responsive) for the "Opening and Closing of Schools". (The latter
type of service was originally intended for inclusion in the
Provisional Liturgy; however, time and space prevented it.)

The lengths to which Harbaugh was willing to go in an
effort to introduce and defend the Liturgy can be seen in
his hypothetical dialogue between Fannie and Mary, called
"Excercises on the Liturgy". Mary's Sunday School superin-
tendent refuses to use the Provisional Liturgy, and she visits
Fannie, whose Sunday School is liturgical:

> *Mary:* My Auntie, who was here last summer
> some time, told me ever so many nice things
> about your school; that you used a Liturgy
> and that all the teachers and scholars
> joined in with the Superintendent and
> Pastor in the worship, and it was so nice.
> I thought I *must* come over and see it too.

Fannie informs Mary that were it not for the Liturgy, the
"scholars" would know neither the Apostles' Creed nor the
Lord's Prayer. Mary agrees, because in her Sunday School

precisely that is the case. She then goes on to ask all the right questions about using a Liturgy, and Fannie and her sister, Louisa, answer them handily and convincingly, of course. Whether Harbaugh's efforts had any substantial influence beyond his own congregations is difficult to assess; however, in Lancaster and in Lebanon he did manage to use the Provisional Liturgy in all the services of the church.

Reception of the Provisional Liturgy

Just how widely was the Provisional Liturgy used throughout the churches of the denomination? The answer to that would seem to depend upon whom one trusts as his reporter. Those favoring and advocating the Liturgy were quick to point out its every use in the hope that this meant a general acceptance by the denomination. Others, more realistic or more opposed, hastened to stress that the Liturgy was clearly not winning its way among the congregations. The latter estimation is nearer the truth--witness Nevin himself: "Such as it is, however, the Provisional Liturgy has not come thus far, as we know, into any general use in the Church."[21] Neither had it received a fair trial, Nevin is quick to point out, having been "scanned only in an outside way, or at best experimented upon in broken parcels, sundered from their proper adjuncts, and tinkered at pleasure into other connections and other shapes....A true liturgy, in this respect, is like a piece of music; it must be judged from within; it must be actually sung or performed, in order that it may be rightly understood."[22]

As reported in the *Weekly Messenger*, the forms most frequently used were the occasional services--especially church consecrations and dedications and ordinations and installations

Between January, 1858, and September, 1866, the following
services were reported in the *Weekly Messenger*:[23] (unless
otherwise designated, all are in Pennsylvania)

> *Preparation service:* Lancaster (twice); Mt.
> Bethel; Norristown.
>
> *Eucharist:* Lancaster (twice); Mt. Bethel;
> Norristown.
>
> *Ordination-Installation:* Sulphur Spring;
> Gettysburg; Carlisle; Jacksonville, Va.;
> Huntingdon.
>
> *Funeral:* (Dr. Hoffeditz) no place given.
>
> *Church consecration:* Martinsburg, W. Va.;
> Burkettsville, Md.; Hartstown.
>
> *Cornerstone:* Lebanon; New Chester; Doyles-
> town; Clearspring, Md.

General introductions of the Provisional Liturgy were attempted
with some success in Lancaster (at both the First Reformed
Church and the Franklin and Marshall Chapel), Lebanon, Burketts-
ville, Norristown (one of the strongest liturgical churches
throughout the entire controversy), Frederick, Maryland, and
Third Reformed Church, Baltimore. The statistics are hardly
overwhelming and certainly support Nevin's admission noted
above. The influence which the Liturgy had as a pulpit manual
(even though it was not designed to be that), as a guide to
family devotion, and, especially, as a means of Christian education in the Sunday Schools was considerably greater, however, and an assessment of the extent of this influence will
subsequently be made.

The countless articles concerning the Liturgy, published
in the *Weekly Messenger* during the eight years between the

Provisional Liturgy and the *Order of Worship*, fall into three categories: favorable, general, and unfavorable. The penchant for using pseudonymns means that most of the correspondents cannot be identified for certain; however, Nevin and Harbaugh absorbed the brunt of the attacks made on the Liturgy and responded with series of articles defending it historically and theologically. Their strategy seemed to be to prove that the Provisional Liturgy and the form of worship it represented are the ancient and Reformed way, and that current (Puritan) practices are the innovations.

Articles in the "maybe-yes-maybe-no" category are primarily those asking for more information (or complaining because there is too much) and those raising the constitutional question, discussed above. In that connection, the consensus of the Mercersburg advocates was that a problem definitely existed; however, "the Constitution is not the norm or rule for our catechism, hymnbooks, and liturgies, but these are the norm for it. The Constitution may easily be changed or amended, as is done frequently, but catechisms not so readily."[24] The only reasonable thing to do, the correspondent continued, was to live with the several discrepancies until Synod resolved the issue in regard to the Provisional Liturgy. If it was adopted, then the Constitution would have to be amended.

Those opposing the Provisional Liturgy had a variety of complaints in addition to the problem of constitutionality. For example, Samuel Helffenstein, Jr. stated his complete opposition, specifically disagreeing with the Ordination service because it presumably implied apostolic succession and investiture.[25] Typical of those who find the use of liturgical forms objectionable is "Beta", who is afraid that forms are more liable to be abused than free prayer.[26] "J. W. H."

admits that the Provisional Liturgy has "literary merits"
and a "devotional spirit", but he concludes that the Church
is simply not "prepared for a liturgical form of worship".[27]
The Western church's position is ably represented by "M. S."
of Galion, Ohio, who argued at length that the Provisional
Liturgy is disruptive and will lead to schism if the "High-
churchmen" continue to force it on the congregations. Furthermore, the Reformed tradition is not a liturgical tradition in the sense of the Provisional Liturgy; rather, "The
sermon was always in the Reformed churches the main part of
the service, and anything which pushes that aside is Anti-
Reformed."[28] "Piscator" led those who objected to the responses, claiming that they were not in the best Reformed
tradition; and, even if they were, they were not a part of
the Reformed tradition in this country.[29] It is interesting
that those who were shown that the Provisional Liturgy was
not entirely unlike certain sixteenth century Reformed fore-
bearers immediately shifted their historical norm to claim
eighteenth and early nineteenth century America as the liturgical standard. "Heidelberg" summarized a lengthy series of
articles denouncing the responsive nature of the Liturgy in
this fashion:

> First, the paucity of Liturgies in this
> country clearly proves, that the member-
> ship could not have been supplied with
> them, and were therefore only in the hands
> of the ministry. Second, the absence of
> a responsive service in those Liturgies.
> Third, the testimony of the Church in this
> country. Any one of these proofs would be
> conclusive; but the three combined, render
> the case clear, even beyond a shadow of a
> doubt.[30]

This appeal to the American "Fathers" was undoubtedly
the most sentimental argument against liturgical worship,
and likely had not a little influence among the laity. "Will
it be said, that because they ["the Schlatters, the Hendels,
the Helffensteins, Hoffmeier, Becker, Geistweit, Hilster,
Mayer, Gloniger, Rahousers"] were not in the habit of reading their prayers, and having their congregations to respond
from books; that, therefore, they had no congregational worship, and that the people were, as a consequence, thus de-
prived of a most important benefit?"[31] Elizabeth Clarke
Kieffer summarizes these years of discontent in this fashion:
"The opponents of the [Provisional] Liturgy were, first, those
who altogether disapproved of 'printed prayers' and demanded
'free worship'; next, those who thought the English liturgy
should be a bare translation of the German Liturgy still in
use in many churches; and third, those who, ready to receive
and use a liturgy, still managed to ferret out in *this* liturgy
the cloven hoof of Mercersburg theology."[32]

Calls for Revision

The story of the agitation within the denomination which
led to a revision of the Provisional Liturgy is, in many ways,
the story of John Henry Augustus Bomberger. While his was
certainly not the only voice raising questions about the Provisional Liturgy, it was unquestionably the strongest and most
influential one.

Bomberger first drew the favorable attention of the Mercersburg professors when he succeeded Wolff at Easton. While
there Bomberger wrote his notable defense of Nevin, mentioned
above. Granted, he had certain reservations; however, by and

large Bomberger was decidedly pro-Nevin and Mercersburg in
1853. It will be recalled that it was Bomberger who first
expressed the growing desire within the denomination for
liturgical renewal. His Norristown proposals in 1849 marked
the serious beginning of the liturgical movement. In 1852
Bomberger accepted the Baltimore proposals without dissent;
and in 1857 he was the first member of the committee to introduce the Provisional Liturgy to the denomination. It was
appropriate for him to do so, since he worked as long and
hard on its completion as any other member, seeing it through
the press and sending Schaff frequent reports concerning its
progress.

The position taken by Bomberger in the *Weekly Messenger*
of November 11, 1857, was used against him on so many subsequent occasions that a brief résumé is helpful. In a lengthy
article he gave a history of the movement which resulted in
the Provisional Liturgy, assured the denomination that the
"Plan and Principles" adopted by the Synod in 1852 "have been
faithfully adhered to in the execution of the work", and described it as one which combined the "rich treasures of the
Church" with an "ultimate reference to our old standard
Palatinate Liturgy. So that whilst such modifications as
were felt to be expedient and necessary, have been freely
allowed, the new work will be found to be in essential agreement with the old. *It may be said to be what the original
framers of the Palatinate Liturgy would have made it, had
they lived and labored in such a period as ours.*" Bomberger
urged that the Provisional Liturgy be "tried in candor", and
that the "sacramental, festival, and special forms of the new
work should come into general public use". He even went so
far as to commend the Liturgy to families as a book of private
devotions, especially calling their attention to the baptismal

service, and concluded thus: "It is a book which parents may
safely put into the hands of their children, and which Christian friends may give, as a friendly momento to Christian
friends."

The mind and mood of Bomberger changed during the three
years following the publication of the Provisional Liturgy,
however, and the reasons for that change are not entirely
clear. It is perhaps first noticed in 1860, when certain
lines of division between Bomberger and Mercersburg are
drawn in an article entitled "The Church and Charitable Institutions".[33] His principle concern at that time was "for
the lack of dynamic denominational participation in the work
of the leading voluntary societies of the day. He decried
the quietism inherent in the pursuits of a wholly theological,
liturgical, or parochial sort, be they found at Princeton or
at Mercersburg.[34] Then, in the *Weekly Messenger*, March 27,
1861, one finds the first public notice of Bomberger's change
of heart in regard to the Liturgy. "He dwelt mainly upon the
dangers inherent in continuing an exchange of views wholly
without reference to eventual classical or synodical action.
He urged that a decision at both levels of the denomination's
policy be made, suggesting also that that decision be a call
for a revision of the Provisional Liturgy."[35] That any member
of the liturgical committee would call for a revision of the
Provisional Liturgy, let alone six years before its decade
of grace had been completed, was unthinkable to Nevin and
Harbaugh; thus the polemic began which was to continue for
twenty years.

Bomberger's turn-about was not quite 180 degrees; however, it was almost that. What made him change his mind?
There is no clear answer--no extant letter or diary which
would give any single source for the change. The Mercersburg

contingent did not press for a reason; rather they accepted the fact that Bomberger had either simply changed his mind, or was an anti-liturgical wolf in liturgical clothing all along. The seeming inconsistency between his position in 1857 and that taken in 1861 was hammered home, however; but Bomberger and his later apologists persistently maintained that no inconsistency existed. Rather he consistently urged a "medium liturgy", the essence of which was contained in the Provisional Liturgy: "We have all the *material* for such a book in our New Provisional Liturgy. If, instead of stubbornly adhering to what are, or at least are thought to be, objectional peculiarities, such modifications are made of it, as the voice of the Church requires, we still have a book of which we need not be ashamed...."[36]

To give Bomberger the benefit of any doubt, the following things must be said: he was not as "liturgical" as his "esteemed brethren" from the beginning, and he admitted as much to Steiner.[37] He wanted a "medium liturgy", which, by his definition, was far from anti-liturgical. The Provisional Liturgy was loose enough in its construction--offering a variety of forms--and it provided sufficient liturgical latitude in the rubrics to satisfy Bomberger's tastes; therefore there is no reason to disbelieve him when he argued that with a few minor changes the Provisional Liturgy would satisfy his desires completely. For this reason Bomberger felt he could endorse the Liturgy and urge its use by the congregations.

After the publication of the Provisional Liturgy, Bomberger waited to see how it would fare with the denomination. As has been noted above, it did not quickly capture the imagination of most of the clergy and was not being used with any frequency in the worship of the congregations. From the first Bomberger was interested both in liturgical unity (not necessarily uniformity) and in a Lord's Day service which would be widely used; therefore his initial argument that the Provisional Liturgy should be revised need reflect nothing more serious than his realistic appraisal of the extent to which the Liturgy was not being used and, apparently, not meeting the needs and desires of the denomination. In making this judgment Bomberger assumed that the people were the ultimate standard of what was proper liturgically and that they were capable of determining their own liturgical needs. He would never have accepted Thomas Apple's remark in a letter to his brother, Theodore: "The only real difficulty with our people, after all, is the apparent novelty of the new order of worship. The people will have no difficulty with the doctrines, but with their order of intelligence, any change must be affected slowly, and gradually. The Revised Liturgy will stand, but it will require time to introduce it. Our people are more governed by habit and custom, than an intelligent judgement as to a proper order of worship."[38]

The more questions Bomberger raised, the more abuse was heaped upon him by Nevin, Schaff, Harbaugh, Gerhart, and Steiner--all close personal friends for many years. Simply put, the more abuse the madder he got, and the madder he got, the further Bomberger moved from his medium-liturgical moorings, until he was finally making charges and advocating positions quite inconsistent with his own earlier statements.

Sufficient question had been raised concerning the constitutionality of the Provisional Liturgy that the Synod of 1860 appointed a committee to study "discrepancies between certain forms in the New Liturgy and the Constitution". The conclusion was that since the Constitution was "a changeable system of rules", it could not become the norm for a liturgy; therefore the committee recommended that the church now take

up the question of revision of the Liturgy, in order that it
might be sent to the Classes for approval. It will be remembered that the Synod of 1857 made no resolution concerning
the Liturgy; rather agreed to follow the recommendation of
the liturgical committee that the church use the book for a
period of ten years before any action was taken. The Synod
of 1860, however, resolved "that the Provisional Liturgy be
submitted to the several Classes of this Synod for their
examination, and that they report their views upon the same
to the next meeting of Synod".

If the *Weekly Messenger* had not labored previously under
the weight of articles concerning the Liturgy, this action by
the Synod provoked a veritable deluge of debate in its columns.
As noted above, Bomberger first drew blood on March 27, 1861,
when he charged that "some peculiar views privately enter-
tained, but not current in the Church, were allowed so far
to prevail, as to secure admission into it [the Provisional
Liturgy]".[39] Steiner and even Fisher quickly pointed out that
if so, then these "peculiar views" also went out under Bomberger's own "imprimatur". Gradually these exchanges forced
Bomberger to articulate precisely what he desired in a liturgy and what he despised in the Provisional Liturgy. In
answer to his own question--"What keeps it [the Provisional
Liturgy] from being generally used?"--Bomberger replied that
the first "peculiarity" and the one most offensive to the Reformed tradition was the *responsive* form of public worship".
What may be liturgically proper is of little consequence, for
the people clearly do not want the responses. The great
length of some of the forms and "we might, at the same time
add, their didactic character, which probably led to their
being made so long" was a second objection. Especially the
sacramental forms were too "intricate" "for congregations not

long trained to its use". His final objection was to "certain sacramental doctrines, and high church views"--particularly ministerial absolution, baptismal regeneration, and "the priestly character of the ministry". The first and last of this trio of concerns are a part of the Mercersburg doctrine of the ministry discussed above and to be developed further subsequently in this chapter. Baptismal regeneration was a question often debated. Mercersburg's high doctrine of the church and sacraments created not a little discomfort among many in the German Reformed Church, Bomberger chief among them. On more than one occasion Nevin stated flatly that he did not believe in baptismal regeneration "in the sense of a change necessarily brought about at the time in the recipient of baptism".[40] In baptismal grace, however, Nevin declared a firm belief. "With baptism, as with the Lord's Supper, Nevin evidently believed in an objective communication of grace which was not, however, effective apart from faith";[41] yet neither Nevin nor Schaff was anxious to attempt an explanation of the mechanics of that grace. The confusion in Bomberger's mind was the difference between Baptism as grace-bearing and Baptism as the source of grace. Mercersburg never claimed the latter, as this rhetorical question posed by Gerhart makes clear: "Is the moon the source of light because it reflects the light of the sun?"[42] In spite of all the printed words exchanged on the matter, the subject was never satisfactorily clarified for Bomberger, who steadfastly maintained that the forms for Baptism in the Provisional Liturgy and the *Order of Worship* implied baptismal regeneration.

Regardless of these criticisms, which appear rather extensive, Bomberger concluded that "it would probably not cost $50, certainly not more than $100, to make the alterations proposed, in the stereotype plates of the Provisional Liturgy".[43] A month and several articles by Harbaugh and Steiner later, Bomberger again summed up his desires in a single sentence: a liturgy with "no responses for the ordinary Lord's Day service--no baptismal regeneration in such terms as have latterly gained some currency among us-- and no priestly absolutions in the form adopted in the Provisional Liturgy".

The reports from the Classes to the Synod of 1861 were inconclusive for either side. Fisher summarized them in this fashion:

> 1. All the Classes seem to desire a Liturgy. There is no word to the contrary.

> 2. Eight out of the eleven [three did not report] verbally approve of the general plan of the present Liturgy....

> 3. Four express the wish to have it remain under its provisional form for the remaining seven years.

> 4. Eight express the judgment, that, before its final adoption by the Synod, it should undergo a revision by the original committee. Each Classis' action upon it suggests its own changes, additions and commissions; we notice but three that refer to responses, one wishing them omitted in the burial service, and to some extent from the other forms also; one wishing some of them erased from the devotional services, excepting the Litany, and the answers in the Baptismal service, and one desiring them omitted from the regular Sunday services.

The Synod then resolved:

> That the Provisional Liturgy be placed in
> the hands of the original committee for
> final revision; and that the committee be
> instructed to consider the suggestions of
> the Classes as given in the minutes of
> their late meetings, and use them in the
> revision of the work, as far as the gene-
> ral unity of the work will allow, and in
> a way that shall not be inconsistent
> either with established liturgical princi-
> ples and usages, or with the devotional
> and doctrinal genius of the German Reformed
> Church....[44]

Nevin attempted to resign from the committee, still having
"no heart for it", and fearing that the Church would refuse
to accept the revision;[45] however, Synod did not accept his
resignation. He may have also anticipated that Schaff would
become less an influence in the work of revision and that the
bulk of the work would fall on his own shoulders—which is
precisely what occurred.

It became known to Harbaugh and Gerhart that Schaff did
not plan to attend the first meeting of the revision committee,
called for Lancaster on January 6, 1862. Harbaugh's letter of
December 15, 1861,[46] strongly urged Schaff either to come to
the January meeting, or to postpone the meeting until he could
come. Bomberger and F. W. Kremer had been writing letters to
several members of the denomination and to those members of
the liturgical committee whose support they hoped to receive,
and this activity alarmed Harbaugh. "If, at the first meeting, things should be inaugurated that compromise the life of
the Liturgy, it will be more difficult to make them right
after they have placed themselves by that means on a kind of
vantage ground....Now suppose Dr. Nevin does not attend, and

you [Schaff] are absent, what can the rest do?" Gerhart shared Harbaugh's concern, and wrote to Schaff on December 30, 1861:[47] "As the chairman of the committee you ought by all means to be present to participate in the discussions, give your own views, answer objections, and aid in reaching a conclusion that may be satisfactory to all."

The reason for Schaff's absence is nowhere explained. Apparently he was neither sick nor otherwise engaged. If the latter, then the meeting could certainly have been postponed. Rather it appears that Schaff determined not to become deeply involved in the revision--perhaps because he was weary of the whole affair and felt that others should do the work of revision (He did recommend to Synod that an entirely new committee be appointed to revise the Provisional Liturgy.); or perhaps he already anticipated his subsequent resignation from the Seminary (1865). Although Schaff did attend seventeen of the fifty-five revision sessions, the first meeting began on January 6, 1862, without him.

At the first session a plan of revision was suggested; however, upon Bomberger's arrival for the second session, the meeting was occupied "in a free discussion of the general principles according to which the revision should be conducted". Harbaugh made this entry in his diary on January 8, 1862: "Committee sat again. Discussion but no progress in the work. All the discussions are in a friendly spirit, but Dr. B[omberger] raises side issues, and is only bent on revolutionizing the whole work into a puritan shape."

Gerhart's letter to Schaff dated January 23, 1862, is an important summary of the difficulties within the committee and of the two schemes of worship which were so clearly at odds:

Dr. Bomberger took position, in effect,
against the *principle* of the Provisional
Liturgy, or the entire scheme of worship
which under-lied the book; but aimed his
objectives chiefly against the responses.
We argued against him from the instructions of Synod, 1852, and the character
of the resolution adopted by the Synod
of Easton [1861] referring the book to
the Committee for Revision; maintaining
that Synod authorized a Liturgy on the
general basis of the ancient Liturgies
and modified by the Reformation Liturgies so as to be adapted to the needs
of the present age; that the Provisional
Liturgy embodied this idea, and could
not be revised on any other basis; that
a majority of the Classes approve the
plan and substance of the book; and that
the Easton resolution was a reaffirma-
tion of the original Instructions. On
the other hand he maintained that, in
his opinion, the Instructions required
us to make the Reformation Liturgies
the norm of the new Liturgy, and have
reference in the formation of it, to
the ancient Liturgies, that the great
majority of the Church disapproved of
the distinctive character of the work,
especially the responses; that the
action of the Classes must be interpreted as indicating general dissatisfaction with the responses; that the
trial of four years by the Church was
a proper test of its availability and
adaptation to its wants; and that the
Easton resolution sustained the correct-
ness of his views of the whole question. [48]

A complete impass was reached; therefore at the sixth
session the following resolution was passed:

Whereas in the endeavor to revise the
Provisional Liturgy the Committee discovered after a long discussion, pro-

tracted through several days that there is
a radical difference of opinion among its
members, concerning the import of the instructions of Synod, therefore, Resolved
that the Rev. Dr. J. W. Nevin prepare a
report to Synod setting forth a clear,
definite and full idea of both schemes of
Worship advocated in Committee, in order
that Synod may understand the real question
at issue and state in explicit terms what
it requires at our hands.[49]

Nevin complied and presented his report (*The Liturgical
Question*) to an adjourned meeting of the committee in Lebanon
on April 23, 1862. The report was adopted--Bomberger dis-
senting--and ordered published in preparation for its presentation to Synod.

In anticipation of the debate Schaff knew would ensue
at Synod, he sought to summarize the position of the committee
for the denomination in a lengthy article in the *Weekly Messenger* for May 14, 1862. It could hardly be said that he
was entirely objective in presenting the case; however, his
purpose was more to persuade than to inform. He did make it
clear that the debate concerning responses is not an insignificant matter, for it "involves the more general question, which
is now properly before the Church and must be met by the next
meeting of Synod: Shall the new Liturgy be a book of forms
only for the use of the pastor in the study and on the pulpit
(like the Mayer Liturgy and others of the same character), or
shall it be a book of the pastor *and people* for common worship (like our hymn-books, and the first German Reformed
Liturgy made in Switzerland)?" The majority of the committee
felt that their position was sustained both by the Synod of
Baltimore (1852) and the Synod of Easton (1861); however, in
fairness to the minority of one the committee decided to

present the case before the Synod of 1862 and to abide by
its decision.

That decision was arrived at only after two days of
continuous and caustic debate. Since *The Liturgical Question*
had been published in June, 1862, the delegates to Synod had
had ample opportunity to familiarize themselves with it.
Nevin stated Bomberger's position as briefly and unappeal-
ingly as possible, describing it as "simply a mechanical
directory of the manner in which the services of the sanctuary are to be conducted, with written forms of prayer and
other public address, more or less full, thrown together in
an outward and prevailingly independent way".[50] "There is,"
Nevin claimed, "in some way an ominous affinity between free
worship and free thinking in religion...."[51]

By contrast, the liturgical theory of the majority
argues that

> ...a liturgy is not just a collection of
> prayers and other single forms of devo-
> tion, but a whole order or scheme rather
> of public worship, in which all the parts
> are inwardly bound together by their having
> a common relation to the idea of the Chris-
> tian altar, and by their referring them-
> selves through this always to what must be
> considered the last ground of all true
> Christian worship, the mystical presence
> of Christ in the Holy Eucharist.[52]

Such a theory implies that the "sacramental principle" governs
the liturgy throughout--i.e., the Eucharist becomes "a single,
grand system" around which the entire liturgy revolves.[53]
The theory implies, as well, a "priestly character"--i.e., the
focus of worship is the altar rather than the pulpit.[54] So,
too, must the liturgy revolve around the Church Year and the

Apostles' Creed.[55] And, finally, this liturgical theory necessitates the "active co-operation of the people, along with the officiating minister, in its services"--i.e., responses with the body and the voice".[56]

Nevin then proceeded to evaluate the Provisional Liturgy in light of the above principles. He argued that the sixteenth century cannot be the liturgical norm for the Reformed tradition simply because the times were not conducive to "the production of good liturgies". At Baltimore the Synod established the early church as the liturgical norm, with special reference to the sixteenth century, of course, and the Provisional Liturgy has fulfilled that directive.[57] Granted, the Liturgy has not come into general use; yet neither has it been adequately tested.[58]

It was readily admitted, also, that the majority of Reformed liturgies have been of the pulpit variety--such as Bomberger was presumably advocating--however, the question Nevin put to the Synod is this: "Must the past liturgical practice of the church, so far as there has been any such practice, control our universal worship now?"[59] The Provisional Liturgy

> ...is not after the pattern strictly of any system of worship which has prevailed hitherto in the German Reformed Church either in this country or in Europe. It makes no such profession or pretence. It aims to be an improvement upon this whole past cultus, by which it is to be made more thoroughly liturgical than ever before....It is a question of very material change in our church practice, if not in our church life. The new Liturgy is for us, as a Church, in many respects, a new scheme of worship. It is not the pattern according to which our fathers worshipped, either in these United States or elsewhere.[60]

(It will come as little surprise to learn that this statement was quoted back to Nevin *ad infinitum*.)

Nevin's answer to his own question is that Synod may change the liturgical plan entirely if it wishes; however, the Provisional Liturgy cannot be fundamentally changed. "Like a work of art, it has in this view its own plan, and is governed throughout by its own reigning idea....As a work of literature at least, if nothing more, let the Liturgy live."[61] In the final analysis, "the question with us, as we stand at present, is not whether we shall have an altar liturgy or a pulpit liturgy--a liturgy with responses, or a liturgy without them--but whether we shall have a liturgy in any form or shape whatever".[62]

The Synod of Chambersburg (1862) marked the first full discussion of the merits and demerits of the Provisional Liturgy, and tempers were high. Immediately after Schaff made the majority report, Bomberger surprised the committee and the Synod by requesting permission to offer a minority report. The protocol of this move resulted in a lengthy debate, for Bomberger had not informed Schaff that such a report was to be forthcoming. Nevin insisted that it be heard; therefore both Bomberger's report (signed also by Heiner and Fisher) and *The Liturgical Question* were *read* to the Synod.

Before discussing the contents of the minority report, an important parenthesis concerning Heiner and Fisher will be helpful. As noted in Chapter IV, Heiner was a cooperative, if conservative member of the liturgical committee and initially expressed no serious objections to the Provisional Liturgy. In fact, he seemed rather pleased with it. Something occurred between 1857 and 1862, however, to change

Heiner's mind completely. Perhaps he came to his conclusions alone; more likely he was one whom Bomberger managed to influence. Whatever the reason, he wrote to the liturgical committee on April 21, 1862, to this effect:

> I have carefully weighed, I think the whole subject, and am more and more convinced that the Provisional Liturgy in some important particulars is at variance with the spirit, history, and customs of the Reformed Church. I desire this to apply especially to the *responsive* forms in the New Liturgy. Our [illegible word] and German Churches from the Reformation down seem to have virtually rejected them. The Liturgy in question was brought to the notice of the Church under the most favorable circumstances, and yet after a fair trial of four years, only three congregations, I believe ([illegible word], Lebanon, and Burkettsville) out of more than 600 have introduced the responsive form of public worship....Our people have no taste or inclination for, or patience with, such innovations (may I say?) upon the practices of their fathers....I think that by simply erasing the responses, and abridging some forms, and modifying some doctrinal expressions, and omitting the declaration of the remission of sins, and adding a service for sea, thanksgiving, fast days, etc., we would have a book to meet our wants, and promote our peace.[63]

Heiner's death the following year precluded any further personal influence he might have had on the course of liturgical revision; nevertheless his name added prestige to Bomberger's cause.

Part of the interesting story of Samuel R. Fisher has already been told in connection with the printing of the Provisional Liturgy. As late as April, 1857, Fisher still

believed that M. Kieffer & Co., the Synod's printing firm,
would publish the Provisional Liturgy. Since Synod had con-
tracted with M. Kieffer & Co. to publish all the denomination's documents, Fisher refused to pay the "bonus by way of
inducement for the *privilege* of printing" the Liturgy, as
the committee had requested.[64] Acting quite on its own
authority, the committee then turned to Lindsay & Blakiston
in Philadelphia. In short, Fisher was enraged. The next
year Schaff further angered him by publishing his *Deutsches
Gesangbuch* privately. A bitter interchange took place between the two men in the *Weekly Messenger* for January 5, 1859.
In an effort to defend his and the committee's actions, Schaff
insisted that Fisher would never have been placed on the
liturgical committee had Synod foreseen "at that time [1852]
that, instead of helping the Committee, you would prepare a
Prayer book of your own and publish it just a few months before the Church's book was expected to appear". Fisher
"corrected" Schaff's memory as to the reason he was placed
on the committee--*viz.*, to see the work through publication
and nothing more--then defended his publication of "The Family
Assistant", claiming that he had no intention of "trespassing
upon the province of the Liturgy".

The fact that the pages of the *Weekly Messenger* from
1859-1862 literally teem with articles *critical* of Mercersburg in general and the Provisional Liturgy in particular can
hardly be an accident. Fisher was mad and knew well how to
use his editorial position to influence the opinion of the
denomination. His signature on the minority report was, then,
no surprise.

The report itself was subsequently published in the
Weekly Messenger, October 29, 1862. It offers four principal
reasons for objecting to the consensus of the majority:

(1) The directions given the revision committee by the Synod
of Easton (1861) specified that the revision be "not inconsistent either with established liturgical principles, and
usages, or with the devotional genius of the German Reformed
Church". In Bomberger's opinion, the Provisional Liturgy is
clearly not within the German Reformed tradition; therefore
to maintain it would be inconsistent with the directions of
Synod. (2) *The Liturgical Question* does not fairly state
both sides of the issue. (3) Nevin's report attempts "to
persuade the Church to repudiate the principles of its past
cultus...." For example, the Provisional Liturgy at least
permits free prayer; whereas the majority report "explicitly
disapproves of all such subjective libertinism". (4) Bomberger completely disagrees with Nevin's argument that to
modify the Provisional Liturgy "would destroy [its] integrity or unity".

To illustrate his liturgical desires Bomberger submitted
to the Synod a "Revised Provisional Liturgy". As Fisher describes it:[65]

> The first 128 pages of the Provisional
> Liturgy are not changed. The responses
> are omitted from all the forms except
> that for Good Friday, though even here
> the minority hesitated, fearing the abuse
> and perversion of their admission; yet
> they ventured to allow them to stand be-
> cause of the peculiar solemnity of the
> day. In the forms of absolution or com-
> fort the expression 'I declare' etc. is
> changed to read 'the Gospel declares'
> etc. In the communion service the
> address to the communicants, except the
> first paragraph, is substantially the
> same as that in the Palatinate Liturgy.
> In the baptismal service, instead of the
> first form given in the Provisional Litur-
> gy, the minority report gives the whole

> main form from the Palatinate Liturgy.
> Also the form for adult baptism is from
> the same source.

The Communion service was probably the one which Bomberger submitted to Schaff in 1852.

To highlight the discussion at the Synod and then summarize it, one may fairly say that no new positions emerged. Throughout, Nevin and Schaff held their now familiar position: either the Provisional Liturgy or something entirely different --i.e., do not seriously modify its plan and scheme. Fisher and Bomberger both argued that since the vast majority of the congregations had not adopted the Provisional Liturgy, they must not want it. Schaff countered that the statistical argument was a "sophism". The Provisional Liturgy sold more than any other liturgy attempted by the denomination (4,000 copies); furthermore, it was being used more in the homes than in the congregations; Harbaugh suggested bluntly that the question was not what the people want anyway; rather what they need. Foulk argued his familiar thesis that it took 100 years to make the people what they are today, and it is therefore foolish to expect them to change in 10 years. Nevin made a lengthy defense of the doctrine of sacramental grace, articulated by the Provisional Liturgy and found entirely unacceptable by Bomberger: "Is ordination more empty than the paper commission of an officer of the government? In and after baptism, is a man just where and what he was before? Is there no room for speaking of an actual transfer from the one kingdom to another?" Schaff argued at length that responsive worship was indeed the Reformed tradition; and that, contrary to Bomberger's charge, he was personally in favor of the maintainance of free prayer and would not support a liturgy which excluded it. Rust reported that the Western Synod had over-whelmingly defeated a resolution to introduce the Provisional Liturgy into its congregations. G. B. Russell (also from the Western Synod) as much as called Rust a liar, since the reso-lution to which he referred was defeated by only two votes.

In short, the entire discussion, if faithful reporting can be assumed (and there is no reason to doubt it), was bitter and prolonged; nevertheless, it made the Synod and the denomination aware of the depth of the division, even if an immediate answer was not clear. Elder William Heiser's simple question for information regarding the committee's contractual arrangement with Lindsay and Blakiston permitted the antagonists to silence their theological guns and settle the issue on the basis of a moral obligation to honor the ten-year contract with the publisher.

> Whereas, It appears after full discussion
> of the subject, that the way is not open
> for the Synod to take any further action
> in regard to the Provisional Liturgy,
> therefore *Resolved*, That the optional use
> of it, as heretofore allowed among our
> churches, be suffered still to continue
> till the end of ten years from the time
> of its first publication, and that the
> whole question of its revision be now
> indefinitely postponed.

This resolution carried by a vote of 43 to 13. Although the margin of victory for the Mercersburg position was decisive (better than 3 to 1), it cannot be interpreted as overwhelming support for the concept of the liturgy as argued by Nevin and Schaff. A Mr. Giesy, for example, clearly was not in favor of the Provisional Liturgy; rather: "What most affects me is the moral obligation of Synod to Lindsay and Blakiston. I am sorry to say, yea."

Whatever the dynamics, there the matter stood until the General Synod,[66] organized in 1863 in an effort to bring the East and West closer together, requested the East to proceed with its revision of the Provisional Liturgy, and the West to continue with the preparation of its proposed liturgy; so that the two liturgies could both be before the church at the next meeting of General Synod (1866).[67] The Eastern Synod complied with General Synod's request and appointed a committee of revision in 1864. It is interesting to note that in spite of Schaff's plea for an entirely new committee (made during the discussions of 1862), the original committee was reappointed with the additions of T. G. Apple and L. H. Steiner--both Mercersburg advocates! Here, then, begins the story of the revision of the Provisional Liturgy.

The *Order of Worship*

Procedures of Revision

The revision committee held six meetings and forty-five sessions, as follows:

I.	Lancaster:	3-7-65 to 3-9-65	sessions 1-6
II.	Lancaster:	6-13-65 to 6-17-65 . . .	sessions 7-15
III.	Frederick:	8-16-65 to 8-18-65 . . .	sessions 16-21
IV.	Lancaster:	12-5-65 to 12-7-65 . . .	sessions 22-27
V.	Lancaster:	3-6-66 to 3-8-66	sessions 28-35
VI.	Lancaster:	3-24-66 to 3-28-66 . . .	sessions 36-45

No fundamental changes were made either in the particular services or in the general structure and design, as a comparison of the Table of Contents will show.[68] The major design changes

came in the order or sequence of certain of the services.
Harbaugh sums up the process of revision as essentially one
of abridgment:

> The principal changes, so far as the com-
> mittee proceeded, are in the way of abridg-
> ment. Thus, the Scripture passages fur-
> nishing warrant for the different parts of
> worship from p. 7 to p. 14 [Christian Wor-
> ship], were stricken out as having served
> their purpose. In the Primitive Forms
> verbal corrections, corrections in punctua-
> tion and in capitalizing were made; and all
> notes, marginal or under the headings, and
> all Scripture references, were omitted as
> not essential in a Liturgy. The Table of
> Scripture Lessons from page 30 to page 33
> is in like manner omitted, since all here-
> in contained is repeated in connection
> with the Lessons and Collects....[69]

More forms were added than omitted. As noted above, the
section of Scripture readings (Christian Worship) was omitted,
as were the Guide to Private Devotions and the Hymns. The
only specific services to be omitted were the three optional
forms for the Lord's Day. These omissions afforded sufficient space to include several of the services which were
originally considered for the Provisional Liturgy: the
Evening Service, Prayers and Thanksgivings for Special Occasions, a Service to be Used at Sea, and an Order of Scripture Readings for the Family. The result was a volume of
288 pages,[70] which will now be examined in detail.

General Structure and Design

Title: An Order of Worship for the Reformed Church.
Action on the Title was saved for the final session of the
committee on April 28, 1866, when it was unanimously adopted.
"The word liturgy has become offensive to many persons and in
view of that fact, the work was called simply, 'An Order of
Worship for the Reformed Church'."[71] If this was in fact a
consideration of the committee, it may well reflect a growing
realization that in the matter of details, at least, political
awareness was necessary.

Table of Contents: Although there must have been one,
the particular rationale for the change in sequence of some
of the services is not readily apparent. Certainly the abridg
ments Harbaugh described were designed to make the *Order of
Worship* a more compact volume, whereas the additions had been
long desired by many in the denomination. The Liturgy remains
a unit, ruled throughout by the Church Year; and, as shall be
shown below, the several services bear an even more direct
relationship to the Eucharist, as the dominant and controlling
focus for the entire worship of the Church--regular and occasional.

The Church Festivals: Steiner was responsible for pre-
paring the table for determining Easter and the Table of the
Movable Festivals from 1867-1890, according to the minutes of
June 15, 1865.

A Table of Scripture Lessons: A sub-committee of Steiner
Zacharias, and Bomberger was appointed on March 8, 1865, to
prepare "a Calendar of Scripture readings for the Sundays and
Festivals of the Christian Year" and also "a Calendar for
family use". On April 25, 1866, "'The Table of Scripture
Lessons for all the Lord's Days Throughout the Year', containe

in the Book of Common Prayer as revised by the Westminster Divines, was adopted." In short, the committee adopted the lectionary entirely from Shields' *Presbyterian Book of Common Prayer*.[72] Old Testament readings were now regularly available, and a series for evening worship was provided.

The Regular Service on the Lord's Day: On March 8, 1865, the committee resolved that "the four services for the Lord's Day be stricken out with a view to reconstruction....The Committee then, in accordance with a resolution, proceeded to discuss the principles and order which should control the preparation of the Lord's Day service." Following a series of resolutions governing the structure of the Lord's Day service--e.g., "That the General Petition of the Second Series in the present Liturgy be the general basis of the General Petition in the Proposed Lord's Day Service."--the committee then appointed a sub-committee of four "to prepare a Lord's Day Service, in accordance with the resolutions already adopted concerning its structure." That sub-committee consisted of "the members resident in Lancaster (Rev. Dr. J. W. Nevin, Rev. Dr. B. C. Wolff, Rev. Dr. E. V. Gerhart, and Rev. Prof. Thos. C. Porter)". On June 15, 1865, Nevin reported the Lord's Day office, and, "after hearing same, the Committee was instructed to introduce the Thanksgiving Prayer as early as possible in the General Prayer". Further instructions were given the sub-committee at the following session, and the matter was referred to them for further work. On August 17, 1865, during the brief meeting in Frederick, Maryland, the Lord's Day service was finally adopted. The internal changes will be detailed below.

The Evening Service: On April 18, 1866, Harbaugh wrote to Steiner: "I have finished an Evening Service after faithful labor on it, and Br. Apple thinks it a success. What the

committee will say is to be seen. I believe it is not bad."[73]
On April 26, 1866, Steiner moved that the committee "proceed
to adopt 'An Evening Service' from materials collected by Dr.
Harbaugh. After sundry considerations and alterations it is
as follows...." Harbaugh's manuscript of this form, dated
April 18, 1866, is extant in the archives of the committee.
The two working copies include a curious combination of Harbaugh's and Steiner's hands. It is quite possible that Harbaugh submitted the form to Steiner early in the meeting which
began in Lancaster on April 24, and together they composed the
form which was finally submitted to the committee. In any
event, Harbaugh definitely did the basic work and Steiner
assisted in the final edition.

The Litany: The Litany is unchanged from the Provisional
Liturgy, except that it is now printed separately as a form in
its own right, following the pattern of both the Catholic
Apostolic Liturgy and the *Book of Common Prayer.* This was
ordered by the committee on April 28, 1866.

Prayers and Thanksgivings for Special Occasions: On
March 9, 1865, Bomberger and Fisher were assigned the prayers
for special occasions. Realizing that he had no support
among the other members and was not likely to get any, Bomberger refused further cooperation with the committee in a
letter dated December 6, 1865. Apple was then given the responsibility for the occasional prayers; however, most of the
prayers were reported in Bomberger's familiar script. He was
definitely responsible for the following prayers: For the
Opening of a Synod or Classis; In Time of Pestilence; In Time
of War (adapted from the Catholic Apostolic Liturgy); For the
Conversion of the Jews; A General Thanksgiving ("Compiled from
Shield [*sic*]"); Thanksgiving for Harvest ("Compiled from
English Occasional Service and Diarium Pastorale"); For

Deliverance from Death ("Chiefly by Shield [*sic*], with the last sentence added"). On April 25, 1866, these prayers were placed in the hands of Porter and Steiner for examination.

The Gospels, Epistles, and Collects for the Church Year: The *Order of Worship* retains all of the Gospel and Epistle readings and the Collects from the Provisional Liturgy, with the addition of new readings and a new Collect for the Second Sunday after Christmas. On March 8, 1865, Nevin and Harbaugh were appointed a sub-committee to revise the series of readings and Collects, and on March 9, 1865, Harbaugh and Apple were assigned the Festival Prayers. On December 6, 1865, Steiner was assigned the readings for review, and was also directed to change the "titles of the 24th, 25th, 26th, and 27th Sundays after Trinity to 'The Fourth Sunday from the end of the Church Year'," etc. On the same day Gerhart and Porter were assigned the preparation of the Festival Prayers.

Preparation for the Holy Communion: Nevin was responsible for the revision of this form, according to the minutes of December 6, 1865. His report consumed most of the two sessions on March 6, 1866.

The Holy Communion: A detailed analysis of this form will be given below; however, it may be said here that its revision was the work of the entire committee. No individual or sub-committee was assigned the specific task, with one exception: Harbaugh was responsible for the opening rubric and for the Scripture sentences to be read during the Offering (December 5, 1865).

Baptism of Infants, Private Baptism of Infants, Baptism of Adults, and *Confirmation* were all referred to Harbaugh for revision, according to the minutes of December 7, 1865.

Marriage: On March 9, 1865, Wolff and Porter were assigned this form for revision. Certain stylistic changes

were made, principally the addition of an address "given in
the Book of Common Prayer as amended by the Westminster
Divines, pages 308, 309, 310"--i.e., Shields.

Ordination and Installation of Ministers: These services were initially placed in Schaff's hands for revision,
according to the minutes for December 7, 1865; however, as
shall be shown in the detailed discussion to follow, Nevin
also was involved in the revision.

Ordination and Installation of Elders and Deacons:
Porter was made responsible for the revision of these services on December 7, 1865. They were discussed and adopted
on April 26, 1866.

Excommunication and Restoration: Gerhart, author of
these forms in the Provisional Liturgy, was given the responsibility for their revision on December 7, 1865. He
reported to the committee on April 25 and 26, 1866. Essen-
tailly no changes were made in the forms.

Visitation and Communion of the Sick: On March 9, 1865,
the committee entrusted Harbaugh with the examination and revision of these forms. He wrote to the committee on June 10,
1865, that "the revision of the Service for the Communion and
Visitation of the Sick, committed to me alone, has been
attended to. The principal prayer in the Visitation of the
Sick has been reconstructed. You will find it in the manuscript."[74] These changes occupied the committee on June 16,
17, 1865. No fundamental alterations were made; however, it
is interesting to note that "the Confession and Declaration
of Pardon [in the Communion of the Sick] were made to conform
to those employed in the Office of the Holy Communion",
according to the minutes for December 5, 1865. This was a
further effort on the part of the committee to express the
centrality of the Eucharist for the entire Liturgy.

The Burial of the Dead.   The Burial of Members of the Church: The first form was assigned to Porter for revision. Except for the addition of one prayer, the service was substantially unchanged.

The Burial of Children: This brief grave-side rite is new to the *Order of Worship* and was assigned to Harbaugh at the final session of the committee, with the provision that it was to be reviewed by the Lancaster sub-committee before printing.

A Service to be Used at Sea: As noted above, this service is new to the *Order of Worship*; and, according to the minutes of March 9, 1865, and April 27, 1866, it was the work primarily of Steiner. So, too, did Steiner report the *Prayers and Thanksgivings for Special Occasions at Sea* and the brief *Burial of the Dead at Sea.*   In a further effort to coordinate and unify the several services, most of the prayers in the Service to be Used at Sea are taken from the regular Lord's Day form.

Public Reception of Immigrants: Harbaugh was assigned this form for revision. It was reported and adopted on March 8, 1866.

Laying of a Corner Stone: On June 17, 1865, Wolff was assigned the examination and revision of this form. On March 8, 1866, Gerhart was assigned the revision of the final prayer in this service. The changes are slight.

Consecration of a Church: On June 17, 1865, Gerhart was assigned this form for examination and revision. The only significant changes are in the Psalms, which are printed responsively in the *Order of Worship*.

Consecration of a Burial Ground: Porter was to examine the Consecration of a Burial Ground, according to the minutes of June 17, 1865; however, Wolff reported the revisions

(which, again, are slight) on December 6, 1865. Steiner
made the antiphonal arrangement of the Ninetieth Psalm.

An Order of Scripture Readings for the Family: This
table was assigned to Steiner and Zacharias on March 8,
1865, and was reported by Steiner and adopted by the committee on December 6, 1865. It bears some resemblance to
the monthly table in Shields' *Presbyterian Book of Common
Prayer*;[75] however, the selections are original for the most
part. The scheme is constructed around the Christian Year.
The first lesson provides substantial readings in course
throughout most of the Old Testament books, while the second
lesson is chosen principally from the New Testament to illustrate the theme of the Christian Year. This table combines
the best of the pericope and the *lectio continua* systems.

Prayers for the Family: The family prayers were reduced from two series to one by a sub-committee of Harbaugh,
Apple, Zacharias, and Steiner. At the last session of the
committee, "it was resolved that the final revision of the
'Family Prayers'..." be entrusted to the Lancaster sub-committee.

The Canticles, Psalms and Ancient Hymns: The committee
came late to their decision not to include a section of hymns;
therefore, it was only at the last session that the resolution
of the Canticles, Psalms and Ancient Hymns was made. Harbaugh
and Steiner "were authorized to complete the preparation of
the Canticles and Psalms and to report their work to the Committee of Publication".

Theological and Liturgical Examination of Forms

The Regular Service on the Lord's Day

In spite of the several changes made in the Lord's Day service, it is nevertheless defensible to say that the character and nature of the service remains the same. The following order may be compared with that on pages 220-221 above:

> Solemn Declaration
> Call to Confession
> Confession (corporate)
> Declaration of Pardon
> Apostles' Creed
> Versicle
> Gloria in Excelsis
> Gospel
> Epistle
> Gloria Patri (responsive)
> Salutation
> Collect
> General Prayer (thanksgiving, prayers for
>   redemption, church, country, all sorts
>   and conditions of men, supplication)
> [Festival Prayer]
> Psalm or Hymn
> Sermon (to follow the Church Year)
> Prayer (no longer the option for free
>   prayer)
> Lord's Prayer
> Alms
> Announcements
> Psalm or Hymn / Doxology
> Apostolic Benediction

The *Order of Worship* omits the opening anthem by the choir and the invocation, the second declaration of pardon, and the Pax. The general sequence of readings and collect is changed and the Lord's prayer is moved from the general prayer to the prayer after the sermon. While the minutes of the committee record action on all these changes, no rationale is given for any of them.

The Call to Confession is new to the *Order of Worship*, and is composed of 1 John 1:8-9 and a free rendering of the *Book of Common Prayer*. The Confession prayer is the committee's adaptation of Nevin's prayer in the Provisional Liturgy, which, by action of the committee, was made to conform to the Confession in the Eucharist. Here is still another example of the committee's intention to make the Eucharist the focus of the entire Liturgy. As noted above, the second Declaration of Pardon in the Provisional Liturgy is omitted, and the first one is retained essentially intact.

The Creed, Versicle, and Gloria in Excelsis follow the Provisional Liturgy. So, too, is the sequence of Gospel and Epistle maintained in the *Order of Worship*; however, the Collect now follows the Gloria Patri and Salutation. For reasons not given, the committee resolved on March 9, 1865, "that the General Petition of the Second Series in the present Liturgy be the general basis of the General Petition in the proposed Lord's Day Service". Apparently no significance should be attached to this decision, since Schaff was originally responsible for both sets of prayers—the committee simply preferred the second series to the first. The Thanksgiving is that from the *Book of Common Prayer*, and the second prayer for redemption was apparently composed by the sub-committee for the *Order of Worship*.

As in the Provisional Liturgy, the entire service is conducted from the altar until the Psalm or Hymn prior to the sermon, at which time the minister enters the pulpit. The rubric has been changed, deleting the advice concerning the length of the sermon—but retaining the specification that the sermon "should be in harmony with the general order of the Church Year". On June 15, 1865, "the committee was ordered to prepare a prayer which, with the Lord's Prayer, shall follow the sermon...." Thus the two collects take the place of Schaff's prayer in the Provisional Liturgy, and the Lord's Prayer follows. This sequence is found in neither the Catholic Apostolic Liturgy nor in the *Book of Common Prayer*.

The two most important decisions made by the committee in regard to the Lord's Day service were the omission of alternative forms and the intention to relate the service more directly to the Eucharist. In the latter decision, as has been noted above, the committee pointed to the Eucharist as central even on those occasions when it was not celebrated. In omitting the alternative forms, the entire Liturgy became more internally consistent and more expressive of Mercersburg theology; however, the last possibility was removed for those sharing Bomberger's "medium liturgy" sentiments to make use of the *Order of Worship*. Even the token gesture of free prayer, included in the Provisional Liturgy, was omitted in the *Order of Worship*; and, somewhat surprisingly, no opportunity for free prayer was afforded in the Evening Service. These decisions clearly moved beyond the Baltimore proposals, as Bomberger was quick to point out.[76] They specified, it will be remembered, that the Lord's Day service "should embrace several forms... some with and without responses"; and that "a Liturgy ought not to interfere with the proper use of extemporaneous prayer", especially in the afternoon and evening services. The committee—sans Bomberger—definitely decided to proceed on principle with no concession to politics at this point. In the section to follow the results of that decision will be apparent.

The Holy Communion

The most obvious change in the Eucharistic order is in its structure, as the following outline will indicate:

> Solemn Declaration
> Call to Confession (The same as in the revised Lord's Day service.)
> Confession (Essentially the same as in the Provisional Liturgy.)
> Declaration of Pardon (The same as in the revised Lord's Day service.)
> Nicene Creed
> Versicle
> Gloria in Excelsis
> Gospel
> Epistle
> Gloria Patri
> Salutation
> Collect
> Festival Prayer
> Psalm/Hymn
> Sermon
> Offering (The sentences were provided by Harbaugh.)
> Collect (The opening collect from the Provisional Liturgy.)
> Scripture Sentences (Following the opening collect in the Provisional Liturgy.)
> Salutation
> Sursum Corda
> Gratia Agamus
> Consecration Prayer (Essentially the same as in the Provisional Liturgy with the minor exception noted below.)
> Distribution (The same as in the Provisional Liturgy.)
> Benediction on the communicants (The same as in the Provisional Liturgy.)
> Post Communion
> Te Deum
> Benediction (The above three items are all from the Provisional Liturgy.)

The opening portion of the service indicates a return more to a Reformed than to an Anglican pattern, as reflected in the Provisional Liturgy--i.e., the Confession and Declaration of Pardon begin the service in the *Order of Worship*--and it is coordinated with the order for the Lord's Day. The Exhortation, familiar to both the Anglican and Reformed traditions, is omitted, likely in an attempt both to reduce the length and the didacticism of the service. Bomberger was quick to point out, however, that the Exhortation was "the only distinctive point of contact between the [Provisional Liturgy] and our ancient mode of administration of the Holy Supper...."[77] The rubrics remain essentially the same in the *Order of Worship*; and, as noted above, the Consecration Prayer is preserved intact with one exception: for no explicable reason the prayer of oblation was reduced nearly to one-half its original length. This is unfortunate by any liturgical-devotional standard, since most of the anamnesis and expectation have been removed. The idea of self-oblation made through the one, perfect sacrifice of Christ remains in the *Order of Worship*, but in a severely truncated form.

These, then, constitute the principle changes in the Holy Communion.

Ordination of Ministers

With minor exceptions the Ordination of Ministers is identical in the Provisional Liturgy and the *Order of Worship*. The form was discussed by the committee on March 8, 1866, at which time Nevin was instructed to review the ordination questions. He reported on April 24, 1866. The final sentence in the second question was omitted: "And do you consent unto the system of Faith set forth in the three Creeds, commonly called the Apostles' Creed, the Nicene Creed, and the Athanasian Creed?" Presumably it was thought that the essence of the question was covered in the third question concerning adherence to the "confessional system of the Heidelberg Catechism". This question was also slightly re-written.

To summarize: several significant changes made by the revision committee resulted in a prayer book more internally consistent, and one more completely expressive of the Mercersburg theology. Alternative forms were omitted; and all services were related more directly to the Eucharist, thus the better expressing its centrality. As suggested above, certain of these revisions did not fulfill the Baltimore proposals—e.g., omission of alternative forms, free prayer, and hymns; neither were they politically expedient. It seems, however, that Nevin and the committee determined rather to proceed upon the basis of what they considered to be liturgically correct, regardless of the consequences; and without Bomberger to deter them, little else stood in their way.

Results of the *Order of Worship*

Eastern Synod of 1866

The debate at the Eastern Synod in 1866 was not so protracted or vitriolic as that which marked the Synod of 1862; however, Bomberger once again presented a minority report, stating "the reasons for his having been unable to co-operate with the committee during the past year, or to unite with them in rendering their final report".[78] This report was not incorporated in the Synod minutes; however, it can be found in *The Revised Liturgy*, published by Bomberger in time for the meeting of General Synod later in 1866. Essentially his position is that the *Order of Worship* is more ritualistic, not less, as it should have been. Furthermore, it is not what the Synod ordered, nor is it in harmony "with the devotional and doctrinal genius of the German Reformed Church". As has been noted above, Bomberger is correct in certain of his criticisms--*viz.*, that the *Order of Worship* does not entirely conform to the principles as outlined at Baltimore in 1852, especially in regard to optional forms and free prayer. He equates "more ritualistic" with the multiplication of responses, and by this definition he is also correct in his observation, if not his complaint. His perennial charge that the two Liturgies are not in harmony with the devotional and doctrinal genius of the German Reformed Church is not so clear cut, nor is Bomberger quite so convincing. He insists that Nevin took the early church--i.e., the church of the fourth and fifth centuries--as his model, rather than the primitive or Biblical church; and everyone knows (according to Bomberger) that by the fourth century doctrines were perverted. Instead one should take the worship of the New Testament as his model, for there it is discovered that worship is "subjective" and Word [i.e., preaching] centered. Inevitably Bomberger's criticism reaches a climax in his familiar argument that to forsake the worship of the (*American*) Fathers will unquestionably bring the church to ruin: "And so our beloved Zion would be as a woman bereaved of her children, and sit solitary and forlorn in her desolate places, as a widow stripped of her glory, and covered with the sackcloth of her shame."

The minority report apparently had little effect on the
Eastern Synod. A committee was appointed to examine the
majority report and the *Order of Worship*. Its presentation
to the Synod consisted of a lengthy summary of the history
of the liturgical action of past Synods, leading up to these
resolutions:

> That our thanks are due, and are hereby
> rendered to the great Head of the Church,
> that this work, so far as Synod is con-
> cerned with it, has been brought to a
> termination.
>
> That the thanks of the Synod are hereby
> tendered to the committee, for the zeal,
> ability and unrequited toil which they
> have displayed in the prosecution of
> their work, from the beginning to the
> end.
>
> That the *Revised Liturgy* be referred to
> the General Synod for action, and that,
> in the mean time, the optional use of
> the *Revised Liturgy* be authorized, in
> the place of that of the Provisional
> Liturgy, within the limits of the
> Eastern Synod, until the whole question
> be finally settled by the various
> Classes and the General Synod, accord-
> ing to the Constitution of our Church.[79]

The final clause of the last resolution caused some debate;
however, it was passed by a vote of 53 to 14.

General Synod of 1866

In these lines penned by the warrior, Harbaugh, to his
friend, Steiner, the whole of the General Synod debate is
capsuled:

> You have all the news from Dayton! What a
> panic--what a storm--but it is all over,
> and the skies are brightening. You missed
> a rich scene, and a heroic battle.[80]

The "rich scene" and "heroic battle" lasted for eight
sessions, two and one-half days, and was occasioned by the
following events. It will be recalled that the General
Synod of Pittsburgh (1863) instructed the Eastern Synod to
revise the *Order of Worship* and urged the Synod of Ohio to
proceed with the preparation of another liturgy. Both were
to be presented to the General Synod of 1866. The Ohio Synod
was able only to report progress: no complete liturgy had
been finished, but "a number of forms, however, have been
prepared and published, the optional use of which has been
authorized by the Synod of Ohio and Adjacent States within
its bounds".

The majority report of the Eastern liturgical committee
was then presented, which, in view of Ohio's tardiness in
completing its work, resolved to allow the Western Synod to
continue its work; and further:

> that the Revised Liturgy reported to this
> Synod by the Eastern Synod...is hereby
> allowed as an Order of Worship proper to
> be used in the congregations, and families
> of the Reformed Church.
>
> That this action is not designated to
> interfere in any way with that freedom,
> which is now enjoyed in regard to the
> Liturgy, by all such ministers and congre-
> gations as may not be prepared to intro-
> duce it in whole or in part.

In short, the Eastern Synod asked the General Synod to maintain the status quo until the Synod of Ohio completed its
liturgy.

The now familiar minority report was entered by J. H. Good (professor of theology in the German Reformed seminary at Tiffin, Ohio), David Winters, Edward Swander, and V. C. Tidball. It listed fifteen reasons why the Synod should not endorse the *Order of Worship*. Essentially these amounted to the arguments that the Liturgy was not consistent with Reformed liturgical history; that it could not be introduced into the congregations without division and strife; that it would necessitate a change in church government were it to be effective; that it is doctrinally impure; that it would separate the German Reformed Church from its sister denominations; and that it would have a detrimental effect on missions. Therefore, the minority resolved that the Provisional Liturgy and the *Order of Worship*, along with the specimen material produced by the Synod of Ohio, be referred to a special committee "with instructions to prepare such an Order of Worship (or Liturgy) as shall be in harmony with the doctrinal and devotional principles and genius of the German Reformed Church, and adapted to her present needs and circumstances...."[82] The principles by which the committee should be guided are interesting:

> 1. The doctrines of the German Reformed Church, as set forth in the Heidelberg Catechism and the Liturgical Worship of the Reformation period, as set forth in the Palatinate Liturgy of 1563, and other Reformed Liturgies, shall be made the general *basis* of the proposed Liturgy. [Note: no mention at all of any liturgical point of reference prior to the sixteenth century.]
>
> 2. Those portions of the Liturgy which are most frequently used, such as the morning and evening service on the Lord's

> Day, the celebration of the Lord's Supper,
> Baptism, etc., shall embrace several forms,
> agreeing in substance and spirit, so as to
> adapt them the more readily to the varied
> conditions and wants of our congregations
> at the present time.
>
> 3. The Liturgy shall be so constructed as
> not to interfere with the proper use of
> extemporaneous prayer, either in public
> or private; but rather so as to regulate,
> improve and promote it.[83]

The reader will recognize in the second and third of these
principles an unmistakable echo of Baltimore fourteen years
earlier.

The substance of the discussion which followed the two
reports is chronicled in the *Weekly Messenger*.[84] From this
abbreviated debate it is clear that the Western Synod had one
goal--to "kill" the *Order of Worship*--and two different means
of achieving it. It was first argued that the provisional
use of a liturgy upon which the Synod had not passed was unconstitutional. If Synod must approve a hymnbook before it
was used, how much more a liturgy; therefore, J. H. Good insisted that Synod voice its approval or disapproval of the
Order of Worship and send it to the Classes for their vote.
It was assumed, thereby, that the Classes would reject the
Order of Worship. Failing this, the West's second plan was
suggested by Williard (prominent member of the Western
liturgical committee and editor of the *Western Missionary*)
and is incorporated in the minority report: the creation of
a new committee which would attempt a compromise revision.
This was totally unacceptable to Nevin and company, of course,
who had insisted throughout the liturgical conflict that the
church could reject the *Order of Worship* if it chose, but it

could never compromise the plan and principle upon which it
was constructed. The specific complaints against the *Order
of Worship* were not new--save for the argument that "ritualistic" worship would necessitate an Episcopal form of
government. Familiar doctrinal points were raised in connection with the Eucharist, sacramental grace in Baptism,
and absolution and the priestly character of the ministry
in the Ordination service.

The East was hardly unaware of the West's strategy. So,
too, were Nevin and Harbaugh not unaware that they were defending their cause on their opponents' home ground--Dayton,
Ohio. Apple and Nevin both underscored the presumptuous
discourtesy in the Western Synod's attempt to "mutilate,
deface, and change" the Eastern Synod's Liturgy, without
even having produced one of their own. Nevin hastened to
defend the doctrine in the *Order of Worship* and went on to
suggest that Bomberger's charge of a liturgical committee
conspiracy implied that past Synods had been duped and were
too ignorant to know it.

Bomberger's reply, if accurately reported, was entirely
emotional--a prelude to *Reformed, Not Ritualistic*, issued
the following year. "I hate this book [the *Order of Worship*]," he said, "because it seeks to subvert and sap our
foundations. It seeks to reduce our evangelical religion to
formalism, stiff and starched."[85] Regarding Nevin's explanation of the Eucharist in the *Order of Worship*, Bomberger made
this statement--one he would never have made had he not been
seeking effect: "I could not see any essential difference between the representation of the Lord's Supper given this
morning [by Nevin] and the Romish Mass."

The question was finally called on Thursday, December 7,
1866, at 7 p.m. First, the minority report: it was defeated

55 to 66. The majority report was passed by only 7 votes: 64 to 57.

> Dr. Nevin was well pleased that the liturgy
> had survived so great an obstacle. It
> should be remembered that since the meeting
> of the General Synod took place at Dayton,
> Ohio, the western part of the Church had
> more of their delegates present at the
> meeting than did the Eastern Synod. If the
> meeting had taken place in the East, the
> liturgy would probably have won the day
> with a much greater majority of votes.[86]

Harbaugh voiced a similar sentiment to Schaff: "Many Eastern delegates were not there, but the West were out to a man, and the Western delegates were elected with a view to defeat the liturgy."[87]

The *Order of Worship* had won a hard-fought lease on life: it could be used provisionally for at least the next three years; but how was it introduced, and with what success?

Introduction and Reception

It is somewhat difficult for one a century removed from the liturgical conflict to get an accurate picture of the manner in which the *Order of Worship* was introduced to the denomination and the extent of its reception and use. Not unexpectedly each side was anxious to interpret the facts in light of its own case. Certain defensible conclusions are possible, however. For example, the liturgical committee did learn one important lesson: do not antagonize the journalists in the denomination. On February 20, 1863, Apple wrote to Schaff that he favored M. Kieffer and Company as the publisher

for the *Order of Worship*, "especially since Dr. Fisher yields
the old point and offers a bonus".

> If we give it to the [Printing] Establish-
> ment, we will please the Church at large,
> I think, and not displease the few who may
> have better taste, provided it is respect-
> able in appearance, as I have no doubt it
> will be. It will circulate somewhat out
> of the Church, but *mainly in it*. The Es-
> tablishment have facilities for its en-
> couragement and circulation in our Church,
> which no other firm has. *Besides it will
> conciliate and heal old wounds*--and as it
> is the first book given to the firm, I
> think they ought to have it.[88] [Italics
> mine.]

It is interesting to note that Fisher did a complete
turnabout between 1862 and 1866. After joining Bomberger
and Heiner in the minority report of 1862, Fisher reversed
himself and played a significant role in defeating the
attempt of the Western Synod to block the *Order of Worship*
at the General Synod in 1866. "In the discussion, Dr. Fisher
...explained why he had opposed the Provisional liturgy but
now endorsed the Order; for he says he had been charged with
being a traitor. The Provisional liturgy, he said, had no
unity in it. This [the *Order of Worship* is a unit--one system
--one order of worship. It is far better than the Provisional
and is the result of a compromise."[89]

Perhaps Fisher did make the change through a critical
liturgical analysis; however, the decision of the liturgical
committee, as early as April 24, 1862, to contract with Moses
Kieffer & Co. (i.e., the Printing Establishment) for publication of the revised liturgy, and the tactful manner in which
Fisher was invited to the meeting of the committee on April 27,

1866, to explain the details of publication, did nothing to impede his change of heart. The results of this turnabout by Fisher can be seen in a letter from Thomas Apple to his brother, Theodore, dated April 21, 1867:

> Dr. Fisher has stiffened up most wonder-
> fully. He is straight up and down with
> the anti-liturgical party, makes them all
> father their own article. [It was the
> custom to submit articles to the *Weekly
> Messenger* under a pseudonym.] Under
> this requirement Franklin Kremer [vocif-
> erous in his denunciations of Mercers-
> burg and the *Order of Worship*] squirms,
> who had some half dozen [articles] sent
> on under different signatures....Fisher
> seems to go ahead of us all in zeal--as
> a new convert. George Welker sent a
> scurrilous article against Dr. Nevin
> through Weist. Fisher would not touch
> it.[90]

Members of the committee were also sensitive to the charge that they wanted to force the *Order of Worship* into congregations which did not wish to use it, with the result that, if anything, they went out of their way not to press the issue at any point. Of course, the reason for Bomberger's concern and his attempt to prevent the further provisional use of the Provisional Liturgy or the *Order of Worship* was his fear that within ten to fifteen years the youth would be edu- cated in ritualistic ways through the Sunday Schools, while the younger clergy would be "brainwashed" through use of the liturgies in the Seminary. To counter such a charge, Wolff made this point during the heated discussions of the Eastern Synod in 1862: "Our counsel to them [the students] is this: Do nothing to interfere with the harmony and peace of your congregations; do not introduce the liturgy without the full consent of your people. The faculty would scorn to force it upon you; so should you deal with your people."[91] Responding to the same general criticism, Gerhart said this to the General Synod, 1866: "I have never advocated it [the *Order of Worship*] especially, and shall not introduce it into the congregation I serve, unless they desire it. But it is fair to give it a trial."[92] These may seem strangely curious positions for men who had so recently involved their time and energy in the composition of two liturgies; however, they could hardly have adopted any other. Furthermore, however impractical it may seem today, their philosophy was simply to publish the liturgies, then wait and see what results might follow, apparently believing that if they were of God, they would somehow succeed; if not, then they would fail.

J. S. Foulk was one of the few men who persistently maintained a level head throughout the liturgical dispute; however, there is no evidence that his mature and scholarly articles in the *Weekly Messenger* and the *Mercersburg Review* were heeded. He was definitely in the liturgical camp; but he was also a wise and sensitive pastor. His thesis was that to force even a correct liturgical form on the people is "'to sin against the brethren and wound their weak conscience'." The people

> ...must be prepared by cultivating in them a liturgical spirit....It is impossible to rise at a bound, or by a single effort to the dignity of a Liturgy, which to be adequately admired requires a spirit in sympathy with its forms, and an order of piety which finds its highest and happiest strains of devotion in its fixed channels. The people must be educated and prepared to regard forms of prayer in precisely the same light, in which they look upon familiar psalms and hymns....[93]

Use of the *Order of Worship* as reported by the *Weekly Messenger* reflects the same general pattern as was seen in connection with the Provisional Liturgy. Between February, 1867, and August, 1869, the *Order of Worship* was reportedly used in at least the following churches: (all in Pennsylvania unless otherwise indicated)

> *Ordination--Installation:* Bethlehem;
> Millersville, Jefferson, Md.; Landisburg;
> Duncannon; Taneytown, Md.; Allegheny City.
>
> *Dedication--Consecration:* Meadville; St.
> Paul's, Armstrong Co.; First Reformed,
> Baltimore, Md.; Brady's Bend; Altoona;
> Emanuel, Baltimore, Md.; Clear Spring, Md.;
> Strawberry Ridge, Emittsburg, Md.
>
> *Cornerstone:* Allentown; Emittsburg, Md.;
> Littlestown; Mt. Union.
>
> *Preparation and Eucharist:* Emittsburg,
> Md.; St. Thomas.

The general or complete introduction of the *Order of Worship* is reported in the following locations: Jonestown; Newport and Bloomfield, St. Stephen's Chapel, Franklin and Marshall College; First Reformed, Allentown; Green Castle; Third Reformed, Baltimore, Md.; Frederick, Md.; First Reformed, Lancaster; Norristown; Mercersburg; Bedford; Petersburg.[94] While the occasional services were clearly used most often, the notable difference between reported uses of the Provisional Liturgy and the *Order of Worship* is the greater number of congregations which initiated a general introduction of the Liturgy. Nevertheless, the number, while encouraging to the liturgical advocates, was relative, and Nevin reported in the *Weekly Messenger*, September 15, 1869:

> It is now perfectly plain, if it has not
> been before, that no Liturgy can be intro-
> duced among us, and made to be of general
> binding force, by Church authority. How
> far the *Order of Worship* might have got
> before the people, and gained their favor,
> if no hue and cry had been raised against
> it, no one, of course can say....Enough
> that the hue and cry has been raised, and
> that it has had its effect....It must be
> admitted that the general introduction of
> the book is now out of the question.

The "hue and cry" had indeed taken its toil. So far as
the public debate was concerned, little was accomplished
following the General Synod in 1866, except further to fray
feelings long since tattered. The myriad articles which still
flooded the *Weekly Messenger* were by the same protagonists and
antagonists, arguing the same lines. Nevin and Bomberger each
contributed another volume[95,96] after the meeting of General
Synod; however, both simply reiterated long established positions. Bomberger's work is noteworthy only in this respect:
it reveals the extent to which he had become almost completely
emotional, advocating positions and making allegations his
maturer mind would not have countenanced. He openly charged
that the Synods which approved the designs of the two liturgies
were "out of order, as they were giving approval to a constitutional change which can only be approved by the Classes".[97]
Considerable time was spent on the old argument that Nevin had
forsaken the German Reformed "Fathers", leading Bomberger to
this spurious conclusion: if Ursinus and Olevianus were
qualified to produce the Heidelberg Catechism, which Nevin
lauds, then they were certainly qualified to write an equally
perfect Palatinate Liturgy.[98] Leaving his more defensible
argument for a "medium liturgy" far behind, Bomberger contended
for a subjective form of worship, word-dominated, preacher-

centered, and liturgically free. He permitted himself gross
misrepresentations of the *Order of Worship*: "No one," he
claimed, "can be forgiven, until he has come to the minister
at the altar, there confessed his sins, and thus obtained
pardon".[99] After once stating that the Christology of the
Mercersburg school was its one unassailable feature,[100] he
now insisted that the Heidelberg Catechism proved conclusively that "Christology is not central to the Christian faith"
and that "the incarnation was for the purpose of something else
--namely, atonement".[101] In short, according to Bomberger,
Nevin's "system" is "mechanical, material, or magical".[102]

The Myerstown Convention

The significant events following the General Synod of
1866 occurred privately, not publically. In February, 1867,
an informal conference of those opposed to the *Order of Worship* was held in the house of Emanual Kelker in Harrisburg,
at which time it was decided "to call a general conference of
those opposed to the Liturgy; to found a college; to start a
monthly paper to defend their principles".[103] The activities
leading up to the convention were kept secret, as those
opposed to the *Order of Worship* worked silently in search of
support for their cause. Their manner in this regard was
severely questioned by Fisher and others, who claimed that
often one minister was found "tampering" with another minister's members.[104] In August, 1867, "Plain Member" reported
a "rumor" that a call was being circulated for a convention
"in order to take measures to rid the Church of the great
'Liturgical evil'."[105]

The "rumor" was correct, for on September 24, 25, 1867, 225 ministers and elders (34 ministers, of whom two were from the West) gathered in Myerstown, Pennsylvania, for the purpose "of protesting against the innovations of the Revised Liturgy, as a standard of faith and order of worship in the Reformed Church".[106] The names of Bomberger, F. W. Kremer, and Herman Rust (of the Synod of Ohio) were the most prominent among those directing the acts and proceedings of the Convention. The specific complaints are not new: the *Order of Worship* is not in the Reformed tradition; it has been introduced into congregations without their approval (Harrisburg, Pittsburgh, and Waynesboro were the only congregations named); it has been introduced in the seminaries and schools of the denomination (which belong to the *whole* denomination); continued use of the *Order of Worship* will eventuate in great loss of membership--both clergy and laity (the fact that two of Nevin's sons had joined the Episcopal Church was used as evidence); and, since ministers have now been educated in the "new worship", they and the Synods to which they are delegates no longer represent the majority of the people. Delegates to the Myerstown Convention wanted to make it clear that they were not "anti-liturgical"; rather that they were "liturgical in the sense of our Reformed Church".

The acts and proceedings of the Myerstown Convention were presented to the Eastern Synod in 1867; however, the Synod refused to receive the papers. Rather the Convention was denounced as unconstitutional and potentially schismatic, and a pastoral letter was adopted to be sent to all the congregations in the Synod. After reviewing the actions of the Eastern and General Synods in regard to the *Order of Worship*, the letter stated: "This Synod, after duly examining the proceedings of this Convention, refused to recognize this body, and regarded it as having entered upon an unwise, dangerous, and schismatic course of action in relation to the Church."[107]

The Myerstown committee continued, however, and began the publication of the *Reformed Church Monthly* in 1868, with Bomberger as the editor. Out of the actions of the Myerstown Convention also came the purchase of Freeland Seminary in Collegeville, which became Ursinus College in 1870, with Bomberger as president.[108] A schism had been narrowly averted; however, the feelings which prevailed on both sides were harsh and bitter. Rival congregations were formed and personal friendships broken. "The line of cleavage was definitely drawn, which revealed itself in practically all the agencies and activities of the Church. There was a general scramble to get control of vacant pulpits and to secure membership on the important Boards and Committees of the Church."[109]

Throughout 1868 the debate in the *Weekly Messenger* primarily concerned the pros and cons of the Myerstown Convention; while 1869 was a relatively quiet year in the denominational press, as everyone was apparently awaiting the appearance of the Western Liturgy and the meeting of the General Synod. It was convened in November, 1869, in Philadelphia, and featured a slightly abbreviated version of the General Synod of 1866.

General Synod of 1869

The West now had their Liturgy,[110] which was presented to the Synod by George W. Williard, a member of the committee. Apple, Bossard, Nevin, Ermentrout, and Small, constituted a committee for the purpose of examining the Liturgy, recommended

that General Synod now grant permission to the churches to
use either of the liturgies now before it, and that neither
be sent to the Classes for action, since "We do not believe
that the Church is prepared to unite on any one now."[111]

Western parliamentary strategy had not changed, and a
substitute motion was made: that the two liturgies "be
submitted to the several Classes for their approval or disapproval" permitting the optional use of both in the meantime; and that "neither of these Liturgies, however, shall
in any case be introduced in the regular order of service
without the formal consent of the Consistory and congregation".[112] As Apple analyzed this action, the purpose of the
substitute was "to send the two liturgies down to the Classes
for adoption or rejection, a course which, it was known, would
in all probability result in the non-adoption of either. The
friends of the *Order of Worship* wanted no legislation *for* it,
but they were concerned that there should be no legislation
against it."[113]

The stage was set for another debate after the fashion
of the General Synod of 1866; however, as it was reported by
the *Weekly Messenger*, December 22, 1869, the "discussion"
reflects the fact that neither side had anything new to say
and both were tired of saying it. On Wednesday morning,
December 1, 1869, the vote was taken on the substitute. It
was defeated by 106 nays to 74 yeas, with 2 *non-liquets*.
The original report was adopted by a vote of 117 yeas to 52
nays--a substantial defeat for Bomberger, Good, Rust, Williard
and company, and one which gives support to the claim of some
that the vote on the same question at the General Synod of
1866 would have been substantially larger had the Synod been
held in the East. The result, then, was a standoff; yet the

effect was a decided victory for the advocates of the *Order of Worship*, who still sought time for it to "win its way with the people".

The Western Liturgy

Since it is not the purpose of this essay to document the complete liturgical history of the German Reformed Church in the nineteenth century, only brief comments of a general nature will be made regarding the Western Liturgy. A letter from Herman Rust to Bomberger, dated February 6, 1864, reveals that the latter assisted the Western committee; and that fact alone should give adequate indication of the general nature of the book.[114] Were one to analyze the liturgical thought of Bomberger, the Western Liturgy would be a primary source, since it likely conforms to many, if not all, of his later liturgical desires. The "Preface" tells it all: This work "is designed to be, in the old Reformed sense, *a directory and guide* for the proper and orderly conduct of the public worship of God". It is not intended that the forms provided "shall be of binding force, either as a whole or in part, to the exclusion of free devotional services; but that *Pastors may here find a help and guide to the proper and spiritual discharge of their duty*". In no way is the Liturgy "to interfere with free, or extemporaneous prayer; but rather to improve, regulate, and promote it" according to Apostolic example "and the obvious preference of the great body of our people at the present day".

As Apple stated in his review of the Western Liturgy, it is a pulpit manual or directory, providing the structure

for the services and optional forms to be used at the dis-
cretion of the minister.[115] From the *Order of Worship* the
Festival Calendar is retained, and a lectionary is provided
which is modeled on but not identical with that in the Provisional Liturgy. A section of "ancient liturgical forms"
is provided; however, little opportunity is afforded for
their use. The Lord's Day service illustrates the principal
changes made by the West. Conspicuous by their absence are
confession and absolution, responses of any variety, the
creed, and any attempt to relate the Lord's Day worship to
the Eucharist. Forms are provided for the prayers before
and after the sermon; however, it is explicitly stated that
the prayers may be free. Slifer sums up the relationship
between the orders of the East and West:

> This Western Liturgy was influenced by the
> Eastern order only to the extent that it
> contained a section of ancient forms such
> as the Ecumenical Creeds, the Gloria, the
> Te Deum, the Litany, the Church Year lec-
> tions, but not the Collect for the Day.
> One of the Communion services contains a
> Eucharistic Prayer in modified form.
> Aside from this there is no evidence of
> kinship between the two liturgies. The
> Western Order was strictly a pulpit
> manual for the use of the minister.[116]

The two "tendencies" in the German Reformed Church were
now distinctly two parties, reflecting, as Theodore Appel
observed at the General Synod of 1869, even more a theological
than a liturgical difference; yet around the liturgies the
parties revolved. Labels were plentiful as the opponents
hurled their charges back and forth; and, while it is something of an oversimplification, it may be said, nevertheless,

that the East reflected the "high church" position, the West,
the "low". For more than ten years following the events of
1866-69, the hostility and back-biting continued unabated,
until, wearied by the "war", a Peace Commission was appointed
by the General Synod of 1878. That story will be the subject
of the following chapter.

NOTES TO CHAPTER VI

1. *Constitution of the German Reformed Church in the United States of North America.* (Chambersburg, Pa.: M. Kieffer & Co., 1850), IV: 10.

2. *Ibid.*, IV: 20.

3. *WM*, April 28, 1858.

4. *Constitution*, IV: 22.

5. Letter, George C. Welker to Philip Schaff, January 5, [1857], E & R Historical Library.

6. Nevin, *Vindication of the Revised Liturgy*, p. 25.

7. Nevin's report to the Synod of 1857, quoted in Klein, *History of the Eastern Synod*, pp. 236-237.

8. *WM*, December 30, 1857.

9. John W. Nevin, "The Liturgical Movement," *MR*, I (1849), p. 608.

10. *WM*, June 24, 1868.

11. *WM*, December 8, 1858.

12. *WM*, June 16, 1858.

13. *WM*, December 16, 1857.

14. Letters in the E & R Historical Society.

15. Steiner and Schwing, *op. cit.*

16. E & R Historical Society.

17. Henry Harbaugh, *The Golden Censer; or, Devotions for Young Christians* (Philadelphia: The Publication and Sunday School Board of the Reformed Church in the U.S., 1860).

18. Kieffer, *op. cit.*, p. 218.

19. Letter to Steiner, E & R Historical Society.

20. Henry Harbaugh, ed., *Hymns and Chants: with Offices of Devotion. For Use in Sunday-Schools, Parochial and Week-Day Schools, Seminaries and Colleges. Arranged According to the Church Year* (Philadelphia: Reformed Church Publication Board, 1861).

21. Nevin, *The Liturgical Question*, pp. 51-52.

22. *Ibid.*, p. 52.

23. *WM*, July 7, September 15, 1858; May 22, 29, June 8, August 24, September 28, 1859; June 19, October 23, December 11, 1861; March 26, May 28, 1862; November 9, 1864; February 1, 1865; September 12, 1866. See also entries in Harbaugh's Diary: January 10, April 3, 4, May 22, 1858.

24. *WM*, April 27, 1859.

25. *WM*, April 7, 1858.

26. *Ibid.*

27. *WM*, July 7, 1858.

28. *WM*, January 19, 1859.

29. *WM*, March 30, 1859.

30. *WM*, January 1, 1862.

31. *WM*, March 10, 1858.

32. Kieffer, *op. cit.*, p. 211.

33. J. H. A. Bomberger, "The Church and Charitable Institutions," *MR*, XII, (1860), pp. 64-85.

34. Gerald Hahn Hinkle, *The Theology of the Ursinus Movement: Its Origins and Influence in the German Reformed Church* (unpublished Ph.D. dissertation, Yale University, 1964), p. 111.

35. *Ibid.*, p. 123.

318

36. *WM*, March 12, 1862.

37. Letter, March 1, 1860, E & R Historical Society.

38. Letter, March 21, 1867, E & R Historical Society.

39. *WM*, March 27, 1861.

40. Nichols, *Romanticism*, p. 245.

41. *Ibid.*

42. *WM*, February 12, 1868.

43. *WM*, April 17, 1861.

44. *Acts and Proceedings of the Eastern Synod*, 1861, pp. 34-48, 77-78.

45. Nevin, *Vindication*, p. 29.

46. E & R Historical Society.

47. *Ibid.*

48. E & R Historical Society.

49. *Order of Worship* committee minutes, January 9, 1862.

50. Nevin, *The Liturgical Question*, p. 1.

51. *Ibid.*, p. 15.

52. *Ibid.*, p. 23.

53. *Ibid.*, p. 26.

54. *Ibid.*

55. *Ibid.*, p. 29.

56. *Ibid.*, p. 31.

57. *Ibid.*, pp. 45-51.

58. *Ibid.*, p. 52.

59. *Ibid.*, p. 61.

60. *Ibid.*, p. 62.

61. *Ibid.*, p. 65.

62. *Ibid.*, p. 70.

63. E & R Historical Society.

64. Fisher's letter is incorporated in the minutes of the liturgical committee, following the forty-eighth session.

65. This description is in an unpublished transcript of the liturgical discussion during the Synod of 1862 in the E & R Historical Society.

66. The General Synod of the German Reformed Church in the United States first met in Grace Reformed Church, Pittsburgh, on November 18, 1863. Through the westward migration German Reformed settlements appeared far outside the geographical boundaries of the Eastern or "Mother" Synod--the first and largest of these German Reformed centers being in Ohio. Soon there was a sufficient number of congregations to justify a separate Synod. To facilitate correspondence between these Synods--known popularly as the Eastern and Western --the General Synod was established to meet every three years. It was, of course, the highest judicatory of the denomination, exercising control over the several District Synods.

67. As shall be noted in more detail at the conclusion of this Chapter, the Western Synod found little favor with the Provisional Liturgy, sympathizing more with Bomberger's later position. A committee was appointed by the Western Synod to prepare another liturgy more to its liking, and the action by the General Synod in 1863 simply encouraged both District Synods to proceed with their work in order that the second General Synod could take some action on the two liturgies.

68. Appendix VII.

69. *WM*, March 22, 1865.

70. *An Order of Worship for the Reformed Church* (Philadelphia: S. R. Fisher & Co., Publishers, 1867).

71. Linn Harbaugh, *op. cit.*, p. 245.

72.   Charles W. Shields, *The Book of Common Prayer and Administration of the Sacraments and Other Rites and Ceremonies of the Church as Amended by the Presbyterian Divines in the Royal Commission of 1661 and in Agreement with the Directory for Public Worship of the Presbyterian Church in the United States* (New York: Charles Scribner's Sons, 1864). Shields wrote an essay in 1860 commemorating the bicentennial of the Savoy Conference in 1661. He advocated and subsequently produced a *Presbyterian Book of Common Prayer*, revised in light of the criticisms made of the Anglican *Book of Common Prayer* at Savoy. Hodge "doubted that Presbyterians would ever generally use the book in worship, but gloated over how Shields had made inroads into the exclusive claim of Episcopalians to the *Book of Common Prayer*". [Melton, *op. cit.*, p. 87.] The denomination did not adopt the book, as Shields had hoped, perhaps because he attempted to rush a communion which still resisted any formal action in matters liturgical.

73.   E & R Historical Society.

74.   Letter incorporated in the minutes of the committee.

75.   Shields, *op. cit.*, pp. xiii-xviii.

76.   *The Revised Liturgy*, pp. 39-43.

77.   *Ibid.*, p. 71.

78.   *Acts and Proceedings of the Eastern Synod*, 1866, p. 94.

79.   *Ibid.*, p. 98.

80.   December 10, 1866, E & R Historical Society.

81.   *Acts and Proceedings of the Eastern Synod*, 1866, p. 61.

82.   *Ibid.*, p. 72.

83.   *Ibid.*, pp. 72-73.

84.   *WM*, December 26, 1866; January 2, 9, 23, 30, 1867.

85.   *WM*, January 9, 1867.

86. Binkley, *op. cit.*, p. 107. This interpretation is drawn largely from Nevin's *Vindication*, pp. 46, 47.

87. Letter, Henry Harbaugh to Philip Schaff, December 10, 1866, E & R Historical Society.

88. E & R Historical Society.

89. Good, *op. cit.*, p. 429.

90. Letter, Thomas Apple to Theodore Appel, April 21, 1867, E & R Historical Society.

91. Unpublished typescript, E & R Historical Society.

92. *WM*, January 9, 1867.

93. J. S. Foulk, "Forms of Prayer," *MR*, XV (1868), pp. 149-150.

94. *WM*, February 20, 27; March 20; April 17; May 22; June 12, 19; July 10; August 14, 21, 28; October 9, 16; November 20; December 18, 1867. June 10, 24; July 1, 8, 15; August 5, 12, 22; September 9; October 7, 14, 21, 1868. January 7, 27; February 24; April 14, 28; May 12; June 16; July 14, 21; August 11, 25, 1869.

95. Nevin, *Vindication of the Revised Liturgy, op. cit.*

96. J. H. A. Bomberger, *Reformed, Not Ritualistic* (Philadelphia: Jas. B. Rodgers, 1867).

97. *Ibid.*, p. 52.

98. *Ibid.*, pp. 71-72.

99. *Ibid.*, p. 100.

100. J. H. A. Bomberger, "Dr. Nevin and His Antagonists," *MR*, V (1853), p. 164.

101. Bomberger, *Reformed, Not Ritualistic*, p. 128.

102. *Ibid.*, p. 134.

103. Schaeffer, *History of Philadelphia Classis*, pp. 74-75.

322

104.   *WM*, September 11, 1867.

105.   *WM*, August 14, 1867.

106.   *Proceedings of the Convention of Ministers and Laymen belonging to the German Reformed Church, held at Myerstown, Lebanon County, Pa., September 24th and 25th, 1867* (Lancaster, Pa.; Pearsol & Geist, 1867).

107.   *WM*, October 30, 1867.

108.   Binkley, *op. cit.*, pp. 117–118.

109.   Schaeffer, *History of Philadelphia Classis*, p. 75.

110.   *Liturgy, or Order of Worship for the Reformed Church* (Cincinnati: T. P. Bucher, Publisher, 1869).

111.   *Acts and Proceedings of the General Synod*, 1869, p. 46.

112.   *Ibid.*, p. 47.

113.   T. G. Apple, "The General Synod," *MR*, XVII (1870), pp. 156–162.

114.   J. H. A. Bomberger, *The Reverend John H. A. Bomberger, Centenary Volume*, p. 190.

115.   T. G. Apple, "The Western Liturgy," *MR*, XVIII (1871), pp. 92–114.

116.   M. Slifer, *op. cit.*, p. 239.

CHAPTER VII

The Liturgical Conflict: Resolution and Results

The Mercersburg liturgical controversy was finally resolved, on the surface at least. How was it resolved? What
was the effect of "the thirty-years' war"? Did it have any
abiding influence? These are the questions to which attention is directed in this chapter.

The Peace Commission

During the decade which followed the General Synod of
1869, the controversy within the denomination moved from the
public presses into the back rooms of ecclesiastical politics.
Personal qualification became less the prerequisite for pulpits and positions on the boards and agencies of the church
than the "party" to which the candidate expressed allegiance.
No liturgical business appeared on the docket of the General
Synod in 1872; and the General Synod of 1875 was not anxious
to debate the subject again. In response to an overture from
the North Carolina Classis seeking Synod action "to correct
alleged evils arising from the existing freedom in regard to
the use of two different 'Orders of Worship'," the Synod refused to question the "legitimacy or the wisdom of the Synod's
past action".

The extent to which the denomination had become weary of
the war is to be felt at the following General Synod in 1878,

however. With no advance warning, Clement Z. Weiser took
the floor during the evening session on Monday, May 20, and
read a brief paper pleading for peace, and warning the Synod
of "the impending ecclesiastical suicide, if we bite and de-
vour our inheritance". Weiser had a concrete plan: the
creation of a "Peace Commission", composed of members representing the several District Synods and "proportionally
representing the true tendencies in the Church". The purpose
of the commission would be to devise a plan "guaranteeing
unity in essential, liberty in doubtful, and charity in all
things pertaining to the Church". The proposal was adopted
unanimously and a strategy devised for immediate implementa-
tion, calling on all individuals and "ecclesiastical bodies"
within the denomination to "conduct their business so as to
cultivate and advance the cause of peace and good will".

Following the ancient principle that he who proposes
presides, the Synod made Weiser chairman of the Peace Commission. On behalf of the Commission he presented a three-
part peace plan to the General Synod meeting in Tiffin, Ohio,
in 1881. Ten doctrinal theses were set forth as essential to
unity. With reference to cultus the Commission recommended a
committee "whose duty it shall be to prepare an Order of Worship, containing such offices as may be required for the
services of the Church"--i.e., a compromise liturgy. Pend-
ing the adoption of such an Order of Worship, "the various
Liturgies now in use in the Church [shall] be allowed in
public worship, provided none of them be hereafter introduced into any congregation without the consent of the majority of its communicant members". In short, this amounts to
Williard's minority proposal made at the General Synod in
1866. The Commission further recommended that Synod under-
take a thorough revision of the Constitution. A committee

appointed by Synod to examine the Commission's report recommended its adoption, and further recommended that the members
of the Peace Commission be appointed a committee to carry
out its suggestion in regard to a Directory of Worship.

The Peace Commission--now the Liturgical Commission--
met briefly to organize on May 27, 1881. At that time a sub-
committee of nine was appointed to prepare the *Directory of
Worship*: T. G. Apple, J. H. Good, S. N. Callender, J. M.
Titzel, F. W. Kremer, J. Kuelling, P. Greding, L. H. Steiner,
and C. Z. Weiser. The opposing "tendencies" were fairly
represented within this subcommittee: Apple and Steiner
having assisted in the preparation of the *Order of Worship*,
Good and Kremer having devoted most of their energies since
1866 to foiling its acceptance by the denomination.

Four meetings, each of three days' duration, were held:
November 17, 1881, April 25, 1882, August 8, 1882, and November 20, 1883. The full Commission convened in Harrisburg on
November 23, 1883, to hear the report of the subcommittee;
and, after four days' deliberation, unanimously approved the
revision. The work was presented to the General Synod in
1884, and that body resolved to refer the *Directory of Worship* to the Classes "for approval or rejection". The result
of that action is as follows:

```
        Number of Classes in 1884 . . . . . . . . 52
        Number required to make the Directory
            an "ordinance of the Church" (2/3) . 35
        Number approved . . . . . . . . . . . . 39
        Number rejected . . . . . . . . . . . .  8
        Number approved conditionally . . . . .  1
        Number not reporting. . . . . . . . . .  2
        Number abstaining . . . . . . . . . . .  2
```

The General Synod of 1887 was able to take the following action:

> Whereas, The Directory of Worship has re-
> ceived the affirmative vote of the number
> of Classes required by the Constitution
> for adoption of an ordinance in the Church;
> therefore, Resolved, That the said Direc-
> tory of Worship is hereby declared to be
> constitutionally adopted as the Directory
> of Worship in the Reformed Church in the
> United States.[1]

What was this *Directory of Worship*[2] and how was it received? J. H. Derr, an ardent advocate of the *Order of Worship*, could not contain his tongue during the General Synod
of 1884, and disturbed the "peace" by announcing that "to
adopt this book [the *Directory*] will be to go back one hundred
years".[3] Sixty years later Elizabeth Clarke Kieffer described
the *Directory* as a "hermaphrodite form which satisfied no one,
but which the Synod tried for several decades to enforce as a
required ritual".[4] Morris Slifer, on the other hand, provides
a more tempered description:

> The Directory of Worship of 1884 is very
> much like the Revised Liturgy of 1866 if
> we allow for the following changes: the
> erasure of a few versicles and congrega-
> tional responses which, it was thought,
> gave the old Order a ritualistic charac-
> ter, the altering of several phrases
> which were theologically distasteful to
> some of the brethren and the rubrical
> recognition that there is such a thing
> as free prayer.

A comparison of the Tables of Contents in the *Directory*
and the *Order of Worship* reveals that few changes were made.
Nothing was added by the *Directory*, while the Evening Service
and Services to be Used at Sea and for the Reception of Immigrants were dropped. The Lord's Day Service is indicative of

the principal changes made in the *Directory*. Rubrics specify the points at which free prayer may replace prescribed prayer --e.g., "The congregation standing, the Minister shall begin the service with a free *Invocation*; or, he may say...." In place of the Prayer of Confession from the *Order of Worship*, a modified form of the Collect for Purity may be used. The Assurance of Pardon in the *Directory* removes the much debated declaration of forgiveness; nevertheless, what remains is far stronger than merely a prayer for forgiveness. All responses except the "Amen" are removed; the Creed is printed but optional; and that portion of the rubric in the *Order of Worship* which prescribes that the sermon "should be in harmony with the general order of the Church Year" is omitted. Otherwise, the prayers which are printed and the order of service which is prescribed generally follow the *Order of Worship* exactly.

Essentially the same type of revision is to be found in the Eucharist. Rather than providing a complete service, the *Directory of Worship* directs that the regular Lord's Day order shall be used through the sermon and offering. Responses are omitted throughout--the Salutation, Sursum Corda, and Pax. The Seraphic Hymn *may* be corporate. In the Eucharistic Prayer certain changes in wording reflect the feeling of Bomberger and others that the *Order of Worship* was too "Roman". One example from the Oblation will suffice:

> *Order of Worship:* And be pleased now, O most merciful Father, graciously to receive at our hands this memorial of the blessed sacrifice of Thy Son; in union with which we here offer and present unto Thee, O Lord, the reasonable sacrifice of our own persons....

> *Directory of Worship:* And be pleased now,
> O most merciful Father, to accept our sacri-
> fice of thanksgiving and praise, which we
> here offer unto Thee, in union with this
> memorial of the blessed sacrifice of Thy
> Son....

Curiously, the intercessions have been omitted from the Eucharistic Prayer in the *Directory*. There is no apparent reason
for this excision, save the desire for brevity.

One final change should be noted: the rubric prescribing
the distribution of the elements has been significantly revised.

> *Order of Worship:* While a sacramental hymn
> is sung, the people shall present themselves
> *in front of the altar*, reverently and de-
> voutly standing.

> *Directory of Worship:* While a sacramental
> hymn is sung, the people shall present
> themselves *at the communion table* reverent-
> ly and devoutly standing.

Mercersburg's persistent use of "altar" had long irritated
Bomberger--not without historical justification. The divided
chancel with the separation of pulpit and lectern and the
center aisle reaching its destination and climax in the elevated *altar* fixed to the East wall was the architectural style
Nevin believed the Provisional Liturgy and the *Order of Worship* demanded. He was not ignorant of the distinction between
the connotations of altar and table, and he chose the former
because he felt it better expressed "that mystical union which
takes place between Christ and his people in every act of
Christian worship".[6] Furthermore, he was reacting so strongly
against a pulpit-dominated architecture and worship that he

went to the other extreme. Harbaugh also argued the use of altar instead of table,[7] claiming that this term expressed better the objective action of God in worship generally and the Eucharist particularly. Nichols suggests that Nevin "gave no sign whatever of being aware of the classical Reformed view of this subject".[8]

If Nevin was not aware (a circumstance which this writer cannot conceive), Bomberger certainly was. He claimed, and with not a little justification, that Nevin's concept of sacrifice was propitiatory. By changing the terminology from altar to table Bomberger hoped both to reclaim the historic Reformed note of communion as fellowship and to correct both the ritual and the theology imperceptibly implied in Nevin's unfortunate choice of words. In the *Directory of Worship* Bomberger finally got his way.

It is interesting that only one substantial change was made in the Ordination of Ministers--and that not where one might expect. The paragraph containing the heart of Nevin's doctrine of the ministry was left untouched: "The office is of divine origin, and of truly supernatural character and force...." (See Appendix VI for the remainder of this paragraph.) The single change came in the fourth ordination question. Both *Directory* and *Order* begin the same:

> Are you truly persuaded in your heart, that you are called of God to the office of the holy Ministry, and do you desire and expect to receive, through the laying on of our hands,...

The *Order* proceeds thus:

> the gift and grace of the Holy Ghost, which shall enable you to fulfil this heavenly commission and trust?

The *Directory* reads instead:

> official authority for the sacred office,
> and trust in the grace and aid of the
> Holy Spirit that you may rightly dis-
> charge the duties of your high calling?

It was doubtless felt that in this revision the objective, sacramental nature of the ministry, which the low churchmen so thoroughly opposed, was removed. In retaining the prior paragraph which sets forth Nevin's objective, sacramental view of the ministry, however, the *Directory* succeeded only in creating an inconsistency.

Finally, any comparison of the *Directory* and the *Order* must be made with these two facts in mind: first, the changes made in the *Directory* were more politically than liturgically motivated; second, the extent of those changes was minimal.

Whatever success the peace movement and the *Directory of Worship* had during the decade of the '80's can be attributed largely to Thomas G. Apple, who emerged during these years as both the peacemaker and political strategist par excellence. He carried on a sizable correspondence with the potentially volatile men in the Lancaster-Mercersburg axis,[9] counselling acceptance of the *Directory* and insisting that they must advocate peace and freedom in matters liturgical, else Bomberger would have a legitimate case against them. In one of Apple's letters to Jacob Heyser it is learned that Bomberger worked diligently during the early years of the peace movement to "poison" the members of the Commission and influence them against Lancaster; therefore Apple insisted that communication lines between the liturgical advocates and members of the Commission remain open in order to insure that the position of the former was not misrepresented.[10] Earlier he had written to Heyser: "Much as I love and prefer our Order of Worship, I would be willing to have it modified so that it might be really introduced into our Churches...."[11] To Higbee, Apple insisted that the peace movement must not be allowed to come under Bomberger's influence; however, "We have grown beyond those old kinks which Bomberger has been fighting all along."[12] Once the work on revision began, Steiner complained that the *Order of Worship* was being compromised. Apple replied:

> I agree with you that our work will prove a deformation of the Order of Worship, and the only thing that reconciles me at all to it is, 1st, that it is better to have an inferior liturgy in actual use than a superior one merely in a book that is not used; and 2nd, that we are gaining time to allow prejudices to wear away, so that possibly when our work goes through some years of examination and criticism the Church may yet come to see the superiority of the Order of Worship and become reconciled to its use.[13]

Apparently Bomberger never suspected for a moment that those advocating the *Order of Worship* would accept, let alone advocate, the *Directory of Worship*. If the *Directory* passed General Synod, Bomberger supposed that it would be binding on the more liturgical wing of the church (if they chose to use a liturgy at all), while the rest could then return to free worship. On the contrary, Synod action made the *Directory* binding in so far as the sacraments and ordinances were concerned, without rescinding past actions permitting use of the *Order of Worship*--a parliamentary blunder by any standards. Apple wrote a lengthy letter to Davis, then editor of the *Weekly Messenger*, stating:

The *whole Church* is committed to the Directory, and that is a great deal, considering
how largely that book is a reproduction and
repetition of the Order of Worship. If now
our men use the Directory, it deprives them
[Bomberger, *et al.*] of raising any controversy any more on the subject of the liturgy.
That is one advantage. Then secondly, it
puts us in harmony with the action of the
General Synod, and them in opposition to
said action so far as they refuse to use
the Directory. In the third place, it
divides their ranks, because *some* of their
men *will* use the Directory. That book,
faulty though it may be, will educate right
in the line of the Order of Worship....In
arguing *for* the Directory we have them at
an immense disadvantage; and they feel it.[14]

In truth both sides won something of a victory as the
result of the peace movement and the *Directory of Worship*;
and certainly the denomination was now free to turn its
energies and attention to missions, which it quickly did.
There is evidence, however, that liturgically there was no
real compromise, for "the anti-liturgical congregations
slipped back into the use of 'free worship' and the liturgical congregations got out the 'Order of Worship' again".[15]
Surviving members of the publishing committee for the *Directory of Worship* complained to the General Synod in 1893 that
the *Order of Worship* was still being used, especially in
regard to admission to church membership. The General Synod,
fully aware of the constitutional inconsistency in permitting
use of both the *Order of Worship* and the *Directory of Worship*,
simply turned its back, stating that "in this era of peace
and good will" it would be unwise to open the liturgical
question again, "for unprofitable and unedifying discussion".[16]
Kuhns complained in 1896 that the *Order of Worship* is still
being printed and used.[17]

It is difficult, if not impossible, to make any reliable estimate of the extent to which the *Directory* was actually used. Perhaps a detailed examination of the *Weekly Messenger* from 1887 to 1900 would yield certain clues; however, the virtually complete moratorium on liturgical debate in the denomination's publications, in effect well in advance of the Peace Movement, continued after the General Synods of 1884 and 1887. Furthermore, it can be argued with some justification that public interest in liturgical matters diminished after the Peace Movement. The general works on the German Reformed Church—Good, Appel, Dubbs, and even Richards—barely mention the *Directory of Worship*. Good alone describes it in any detail. He appears to be satisfied that a compromise liturgy was the final result, and shows no interest in the extent of its use. Kieffer's observation (noted above) is likely true: after 1887 the liturgical pattern was simply "to each his own". Only two of the liturgies available to the denomination in 1887 had received the official sanction by the Synod—the Mayer Liturgy and the *Directory of Worship*; however, when the Synod of 1893 refused to restrict the use and continued publication of the *Order of Worship*, the policy of liturgical laissez faire was established. No doubt the *Directory* was used to some extent by both the high and low churchmen, for it did represent something of a compromise between the "opposing tendencies"; yet it is interesting to note that *The Book of Worship*[18] of 1923 "restored most of the responses that had been removed from the liturgy of 1884. It, too, reflects the essential spirit of the Revised Liturgy."[19] Simply put, then, the *Directory of Worship* was a political more than a liturgical success; however, as Slifer suggests, it retained not only the spirit but most of the content of the *Order of Worship*. In retrospect it is clear

that few, if any, of Mercersburg's positive liturgical contributions were seriously compromised by the Peace Movement
and the *Directory*.

With the *Directory of Worship* this German Reformed
chronicle comes to a close; however, a brief review of the
Dutch Reformed and Presbyterian liturgical activity in the
late nineteenth and early twentieth centuries will complete
the pan-Reformed story begun in Chapter III.

The Dutch Reformed Church

The 1873 revision of the Dutch Liturgy[20] received
approval for provisional use by the Synod of 1874; however,
in the following year the Classis of New York argued that
even provisional liturgical forms could not be used without
constitutional amendment. The Synod accepted this reasoning
and sent the revision to the Classes for action. Voting was
slow and not before 1878 was the two-thirds majority obtained.
Printing was even slower than the voting, and the volume was
not available until 1882.[21] This was the first approved
Liturgy of the Dutch Reformed Church to be printed as a
separate book. In light of the 1875 overture by the New York
Classis, it is interesting to notice that certain changes
were made--without Synod action or constitutional amendment--
in the order of the Lord's Day service;[22] however, the 1882
publication is essentially the same as the 1873 revision.

Throughout the series of revisions undertaken by the
Dutch Reformed Church in the nineteenth century, the doctrinal forms--particularly Baptism and the Lord's Supper--had been
virtually avoided. Hageman does not detail the specific
problem; however, widespread disfavor with the Baptism forms

forced the Synod of 1902 to appoint a committee for the purposes of revising the Liturgy of 1882.[23] The committee presented its report in 1903, recommending revisions in the forms
for both Baptism and the Lord's Supper. These recommendations
amounted to little more than abridgments and they were rejected by the Classes. A new committee was appointed, which
suggested further revisions--mainly in the Baptism forms--to
the Synod of 1905. Classes' approval was secured and the
Liturgy of 1906 became a part of the Constitution. Provi-
dentially, according to Hageman, the Synod of 1906 directed
Edward B. Coe, minister of St. Nicholas Church in New York,
to make a selection of prayers to be printed in the Liturgy
for optional use. Through Coe's editorship a number of canticles, morning and evening prayers, collects for the Christian
Year, and a table of Psalms appropriate for the seasons of
the Christian Year were added to the 1906 revision of the
Dutch Reformed Liturgy.[24]

By the turn of the century, then, the Dutch Reformed
Church had expended no little liturgical energy on a series
of interesting revisions; yet the final official result of it
all was disappointing: "The 1906 revision contained nothing
new. It was a very conservative revision made almost solely
in the interest of brevity. There was nothing in it to
create ferment, raise questions and discussion. I suggest,
therefore, that it had a mummifying effect on the liturgical
situation in our church." Nevertheless, the nineteenth century liturgical experimentation was creative, if conservative,
and likely had not a little influence even in provisional
form. "Little as was actually approved by the Synod, the
mere issuance of those provisional books of 1857 and 1873
put forth numbers of new liturgical ideas. Even though Synod
re-called its approval of them, it did not collect the books

together and burn them. The books were out where people read
them, and used them. It is very significant to see how much
material put forward experimentally in one is used in the
next."[25]

The Presbyterian Church

During the latter part of the nineteenth century the
Presbyterian Church still resisted an official book of wor-
ship; however, the denomination's press did publish Archibald
Alexander Hodge's *Manual of Forms* in 1877. In the Preface
Hodge wrote:

> The action of our recent General Assemblies
> from 1873 to 1875 proves that the mind of
> the Church is decidedly averse to the
> recommendation *by authority* of even the
> simplest forms for special services. With
> this jealous care for the freedom and
> spirituality of the Church the compiler of
> this little manual is in perfect sympathy.[26]

He further confessed, however, that adequate verbal preparation
for the "edifying performance of certain special services, as,
for instance, the administration of Baptism and the Lord's
Supper" was necessary. "Any approximation to a uniformity of
method in these particulars which can be secured without the
sacrifice of freedom and adaptability to varying circumstances
will be generally welcomed."[27] The services Hodge presented
were in every way "conformed to the doctrinal principles of
the 'Confession of Faith' and to the regulative injunctions
of the 'Directory for Worship'."[28] To insure that his requirement was met, quotations from the *Larger Catechism, Directory,*

and Constitution were printed on the pages opposite the text.
No form for the regular Lord's Day service was prescribed and
all the prayers, including the Consecration Prayer in the
Lord's Supper, were free except for the brief prayer of supplication in the Marriage service. After the fashion of *The
Westminster Directory*, rubrics specified the general structure of the prayers, such as this for the prayer of Consecration: "Then the minister shall offer a solemn prayer of—
Invocation, Consecration, Confession and Supplication for the
indwelling and communion of the Father and the Son through
the Spirit."[29]

In his Preface to the "new and rewritten edition" of
1882, Hodge acknowledged that "a permanent and somewhat
general demand for it [the edition of 1877] seems to have
been established in the Church"; therefore this considerably
expanded second edition, doubled the size of the first.[30]
Forms were added for the Ordination of Elders and Deacons,
the Dedication of a Church, Scriptures and Prayers for the
Sick Room, Hymns for the Sick Room and for Funerals, the Decalogue, Lord's Prayer, and the Nicene and Apostles' Creeds.
Portions of the Baptism of Infants, Ordination of Elders,
and Funeral forms were taken from the Liturgy of the Reformed
Dutch Church in America.

Melton sums up the result of the myriad private compilations during the latter half of the nineteenth century in this
fashion: "The peculiarities of individual compilations were
causing more and more Presbyterians to see some value in the
denomination itself stepping in to produce a manual to assist
its people in their worship."[31] It took the formation of the
Church Service Society in America in 1897, however, to provide
the impetus for denominational action. A detailed account of
the work of Henry van Dyke, Louis Benson, and others in bring-

ing about the publication of the *Book of Common Worship* in
1906 goes beyond the scope of the present research. Furthermore, the Presbyterian "way" in the nineteenth century has
already been demonstrated. It was, to quote Charles Hodge
again, the "wide and safe middle ground" between an obligatory liturgy, such as the *Book of Common Prayer* and the sheer
liturgical chaos of complete freedom. Such a private compilation as Hodge advocated in 1855 never received sanction by
the denomination, however; and the Presbyterians finally
came to the same general liturgical procedure as had the
Germans and Dutch before them--a committee. The four cri-
teria established by the General Assembly in 1903 are interesting:

> In the first place, the 1903 Assembly felt
> that for a service to be Christian it
> should be biblical; therefore it advised
> using biblical materials and forms and
> keeping the service firmly based on Scrip-
> ture. Second, it thought a service for
> denominational use should embody the basic
> faith and experience of the denomination.
> In the third place, for the service to
> buttress Presbyterianism's claim to a
> place in the universal church it should
> express elements universal in Christian
> experience. Finally, the service should
> avoid being esoteric by relating itself
> consciously to the realities of the life
> of the church members.[32]

Van Dyke had most of the book completed in time for the General
Assembly in 1905. Despite extensive explanations and justifi-
cations of their work, the committee encountered an Assembly
anxious to debate. After three hours of speeches (limited to
five minutes each), the book was recommitted to the committee
for minor revisions and completion of the occasional services.
It was published the following year.

The Preface to the 1906 *Book of Common Worship*[33] took great pains to stress the voluntary nature of the volume: "This book of Common Worship is...not to be taken in any wise as a liturgy imposed by authority. Nor is it a substitute for the Directory of Worship, but rather a supplement to it...." The committee urged that "in those churches which choose to make use of the following Orders and Forms of Service, every member of the Congregation should be supplied with a copy of this Book...." Considering the fear, if not the expressed hostility for such a project in the Presbyterian Church, van Dyke and his committee had remarkable success, and the volume reflects sound liturgical scholarship and a wide range of sources—Calvin, the *Book of Common Prayer*, the *Directory for Worship*, the *Euchologion*, Shields, and the Dutch Reformed Liturgy being among the more conspicuous ones.

In the Lord's Day service one finds a corporate prayer of Confession, Versicles, and the Apostles' Creed. Divisions and subjects are prescribed from the *Directory for Worship*, but the "General Prayer" before the Sermon is free. A rubric notes that instead of free prayer, "the Minister, if he will, may use any of the *Prayers* given in this Book, under the title of *Treasury of Prayers*". The General Prayer concludes with the Lord's Prayer. The "Treasury" includes what Melton describes as a "cautious espousal of the Christian Year"—*viz.*, prayers for Good Friday, Easter Day, Advent, and Christmas. No lectionary is provided in this first edition of the *Book of Common Worship*.

The form for the Lord's Supper draws heavily from the *Directory for Worship* and the *Westminster Confession of Faith*; yet, the service is not lacking in devotional warmth. The Eucharistic Prayer included the Salutation, Sursum Corda, Gratia Agamus, Vere Dignum, and a corporate Sanctus and Benedictus.

The 1906 *Book of Common Worship* is not as extensive or
as complete as the *Order of Worship* or even the *Directory
of Worship*; and, although it does not contain certain of the
faults in the Dutch revision of 1873--e.g., the Confession
and Assurance are in the Lord's Day service and the Communion
service is more historically defensible--neither does it reflect the refinement which comes through a succession of revisions. Nevertheless, drawing upon their own considerable
liturgical sophistication, the many private compilations
offered by nineteenth century Presbyterians, and the experience of their German, Dutch, and Scottish siblings, van Dyke,
Benson, *et al*. produced a Liturgy in 1906 of which their denomination need not have been ashamed.

Liturgical Influence on the German Reformed Church

What was the effect of the liturgical controversy on the
German Reformed Church in the nineteenth century? It is interesting to compare the answers given that question by those
writing during the last stages of the controversy and those
assessing its influence a century later.

Kuhns is typical of those who believed the conflict to
be injurious to the denomination. "During the years of controversy our Home and Foreign Mission work languished, our people
were disheartened, our congregations in many instances were
divided."[34] He then goes on to point to the number of ministers who left the German Reformed Church for the Episcopalian
and Roman Churches, and the number of laity who "found refuge
in sister churches"--principally the Dutch Reformed and Presbyterian Churches. It is true that during the decade of the
'60's the denomination was primarily occupied with liturgical

matters, and this doubtless did have an effect upon missionary interest and benevolence giving; however, to suggest as
Kuhns does that the liturgical controversy was thereby all
bad is hardly an accurate assessment. Apple acknowledged
that the controversy had in some measure impeded the practical activity in the Church, but he disagreed "with those who
think that theological interest and controversy are hindrances
to practical activity in the Church".[35]

The weight of evidence indicates that the period was
more beneficial than detrimental. Nevin was certainly interested in underscoring the better aspects of the period;
nevertheless there is truth in his remarks: "The [Provision-
al] Liturgy, in fact, did not get into any general use. In
that respect it proved a failure. Yet it was wonderful to
see how it worked notwithstanding as a silent influence among
us, in favor of sound ideas on the subject of Christian worship. It wrought a change, far and wide, in the spirit and
form of our sanctuary services. It served to deepen among
us the power of the liturgical movement, which had given it
birth."[36]

In two *Messenger* articles[37] "G" (not Gerhart) argued a
number of benefits which were the result of the liturgical
movement: the denomination now has an historical knowledge
of itself which it did not have before the controversy; and
the Creed and Lord's Prayer were introduced to the church and
made a part of its worship, as "had not been for many years
before". The "sacred altar" was no longer "the mere convenient place for counting out the collection money, or the
writing table on which the secretary of the consistory might
record the minutes of business meetings. It is a holy and
sacred place, consecrated to the most momentous transaction
in the Church of Christ." Furthermore, the Heidelberg Cate-

chism was now more central to the faith of the denomination; the Eucharist was generally acknowledged to be central to worship; the quality of hymns improved; ideas in church architecture were "elevated"; and, claimed "G" in contrast to Kuhns' comments noted above, the liturgical movement has contributed to the cause of missions by waking the denomination out of its general sluggishness.

"G's" one comment concerning the general educational value of the liturgical movement--even the "plainest member" is far better educated in Reformed theology and worship than he ever was before--is unquestionably true; and it is to this "benefit" which those writings in both centuries most often point. J. Spangler Kieffer, a liturgical moderate, wrote in 1884: "A higher grade of intelligence as to matters of doctrine has been attained, and more satisfactory ideas as to the nature of Christian Worship have come to prevail."[38]

Did the "practical activity" of the church suffer seriously during the thirty years' war? Harbaugh contended that it did not: "The Church increase was greater at that period than at any time in her history in America."[39] So, too, did Dubbs claim that while some important clergymen and congregations were lost, "we must recognize the fact that during this stormy period the Reformed Church in the United States [i.e., the German Reformed Church] grew more rapidly than it ever had done before. Though there were many discouragements, there was also much energy and enthusiasm; and for earnest study and productive literary activity the Mercersburg period is unequalled in the history of the Church."[40]

It is not surprising that those advocating the Mercersburg liturgical endeavors found the controversy beneficial, while those opposing Mercersburg were convinced that the controversy was detrimental and would surely have ruined the denomination were it not for their opposition. It was claimed, for example, that Bomberger's *raison d'etre* was to be found "in his able, dauntless, and unrelaxing opposition to ecclesiastical influences which at one time threatened to sweep the whole Reformed Church away from its evangelical moorings. This was the supreme work to which he dedicated his life."[41] It would seem that Dubbs' evaluation of the controversy is nearer the truth than Kuhn's. In the first place, there is no evidence of missionary zeal--in bud or in bloom--on the part of the denomination prior to 1857; and simply because such an interest did develop in the 1870's and 1880's, there is little reason to conclude that the liturgical controversy prevented its earlier appearance. Second, in spite of the loss of certain clergymen and congregations, the fact remains that the denomination did grow rapidly during the "thirty-years' war".

It was pointed out from time to time that the controversy alienated sister denominations. As has been shown, this was certainly the case with the Dutch; however, it is mere speculation to suggest that the Triennial Conventions would have led to union had it not been for the liturgical dispute. Any temporary alienation was a small price to pay for the creative discussions and research provoked and conducted by Nevin and Schaff. The increased "intelligence"--to use J. Spangler Kieffer's term--which resulted from the controversy is surely one of its greater benefits. Whether this increase was as extensive as "G" would have his readers believe is debatable; yet it is not too much to argue that the denomination as a whole did have a greater historical consciousness and a more reverent sense of the high act of worship in 1880 than it had in 1840.

Those assessing the liturgical movement a century later all seem to agree that the influence was generally good and, in some cases, abiding. George Richards wrote this:

> Notwithstanding the deplorable animosities
> and suspicions which were awakened in every
> section of the Church, the outcome was by
> no means without beneficent results. It
> was a creative rather than a destructive
> controversy; for on both sides there were
> men not only of sincere devotion to the
> cause of Christ but also of profound
> scholarship. Now that a century has elapsed
> since its beginning, we are able to evaluate
> without prejudice the character of its
> leaders and to say that there were giants
> in those days.[42]

As for the specific liturgical influence of the Mercersburg liturgies, Slifer indicates that "the theological and
liturgical insights of the Mercersburg Movement took root in
our liturgies and ultimately shaped not only the liturgical
tradition of the former Reformed Church in the United States,
but also the liturgical tradition which is in process of
establishing itself in the Evangelical and Reformed Church".[43]
Writing after still another denominational merger, Horton
Davies notes that the "liturgy and a high church viewpoint",
which many in the Evangelical and Reformed Church "inherited
from John William [sic] Nevin and Philip Schaff", was a factor
to be contended with in the composition of the new provisional
liturgy for the United Church of Christ.[44] Likely a number of
congregations--e.g., Norristown and Third Church, Baltimore--
continued to use the *Order of Worship* until the turn of the
century; however, according to Elizabeth Clarke Kieffer, the
only congregation in the denomination currently using any
parts of the *Order of Worship* directly is First Reformed Church
in Lancaster. Generally, however, Miss Kieffer believes that
the *Order of Worship* developed and preserved throughout the

denomination a love of form and the poetry of devotional
language.[45] Undoubtedly this is true. Even among those
congregations which did not use any of the specific services
of the *Order of Worship*, an increase in the use of the Creed,
the Lord's Prayer, and certain of the ancient hymns and canticles was generally reported in the *Weekly Messenger*. Furthermore, as has been noted, save for a reduction in the number of
congregational responses, the *Directory of Worship* remained
essentially as "liturgical" as the *Order of Worship*; therefore,
one can defensibly conclude that there was a general move toward a more historic, Reformed pattern of worship throughout
the German Reformed denomination by the turn of the century.

Reasons for the Controversy

By far the more tantalizing question concerns not the
effects of the liturgical controversy, but whether there
should have been one at all. Within any denomination there
are "high" and "low" church sentiments; therefore the differences of opinion which followed *The Principle of Protestantism*
and *The Mystical Presence* were to be expected. Beyond this,
however, the controversy would likely never have gone, had it
not been for the following reasons, only one of which--alone--
provoked the controversy; but all of which, in combination,
sustained it. (Since most of these reasons will be evaluated
at greater length in the following chapter, they are mentioned
here only briefly.)

The theoretical mistake which the denomination made in
the beginning was the prevailing notion that liturgical unity
necessarily meant liturgical uniformity. When the clergy came
to realize that it was the Provisional Liturgy or nothing, a

sizable minority of them resisted vociferously. Only in the
end did Nevin and others come to see that "as desirable as
liturgical uniformity may be, Church unity is possible without it".[46]

A second reason is one of five which may be classed under
the general heading of procedural matters. The hasty manner
in which the Synod of 1852 accepted the Baltimore proposals,
and then the dispatch with which the Synod of 1857 agreed to
the Provisional Liturgy (never having examined a copy) created
the impression in later years that the denomination had been
duped. Third, the question concerning the constitutional
status of a provisional liturgy was never answered satisfactorily. The effect of this constitutional indecision was
to create an atmosphere of doctrinal and liturgical suspicion
from which the *Order of Worship* was never completely free.
Fourth, there was no strategy for introducing the Liturgies
to the congregations. Had this been worked out in advance of
the publication of the Provisional Liturgy, there is reason
to believe that much of the fear and distrust could have been
prevented; however, by 1862--the stormy Synod of Chambersburg
at which Bomberger presented his minority report--the battle
lines had been drawn and a peaceful and quiet introduction
was impossible.

Fisher and the publication fiasco account largely for the
bad press the Provisional Liturgy received: the fifth reason
for the liturgical controversy. Since the *Weekly Messenger*
reached most homes in the denomination (as well as a number
outside the denomination--especially in Dutch Reformed
circles), the liturgical opinion of the editor was a significant consideration. The sixth reason, still of the procedural
variety, concerns the manner in which the committee revised
the Provisional Liturgy. Had the rubric acknowledging free

prayer been retained and a second form for the Lord's Day service been offered, two of Bomberger's more serious and defensible arguments would have been met.

The seventh and eighth problems which contributed to the controversy are of an ecclesiastical nature: first, poor communications between the Western and Eastern branches of the denomination. The older generation which founded and taught in the Tiffin college and seminary were trained at Mercersburg either before Nevin and Schaff arrived or before the Mercersburg theology came to be articulated clearly, and it found little favor with them. From Tiffin, then, came a generation of young ministers pioneering in the Synod of Ohio and Adjacent States who were taught all the evils of Mercersburg's theology and her liturgies. Travel was difficult and the press biased; therefore only through an annual exchange of Synod delegates did the West know the Eastern thinking first hand. From 1859 on the debates on the liturgy in the Eastern Synod did little to convince the Western delegates that all was orthodox in the Mother Synod.

An eighth reason for the liturgical controversy concerns the ecclesiastical relations between the German Reformed Church and her sister denominations—particularly the Dutch Reformed Church. As the *Weekly Messenger* and the *Mercersburg Review* became more and more pro-Mercersburg, the *Christian Intelligencer* (of the Dutch Church) became more outspoken against Mercersburg; so that, finally, it became the primary organ of both those Germans and Dutch who opposed Nevin and Schaff. A detailed account of the positions taken by several other denominational papers is beyond the scope of this research; however, it may be safely asserted that the liturgical controversy within the German Reformed Church was fed largely from the outside through the weekly papers and periodicals of the Dutch, Lutheran, Presbyterian, and Episcopalian churches.

This writer would maintain that the final two reasons for the liturgical controversy are the decisive ones. All of the above--the theoretical, the procedural, and the ecclesiastical--could have been overcome had it not been for the personal. Bomberger once said: "Where there are six Germans, there are seven opinions."[47] With no intention of dealing in stereotypes or in casting aspersions, it is contended nevertheless that the ninth reason for the liturgical controversy is simply that these were predominantly stubborn, opinionated, ambitious men who, in the words of Elizabeth Clarke Kieffer, "translated their personal hurts into theological controversy. They were ministers, you know, and they had to act as if the whole of Reformed theology was at stake."[48] Berg, for example, immediately chose a heresy trial rather than the several quieter and more winsome ways of settling his differences with Schaff and Nevin. Nevin and Bomberger were extremely volatile men who, unfortunately, were skilled in caustic debate and preferred the press to private interchange as the means by which their differences of opinion were discussed. When two men of this caliber play to the gallery over a period of twenty years and more, a serious dispute cannot be avoided.

The tenth reason, growing out of the ninth, is the decisive one. It may seem an extreme oversimplification to argue that had Bomberger been treated differently by the men of Mercersburg, there would have been no liturgical controversy; yet the evidence is convincing. There is no indication that at any time after Bomberger first questioned the Provisional Liturgy of 1861 any of the Mercersburg principals attempted to hear him out. Compromise was not a word in the vocabularies of Nevin, Schaff, and Harbaugh. They reacted defensively--and so did Bomberger. The complete breakdown in communication between these men and the unwillingness of Nevin to concede that Bomberger just might have a few insights of his own caused the liturgical discussions to become a liturgical controversy.

There is also ample evidence that Bomberger had at least the expected amount of professional and personal ambition. He was perhaps too young to be given serious consideration for the chair Nevin vacated in 1853; however, Hinkle indicates that "even at that late date" (1863), Bomberger was the only other candidate given serious consideration for the professorial appointment which eventually was granted Harbaugh.

> Harbaugh's victory meant that the Eastern
> Seminary had lost its last opportunity to
> be looked upon by all regions of the Re-
> formed Church as an institution whose
> teachings were truly representative.
> Whatever else resulted (or was alleged to
> have resulted) from Harbaugh's appoint-
> ment, without Bomberger on its faculty
> the Mercersburg school was considered by
> many throughout the second half of the
> nineteenth century to be the seat of un-
> challenged 'Nevinism'.[49]

George H. Bricker, professor of theology and librarian in the Lancaster Theological Seminary, and Miss Elizabeth Clarke Kieffer, formerly librarian of the Historical Society of the Evangelical and Reformed Church, both indicated that the "oral tradition" at Lancaster suggested the same thought--that had Bomberger been elected to a professorship in the Seminary, there would have been no full-scale liturgical controversy.

Linn Harbaugh insisted that his father and Bomberger remained friends in spite of Harbaugh's appointment, and Good maintained that Bomberger had no personal ambition in the matter of the founding of Ursinus; however, neither of these observations can diminish the plain fact that Bomberger felt the denomination had not given him his due. So deeply did he feel this that his liturgical polemics were not unaffected by it.

On the other hand, the Eastern Synod, now fully in Mercersburg's control, could hardly have been expected to give Bomberger the position even if the political implications of such a decision had been clear--as they likely were to not a few. Of course, it was much too late to placate Bomberger in 1868, and by that time the Synod was even less inclined to do so in any event; however, his name was again placed in nomination when the Synod considered a man to fill the chair made vacant by Harbaugh's death. The nominating committee proposed only one name--E. V. Gerhart. Bomberger objected to the procedure, and one of his admirers unwisely placed his name in nomination. Realizing that a contest would bring only ignoble defeat, Bomberger withdrew. Then, "in an interview with a reporter from Philadelphia's *Evening Telegram*" he declared that "the Hagerstown meeting still in session was guilty of irregular proceedings 'unknown even among secular politicians, and without precedent in our Church'."[50] A number of clergy in the Synod had been seeking an opportunity to censure Bomberger ever since the Myerstown Convention, and now they had their opportunity. They succeeded in securing an official censure, and were well along with plans to deny his ministerial standing as well. At this Bomberger issued a satisfactory retraction of his public statements. "Yet even that retraction had its subtle side; for Bomberger retained his standing in Synod by retracting only the rash act of *publishing* his thoughts, without reference to the thoughts themselves."[51]

Bomberger's influence was considerable in the denomination for forty years, and his election to the presidency of the General Synod in 1890--the year of his death--was befitting this influence and the lifetime of creative controversy he largely spawned within his beloved "Reformed Zion".

In sum, then, there was a liturgical *debate* for thirty years because serious issues provoked deep differences of opinion; but there was a liturgical *controversy* for twenty of those thirty years because John Williamson Nevin and John H. A. Bomberger were the brilliant, proud men that they were. Any protracted debate brings a certain measure of diminishing returns, and this one is no exception. Yet the evidence indicates that the Mercersburg Movement awakened a slumbering Zion, improved her worship, and educated more than confused her people. This was the effect upon the German Reformed Church; but did the Movement have wider influence?

Liturgical Influence on Other Reformed Traditions

According to Nichols, "It is indeed possible that neither Nevin nor Schaff had ever heard of Mercersburg before they were first approached about joining the faculty there."[52] This is certainly true in Schaff's case; and, although Nevin had probably heard of Mercersburg, there is no reason to believe that it had interested him, since there was nothing particularly interesting about the seminary and college before he arrived in 1840. Rauch's work was important; however, it

was neither developed nor known prior to Nevin's advent.
"The spirit of the [Mercersburg] movement survived mainly
in the liturgy it had molded";[53] and to that Liturgy attention is now turned. In so far as the Liturgy is an articulation of the Mercersburg theology, the theology also survived;
however, the force of the Liturgy is more discernible today
than any other single aspect of the movement.

Documentation of Mercersburg's liturgical influence is
difficult. In light of the enormous liturgical activity and
interchange during the decades of the '50's, it would seem
safe to suppose that the Mercersburg liturgies had a wide
circulation both in this country and in Europe. In many
cases, however, it cannot be established with certainty
whether Mercersburg was borrowed directly, or whether common
sources were used. Commenting on the liturgical movement in
the Reformed churches, Charles P. Krauth, the Lutheran Professor of Intellectual and Moral Philosophy in the University
of Pennsylvania, wrote: "The Liturgical struggle in the
German Reformed Church is one in which all Protestantism is
interested; for it is not a mere battle between two parties,
but a struggle between two principles; and it is carried on
with an ability which gives promise that the result will be
felt, beyond the bounds of the communion in which it originates."[54]

Howard G. Hageman, a very perceptive liturgical sleuth,
has concluded that "the influence of Mercersburg on Reformed
church worship was indirect....Sometimes there were direct
borrowings from the *Order of Worship*; more often the influence
of the movement in other churches was seen in the stimulation
of liturgical study and publication".[55] As noted above, one
of the reasons Hageman suggests for the revival of liturgical

interest in the Dutch Reformed Church was the realization
among "certain Dutch leaders...they had best get about their
business before they had to deal with the finished product
of their German cousins...."[56]   While it would not be accurate
to attribute later Presbyterian liturgical moves to Mercersburg, it would be defensible to say that the Presbyterian
Church certainly felt the pressure of the general liturgical
revival of which the German Reformed Church was so conspicu-
ously a part during the latter half of the nineteenth century.
The Presbyterian liturgical committee which submitted the
Book of Common Worship to the General Assembly in 1905 was
definitely aware of the Mercersburg liturgies, and at least
one prayer was directly borrowed from the *Order of Worship*.[57]

Hageman has discovered two instances in which the Provisional Liturgy was directly used in Scotland. In 1858 a
"curious little book"[58] was published by Andrew A. Bonar,
minister of the Canongate in Edinburgh. This volume is
greatly dependent upon Baird's *Eutaxia* and the Dutch Reformed
Liturgy published in 1857. In addition Bonar acknowledged
that his Festival Prayers "are extracted from 'Liturgical
Contributions', contained in the 'Mercersburg Quarterly Review' for July, 1856, which was recently forwarded to us by
a gentleman, who takes much interest in the matter...."[59]

The most important instance of Scottish borrowing is
found in the lectures on worship delivered by Dr. George
Washington Sprott of North Berwick, chairman of the committee
to prepare the *Euchologion*. In his list of books "which are
useful either as furnishing materials for prayer, or as
sources of information on the history of worship in our own
and other branches of the Church", Sprott includes the Liturgy of the German Reformed Church in America.[60]

To trace completely the considerable contributions of
the German Reformed Liturgies to the several editions of the
Euchologion would require a chapter in itself; however, since
the *Euchologion* was seminal for both the prayer books of the
Church of Scotland and the Presbyterian Church in America,
some brief assessment of Mercersburg's influence is necessary.
In the 1905 edition of *Euchologion* Sprott acknowledged the
indebtedness of the Church Service Society[61] to the Mercersburg movement.[62] That same edition included source notes--
which are described by W. D. Maxwell as "not wholly accurate,
but still of great value".[63] The Provisional Liturgy, *Order
of Worship*, and *Directory of Worship* (all mistakenly grouped
in Sprott's code as "Provisional Liturgy of the American
German Reformed Church, 1859") appear over fifty times.
Thirty-five notes indicate direct borrowing from the German
Reformed Liturgies, while most of the remainder reflect a
common reliance of Mercersburg and the Church Service Society
on the Catholic Apostolic Liturgy.

The *Euchologion* borrowed twenty-four Collects from the
German Reformed Liturgies. Some of the more interesting
examples are as follows: the prayer, "At the Beginning of
the Year",[64] is noted by Sprott as coming from the *Directory
of Worship*. It was, in fact, written by Harbaugh and first
appeared in the *Order of Worship*. In at least three instances
the *Euchologion* used Collects from the Provisional Liturgy or
Order of Worship, and then the prayer was borrowed from the
Euchologion by van Dyke. The third Passion Collect in the
Euchologion was written by Gerhart and originally appeared
as the Festival Prayer for Good Friday in the *Order of Worship*.
Van Dyke used the same prayer, attributing it to the *Book of
Common Order*.[65] The second Resurrection Collect in the *Eucho-
logion* was written by Schaff. It, too, appeared in the *Book*

of Common Worship, attributed, again, to the *Book of Common Order*.[66] The third Resurrection Collect in *Euchologion* provides an interesting variation. It was written originally by Harbaugh for the Provisional Liturgy, then revised by Porter for the *Order of Worship*. In the *Book of Common Worship* it is attributed to Comegys.[67,68] One final illustration will be sufficient to demonstrate that both the Provisional Liturgy and the *Order of Worship* were used by the Church Service Society. The prayer for a Sick Child was written by Harbaugh for the Provisional Liturgy. He then revised and substantially abridged it for the *Order of Worship*. The *Euchologion* notes the source as the Provisional Liturgy, when in fact the form of the prayer is taken from the *Order of Worship*. The same prayer is amended further and appears in the *Book of Common Worship* credited to the Presbyterian liturgical committee.

In addition to borrowed prayers and Collects, the first Evening Service in the *Euchologion* comes almost entirely from the second Lord's Day Service in the Provisional Liturgy. There would appear to be a closer relationship between the Eucharistic forms in the *Euchologion* and the Provisional Liturgy than actually exists. There is no direct borrowing except for the opening lines in the Prayer for the Communion of Saints.[69] By Sprott's own admission, the *Euchologion* relies largely on the Catholic Apostolic Liturgy--a common source--and this accounts for the several surface similarities.

One final relationship between the *Euchologion* and the Provisional Liturgy should be noted. Much of the Ordination Service in the former is borrowed from the latter.[70] The *Euchologion* adapts the opening address and the statement to the candidate prior to the ordination questions. So, too,

are the ordination prayer and addresses to the newly ordained
and the congregation taken from the Provisional Liturgy; however, the two addresses are given after the laying on of
hands in the *Euchologion* rather than before, as in the Provisional Liturgy. The paragraph which states Nevin's doctrine of the ministry is retained by the *Euchologion*, with
the exception of the phrase, "and of truly supernatural
character and force".

The *Euchologion* was the chief vehicle of German Reformed liturgical influence outside the denomination. Not
only was the *Euchologion* a major source for American Presbyterians, but the Dutch also made no little use of it as well,
borrowing a Eucharistic prayer for the revision of 1873. The
Dutch also made use of the German Reformed Liturgies. Hageman
notes that the lectionary in the Liturgy of 1873 was taken
from the *Order of Worship*;[71] however, he fails to point out
that the *Order of Worship* in turn had borrowed its lectionary
from Shields. "This kind of liturgical exchange, which had
taken place earlier in the sixteenth century, was a hopeful
sign that the Reformed churches, after years of isolation,
were beginning again to find each other."[72] Even more specifically it meant that "the liturgical activity of the various
American Reformed churches was responsible for [influenced, at
any rate] the development of similar activities in Great
Britain".[73]

Strengths and Weaknesses

An assessment of the strengths and weaknesses of the Mercersburg movement offers nothing new, since each has appeared
in various connections and degrees during the historical dis-

cussion; rather, by way of summary, it is in order to underscore the several more striking observations which have already been made. As has been shown above, Mercersburg was
not a failure, either in its legacy to the denomination or
in its broader influence; yet as an identifiable force, it
did indeed "have its day". What were some of its more notable
weaknesses?

The title of Nichols' volume on the Mercersburg Movement
--*Romanticism in American Theology*--is both descriptive and
critical. Nevin and Schaff were clearly the Reformed expo-
nents of Romanticism in America, and, as such, participated
in all that was both defensible and indefensible in this
"appreciation if not emulation of the ways of ancestral
generations...."[74] Hageman calls the second generation of
the nineteenth century the "Gothic Age", and architecturally
and aesthetically it was. A return to the past was necessary
in order to recover a lost liturgical heritage; and in this
sense Protestantism owes a substantial debt to Romanticism.
The sixteenth century was rediscovered as well as the early
church; and that made the nineteenth century the golden age
of liturgical renewal in the Reformed churches.

Yet reaction often means extremes, and so it was in the
nineteenth century. In Hageman's criticisms of Romanticism,
Mercersburg's more serious weaknesses are to be seen. First,
"the historical and the theological began to mean less and
less as the demands of the psychological and the aesthetic
loomed larger".[75] Mercersburg's liturgical theory was complete in that it involved the body as well as the mind, and
had definite implications for church architecture, as has
been noted above. That Mercersburg encouraged the aesthetic
--recognizing the holiness of beauty as well as the beauty
of holiness--is hardly a criticism; yet the extent to which

358

Mercersburg's second generation (and subsequent ones) became preoccupied with architectural frills is indeed a
criticism. This was not, however, Mercersburg's most serious
fault.

Hageman's second criticism of liturgical romanticism
suggests a greater weakness in the Mercersburg enterprise--
viz., that "reading the history of the nineteenth century
certainly gives the impression that the liturgy was so exclusively a clerical pastime that...it was a pother that
was going over the layman's head and one in which he had no
great interest".[76] Many laymen yawned at the whole frilly
affair, while others were convinced that ministers interested
in matters liturgical had surely "lost their gospel". In
theory, as well as in isolated practice, Mercersburg did make
a genuine attempt to include the layman in the liturgical
renaissance. The Liturgy was not to be a pulpit manual; instead, no little time and energy went into the attempt to
make it a peoples' book. Furthermore, as has been noted
above, one of the benefits of the liturgical controversy was
the heightened "intelligence" of many laymen in their history
--ecclesiastical and liturgical; nevertheless, in the end, the
success or failure of the Mercersburg liturgical movement
rested with the clergy. Many of them were not fully informed
concerning the issues involved; yet in the heat of battle
they drew second-hand conclusions and acted, often without
ever having examined either Liturgy. The appallingly poor
strategy for introducing the Liturgy to the denomination is
one of the more important reasons for its failure to gain
widespread acceptance; and, while Hageman does not have Mercersburg specifically in mind, his observation is quite pertinent: "The obvious conclusion is that there was a real
failure to give instruction in the meaning of worship, to

explain to the laymen what all these improvements and additions to the service signified."[77]

A second aspect of this clerical infatuation with the liturgical movement is that a substantial number of Mercersburg's sons left the German Reformed Church for the Episcopal and Roman Churches. The quantity was not as great as the quality of those second-generation ministers whose defections not only gave Bomberger grist for his mill, but robbed the Mercersburg tradition of an on-going leadership. Schaeffer determined that at least eight or ten prominent ministers went over to Rome--four from the Norristown church alone: Edwin O. Forney, George Derring Wolff, John S. Ermentrout, and Daniel Gans. Nevin's two sons joined the Episcopal Church and Wolff's two sons joined the Roman Church the year after their father's death.[78]

Two conflicting interpretations of these defections were offered. Bomberger, of course, attributed them to the high church tendencies in the Mercersburg movement. Apple, on the other hand, insisted that the cause was precisely the opposite: "So far as transitions to the Episcopal Church are concerned, it has not been the liturgy, but the *opposition* to the liturgy, that has been the cause."[79] In his biography of Nevin, Theodore Appel went into more detail, insisting that because the "theological movement in their own Church" did not advance rapidly enough for the second-generation, many of them "fell out of rank, read Catholic authors almost exclusively, differed from their teachers, and in apparent sincerity, for the most part, yet in some sort of bewilderment, they sought refuge in the Roman Church". They were, to use Appel's description, "in an earnest theological movement, but they were not of it...."[80]

Whatever the reason--and there is truth in the observations of both Bomberger and Apple--the force of the Mercersburg movement was seriously diminished by the loss of several
of its brighter sons.

A third criticism of liturgical romanticism in the nineteenth century--that it never seriously faced the deeper
questions of a theology of the liturgy--is also *in part* true
of Mercersburg. As has already been argued, Mercersburg is
generally a paradigm of a theology which articulated itself
liturgically; yet this discussion focussed almost exclusively
on the Eucharist. Important gains were made in that regard;
however, there was no "basic discussion of the relation of
Word to Sacrament".[81] Both Nichols[82] and Hageman[83] argue
that Mercersburg seriously "undervalued" (Hageman's term)
preaching due to its reaction against Puritanism and its
effort to re-establish the centrality of the Eucharist. By
comparison the emphasis was certainly on the sacraments, and
neither Nevin nor Schaff offered any theology of preaching in
the same way that they constantly put forth their theology of
the Eucharist. Nevertheless, to suggest that there was an
undervaluation of the Word is too harsh a judgment. Even in
The Liturgical Question, in which Nevin went out of his way
to establish the architectural and liturgical centrality of
the altar, he insisted that this was not to be done in such
a way as "to disparage the reading-desk or the pulpit, as
being the proper organs of address from the side of God to
the people".[84]

The most detailed comment any of the Mercersburg principals made on preaching *per se* is to be found in a letter
Schaff wrote while on sabbatical in 1854.[85] Many in Switzerland and in America blame preaching for liturgical decay, he
wrote, and want to introduce some sort of mass again. Quite

to the contrary, Schaff argued, for the sermon cannot be
valued too highly. "It produced the Church in the first
century, reformed it in the sixteenth, and must also re-
generate it in the nineteenth century." A strong liturgy
demands a strong sermon; thus, instead of diminishing its
importance, the sermon must be raised up to what it should
be. Schaff suggested four ways in which this may be done:
first, the sermon should not be considered an "historical
declamatory exercise", or "simply instruction"; but "a
communication of life and spirit; a life witness of Christ;
directing to Christ". Second, a greater variety of preaching styles must be used: "cultus-sermons, homilies, exhortations, simple addresses, missionary sermons, etc." Third,
"the choice of the theme dare not be left to the purely
arbitrary will of the preacher; but must be, as a general
thing, regulated by the idea of an ecclesiastical year and
the principal festivals...." Finally, "the other elements
of religious worship, in their place equally as important
[as the sermon], must assert their rights, and support the
sermon; for the latter has suffered the most just from the
fact that it has pushed the former out of its position and
significance". What more classically Reformed statement of
the relationship of the sermon to the liturgy could one desire?

Articles on preaching—most of them concerned with its
practical aspects—are in virtually every issue of the
Weekly Messenger throughout the liturgical controversy.
These do not speak directly to the subject at issue here;
however, they do certainly indicate that preaching was hardly
"undervalued" within the denomination at large. The articles
which do appear from the pens of those seeking to delineate
the relationship of preaching to the liturgy all argue

essentially the same theme: that preaching is "a part, an important part, the most prominent part of worship, if you please"; however, "he who goes to the house of God and returns, having heard only a sermon, has not worshipped God according to his requirement and our deepest spiritual wants".[86] In an article appearing in the *Mercersburg Review*, George Lewis Staley, minister of St. John's Reformed Church near Petersville, Maryland, provides his readers with a remarkably sound description of preaching: "...the preaching of the word, which is truly a sacramental power, is not a dry, lifeless discussion of doctrine, but a vivid reproduction and *re*-presentation of the facts and mysteries of our Holy Religion."[87]

So what may one conclude? Just this: a comparison of the weight of the words written about the sacraments and about preaching certainly reveals an imbalance; yet, when the Mercersburg men did speak concerning preaching, what they said indicates a genuine appreciation of its importance within the liturgy. Even more, as in Staley's description, some of them considered preaching to be something of a sacrament itself. This writer is of the opinion, then, that preaching was neither "undervalued" nor suffered seriously from neglect. Rather there is every indication that the quality of preaching improved in just the manner Schaff predicted in his fourth suggestion--by rediscovering its proper liturgical context.

If the principal liturgical weaknesses of Mercersburg are those of romanticism, then so are the principal strengths also those of romanticism. First, Mercersburg participated--if not led the way within the Reformed ranks--in a rediscovery of the past. Nichols calls it a "polarity between the theologies of Protestantism and of the early Fathers". Schaff described it as "a bond of union with the ancient Catholic

Church and the Reformation, and yet...the product of the
religious life of our denomination in its present state".
In short, the Mercersburg movement, through its theological
investigations, philosophy of history, and liturgical studies,
assisted in breaking the back of provincial sectarianism and
in introducing American Protestantism to the Church catholic.

Liturgical renewal both contributed to and reflected
the strong ecumenism of the Mercersburg movement. This, perhaps more than any other aspect of the movement, has led to
its rediscovery a century later and made it both interesting
and paradigmatic for today. It comes as little surprise to
discover Michael J. Taylor writing of Mercersburg: "Liturgical scholars here and in Europe now look upon the Mercersburg
theology as making a positive contribution to the liturgical
renaissance."[88]

Neither Schaff nor Nevin were interested in what Nichols
calls "an impoverished least common-denominator Christianity".[89] Church unity was, for Nevin, "the most important
interest in the world"; yet he felt it must be reached through
what Wentz has called "ecumenical theology with integrity".[90]
Years before Faith and Order made a similar discovery, Nevin
argued that "the debates over church order, polity, and the
ministry were less important than those over sacramental
grace, for the sacraments were the sign and seal of whatever
power was recognized to be in the church".[91] The Hegelian
dynamic led Schaff to his eschatological church or Protestant
Catholicity. This was more than an intellectual principle;
it was rather Mercersburg's dream. In light of events during
the twentieth century, who is to say that the dream may not
yet come true?

Still another of Mercersburg's strenths--considerably
more practical than the above named, yet of equal significance

--is the quality of men who served on its liturgical committee. They had the intellectual stature and vision to hammer out a neo-Reformed theology; and, further, they had the talent of poetic compilation required to give that theology a devotional voice. The *Order of Worship* they produced is a paradigm of literary, liturgical, and theological unity.

The historical discoveries, the ecumenical vision, and the liturgical fruits of Mercersburg make it a movement within the Reformed tradition worth remembering. But there is more to be said. The issues--both theoretical and practical-- which emerged during the Mercersburg liturgical controversy still face liturgical committees within the Reformed tradition today. This study has been undertaken primarily in order to gain some insights into those issues, that certain practical guidelines may be suggested to contemporary liturgical committees at work with the Reformed tradition. By way of summarizing this historical investigation, then, and of accomplishing its purpose, attention is turned now to the liturgical lessons of Mercersburg.

NOTES TO CHAPTER VII

1. *Acts and Proceedings of the General Synod*, 1881, quoted in Benjamine Kuhns and Rudolph F. Kelker, *The Liturgical Conflict and the Peace Movement of the Reformed Church in the United States as Exhibited by the Official Records of the General Synod* (Dayton, Ohio: Press of U. B. Publishing House, 1896).

2. *The Directory of Worship for the Reformed Church in the United States* (Reading, Pa.: Daniel Miller, Publisher, 1884).

3. *WM*, May 21, 1884.

4. Kieffer, *op. cit.*, p. 223.

5. M. Slifer, *op. cit.*, p. 239.

6. Hageman, *Pulpit and Table*, p. 95.

7. *WM*, January 10, 1855; *Tercentenary Monument*, p. 261.

8. Nichols, *Romanticism*, p. 294.

9. The Seminary moved to Lancaster in 1871.

10. Letter, Apple to Heyser, November 4, 1881. E & R Historical Society.

11. *Ibid.*, November 22, 1879.

12. Letter, Apple to E. E. Higbee, January 22, 1879. E & R Historical Society.

13. Letter, Apple to Steiner, January 13, 1883. E & R Historical Society.

14. Letter, Apple to Davis, October 23, 1887.

15. Kieffer, *op. cit.*, p. 223.

16. *Acts and Proceedings of the General Synod*, 1893, pp. 80-81.

17. Kuhns, *op. cit.*, p. iv.

18. *The Book of Worship for the Reformed Church in the United States* (Philadelphia: The Publication and Sunday School Board of the Reformed Church in the United States, 1923).

19. M. Slifer, *op. cit.*, p. 239.

20. See page 115 above.

21. *The Liturgy of the Reformed Church in America* (New York: The Board of Publication of the Reformed Church in America, [1882]).

22. The responsive Psalter could be used as the first Scripture lesson and the Lord's Prayer was moved to the beginning of the service.

23. Hageman, "Lectures," III, p. 18.

24. *Ibid.*, p. 25.

25. *Ibid.*, p. 27a.

26. Archibald Alexander Hodge, *Manual of Forms for Baptism, Administration of the Lord's Supper, Marriage, and Funerals. Conformed to the Doctrine and Discipline of the Presbyterian Church* (Philadelphia: Presbyterian Board of Publication, 1877), p. 3.

27. *Ibid.*

28. *Ibid.*, p. 4.

29. *Ibid.*, pp. 34-35.

30. Archibald Alexander Hodge, *Manual of Forms for Baptism, Admission to the Communion, Administration of the Lord's Supper, Marriage and Funerals, Ordination of Elders and Deacons, etc.* (Philadelphia: Presbyterian Board of Publication, 1882), p. 4.

31. Melton, *op. cit.*, p. 111.

32. *Ibid.*, p. 136.

33. *The Book of Common Worship* (Philadelphia: Presbyterian Board of Publication and Sabbath-School Work, 1905).

34. Kuhns, *op. cit.*, p. iii.

35. T. G. Apple, "The Late General Synod," *MR*, XXV (1878), p. 344.

36. Nevin, *Vindication of the Revised Liturgy*, p. 26.

37. May 8, 1867; May 15, 1867.

38. *WM*, July 2, 1884.

39. Linn Harbaugh, *op. cit.*, p. 250.

40. Dubbs, *op. cit.*, p. 312.

41. J. H. A. Bomberger, *et al.*, *The Reverend John H. A. Bomberger, Centenary Volume*, pp. 2-3.

42. Richards, *History of the Theological Seminary*, pp. 339-340.

43. M. Slifer, *op. cit.*, p. 239. The German Reformed Church changed its name in 1867 to the Reformed Church in the United States. Then in 1934 a merger was consummated with the Evangelical Synod of North America to form the Evangelical and Reformed Church.

44. Horton Davies, "Reshaping the Worship of the United Church of Christ," *Worship*, 41 (November 1967), pp. 542-543.

45. Private conversation.

46. J. S. Kieffer, *WM*, July 2, 1884.

47. *WM*, March 6, 1867.

48. Personal conversation.

49. Hinkle, *op. cit.*, p. 126.

50. *WM*, November 4, 1868, quoted in Hinkle, *op. cit.*, p. 141.

51. Hinkle, *op. cit.*, p. 141.

52. Nichols, *The Mercersburg Theology*, p. 3.

53. Nevin, "Anglican Crisis," *MR*, III (1851), p. 396, quoted in Nichols, *Mercersburg Theology*, p. 30.

54. Charles P. Krauth, "The Liturgical Movement in the Presbyterian and Reformed Churches," *MR*, XVI (1869), p. 610.

55. Howard Hageman, *Pulpit and Table*, pp. 97-98.

56. *Ibid.*, unpublished Lectures, II, pp. 10-11.

57. The prayer "For our Country" on page 129 is attributed to the "German Reformed Liturgy, U.S.A."

58. Hageman, *Pulpit and Table*, p. 73.

59. Andrew A. Bonar, *Presbyterian Liturgies with Specimens of Forms of Prayer for Worship as Used in the Continental Reformed, and American Churches; with the Directory for the Public Worship of God agreed upon by the Assembly of Divines at Westminster; and Forms of Prayer for Ordinary and Communion Sabbaths, and for other Services of the Church* (Edinburgh: Myles MacPhail, 1858), p. 32.

60. George W. Sprott, *The Worship and Offices of the Church of Scotland* (Edinburgh and London: William Blackwood and Son, 1882), pp. 52-53. Other liturgies and individuals included are Ebrard, Bersier, the Hugenot Liturgy of Charleston, the Dutch Reformed Church in America, *Eutaxia*, and the Catholic Apostolic Liturgy. It can be presumed that all of these were consulted in the preparation of *Euchologion*.

61. Organized on January 31, 1865, for the purpose of studying "the liturgies--ancient and modern--of the Christian Church, with a view to the preparation and ultimate publication of certain forms of prayer for public worship, and services for the administration of the Sacraments, the celebration of marriage, the burial of the dead, etc."

62. George W. Sprott, ed., *Euchologion. A Book of Common Order: Being Forms of Prayer and Administration of the Sacraments, and other Ordinances of the Church* (Edinburgh: William Blackwood and Sons, 1905), p. xv.

63. W. D. Maxwell, *A History of Worship in the Church of Scotland* (London: Oxford University Press, 1955), note 1, p. 177.

64. *Euchologion*, p. 225; *Order of Worship*, p. 29.

65. *Euchologion*, p. 239; *Order of Worship*, p. 87; *Book of Common Worship*, p. 119.

66. *Euchologion*, p. 241; *Order of Worship*, p. 96; *Book of Common Worship*, p. 119; Provisional Liturgy, p. 79.

67. *Euchologion*, p. 241-42; Provisional Liturgy, p. 167; *Order of Worship*, p. 91; *Book of Common Worship*, p. 120.

68. E. B. Comegys, ed., *Euchologion*, 2nd ed. (Philadelphia: Sherman & Co., 1898).

69. *Euchologion*, p. 300; Provisional Liturgy, p. 200.

70. *Euchologion*, p. 378; Provisional Liturgy, p. 240.

71. Lectures, III, p. 2.

72. Hageman, *Pulpit and Table*, p. 76.

73. *Ibid.*, p. 73.

74. Melton, *op. cit.*, p. 59.

75. Hageman, *Pulpit and Table*, p. 81.

76. *Ibid.*

77. *Ibid.*, p. 82.

78. Schaeffer, *History of Philadelphia Classis*, p. 77.

79. Letter, T. G. Apple to Jacob Heyser, April 22, 1882.

80. Theodore Appel, *The Life and Work of John Williamson Nevin*, p. 410.

81. Hageman, *Pulpit and Table*, p. 82.

82. Nichols, *Romanticism*, p. 106.

83. Hageman, *Pulpit and Table*, p. 97.

84. Nevin, *The Liturgical Question*, p. 27.

85. *WM*, November 22, 1854.

86. *WM*, February 23, 1859.

87. George Lewis Staley, "Preaching," *MR*, XVI (1869), p. 308.

88. Michael J. Taylor, *The Protestant Liturgical Renewal: A Catholic Viewpoint* (Westminster: The Newman Press, 1963), p. 10.

89. Nichols, *Romanticism*, p. 164.

90. Richard Wentz, "The World of Mercersburg Theology," (Introduction to *The Mystical Presence*, Hamden: Archon Press, 1963), p. xvi.

91. Nichols, *Romanticism*, p. 167.

CHAPTER VIII

The Liturgical Lessons of Mercersburg

During the course of the Mercersburg liturgical controversy questions of both a practical-procedural nature and of
a theoretical-theological nature were asked and, in whole or
part, answered. All of these have quite contemporary implications, and they represent the essence of Mercersburg's
liturgical legacy. Some of these lessons may seem tame and
elementary, but Mercersburg discovered them to be otherwise.
Who is to say that the story told above would have been the
same had the actors and events been different? And who is
to say that frustrated personal ambition, an angered editor,
or unresolved questions of church polity may not make a
significant difference in the outcome of any liturgical
venture--even a century later?

The intention of this chapter is to summarize, to
highlight, and to exegete. No attempt has been made to
establish a list of Reformed liturgical principles by which
Mercersburg is then criticized. Rather, as stated in the
Introduction, the purpose of this study is to examine the
issues which emerged during the Mercersburg liturgical controversy with a view to establishing procedural and theoretical principles *for contemporary liturgical committees
in the Reformed tradition.*

The Constitutional Question

As has already been noted in several connections above, one of the most debated issues during the Mercersburg controversy concerned the constitutionality of a provisional liturgy. What is the proper polity in the matter of a provisional liturgy? And, what are the advantages and disadvantages of issuing any liturgy in provisional form?

The Dutch Reformed Church encountered something of the same problem as did the Germans; however, since the Dutch conducted their liturgical debate--such as it was--with considerably less heat than did the Germans, the constitutional question remained simply a question and never did become a divisive issue. The Dutch Synods assumed that provisional use of a revised liturgy was proper until such time as the Classes were prepared for final action on the matter, and followed that course until the New York Classis raised the constitutional issue in 1875. In its overture the Classis insisted that since the liturgy was actually incorporated into the Constitution itself, procedures for constitutional amendment must be followed before any use could be made of the revision. This prompted Synod to rescind its action taken the previous year granting that provisional use.

Synods of the German Reformed Church never honestly debated the issue of constitutionality, although the matter was raised both in the general public discussion and in debate on the floor of Synod. The German Reformed Constitution established the questions to be used at Baptism and Confirmation, and it prescribed the basic elements which constitute the "public worship of the sanctuary". Further it stated that any hymnbook used by the churches must have been "approved and recommended by the Synod". While no

article specifically dealt with liturgical revision and the
liturgy was not itself a part of the Constitution, the spirit
of that document did imply that Synod must "approve and recommend" any liturgy which was issued provisionally. Some
clear action would seem to be necessary also regarding revised forms of Baptism and Confirmation when different questions are proposed.

This problem was never seriously considered to be significant in itself, it must be pointed out; rather those
opposed to the Mercersburg liturgies recognized the ambiguity
in the constitutional question and pressed it in the hope
that were the Liturgies of the Eastern and Western Synods
sent to the Classes for their action, enough support would
be generated to reject them. The issue becomes legitimate
only when the entire liturgy is actually a part of the constitution; or when the sacramental forms are incorporated in the
constitution; or when Baptism, Confirmation, and Ordination
questions are prescribed by Synod or General Assembly action.[1]

The solution to the problem would seem to be a relatively
simply one: the superior church judicatory should appoint a
competent committee to examine any proposed liturgical form,
particularly at points where doctrine is specifically expressed and changes in sacramental questions proposed. If
the committee and the judicatory then approve, there would
appear to be no serious error in permitting provisional use
of the forms until such time as the liturgical committee of
the denomination was prepared to make its final report. The
judicatory should again examine the forms and follow procedures for constitutional amendment.

Assuming the propriety of the polity involved, the
question of the wisdom in using liturgies provisionally

remains. That virtually every Reformed liturgical revision has had its provisional stage testifies to the widespread use of such a procedure; however, what are the disadvantages and advantages?

The only serious problem created by a provisional liturgy which makes extensive changes at any significant point is the creation of liturgical diversity. Such was the opinion expressed by those in both the German and Dutch churches. Presumably one of the fruits of revision was to be an increase in liturgical uniformity; yet permission to use provisional liturgies simply increased the diversity.

In the long run the theoretical advantages of a period of provisional use outweigh the disadvantages. There is definitely something to be said for testing the reaction of the laity to liturgical changes, especially if it can be assumed that they have studied those changes under objective and competent guidance. Mercersburg clearly revealed that in the end a liturgy succeeds or fails by virtue of where the clergy stand; therefore the formal acceptance or rejection of liturgical changes will be made at the Classis or Presbytery level. Yet the extent to which any liturgy is used will be determined by the individual minister and his consistory or session as together they evaluate the proposed liturgy and plan their strategy for its introduction into the worship of their specific congregation.

Constituency of a Liturgical Committee

A second lesson to be learned from Mercersburg concerns the politics and procedures of the liturgical committee. In the preceding pages the members of the Mercersburg committee have been discussed in some detail, and that material will not be repeated here. Let it be said by way of summary, however, that during the sixteen years following the Norristown Synod in 1849, the committee consisted of five professors (Nevin, Schaff, Porter, Gerhart, and Apple), five pastors (Wolff, Harbaugh--both of whom became professors during the course of the liturgical controversy--Heiner, Zacharias, and Bomberger), one clergyman-editor (Fisher), and five laymen of whom only Rodenmayer and Steiner deserve mention. The liturgical opinions held by these men were essentially of a piece, with the exception of Heiner, who died before he could influence the Liturgy for good or ill, and Bomberger, whose story has already been told. The effect of this type of constituency meant that the *Order of Worship* became representative only of the "high" church position within the denomination, all optional forms and rubrical latitude having been removed. The result was a Liturgy with more internal consistency, but a Liturgy which was totally unacceptable to a sizable minority in the Synods.

The lesson here is that membership on liturgical committees must include those of differing liturgical opinions-- a simple lesson, but profound in Mercersburg's case. Granted, these differences will likely prolong the work of the committee; nevertheless, contrary opinions should mean that significant questions are raised and debated--questions the answers to which could easily be presumed were the members all of like liturgical mind. Hopefully the presence of varied opinions would not lead to a wearisome controversy like that experienced by the German Reformed Church; rather to a clearer reflection of the mind of the denomination and to a wider base of support for the liturgy.

Most Reformed denominations in America still do not have
a significant number of liturgiologists, but it should be
expected that extensive use be made of these persons when
they are found--either as members of the liturgical committee
or as consultants to it. While it is not desirable to repeat
the mistake of romanticism and permit liturgical revision to
fall exclusively into the hands of the dilettantes, it must
nevertheless be admitted that this is fundamentally a work
for those who are trained. The committee chairperson should
never be a political appointee, but rather one who is well-
grounded both in Reformed doctrine and liturgical history.
That someone on the committee have certain poetic gifts is
more than a little desirable.

The procedure followed by the German Reformed liturgical
committee is routine. Most, if not all, the services were
first assigned to individuals to prepare or to revise; then
the entire committee would examine the proposals. There is
evidence that especially the sacramental forms and the Lord's
Day services received more of the entire committee's time.
Since these forms will be those most often used, such a procedure is desirable.

Although one familiar with the Provisional Liturgy and
the *Order of Worship* can detect certain stylistic differences
in various forms, the two liturgies (especially the latter)
are remarkably consistent in syntax and devotional quality.
Doubtless this bespeaks some single individual acting in an
editorial capacity. It is the contention of this writer that
Bomberger served that function in the last weeks before the
Provisional Liturgy went to press; and Porter's credentials
lead one to accept rather than doubt the "hunch" of Elizabeth
Clarke Kieffer that he edited the *Order of Worship*. If a

liturgy is not to resemble the proverbial camel, then one individual—well versed in the language of devotion—should edit the entire volume.

Strategy of Publication and Introduction

In a tactical consideration of the publication and introduction of the two German Reformed liturgies, a third lesson is to be learned. As has been indicated in the preceding chapters, an unfortunate and unwise decision was made regarding publication of the Provisional Liturgy. Fisher was snubbed at a time when the liturgical enterprise needed a journalistic friend. This tactical blunder can be attributed solely to Schaff. Not only did he make the initial decision to seek a publisher other than the Printing Establishment, but he chose also to attack Fisher during the Synod of 1858, and further complicated matters by criticising the editor's lack of cooperation with the liturgical committee in the *Weekly Messenger*.

The broader question is what role can the denominational press play today in matters liturgical? No single denominational publication or editor is so widely read and influential today as were the *Weekly Messenger* and Fisher a century ago. Yet through the corresponding journals in the several denominations, news of this type reaches most of the clergy if not the laity. There is no particular need for the editor of such publications to be on the liturgical committee, unless his or her qualifications are more than journalistic; however, he or she should be well informed and educated in any liturgical changes proposed by the denomination. In the final analysis, assuming the quality and historical accuracy of the liturgy, the success of its introduction to the denomination depends largely upon how convincingly it is introduced to the membership.

Regarding that introduction, Mercersburg's lesson is negative--i.e., one learns more what not to do than what to do. It has already been suggested that the Mercersburg principals could have done little more than they did by way of "selling" their product. Clearly they were committed to it and argued it theoretically, if, as in the case of Harbaugh, not practically within their parish situations. The Mercersburg theology had already polarized a substantial segment of both clergy and laity, however, such that whatever the one group proposed, the other automatically rejected. So sensitive did the Mercersburg advocates become to the charge that they were attempting to force the liturgy upon the congregations, that Nevin, Wolff, and Gerhart seemed almost to go out of their way not to use either the Provisional Liturgy or the *Order of Worship*.

In a different context--i.e., one which is not in the midst of a theological and liturgical controversy--a carefully devised and timed plan of introduction seems quite desirable. A study guide for sessions or consistories is in order. Beyond this, articles by competent pastors and scholars should appear regularly in the principal periodicals of the denomination. Written primarily for the layperson, these articles should discuss such matters as Reformed liturgical history, the Reformed liturgical contribution to the ecumenical enterprise, the liturgical principles upon which the new or revised liturgy is constructed, and something of the manner in which the committee operates and who the members are. It is fanciful to expect any intelligent use of

or action on a liturgy unless both clergy and laity are informed and persuaded as much as possible well in advance. If
such measures are taken, controversy is less likely to occur.
Also, it is hoped that serious dialogue and experimentation
in liturgical matters would develop.

Relationship of Theology and the Liturgy

That there is a relationship between theology and the
liturgy is obvious; the specific nature of that relationship,
however, is not so clear. Patrick Cowley states the general
principle this way:

> It is theology that makes worship, and wor-
> ship is always the expression of theology.
> It is only in theology that worship has its
> legitimate origin and sanction, and so the
> faith of the Church is revealed in the wor-
> ship of the Church, as also in its daily
> work. Worship is the dramatization of the-
> ology, and is its living technicolour film.
> As emphases in theology alter, so one finds
> changes in, or additions to, worship.[2]

The Roman and Orthodox traditions would likely agree in principle with Cowley's characterization of the relationship of
theology and the liturgy; however, in his last sentence they
could not concur. The Orthodox Church considers the Divine
Liturgy to be the center of its theology. It *is* its theology
in fact. The Liturgy itself proclaims and teaches the faith,
therefore the traditional Orthodox de-emphasis on both preaching and teaching. Whereas Cowley suggests that the liturgy
articulates a given theology, the Orthodox would insist that
theology is what the liturgy articulates.

The Roman Church might sum up the relationship between theology and liturgy with this dictum: *lex orandi-lex credendi*. Liturgy is the source of doctrine and doctrine is the norm of the liturgy; and between the two there is constant cross-fertilization and modification. While the source of theology is scripture and tradition, the sacrifice--the central mystery--takes place under the form and content of the liturgy. The Divine Liturgy proclaims; the Mass effects.

The Lutheran and Reformed traditions would share fundamentally the same characterization of the relationship of theology and the liturgy--*viz.*, that theology and preaching determine the form and content of the liturgy; the liturgy is not determinative of theology and preaching. The self-revelation of God through Word and Sacraments occurs within a liturgical framework; however, that framework is not itself an integral part of the self-revelation. In short, the liturgy is a functional instrument for the Lutheran and Reformed traditions, and its effectiveness is judged by the adequacy with which it facilitates God's address in preaching and the sacraments, the peoples' response in prayer and praise. Theological re-definition should lead to liturgical revision; and, the obverse: liturgical revision should begin in theological re-definition. According to Luther, in his admonition to the clergy of Lubeck in 1530: "Do not begin with innovations in rites....Put first and foremost what is fundamental in our teaching....Reform of impious rites will come of itself when what is fundamental in our teaching has been effectively presented, has taken root in our pious hearts."[3]

It was to the theology rather than the liturgiology of the Reformation that Mercersburg looked. Perhaps Nevin and

Harbaugh were too critical of the liturgies which emerged from "rigid, didactic Calvinism";[4] however, the plain fact is that neither Calvin nor Luther had the liturgical data or the time to work out the "perfect" Reformed-Lutheran liturgy. Perhaps Bucer in the relative peace of Strassburg came closest to doing that; however, it is generally conceded that while one can find a number of liturgical principles in the sixteenth century, the specific liturgies which emerged from that period were neither as appropriate to the sixteenth century as they could have been, nor are they devotional models for liturgies in the twentieth century.

Parenthetically it should be noted that the Anglican tradition represents a different position with respect to the relationship of theology and liturgy. Generally the observation holds that the Reformed and Lutheran traditions have insisted on common theological ground and allowed the liturgies to vary widely in both form and content. The Anglican position has rather been to insist upon liturgical uniformity and, within that, to permit quite widely divergent theological positions. Both approaches--the Reformed-Lutheran and the Anglican--result in certain inconsistencies. The Reformed Eucharistic doctrine, for example, is basically Calvinistic, as Gerrish has shown through an examination of Reformed catechisms and confessions;[5] yet the Reformed liturgical tradition has witnessed to a theology more nearly Zwinglian than Calvinistic. On the other hand, the Anglican ritual would imply a high Eucharistic doctrine, when the theology of the liturgy is, in fact, more an expression of Zwingli than of Calvin.

The point of the above is simply this: prior to Mercersburg, Reformed theology and Reformed liturgics never came

together in any self-conscious, practical way. To quote
Hageman: "What made the liturgical movement [at Mercersburg]
remarkable was not the *Order of Worship*, despite its high
degree of liturgical skill. It was rather the fact that it
was the first liturgy in the Reformed Church to articulate
a theology. Indeed, it was at Mercersburg that there was
worked out, often in the heat of battle, for the first time
in the Reformed churches what could be called a theology of
the liturgy."[6] The details of that articulation have been
documented throughout this essay.

If the fact that "cultus must express creed" is a Reformed liturgical principle, as Hageman claims,[7] then the
nature of the creed becomes the prior question. What is
Reformed theology? Where does one--especially the liturgi-
ologist--go to find it? As has already been shown, the Mercersburg movement began as a re-definition of church history
and Reformed theology. Out of that re-definition came the
Provisional Liturgy and the *Order of Worship*. In the absence of a "movement"--theological and historical--what is
a liturgical committee to do?

Gerrish has argued the thesis that Reformed theology
amounts to a consensus of the catechisms and confessions
within the Reformed tradition; and that, unless it is the
particular theological system of a given individual which
one seeks to follow, this consensus then becomes the norm.
The plain fact is that a liturgical committee which does not
do serious theological study prior to liturgical revision
runs the risks of either Romanticism or a love affair with
the radically contemporary--both theologically and linguisti-
cally. Those who know nothing of Mercersburg can learn the
same liturgical lesson from the ecumenical movement. The

Faith and Order Commission has discovered that the theological and biblical "why's" must precede the liturgical "how's". Beginning with comparative ecclesiology, Faith and Order shifted its methodology at Lund from the centrifugal to the centripetal--i.e., the aim since 1952 (Lund) has been to go beyond ecclesiological comparison and to search out the theological issues which are behind liturgical differences.[8] In all of this, Mercersburg was a paradigm. Not all of the questions were raised, let alone answered. For example, if one can defensibly develop a basic outline of Reformed theology, the question remains: How great a shift in theological emphasis is required to necessitate a new liturgical articulation? Specifically within the American Presbyterian tradition, a question which must be considered is: What are the liturgical implications of the Confession of 1967?

Mercersburg's lesson, then, is methodological, providing the Reformed tradition with its best illustration of Cowley's dictum noted above: "It is theology that makes worship, and worship is always the expression of theology.... Worship is the dramatization of theology, and is its living technicolour film."

Relationship of Word and Sacraments

An issue of considerable concern within the Reformed tradition today is the liturgical and theological relationship of Word and Sacraments. There are doubtless many who would need convincing, yet the principle of a balance between Word and Sacraments surely need not be debated. It is biblically sound and common--in theory at least--to every major Christian tradition. That worship is incomplete without both Word and Sacrament was acknowledged by every major reformer except Zwingli. So, too, the vast number of Protestant liturgical authorities writing today argue the same principle--again, in theory; yet the fact is that in practice liturgical incompleteness appears to be here to stay. The question then becomes: What arrangement can be devised, other than a weekly celebration of the Eucharist, which will still constitute a defensible "balance" between Word and Sacraments? Furthermore, until serious consideration is given to the relationship of discipline and the Eucharist, to what extent is an increase in the frequency of celebration desirable?

Mercersburg contributes little to the discussion of church discipline, simply because it was not an issue in the nineteenth century. The session minutes of a Presbyterian church in Arkansas[9] bear awesome testimony that church discipline was faithfully exercised and rigidly enforced well into the first two decades of the twentieth century. Liturgical rather than judicial or constitutional forms were provided in the *Order of Worship*, and one gets the impression that they did not go unused. The "Preparation for the Holy Communion"--a service rarely used in Reformed congregations today--was maintained by the German Reformed Church in the nineteenth century and is still found with some frequency in those United Church of Christ congregations which trace their lineage to the German Reformed. The fencing of the Table in the *Order of Worship* is neither as detailed or extensive as that in Calvin's Genevan liturgy; however, the same point is clearly made:

> These holy mysteries are not for the ir-
> reverent, the worldly, or the profane. If
> any of you who are here present...know your-
> selves to be the willing servants of sin,
> being without repentance and faith, and
> yielding yourselves to the power of worldly
> affections and lusts, we solemnly warn and
> admonish you, that ye presume not, so long
> as this is your character, to come to the
> table of the Lord.

The exercise of church discipline is of no little concern today, when sessions and consistories recoil at the
prospects of censure or excommunication, and when national
attention is given to those rare occasions when such action
is taken. Furthermore, one could wonder if those sessions
and consistories willing to take such measures where appropriate do not consider it rather an insignificant gesture
when absence from communion is no longer the punishment it
was once considered to be. Perhaps it is too great a gener-
alization to make without some documentation; nevertheless,
the widespread ignorance among clergy and laity in matters
eucharistic seems to be the fundamental problem in matters
judicial. Discipline and the Eucharist are inextricably re-
lated--the former being exercised primarily for the purpose
of protecting the latter from unworthy partakers, of protecting the unworthy partaker from the Eucharist, of protecting the Eucharistic fellowship from the unworthy, and
of restoring the unworthy to his or her rightful place among
the faithful--therefore, any consideration of an increase in
the frequency of celebrating the Eucharist must involve
serious consideration of church discipline. Nichols and von
Allmen both speak to this matter, and each arrives at a
different conclusion. Commenting on the otherwise commend-
able attempt of the Provisional Liturgy of the United Presby-

terian Church to increase the frequency of the Eucharist,
Nichols wrote: "Where there is as much unfinished business
as with us in the theological understanding of the Communion
and devotional preparation for it, a weekly celebration seems
a desperately risky expedient. A monthly norm might be wiser
with most of our congregations."[10] In short, when the widespread liturgical uncertainty among clergy and laity is considered, is it not entirely un-Reformed to open the Eucharist
to virtually all and sundry? The monthly norm which Nichols
suggests would give adequate time for some measure of preparation by both minister and congregation--a preparation hopefully supported by a thorough-going educational process in
the church school and from the pulpit.

Von Allmen recognizes the problem, although he comes at
it from a slightly different direction. Discipline must be
exercised in order for the Eucharist...

> to mark the difference between the Church
> and the world in a way which is not sub-
> jective, self-centered and moralizing, but
> objective. Listening to the Word is for
> all; but communion is for those who have
> not only listened to the word, but have re-
> ceived it and keep it; and I am convinced
> that if in our Church there is such con-
> fusion about the theological interpretation
> of the relation between the Church and the
> world, it is because our sacramental life
> has become so atrophied.[11]

In a footnote von Allmen continues:

> I do not mean that the Eucharist auto-
> matically guarantees the maintenance of
> church discipline....But it is clear that
> it is not with reference to preaching

> that discipline can be exercised, but with
> reference to sacramental life. If among
> ourselves discipline has disappeared, it is
> largely because of the atrophy of sacra-
> mental life; and if it [discipline] is so
> difficult to restore, it is because its
> point of reference is normally lacking.[12]

In short, von Allmen argues that discipline will not be restored until the frequency of the Eucharist is measurably
increased.

Certainly both Nichols and von Allmen have a point. If
discipline and the Eucharist are inextricably related, then
it is of little avail to exercise a more responsible discipline when the Eucharist is celebrated only quarterly.
Granted, discipline should be properly exercised regardless
of the number of celebrations; however, does a quarterly
celebration sufficiently testify to the significance and
centrality of the Eucharist to make the reasons for a strin-
gent discipline clear and acceptable? In the opinion of
this writer, it does not; therefore it will take a substantial increase in the number of celebrations to force the
issue of discipline. On the other hand, Nichols' point that
a completely open and undisciplined celebration of the Eucharist is entirely un-Reformed is true. "One cannot...attempt
to recover Calvin's communion service with sermon for every
Lord's Day without coming to terms with Calvin's insistence
on a disciplined congregation....Forms of worship are secondary matters. The primary questions are the faith and discipline of the Church and unless these are healthy there will
be no significant reform in worship."[13]

In the absence of a weekly celebration of Communion,
what measures can be taken to realize and maintain a "balance" between Word and Sacraments? Oddly enough, Mercers-

burg's liturgical accomplishments in this regard speak more
eloquently than its writings, for virtually nothing was
written regarding either the matter of frequency or balance.
One cannot avoid the hunch that the liturgy committee would
have liked to urge an increase in the celebrations of Communion; however, the members were undoubtedly aware that such
a recommendation would open them to even more criticism.
There is nothing in the minutes of the committee to indicate
that the matter was ever discussed. The opening rubric in
the *Order of Worship*, written by Harbaugh, merely states
the requirement of the Constitution, with the addition of a
final phrase: "The Sacrament of the Lord's Supper shall be
administered publicly in the Church, in every Congregation,
at least twice a year, *and if possible oftener*." [Italics
mine.]

As has been noted above, neither of the Mercersburg
liturgies adopted the ante-communion structure, devised
originally by Bucer and maintained by Calvin. Certainly
this pattern--if explained to a congregation--can indeed
point to the centrality of even an absent Eucharist. During
the past ten years this writer has been associated with congregations in which such liturgical education and change
have taken place, and in his opinion they have been remarkably effective in restoring a weekly Eucharistic consciousness. The entire liturgy, except for the readings and the
sermon, is conducted from the Table--a recommendation urged
by Mercersburg. Such a procedure focuses attention upon the
center of Eucharistic action, made even more pointed if the
chalice and nothing more adorns the Table.

The manner in which the liturgical committee sought to
correlate the Lord's Day service and the occasional services
with the prayers and form of the Eucharist is yet another way

to make Communion central. If, for example, the prayers regularly begin with the Salutation, Sursum Corda, Gratia Agamus and Vere Dignum, the Eucharistic Prayer is recalled to the minds of the congregation.

As stated above, it is the opinion of this writer that some substantial increase in the frequency of Communion must be expected before the discipline question can be answered, or before the Eucharist is recognized as the central ritual of Christian worship. The monthly rhythm proposed by Nichols would certainly seem a proper beginning. If this is supported by a thorough education in both the church schools and the seminaries, it just could be that future generations--And who is so optimistic as to believe that it will be accomplished in one or two?--may yet recover this imperative balance between Word and Sacrament, established in the New Testament and early church, and recaptured by the Reformation.

The Corporate Factor

Whatever else the Reformation meant for worship, it did return the liturgy to the people. Although Luther moved cautiously in this area, Protestant worship soon was conducted in the vernacular. Prayer books--a Protestant phenomenon-- were owned and used by the people; and worship reclaimed its historic notes of joy and adoration as the people again sang the liturgy. The distinctive use to which Calvin put the Psalter has been well-documented by Nichols and others. "The Reformers, by putting the [liturgical] texts in the vernacular, and in meter adapted to musical settings in the current musical idiom and within the scope of the common man, gave a liturgical voice to those who had been kept mute and passive for centuries."[14] Calvin was especially fond of sung responses because he observed "that the congregation could actually pray the words more effectively than when they labored to read the several parts".[15]

The corporate nature of Reformed worship, so characteristic of the sixteenth century, degenerated somewhat during the centuries that followed, due largely to the Puritan Revolution and revivalistic evangelicalism. The Separatist doctrine of the Church and anti-liturgical ideas gradually penetrated the historic Reformed liturgical pattern, with the result that much of the corporate character was lost. Revivalistic evangelicalism changed the purpose of worship: no longer was the "liturgy" designed to facilitate the peoples' corporate adoration and prayer; rather the goal was now individual conversion, and the "liturgy" became an instrument in the hands of clergy and choir through which that conversion was hopefully precipitated. In a sense Protestant worship had come full circle--from sacerdotalism of the Roman variety to sacerdotalism of the revivalistic variety. "How much better is the congregation that listens to a liturgical performance almost completely dominated by minister and choir than a medieval congregation which watched a liturgical performance almost completely dominated by priest and singers?"[16]

Briefly put, this clerically dominated worship was the context in which the Mercersburg liturgical movement began; and by contrast with the general liturgical surroundings Mercersburg's attempt to reclaim the corporate and congregational character of Reformed worship is all the more remarkable. The sixth Baltimore proposal makes the intention quite

clear: "Like the Bible, the Catechism, and the Hymn Book,
[the Liturgy] ought to be the common property and manual of
every member of the Church. The laymen will take a far
deeper interest in the devotional exercises, if they can
follow the minister by their book, and respond at least
with an audible Amen at the end of each prayer." The
strategy for the restoration of the peoples' part in worship
also involved including a lengthy section of family prayers--
and, it will be remembered, family worship was not at all an
uncommon thing in the mid-nineteenth century--a selection of
the best historic hymns bound with the liturgy; and a number
of spoken responses in addition to the Amen were provided.

The spoken responses were the most controversial issue
during the Mercersburg liturgical controversy. Originally
Bomberger's primary objection was to the *number* of responses,
and in the revised version of the Provisional Liturgy he submitted to the Synod of 1862, he retained certain of them.
The Mercersburg advocates then argued that once a single
response was permitted--even the Amen--the principle was
conceded and the question as to the number became academic.
This pushed Bomberger to the extreme and his final position
was to tolerate no responses at all other than the brief
answers to the constitutional questions in the services of
Baptism, Confirmation, and Ordination.

Clearly the *Order of Worship* does become somewhat
fussy with its many versicles and responses. In addition
to confusing congregations accustomed to little more than
the Lord's Prayer--if that--the responses prolong the service. This, too, became an issue, likely because the responses made the liturgy seem longer than it actually was.
Historically and practically Nichols' argument that the Reformed congregation has traditionally been a singing rather

than a speaking congregation is well-taken.[17] In the
opinion of this writer, the versicle responses should be
kept to a minimum in Reformed liturgies--not only because
they are untraditional, but because congregations are so un-
familiar with them. There are other ways in which the people
may become actively involved in the liturgy. With some instruction and a well-rehearsed choir, a number of the responses in the communion service may be sung--e.g., Kyrie,
Sanctus, Agnus Dei, and Nunc Dimittis. The hymnbooks of
most Reformed denominations now provide several musical
settings for these historic responses, the continued use of
which (said or sung) keeps a twentieth-century congregation
in communion with the saints. Certainly a minimum of three
well-chosen hymns should be expected in a normal Lord's Day
service. Whereas Mercersburg provided no rubrication as to
the types of hymns which should be used, this is a helpful
and educational service which liturgical committees can perform. Traditionally Reformed worship begins on a note of
adoration and praise, and the rubric should specify this.
The "middle" hymn, which often follows either the New Testament lesson or the Sermon, is customarily associated themati-
cally with the sermon and lessons; while the final hymn could
well reflect the sense of mission and witness with which the
service of worship concludes. Nichols has wisely observed
that any attempt to revive the metrical Psalter of Calvin's
Geneva would be a fruitless and antiquarian venture. "Rather
it is for us to follow the principles which led to the metrical psalms, to use Biblical themes and materials in worship
and put them in the literary and musical idiom of the common
man, so that he may make the worship really his."[18]

The Psalter need not be lost, however. This writer
would agree with Nichols that the best alternative now

available is the responsive reading, still retained by many
Reformed congregations in America, and that the most appropriate place in the service for the Psalm to appear is following the Declaration of Pardon. The Psalm is then followed by
the Gloria Patri, sung by the congregation.[19] It is to be
hoped that someone will yet provide modern congregations with
a musical version of the Psalter, for much of the joy which
the Psalm should convey is lost through the wooden manner in
which it is read responsively.

Still other ways in which the congregation may take an
active part in the liturgy include the repetition of the
Lord's Prayer and the Apostles' Creed, both of which are used
with regularity in Reformed worship today. Then there is the
Amen, periodically called for in worship since St. Paul's
plea for its use in 1 Corinthians 14. A personal note is
again in order in this regard, for this writer has been
associated with congregations which have easily accepted the
Amen and faithfully use it, not only in the regular Lord's
Day worship but around the family table as well. The minister explained the purpose of the Amen to the congregation
through a sermon,[20] during the course of which a "trial run"
was taken simply to accustom the congregation to the sound
of its corporate voice. There has been no need for further
words on the matter.

The custom of inviting laymen to participate in the
service of worship—particularly the reading of the lessons—
is one which appears to be gaining favor today. This is
theoretically defensible; however, practical considerations
may overrule the theoretical in this matter. In this writer's
judgment, the quality of most lay reading leaves much to be
desired. It often becomes a performance in which the congregations' main concern is who will win today, the reader or

the "begats"? Furthermore, once this door is open, can it ever be closed--i.e., must an open invitation be extended to all and sundry? In short, this practice may well create more problems than it solves.

That Reformed prayer books will ever become the cherished property of individuals in the same way that the *Book of Common Prayer* and the Missal are owned and known is doubtful. As in the matter of spoken responses, the people are simply not accustomed to owning and using prayer books. This is certainly not to say that they could not be trained to do so (to a measurable extent) nor that it would be undesirable; however, the clergy must first be trained to use a prayer book and sessions encouraged to make these books available in the pews before the congregation will even know what they are, let alone desire a copy for personal use. Again, through the general education of both youth and adults, it is quite possible for this characteristic Protestant practice to come into general use again. If the prayer book were regularly used in the corporate worship of the congregation, there is every reason to believe that it would find its way into many homes, there to provide a guide for private and family devotion.

Relationship of Free and Fixed Prayer

As James F. White has observed: "Probably all that can possibly be said on the relative merits of free prayers and set forms was said in the seventeenth and eighteenth centuries."[21] All the arguments were rehearsed again, however, during the Mercersburg liturgical controversy; and, as was the case with the disputants in previous centuries, those in the nineteenth refused to acknowledge that there was clearly truth on both sides and that the Reformed way is a balance of both.

It is common knowledge that Calvin's Genevan liturgy provided only two occasions for free prayer--the Collect for the Day and the Prayer for Illumination. This combination of free and fixed prayers was maintained until the Puritan Revolution; and, as has been shown by many liturgical authorities, even the Puritans were not initially opposed to all set forms. The Savoy Liturgy is sufficient proof of this. With a complete reaction against the Church of England and later revivalism, however, the prayers became almost entirely "pastoral".

The original intention of the German Reformed liturgical committee was to maintain the historic balance between the free and fixed forms. One of the Baltimore proposals reads in part: "A liturgy ought not to interfere with the proper use of extemporaneous prayer, either in public or in private, but rather to regulate and promote it." Rubrics in the Provisional Liturgy did provide occasions for the use of free prayer; however, these were removed from the *Order of Worship*. The debate which this omission occasioned followed the traditional lines: free prayer can be more pertinent, specific, spontaneous, and simple; whereas fixed prayer permits the congregation to pray with the saints and protects them from the thematic whims and devotional ineptitude of the minister. On one occasion the question was raised: If one prays in the words of another person, is it not the other person who is praying? The answer came back: No more so than if one sings a hymn, is it the author of the hymn who does the singing. Gerhart addressed himself to the question of free and fixed forms and arrived at this conclusion: public or common prayer demands a different form and language from private prayer. "In Public Prayer *man*, as such, with the wants that are peculiar to him as distinguished from the angels, is the main thing, whilst in Private Prayer the *individual* man, with what may be necessary to him as such, is the prominent thought."[22] White draws something of the same distinction: "Set prayers reflect the changeless aspects of the orders; free prayers seek to interpret the way in which they are changing."[23]

In the end the point is that each form "has its value in certain circumstances; insistence on the exclusive use of either is doctrinaire absolutism".[24] These "certain circumstances" are as much sociological as liturgical--i.e., some congregations and some clergymen are more disposed to one form than the other, and one of the Reformed liturgical insights is precisely that these circumstances can be taken into account. If set prayer is genuinely a stumbling block to many of those in a given congregation, then there is every reason not to force the issue of set forms, for the ultimate question is not whether the prayers be fixed or free; rather, "Whether the prayers be...adequate instruments for corporate prayer?"[25] Through responsible preparation and use of the phrases of the ages, the minister can be fully liturgical and corporate through a judicious use of free prayer. So, too, it must be said, can a minister's manner render the classic devotions wooden and inappropriate as vehicles of corporate prayer.

In the judgment of this writer the balance of free and fixed prayer should be maintained, for both are valuable; and this should be made clear in the rubrics of our liturgies. Furthermore, suggestions concerning which forms of

prayer may most likely be fixed and free would be helpful--
e.g., the prayers of adoration and confession express the
changeless character of man's relationship to God, and at
these points it is particularly appropriate to join the
chorus of the ages. A traditional structure has developed
regarding the prayer of thanksgiving, and such a prayer
should include expressions of corporate gratitude for
creation, preservation, and redemption. The prayers of
supplication and intercession are perhaps the points at
which free (although premeditated) prayer is most appropriate, for they reflect the changing relationship of God with
his people. Through such a use of free and fixed prayer a
local congregation is able to witness both to its catholicity and particularity, as it lives out its life within the
context of God's providence and purpose.

The Church Year and Lectionary

Two systems of Scripture readings have traditionally
been followed in Christian worship: *lectio continua*, the
serialized reading in course, and *lectio selecta*, which
specifies thematic pericopes. According to von Allmen,
"The system of *lectio continua* is more historical, that of
the *lectio selecta* more systematic."[26] While both are defensible and each has its respective merits, the latter
system generally prevailed among Anglicans and Lutherans;
whereas, Zwingli and Calvin restored the patristic *lectio
continua* method and this became a Reformed liturgical characteristic. The custom of combining continuous exposition with
the half-dozen chief festivals of the Church Year was widely
used among the several Reformed traditions until "Puritanism

and revivalism...undermined this Reformed system and left us with the current custom of unorganized topical preaching".[27]

Mercersburg preferred the *lectio selecta* pattern, as has been shown above, and proposed a fully developed Church Year, complete with several of the more widely celebrated saints' days. Although the specific readings have changed somewhat with each version, this system has been followed in all subsequent prayer books of the German Reformed Church, the Evangelical and Reformed Church, and the United Church of Christ. So, too, is the *lectio selecta* and Church Year proposed in the prayer books of the Reformed Church in America and the Presbyterian denominations; however, the extent to which the lectionary is followed except for the chief festivals of the Church Year is debatable.

In an attempt to maintain the best of both systems, Nichols has made an interesting proposal--*viz.*, *lectio selecta* from Advent to Pentecost and *lectio continua* during the long and uneventful Trinity season. Were this procedure followed, it would combine an annual festival-rehearsal of the life of Christ with an opportunity for preaching continuously through a book other than one of the Gospels. "Such a series will do more justice to the propositions and dynamic movement of a biblical book and can be more readily coordinated with Bible study in the educational program of the church."[28]

Such a plan would be desirable in the opinion of this writer. There is, however, one practical drawback. To be most effective, preaching in series presupposes a certain degree of consistency in the congregation's attendance. That cannot be presumed in many congregations today, for summer vacations and week end holidays often force a discontinuation

of the educational program of the church and inevitably mean
uncertain and inconsistent attendance at worship. During the
period from mid-June through mid-September the *lectio continua*
pattern would simply not be feasible in some congregations;
however, there is no reason to doubt that the Sundays from
mid-September to the beginning of Advent could not be profitably used in the manner Nichols describes.

Relationship of the Universal and the Indigenous

According to Schaff, the ideal liturgy is one which "is
a bond of union with the ancient Catholic Church and the
Reformation, and yet...the product of the religious life of
our denomination in its present state". The theoretical
question this raises is: What is the relationship between
the universal and the indigenous in a liturgy? If the continuity in Christian history is acknowledged, and yet if it
is equally affirmed that God did not cease his self-disclosing
with Pentecost, then a tension between the catholic and the
particular must be maintained. To quote Schaff again:
"...every age of the Church has the promise of the Spirit
and a particular mission to fulfil."[29]

J. G. Davies has addressed himself to this issue in
Worship and Mission; however, he deals only at the theoretical level. "Monastic devotions" are clearly inadequate forms
of devotion for twentieth-century man, he insists.[30] Again:
the church's cultus "must not be decided on the sole basis
of past forms, but must be constructed in the light of the
Church's vocation to mission today".[31] Quite rightly he observes that liturgical indigenization is a problem for the

twentieth-century West as well as for Asia and Africa. Yet
in all this there is not a hint at the specifics of what the
theory means. Mercersburg's emphasis on an incarnational
theology and a dynamic understanding of history forced the
liturgical committee to deal with this balance of the universal and the indigenous. How did the committee proceed
and fare?

First, the Baltimore proposals made it quite clear that
the early church was to provide the primary point of liturgical reference. In drawing upon the third and fourth centuries of the Greek and Latin traditions a universal was
established both liturgically and theologically. Nevin and
Schaff wanted one foot firmly planted in the period before
the deep divisions within Christendom developed. Second,
special theological reference was taken of the Reformation.
Sixteenth-century liturgical principles were observed--the
corporate nature of worship, the peoples' prayer book, the
relationship of Word and Sacraments--however, liturgical
forms from this century were rarely adopted. A complete
prayer book was then compiled and created within these two
points of reference; yet a book the character of which was
designed to meet the specific needs (if not wants) of the
German Reformed Church in nineteenth-century America. The
men who selected and adapted the forms were pastors and professors sensitive to their denominational constituency, in
spite of the fact that they almost unanimously represented
one specific theological and liturgical position.

Synod's will was followed in most matters--e.g., a
regular Lord's Day service was provided; the service for
Immigrants was included; an improved Marriage service was
offered; and a selection of hymns was bound with the Pro-

visional Liturgy. In still other ways the committee was not
as sensitive to the denomination as it could have been.
Heiner's complaint that the Provisional Liturgy contained
no services to be used at sea apparently won general support,
for such services were included in the *Order of Worship*.
Beyond this debate over specific forms, however, it must be
said again that the denomination clearly desired alternative
and less liturgically complicated forms, as well as rubrical
latitude in the matter of free prayer. Even though Nevin
stated that he felt the *Order of Worship* would meet with
widespread favor, as the more loosely constructed Provisional
Liturgy did not, he seems to have proceeded with the revision
as if he knew full well the *Order of Worship* would not be
acceptable under any circumstances; therefore, write the
"perfect" liturgy for posterity. In sum, then, Mercersburg
operated on the correct theory--a bond between the universal
and the indigenous--but the practice left not a little to be
desired.

Practically speaking, what are the liturgical implications of this attempt to span the centuries? The form for
celebrating the Eucharist may be taken as a case in point.
What is the universal? And what is the indigenous? Especially since Reformed theology has stressed that the Presence and the benefits are association with the *action* rather
than with the "moment of Consecration" (whatever that "moment" may be), the universal dimension may be maintained in
the construction of Reformed liturgies around the classical
"shape" of taking, blessing, breaking, and receiving. Furthermore, to be consistent with Reformed practice, the Words
of Institution should be repeated before the Eucharistic
Prayer as a warrant for the action. That Prayer, however,

may take on an indigenous character through its language and emphases; retaining a universal dimension all the while through the expression of historic themes: eucharistia, anamnesis, epiclesis, fellowship, eschatology, and mystery.

The very language of devotion is itself a debatable issue. Even though Reformed liturgies are not canonized and are thereby free to change as time and circumstance demand, one may question the wisdom of purposely building semantic obsolescence into a liturgy by changing its language to the radically contemporary. As the content of corporate prayer differs from private prayer, so does corporate language differ from conversational cliché. The liturgy must indeed be contemporary and indigenous; yet it has always been and must always be a conservative instrument, willing to change, but waiting to make certain of God's new direction. The "Now" Testament lesson—a reading from the newspaper as if it were on a par with Scripture—is coming into wider use in those congregations whose ministers fancy themselves *avant-garde* liturgiologists. Such sensationalism is an indigenization of dubious missionary value.

So, too, is the current experimentation with jazz settings for the liturgy open to serious question. As musical performances the works by Ellington, Beaumont, and Guraldi are to be commended; however, as vehicles of corporate worship they are impossible. Jazz is by definition improvisation—the diametrical opposite of the liturgy's regularity and order. Often the missionary argument is used to justify these experiments, and perhaps their sensational nature does attract some who would not be disposed to associate themselves with the institutional church; however,

this writer is inclined to agree with Eric Routley's
assessment of this musical innovation: "At present I am
not persuaded that the enterprise, considered as missionary
work is sound, for it appears to have some of the defects
of end-gaining, effect-hunting, and a desire for quick influence that have brought plenty of similar evangelistic
adventures to grief."[32]

In short, the issue is surely resolved in this:
establish the great Biblical themes which have been historically expressed in the liturgy; then charge a poet,
familiar with the liturgical past and sensitive to the social
present with the task of articulating these themes in a
manner which expresses man's contemporary self-understanding
in the light of God's contemporary self-disclosure. This
represents the ideal, of course, and it will seldom be
attained in a liturgy; however it is the goal toward which
the imperative tension between the universal and indigenous
points.

Degree of Liturgical Freedom

The relationship of the universal and the indigenous
gives rise to this final question: What is the degree of
liturgical freedom demanded by and desirable within the Reformed tradition? It is common knowledge that Reformed
churches have never canonized the liturgy--any liturgy. At
various times prayer books or directories have been produced;
yet even when these were designed as peoples' books rather
than pulpit manuals, they remained optional.

From Calvin to the present day one can find no serious
Reformed attempt to legislate liturgical usage.[33] Calvin set
the pattern with his principle of "accomodation". He conformed to local usage at Geneva and Strasburg, and advised
Reformed congregations in Lutheran and Anglican lands to
accomodate themselves to certain ritualistic practices such
as bells, altars, candles, and vestments. "There was some
point, he felt, in avoiding uniformity just to make clear
that Christianity cannot be defined by ceremonial practices."[34] Of course, this is not to suggest that Calvin
had no liturgical mind of his own; however, he made it quite
clear that no Lutheran or Anglican ceremonial peculiarities
"could justify the denial of intercommunion".[35]

On the question of liturgical uniformity, one obtains
a remarkable consensus from Reformed liturgical scholars
today. Reformed worship is of the tabernacle, not of the
temple, Hageman argues. It is a conversation between God
and man--a conversation which is constantly changing.[36] God
cannot be imprisoned in any one liturgical form. He may be
present in any--or none! Jansen[37] and Niesel both argue that
Reformed liturgical form is strictly functional. The latter
puts it this way: "The order has no value of its own, but
only in so far as it serves to build up the Body of Christ.
Since the matter there at issue is the gathering and perfecting of the congregation, the form of worship must be adjusted
with this eschatological goal in view. That is to say, there
is no classic order of service."[38]

The point each is making reflects the Reformed principle
of indigenization, discussed above. While there must be
continuity with the past (As Nichols points out: the bulk
of Calvin's service "consisted of set liturgical forms in
which the congregation could sense its unity with the whole

praying Church of all generations."),[39] Reformed liturgics
should nevertheless be designed "to reflect the sociological
conditions of each individual congregation".[40]

Why *must* this be so? Sociological sensitivity--or
"eschatalogical" concern, to use Hageman's and Niesel's
term--surely reflects in some measure the Reformed principle
that, fundamentally, liturgy articulates theology. As the
Confession of 1967 has made the United Presbyterian Church
aware, the emphases and expressions of theology change as
new historical and sociological situations confront the
church. To the extent that the form and content of the
liturgy emerge out of that theology, so, too, must they
change. For example, as beautiful and devotional as it
surely is, the fact remains that the *Book of Common Prayer*
is basically a product of sixteenth-century England. To
suppose that it provides the best liturgical vehicle for the
twentieth-century West, let alone Asia and Africa, expects
far too much from even this masterpiece. Similar Biblical
themes can certainly be expressed, and the object of worship
will always remain the same; however, cultural differences
as well as changing theological emphases may necessitate
different liturgical forms. Surely this is an insight
which the Reformed tradition can contribute to the wider
ecumenical enterprise.

What was Mercersburg's answer to the question of
liturgical order? As has been indicated in the discussion
of indigenization, Schaff was not unaware of the sociological demands made by Reformed liturgics. The fourth Baltimore proposal specified that alternative forms, "some
shorter, some larger, some with and without responses",
should be provided, "with a view to avoid monotony, and to
adapt them the more readily to the condition and wants of

our various ministers and congregations which are evidently
not prepared for an entire uniformity". The Provisional
Liturgy was partially true to Baltimore's word, offering
four forms for the Lord's Day; however, no alternative form
was provided for the Holy Communion, as was originally suggested. At no time did Schaff desire legislated liturgical
uniformity; however, when commenting on Baird's *A Book of
Public Prayer*, he did make it clear that "a simply optional
or discretionary liturgy will never answer the true idea of
public worship. A liturgy, like the catechism, the constitution, and the hymn book, should have the sanction of ecclesiastical authority, and be the law of the Church which
adopts it, so long as it is found to answer its purpose. It
is in this way only that that order, dignity and unity of
worship can be maintained and promoted, which is one of the
chief objects in the adoption and use of a good liturgy."[41]

The *Order of Worship* removed the internal latitude afforded by the Provisional Liturgy; however, in 1866 it was
clear that the Western Synod would eventually produce a
liturgy of its own and that it would offer a genuine alternative to the *Order of Worship*. The realization that were
liturgical uniformity desirable, it was politically impossible, and that the denomination would likely have before it
two different liturgies for optional use, may have encouraged
Nevin and the liturgical committee to proceed with their revision of the Provisional Liturgy along theoretical rather
than political lines. If Nevin had ever felt that liturgical
uniformity was desirable--and there is every reason to believe that he had at least considered the possibility--he
disclaimed the idea in 1869. "There is no reason at all for
insisting on full uniformity of worship in our churches.

The general scheme should be one; but the ways of carrying it out may be various....The idea of a Procrustean Liturgy-- one exact frame of worship for all our churches--has nothing to do with our proper church unity. We may have half a dozen liturgies and still be one church."[42]

The question remains: Is it possible or desirable to legislate some minimum liturgical uniformity, at least to the same extent that minimum doctrinal uniformity is required? This writer would answer in the affirmative. Because of the specifically doctrinal nature of Confirmation, Ordination, Baptism, and the Eucharist, all congregations should strictly follow the denominationally approved orders for these services. With regard to the Eucharist, especially, alternative forms should be provided, which permit options as regards length and liturgical complexity (responses, etc.); however, the "canon"--i.e., the Eucharistic Prayer--should be fixed.

No legislation would appear to be either possible or desirable regarding the regular Lord's Day service. It is possible, again, to include a variety of alternative forms, differing sufficiently in particulars to meet the needs of most congregations. The advantage in this is simply to aid the liturgically untutored by providing forms for the clergy which reflect the best scholarly opinion and which have received the examination and sanction of the denomination. Furthermore, guidance by way of rubrics and examples should be available regarding the selection of hymns; and a clear rationale and explanation of the lectionary and Church Year is needed to permit the minister to make an intelligent decision regarding his or her homiletical and liturgical procedures. Much of this would be unnecessary, of course, if the Reformed traditions in America would take the liturgy seriously enough at the level of seminary education to train the clergy in matters such as those outlined above.

NOTES TO CHAPTER VIII

1. Since certain of these conclusions are drawn with the Presbyterian Church in mind, the terms, Presbytery and General Assembly, may be used interchangeably with Synod and Classis at certain points. When past actions are considered, the appropriate nomenclature will be followed.

2. Patrick Cowley, *The Eucharistic Church* (London: The Faith Press, Ltd., 1953), pp. viii-ix.

3. Quoted in J. G. Davies, *Worship and Mission* (New York: Association Press, 1967), p. 142.

4. Harbaugh, *Tercentenary Monument*, p. 294.

5. B. A. Gerrish, "The Lord's Supper in the Reformed Confessions," *Theology Today*, XXIII (1966), pp. 224-243.

6. Hageman, *Pulpit and Table*, p. 92.

7. *Ibid.*, p. 119.

8. See especially Lukas Visher, ed., *A Documentary History of the Faith and Order Movement, 1927-1963* (St. Louis: The Bethany Press, 1963), and Howard G. Hageman, "The Coming-of-Age of the Liturgical Movement," *Studia Liturgica*, II (1963), pp. 256-265.

9. Currently in the possession of this writer's family.

10. James H. Nichols, "Is the New 'Service' Reformed?" *Theology Today*, XXI (1964), p. 363.

11. J.-J. von Allmen, *Worship: Its Theology and Practice* (New York: Oxford University Press, 1965), p. 155.

12. *Ibid.*

13. Nichols, "The Liturgical Tradition of the Reformed Churches," p. 224.

14. *Ibid.*, p. 222.

15. *Ibid.*

16. Hageman, *Pulpit and Table*, p. 120.

17. Nichols, "Is the New 'Service' Reformed?", p. 366.

18. Nichols, "The Liturgical Tradition of the Reformed Churches," p. 223.

19. Nichols, "Is the New 'Service' Reformed?", p. 368.

20. Jack M. Maxwell, "The Little Word 'Amen'," *Princeton Seminary Bulletin*, LXII, 1 (Winter 1969), pp. 58-63.

21. James F. White, *The Worldliness of Worship* (New York: Oxford University Press, 1967), p. 77.

22. *WM*, April 27, 1868.

23. White, *op. cit.*, p. 77.

24. Nichols, "Is the New 'Service' Reformed?", p. 361.

25. Hageman, *Pulpit and Table*, p. 121.

26. Von Allmen, *op. cit.*, p. 134.

27. Nichols, "Is the New 'Service' Reformed?", p. 364.

28. *Ibid.*, pp. 364-365.

29. Baltimore proposal, number three.

30. Davies, *Worship and Mission*, p. 145.

31. *Ibid.*, p. 147.

32. Eric Routley, *Church Music and Theology* (London: SCM Press, Ltd., 1959), p. 107.

33. The Dutch Reformed Church in America and others have sought to prescribe the usage of the sacramental forms; however, such a prescription has never been successfully enforced.

34. Nichols, "The Liturgical Tradition of the Reformed Churches," pp. 211-212.

35. *Ibid.*

36. Hageman, *Pulpit and Table*, p. 124.

37. John F. Jansen, "Calvin on a Fixed Form of Worship
--A Note in Textual Criticism," *Scottish Journal of Theology*,
15 (1962), pp. 282-287.

38. Wilhelm Niesel, "The Order of Public Worship in
the Reformed Churches," *Scottish Journal of Theology*, 2
(1949), p. 386.

39. Nichols, "The Liturgical Tradition of the Reformed
Churches," p. 213.

40. White, *op. cit.*, p. 160.

41. Schaff, Review of *A Book of Public Prayer*, *MR*,
VIII (1857), p. 325.

42. *WM*, September 15, 1869.

EPILOGUE

Since ours "must always be a liturgy of the tabernacle, never of the temple", that liturgy will change as God's pilgrim people continue to wander in and out of wilderness and promised land. Mercersburg was but a way station on that pilgrimage; yet if we remember those way stations in our past, we are better able to distinguish between the mirage and the oasis which constantly shimmer across our present horizons. Many are the liturgical lessons which Mercersburg can teach those willing to learn, and the more lasting among her successes and failures have been detailed here. But perhaps the most important lesson of them all is this: Whatever else the liturgy may be, it is the rhythmical heartbeat of that conglomeration of sinners who become a community of saints when bread is broken and wine poured out in remembrance of Jesus Christ.

> Blame us not if we value our Liturgy:
> it embodies the anthems of Saints; it
> thrills the heart with the dying songs
> of the faithful; it is hallowed with the
> blood of martyrs; it glows with sacred
> fire.[1]

Mercersburg was not the first to make that discovery; but in the manner of her rediscovery, she has left to us the richest of liturgical legacies.

NOTE TO THE EPILOGUE

1. J. S. Foulk, "Forms of Prayer," p. 148.

APPENDIX I

Attendance Roll

The secretary of the liturgical committee, Henry Harbaugh, faithfully noted the members present at each session. Such a record aids in evaluating the contribution each member made and the influence he had on the work of the committee. Abbreviations are as follows:

    PS   - Philip Schaff
    JWN - John Williamson Nevin
    BCW - Bernard C. Wolff
    JHAB - John Henry Augustus Bomberger
    HH   - Henry Harbaugh
    EH   - Elias Heiner
    DZ   - Daniel Zacharias
    TCP - Thomas C. Porter
    EVG - Emanual V. Gerhart
    SRF - Samuel R. Fisher
    TGA - Thomas G. Apple
    JR   - John Rodenmayer
    LS   - Lewis Steiner

Not included are William Heyser, George Schaefer, and George C. Welker, none of whom attended any meetings of the liturgical committee.

SESSIONS	PS	JWN	BCW	JHAB	HH	EH	DZ	TCP	EVG	SRF	TGA	JR	LS
3/13-26/56													
1	*	*	*		*		*	*	*				
2	*	*	*		*		*	*					
3	*	*	*		*		*	*	*				
4	*	*	*		*	*	*						
5	*	*	*	*	*		*	*	*				
6	*	*	*	*	*		*	*	*				
7	*	*	*	*	*			*	*				
8		*		*	*		*	*	*				
9		*		*	*		*	*	*				
10		*		*	*			*					
11	*	*	*		*			*	*				
12	*	*	*	*	*			*	*				
13	*	*	*	*	*			*	*				
14	*	*		*	*			*	*				
15	*	*	*	*	*			*	*				
16	*	*	*		*								
17	*	*	*		*			*	*				
18	*	*	*		*			*					
19	*	*	*		*			*	*				
20	*	*			*			*	*				
21	*	*			*			*	*				
22	*	*			*			*	*				
23	*	*			*			*					
24	*	*			*			*	*				
25	*	*			*			*					
26	*	*			*			*					
27	*	*			*			*	*				
28	*	*			*			*					
29	*	*			*			*					
1/2-9/57													
30					*			*	*			*	
31	*				*			*	*			*	
32	*				*			*	*			*	
33	*				*			*	*			*	
34	*				*			*	*			*	
35	*	*			*			*	*			*	
36	*	*			*			*	*			*	

SESSIONS	PS	JWN	BCW	JHAB	HH	EH	DZ	TCP	EVG	SRF	TGA	JR	LS
1/2– 9/57 (cont.)													
37	*	*		*				*	*			*	
38	*	*		*				*	*			*	
39	*	*		*				*	*			*	
40	*			*				*				*	
41	*	*		*								*	
42	*	*		*				*					
43	*	*		*								*	
44	*	*	*	*				*	*				
45	*	*	*	*				*	*				
46	*	*	*	*									
47	*	*		*				*					
48	*	*		*				*					
4/20– 24/57													
49	*	*		*	*			*	*				
50	*			*	*			*	*				
51	*	*		*	*			*	*				
52	*	*			*			*	*				
53	*	*		*	*			*	*				
54	*	*		*				*	*				
55	omitted for purposes of review and research												
56	*			*	*			*					
57	*	*		*	*			*	*				
58	*	*		*	*			*	*				
8/25– 9/3/57													
59				*		*		*					
60		*		*				*					
61		*		*			*	*					
62	*	*		*			*	*		*			
63	*	*		*			*	*					
64	*	*		*		*	*	*					
65	*	*		*		*	*	*		*			
66	*	*		*		*	*	*					

SESSIONS	PS	JWN	BCW	JHAB	HH	EH	DZ	TCP	EVG	SRF	TGA	JR	LS
8/25- 9/3/57 (cont.)													
67	*	*			*	*	*	*	*				
68	*	*			*	*	*	*					
69	*	*			*	*	*						
70	*	*			*	*	*	*	*				
71	*	*			*				*				
72	*	*			*	*	*		*				
73	*	*			*	*	*	*	*				
74	*	*			*	*	*						
75	*	*			*	*	*	*	*				
76	*	*			*	*	*	*	*				
77	*				*	*	*	*	*				
78	*	*			*	*		*	*				
79	*	*			*	*	*	*	*				
80	*				*	*		*	*				
81	*	*			*			*	*				
82		*			*			*	*				
10/13- 21/57													
83	*	*		*					*			*	
84		*		*					*			*	
85	*	*	*	*					*				
86	*	*	*			*	*		*				
87	*	*		*	*	*	*		*			*	
88	*	*		*	*	*	*		*			*	
89	*	*	*	*	*	*	*					*	
90	*	*	*	*	*	*	*					*	
91	*	*	*	*	*	*	*					*	
92	*	*	*	*	*	*	*					*	
93	*	*	*	*	*	*	*					*	
94	*	*	*	*	*	*	*					*	
95	*	*	*	*	*	*	*					*	
96	*	*		*								*	
97	*	*	*	*		*						*	
98	*	*	*	*		*						*	
99	*	*	*	*		*						*	
100	*	*	*	*		*						*	
101	*	*	*	*		*						*	
102	*	*	*	*		*							

SESSIONS	PS	JWN	BCW	JHAB	HH	EH	DZ	TCP	EVG	SRF	TGA	JR	LS

ORDER OF WORSHIP

SESSIONS	PS	JWN	BCW	JHAB	HH	EH	DZ	TCP	EVG	SRF	TGA	JR	LS
1/6–9/62													
1		*			*			*	*			*	
2		*		*	*			*	*			*	
3		*		*	*			*	*			*	
4		*		*	*			*	*			*	
5		*		*	*			*	*			*	
6		*		*	*			*	*			*	
4/23–24/62													
1	*	*			*			*				*	
2	*	*		*	*			*	*			*	
3	*	*		*	*			*	*			*	
4	*	*		*	*			*	*			*	
3/7–9/65													
1	*	*	*	*	*		*	*	*		*		*
2	*	*	*	*	*		*	*	*		*		*
3	*	*	*	*	*		*	*	*		*		*
4	*	*	*	*	*		*	*	*		*		*
5		*	*	*	*		*	*	*		*		*
6		*	*	*	*		*	*	*		*		*
1/13–17/65													
7		*		*				*	*				
8		*	*	*				*	*				*
9		*						*	*				*
10		*	*	*				*	*				*
11		*	*	*				*	*				*
12		*		*				*	*				*

SESSIONS	PS	JWN	BCW	JHAB	HH	EH	DZ	TCP	EVG	SRF	TGA	JR	LS
1/13–17/65 (cont.)													
13		*	*	*				*	*				*
14		*	*	*				*	*				*
15		*	*					*	*				*
8/16–18/65													
16		*			*		*		*			*	*
17		*			*		*		*			*	*
18		*			*		*		*			*	*
19		*			*		*		*			*	*
20		*			*		*		*			*	*
21		*			*		*		*				*
12/5–7/65													
22		*	*		*			*	*		*		*
23		*	*		*			*	*		*		*
24	*	*	*		*			*	*		*		*
25	*	*	*		*			*	*		*		*
26	*		*		*				*		*		*
27	*		*		*			*	*		*		*
3/6–8/66													
28		*			*		*	*	*				*
29		*			*		*	*	*				*
30		*	*		*		*	*	*				*
31	*	*	*		*		*	*	*				*
32	*	*			*		*	*	*				*
33	*	*	*		*		*	*	*				*
34	*	*	*		*		*	*	*				*
35	*	*			*		*	*	*				*

SESSIONS	PS	JWN	BCW	JHAB	HH	EH	DZ	TCP	EVG	SRF	TGA	JR	LS
4/24–28/66													
36		*			*			*	*				*
37		*			*			*	*				*
38		*	*		*			*	*				*
39		*			*			*	*				*
40		*	*		*			*	*				*
41		*			*				*				*
42		*	*		*				*				*
43		*			*				*				*
44		*	*		*			*	*	*			*
45		*	*		*			*	*	*			*

Synod of
  York

| Oct. 17, 1866 | | * | * | | * | | | | | * | | * | |

APPENDIX II

Index of Authors in Deutsches Gesangbuch
(See note 13, page 190.)

Anonymous: 31, 56, 93, 103

Blakewell: 28

Brydges: 91

Cawood, J.: 13

Collyer: 23

Cowper: 69

Doane: 98

Doddridge: 16, 22, 41, 48, 51, 53, 76, 79, 101

Duncan: 34

Dwight: 40

Eastburne, J. W.: 37

Edmeston: 99

Gellert: 61

Gerhardt: 20

Grant, Robert: 58

Hart: 19

Kel: 27

Kenn: 96

Mackay, Mrs.: 84

Madan: 25

Medley: 32, 72

Montgomery: 3, 36, 43, 45, 63, 67, 86

Muhlenberg: 66, 92

Needham: 7

Palmer: 80

Plymouth Collection: 102, 104

Pratt's Collection: 55

Rippon: 75

Steele, Miss A.: 31

Stennett: 42

Stowell: 50

Sternhold: 5 (Ps. xviii)

Toplady: 52

Watts: 1 (Ps. c), 2 (Ps. xcv), 4, 6 (Ps. cxxxix),

APPENDIX III

Lectionary

The Lectionary from the Provisional Liturgy is color-coded to indicate sources. That code is as follows:

> GREEN: Original in the Provisional Liturgy
>
> RED: *Book of Common Prayer*
>
> ORANGE: Catholic Apostolic Church.

THE CHURCH YEAR

TABLE OF SCRIPTURE LESSONS

I. CHRISTMAS SEASON

	Old Series	*New Series*
First Sunday in Advent......	Gospel, St. Matthew xxi.8-11.	St. John i.1-18.
" " " "	Epistle, Romans xiii. 11-14	1 John i.1-ii.2.
Second Sunday " "	Gospel, St. Luke xxi.25-33	Matt. xxv.1-13.
" " " "	Epistle, Romans xv. 4-13.	Heb. x.1-9.
Third Sunday " "	Gospel, St. Matt. xi.2-10.	Luke xvii.20-37.
" " " "	Epistle, 1 Cor. iv.1-5.	1 Thess. v.1-8.
Fourth Sunday " "	Gospel, St. John i.19-34.	John iii.22-36.
" " " "	Epistle, Phil. iv. 4-7.	Gal. iii.21-29.
Christmas Day..............	Gospel, St. John i.1-14.	Luke ii.1-20.
" "	Epistle, Heb. i. 1-12.	Phil. ii.5-11.
St. Stephen's Day...........	Gospel, St. Matt. xxiii.34-39.	
" " "	Epistle, Acts vi. 8-vii.60.	
St. John's Day..............	Gospel, St. John xxi.19-24.	
" " "	Epistle, 1 John i. 1-10.	
Innocents' Day..............	Gospel, St. Matt. ii.13-18.	
" "	Epistle, Rev. xiv. 1-5.	

CHRISTMAS SEASON
(cont.)

	Old Series	*New Series*
Sunday after Christmas	**Gospel,** St. Matt. i.18-25.	Luke ii.23-35.
" " "	**Epistle,** Gal. iv. 1-7.	1 John iv.1-10.
Circumcision (New Year's Day)	**Gospel,** St. Luke ii.15-21.	Psalm xc.
	Epistle, Col. ii. 8-17.	Heb. xi.8-16.
Epiphany	**Gospel,** St. Matt. ii.1-12.	Is. lx.1-15.
"	**Epistle,** Eph. iii. 1-12.	Rom. xv.8-12.
First Sunday after Epiph	**Gospel,** St. Luke ii.41-52.	Matt. iii.13-17.
" " " "	**Epistle,** Rom. xii. 1-5.	Rom. vi.3-11.
Second Sunday " "	**Gospel,** St. John ii.1-11.	Luke iv.1-13.
" " " "	**Epistle,** Rom. xii. 6-16.	Heb. ii.14-18.
Third Sunday " "	**Gospel,** St. Matt. viii.1-11.	Mark i.14-22.
" " " "	**Epistle,** Rom. xii. 17-21.	1 Cor. i.17-25.
Fourth Sunday " "	**Gospel,** St. Matt. viii.23-27.	Luke iv.14-24.
" " " "	**Epistle,** Rom. xiii, 1-7.	2 Cor. iv.1-6.
Fifth Sunday " "	**Gospel,** St. Matt. xiii.24-30.	Matt. xiii.1-9.
" " " "	**Epistle,** Col. iii. 12-17.	1 Pet. i.22-25.
Sixth Sunday " "	**Gospel,** St. Matt. xvii.1-9	Matt. xiii.44-52.
" " " "	**Epistle,** 1 John iii.1-10.	1 Pet. ii.1-10.

II. EASTER SEASON

	Old Series	*New Series*
Septuagesima...............	Gospel, St. Matt. xx.1-16	Matt. xiv.22-33.
"	Epistle, 1 Cor. ix.24-x.5.	Rom. viii.31-39.
Sexagesima..................	Gospel, St. Luke viii.4-15.	John x.1-18.
"	Epistle, 2 Cor. xi.19-xii.9.	1 Pet. ii.17-25.
Quinquages., Estomihi*......	Gospel, St. Luke xviii.31-43.	Matt. xvi.21-23.
"	Epistle, 1 Cor. xiii.1-13.	1 Pet. iv.12-19.
Ash Wednesday..............	Gospel, St. Matt. vi.16-21.	Psalm li.
" "	Epistle, Joel ii.12-18.	Rev. iii.14-22.
First Sunday in Lent, Invocavit................	Gospel, St. Matt. iv.1-11.	Matt. vi.1-21.
" " " "	Epistle, 2 Cor. vi.1-10.	Eph. vi.10-20.
Second Sunday in Lent, Reminiscere..............	Gospel, St. Matt. xv.21-28.	Luke xi.29-36.
" " " "	Epistle, 1 Thess. iv.1-8.	Heb. ii.1-4.
Third Sunday in Lent, Oculi....................	Gospel, St. Luke xi.14-28.	Matt. xii.22-32.
" " " "	Epistle, Eph. v. 1-9.	Heb. x.26-31.
Fourth Sunday in Lent, Laetare..................	Gospel, St. John vi.1-14.	John vi.47-59.
" " " "	Epistle, Gal. iv. 21-31.	1 John v.11-21.

*This title, as also *Invocavit, Reminiscere*, etc., are the initial words of the introductory Psalms appointed for these several Sundays, in the service of the Latin Church.

EASTER SEASON
(cont.)

	Old Series	*New Series*
Fifth Sunday in Lent, Judica.....................Gospel, St. John viii.46-59.		John xii.20-32.
" " " " ....Epistle, Heb. ix. 11-15.		2 Cor. v.14-21.
Sixth, or Palm Sunday.......Gospel, St. John xii.1-16.		Luke xix.28-46.
" " " " ....Epistle, Phil. ii. 5-10.		Rev. i.4-8.
<u>Good Friday</u>.................Gospel, St. John xix.1-37.		Matt. xxvii. 33-54.
" " ....Epistle, Heb. x. 1-25.		Is. liii.
<u>Easter Day</u>..................Gospel, John xx.1-10.		Matt. xxviii. 1-10.
" " ....Epistle, Col. iii. <u>1-11.</u>		1 Cor. xv.1-20.
Monday in Easter Week.......Gospel, St. Luke xxiv.13-35.		John xx.11-18.
" " " " ....Epistle,		1 Cor. xv.51-58.
<u>First Sunday after Easter</u>...Gospel, St. John xx.<u>19-31.</u>		Luke xxiv.36-47.
" " " " ...Epistle, I John v.4-12.		2 Tim. ii.7-13.
<u>Second Sunday after Easter</u>..Gospel, St. John x.11-16.		John xxi.15-19.
" " " " ..Epistle, 1 Pet. ii.19-25.		Rev. vii.13-17.
<u>Third Sunday after Easter</u>...Gospel, St. John xvi.16-22.		Matt. x.16-20.
" " " " ...Epistle, 1 Pet. ii.<u>11-19.</u>		Acts iv.8-20.

III. PENTECOSTAL SEASON

	Old Series	*New Series*
<u>Fourth Sunday after Easter</u>..**Gospel,** St. John xvi.5-15.		Matt. x.24-33.
" " " " ..**Epistle,** St. James i.<u>16-21</u>.		1 Thess. ii.9-13.
<u>Fifth Sunday after Easter</u>...**Gospel,** St. John xvi.23-33.		Luke xi.9-13.
" " " " ...**Epistle,** St. James i.22-27.		1 Tim. ii.1-6.
<u>Ascension Day</u>..............**Gospel,** St. Mark xvi.14-20.		Luke xxiv.49-53.
" " ....**Epistle,** Acts i. 1-11.		Eph. i.15-23.
<u>Sunday after Ascension</u>.....**Gospel,** St. John xv.26-<u>xvi.1</u>.		John vii.33-39.
" " " .....**Epistle,** 1 Pet. iv.7-11.		Acts xix.1-7.
<u>Whitsunday</u>..................**Gospel,** St. John xiv.15-31.		Joel ii.28-32.
" ....**Epistle,** Acts ii. 1-11.		Acts ii.22-41.
<u>Whitmonday</u>..................**Gospel,** St. John iii.16-21.		John iv.13-24.
" ....**Epistle,** Acts x. 34-48.		Acts x.34-48.

IV. CHURCH SEASON

Trinity Sunday	St. John iii.<u>1-15</u>.	Matt. xxviii. 18-20.
" "	Rev. iv. 1-11.	1 John v.1-12.

CHURCH SEASON
(cont.)

	Old Series	*New Series*
First Sunday after Trinity ..**Gospel,** St. Luke xvi.19-31.		Matt. xvi.13-20.
" " . " " ..**Epistle,** 1 John iv.7-21.		Eph. ii.19-22.
Second Sunday " " ..**Gospel,** St. Luke xiv.16-24.		Matt. xviii.11-20.
" " " " ..**Epistle,** 1 John iii.13-24.		Eph. iv.4-16.
Third Sunday " " ..**Gospel,** St. Luke xv.1-10.		John xv.1-14.
" " " " ..**Epistle,** 1 Pet. v.5-11.		1 Cor. xii.12-27.
Fourth Sunday " " ..**Gospel,** St. Luke vi.36-42.		John iii.1-8.
" " " " ..**Epistle,** Rom. viii. 18-23.		Gal. iii.26-29.
Fifth Sunday " " ..**Gospel,** St. Luke v.1-11.		John vi.47-59.
" " " " ..**Epistle,** 1 Pet. iii.8-15.		Acts ii.41-47.
Sixth Sunday " " ..**Gospel,** St. Matt. v.20-26.		Matt. xi.25-30.
" " " " ..**Epistle,** Rom. vi. 3-11.		Rom. iii.19-28.
Seventh Sunday " " ..**Gospel,** St. Mark viii.1-9.		Luke xv.11-32.
" " " " ..**Epistle,** Rom. vi. 19-23.		Acts ix.1-9.
Eighth Sunday " " ..**Gospel,** St. Matt. vii.15-21.		Luke xviii.9-14.
" " " " ..**Epistle,** Rom. viii.12-17.		Phil. iii.3-11.
Ninth Sunday " " ..**Gospel,** St. Luke xvi.1-9.		Matt. viii.5-13.
" " " " ..**Epistle,** 1 Cor. x.1-13.		1 Pet. i.3-9.
Tenth Sunday " " ..**Gospel,** St. Luke xix.41-47.		Matt. xvii.14-21.
" " " " ..**Epistle,** 1 Cor. xii.1-11.		Heb. xi.32-xii. 2.

432

CHURCH SEASON
(cont.)

	Old Series	*New Series*
Eleventh Sunday after Trinity....................	Gospel, St. Luke xviii.9-14.	Luke xii.32-40.
" " "	Epistle, 1 Cor. xv.1-11.	Rom. viii.16-26.
Twelfth " "	Gospel, St. Mark vii.31-37.	Matt. xxii.34-40.
" " "	Epistle, 2 Cor. iii.4-11.	1 John iv.15-21.
Thirteenth " "	Gospel, St. Luke x.23-37.	Luke x.25-37.
" " "	Epistle, Gal. iii. 16-22.	1 Cor. xiii.1-13.
Fourteenth " "	Gospel, St. Luke xvii.11-19.	Matt v.43-48.
" " "	Epistle, Gal. v. 16-24.	Rom. xii.14-21.
Fifteenth " "	Gospel, St. Matt. vi.24-34.	Matt. v.13-20.
" " "	Epistle, Gal. v. 25-vi.10.	James ii.14-26.
Sixteenth " "	Gospel, St. Luke vii.11-17.	Mark xii.41-44.
" " "	Epistle, Eph. iii.13-21.	2 Cor. ix.5-15.
Seventeenth " "	Gospel, St. Luke xiv.1-11.	Mark x.35-45.
" " "	Epistle, Eph. iv.1-6.	Phil. ii.1-5.
Eighteenth " "	Gospel, St. Matt. xxii.34-46.	Luke ix.18-26.
" " "	Epistle, 1 Cor. i.4-9.	2 Cor. iv.8-18.
Nineteenth " "	Gospel, St. Matt. ix.1-8.	Matt. v.3-12.
" " "	Epistle, Eph. iv. 17-32.	2 Pet. i.1-11.
Twentieth " "	Gospel, St. Matt. xxii.1-14.	Mark xiii.32-37
" " "	Epistle, Eph. v. 15-21.	Heb. x.32-39.

CHURCH SEASON
(cont.)

	Old Series	*New Series*
Twenty-first Sunday after Trinity	Gospel, St. John iv.46-54.	Luke xvi.19-31.
" "	Epistle, Eph. vi. 10-20.	Rom. v.12-21.
Twenty-second "	Gospel, St. Matt. xviii.21-35.	John xi.19-27.
" "	Epistle, Phil. i.3-11.	1 Cor. xv.35-50.
Twenty-third "	Gospel, St. Matt. xxii.15-22.	Matt. xxv.31-46.
" "	Epistle, Phil. iii.17-21.	Rev. xx.11-15.
Twenty-fourth "	Gospel, St. Matt. ix.18-26.	John v.24-29.
" "	Epistle, Col. i. 9-14.	Rev. xxii.1-21.
Twenty-fifth "	Gospel, St. Matt. xxiv.15-28.	John xiv.1-4.
" "	Epistle, 1 Thess. iv.13-18.	Rev. vii.13-17.
Twenty-sixth "	Gospel, St. Matt. xxv.31-46.	Matt. xix.27-30.
" "	Epistle, 2 Thess. i.3-10.	Rev. xxi.1-8.
Twenty-seventh "	Gospel, St. Matt. xxv.1-13.	John xvii.20-26.
" "	Epistle, 2 Pet. iii.3-14.	Rev. vii.2-12.

Structural Comparison of the Eucharist
in the Book of Common Prayer,
Catholic Apostolic Liturgy, and the Provisional Liturgy

BOOK OF COMMON PRAYER	CATHOLIC APOSTOLIC LITURGY	PROVISIONAL LITURGY
	Invocation	Invocation
Lord's Prayer		
Collect for Purity		Collect for Purity
Decalogue		
		Scripture Sentences
	Confession	
	Absolution	
	Collect for Forgiveness	
Kyrie Eleison	Kyrie Eleison	
Salutation		
	Gloria in Excelsis	Gloria in Excelsis
		Gospel
		Epistle
Collect of the Day	Collect of the Day	Collect of the Day
Epistle	Epistle	
Anthem	Festival Prayer	Festival Prayer
Gospel	Gospel	
Nicene Creed		
Intercessions		
Sermon	Homily	Homily
	Nicene Creed	Nicene Creed
Offertory	Offertory	Offertory
Sentences		
Prayer for the Church		

BOOK OF COMMON PRAYER	CATHOLIC APOSTOLIC LITURGY	PROVISIONAL LITURGY
		Exhortation
Invitation to Confession		
Confession		Confession
Absolution		Absolution
Comfortable Words		
	Self-Oblation	
	Epiclesis	
	Salutation	Salutation
Sursum Corda	Sursum Corda	Sursum Corda
Gratia Agamus	Gratia Agamus	Gratia Agamus
Preface	Preface	Preface
Vere Dignum	Vere Dignum	Vere Dignum
Proper Preface		
	Thanksgiving: Creation, Preservation Redemption	Thanksgiving: Creation, Preservation Redemption
Sanctus	Sanctus-Benedictus	Sanctus-Benedictus
	Lord's Prayer	
Thanksgiving for Redemption		
Words of Institution (Fraction and Elevation)		Words of Institution (Fraction and Elevation)
	Consecration (Fraction and Elevation)	
		Epiclesis
Anamnesis	Anamnesis	Anamnesis
Epiclesis		
Self-Oblation		
	Intercessions	Intercessions
Lord's Prayer		Lord's Prayer

BOOK OF COMMON PRAYER	CATHOLIC APOSTOLIC LITURGY	PROVISIONAL LITURGY
Humble Access	Humble Access	
	Agnus Dei	
	Benedictions	Benedictions
	Pax	Pax
Communion	Communion	Communion

Post-
  Communion
  Prayer
	Post-
	  Communion
	  Prayer
		Post-
		  Communion
		  Prayer

	Te Deum	Te Deum
Gloria in Excelsis		
Benediction	Benediction	Benediction

APPENDIX V

The Holy Communion

The Holy Communion from the Provisional Liturgy is color-
coded to show the sources of the various parts, as these have
been determined through a comparison with the other Liturgies
Schaff primarily used. A solid line indicates that all the
words are found in the same prayer and in the same sequence
in the respective Liturgy. A broken line indicates adaptation; while a slash (/) indicates an omission. The code is
as follows:

> GREEN: Original in the Provisional Liturgy
>
> RED: *Book of Common Prayer*
>
> ORANGE: Catholic Apostolic Liturgy
>
> GRAY: Palatinate Liturgy
>
> BLACK: Scripture.

The Holy Communion

[When the Communion is celebrated, this service shall take the place of the regular service of the Lord's Day.]

The Minister, standing at the altar, shall
begin thus:

In the name of the Father, and of the Son, and of the
Holy Ghost. *Amen.*

Let us pray.

ALMIGHTY and everlasting God, who by the blood of Thy
dear Son hast consecrated for us a new and living way into
the holiest of all; cleanse our minds, we beseech Thee, by
the inspiration of Thy Holy Spirit, that we, Thy redeemed
people, drawing near unto Thee in these holy mysteries, with
a true heart and undefiled conscience, in full assurance of
faith, may offer unto Thee an acceptable sacrifice in righteousness, and worthily magnify Thy great and glorious name:
through Jesus Christ our Lord. *Amen.*

Then shall the Minister pronounce slowly and
solemnly, either the whole, or some part, of
the following selection of passages from the
Holy Scriptures:

Surely He hath borne our griefs, and carried our sorrows:
yet we did esteem Him stricken, smitten of God, and afflicted.
But He was wounded for our transgressions, He was bruised for
our iniquities: the chastisement of our peace was upon Him:
and with His stripes we are healed. All we like sheep have
gone astray; we have turned every one to his own way; and the
Lord hath laid on Him the iniquity of us all. He was oppressed
and He was afflicted, yet He opened not His mouth: He is
brought as a lamb to the slaughter, and as a sheep before her
shearers is dumb, so He opened not His mouth.--*Isa.* liii.4-7.

The next day John seeth Jesus coming unto him, and saith, Behold the Lamb of God, which taketh away the sin of the world! This is He of whom I said, After me cometh a man which is preferred before me; for He was before me. And I knew Him not: but that He should be made manifest to Israel, therefore am I come baptizing with water. And John bare record, saying, I saw the Spirit descending from heaven like a dove, and it abode upon Him. And I knew Him not: but He that sent me to baptize with water, the same said unto me, Upon whom thou shalt see the Spirit descending, and remaining on Him, the same is He which baptizeth with the Holy Ghost. And I saw, and bare record that this is the Son of God.--*John* i.29-34.

And as Moses lifted up the serpent in the wilderness, even so must the Son of man be lifted up: that whosoever believeth in Him should not perish, but have eternal life. For God so loved the world, that He gave His only begotten Son, that whosoever believeth in Him should not perish, but have everlasting life. For God sent not His Son into the world to condemn the world; but that the world through Him might be saved.--*John* iii.14-17.

This then is the message which we have heard of Him, and declare unto you, that God is light, and in Him is no darkness at all. If we say that we have fellowship with Him, and walk in darkness, we lie, and do not the truth: but if we walk in the light, as He is in the light, we have fellowship one with another, and the blood of Jesus Christ His Son cleanseth us from all sin. If we say that we have no sin, we deceive ourselves, and the truth is not in us. If we confess our sins, He is faithful and just to forgive us our sins, and to cleanse us from all unrighteousness.-- 1 *John* i.5-9.

In this was manifested the love of God toward us, because that God sent His only begotten Son into the world, that we might live through Him. Herein is love, not that we loved God, but that He loved us, and sent His Son to be the propitiation for our sins.--1 *John* iv.9, 10.

Abide in Me, and I in you. As the branch cannot bear fruit of itself, except it abide in the vine; no more can ye, except ye abide in Me. I am the vine, ye are the branches: he that abideth in Me, and I in him, the same bringeth forth much fruit: for without Me ye can do nothing. --*John* xv.4, 5.

I am the living bread which came down from heaven. If
any man eat of this bread, he shall live for ever: and the
bread which I will give is My flesh, which I will give for
the life of the world. The Jews therefore strove among
themselves, saying, How can this man give us his flesh to
eat? Then Jesus said unto them, Verily, verily, I say unto
you, Except ye eat the flesh of the Son of man, and drink
His blood, ye have no life in you. Whoso eateth My flesh,
and drinketh My blood, hath eternal life; and I will raise
him up at the last day. For My flesh is meat indeed, and
My blood is drink indeed. He that eateth My flesh, and
drinketh My blood, dwelleth in Me, and I in him. As the
living Father hath sent Me, and I live by the Father; so
he that eateth Me, even he shall live by Me. This is that
bread which came down from heaven: not as your fathers did
eat manna, and are dead: he that eateth of this bread shall
live for ever.--*John* vi.51-58.

Here shall be chanted the *Gloria in Excelsis*, the Congregation rising; or else in
place of it may be said, or sung, either
the *Te Deum* or the proper *Canticle* for the
season; or a suitable *Hymn* may be sung.

Then shall follow the *Gospel* and *Epistle*
for the day, with their proper *Collect*,
and the *Festival Prayer* for the season.

After this, a brief *Sermon* or *Homily* may
be preached, suitable to the occasion.
Or, instead of this, the Minister may, if
he see proper, read a fit lesson of moderate length, taken from the Holy Gospels
(on the history of Christ's Passion and
Death.)

Having reached this point, the service
shall now go forward with the recitation
of the *Nicene Creed* (p. 16), the people
rising and joining in it, whether spoken
or sung. Instead of which, however, on
the occasion of the last Communion in the
Church year, use shall be made in the same
way of the (*Athanasian Creed*) (p. 17).

Here shall follow a collection of the
Offerings of the people, to be devoted
to the service of the poor, or to some
strictly benevolent purpose; during which
the Minister shall read some sentences
from the Holy Scriptures, such as may
seem to him suitable to the occasion.
When made, the collection shall be brought
by the Deacons, in some proper vessel provided for the purpose, to the Minister;
who shall then reverently place it upon
the altar, in token of its proper meaning,
as an oblation presented unto God. After
which he shall uncover and expose to view
the vessels containing the Bread and Wine
for the use of the Holy Sacrament, and
then proceed as follows:

DEARLY BELOVED IN THE LORD: Our blessed Saviour Jesus
Christ, when He was about to finish the work of our redemption by making Himself a sacrifice for our sins upon the
cross, solemnly instituted the Holy Sacrament of His own
Body and Blood; that it might be the abiding memorial of His
precious death; the seal of His perpetual presence in the
Church by the Holy Ghost; the mystical exhibition of His one
offering of Himself made once, but of force always, to put
away sin; the pledge of His undying love to His people; and
the bond of His living union and fellowship with them to the
end of time. From all this we may understand how great and
glorious the Sacrament is, and with what just reason it hath
ever been regarded in the Church as that act of worship, in
which men are brought most near to God, and, as it were, into
the innermost sanctuary of His presence, the holiest of all,
where more than in any other service it is fit that their
adoration should be joined with sacred reverence and awe.
We have to do here, in a mystery, not with the shadows and
types only of heavenly things, but with the very realities

themselves of that true spiritual world in which Christ, now
risen from the dead, continually lives and reigns. See,
then, as many of you as have it in mind to take part in this
service, that ye be properly clothed for the occasion with
the spirit of humility, self-recollection, penitence, and
prayer. Examine yourselves, whether ye be in the faith;
prove your own selves. Renew inwardly your baptismal en-
gagements and vows. Renounce all sin both in your lives and
in your hearts. Be in perfect charity with all men. **Christ
our Passover is sacrificed for us; therefore let us keep the
feast, not with old leaven, neither with the leaven of malice
and wickedness, but with the unleavened bread of sincerity
and truth. Present** yourselves on the altar of the Gospel,
in union with His glorious merits, **a living sacrifice, holy,
acceptable unto God, which is your reasonable service;
giving thanks unto the Father, which hath made us meet to
be partakers of the inheritance of the saints in light; who
hath delivered us from the power of darkness, and / translated
us into the kingdom of His dear Son: in whom we have redemption through His blood, even the forgiveness of sins.** And
now that we may be able so to compass God's holy altar with
righteousness and joy, let us first of all bow down before
Him, and make humble confession of our sins, that we may
obtain forgiveness of the same through His infinite goodness
and mercy.

All kneeling.

Almighty God, our Heavenly Father, who dost admit Thy
people unto such wonderful communion, that partaking by a
divine mystery of the Body and Blood of Thy dear Son, they
should dwell in Him, and He in them; we unworthy sinners,

approaching to Thy presence, and beholding Thy / glory, do abhor ourselves, and repent in dust and ashes. We have sinned, we have sinned, we have grievously sinned against Thee, in thought, in word, and in deed, provoking most justly Thy wrath and indignation against us. **Our righteousnesses are as filthy rags; our iniquities, like the wind, have carried us away.** The remembrance of our transgressions and shortcomings fills us with sorrow and shame. Yet now, O most merciful Father, have mercy upon us; for the sake of Jesus Christ, forgive us all our sins; purify us, by the inspiration of Thy Holy Spirit, from all uncleanness in spirit and in flesh; enable us heartily to forgive others, as we beseech Thee to forgive us; and grant that we may hereafter serve Thee in newness of life; to the glory of Thy holy name, through Jesus Christ our Lord.

    R.   *Amen.*

      Here the Minister shall rise and say:

    The God of our Lord Jesus Christ, the Father of glory, grant unto you the spirit of wisdom and revelation in the knowledge of Him: the eyes of your understanding being enlightened, that ye may know what is the hope of His calling, and what the riches of the glory of His inheritance in the saints, and what is the exceeding greatness of His power to usward who believe; according to the working of His mighty power, which He wrought in Christ, when He raised Him from the dead, and set Him at His own right hand in the heavenly places, far above all principality, and power, and might, and dominion, and every name that is named, not only in this word, but also in that which is to come; and hath put all things under His feet, and gave Him to be the head over all things to the Church, which is His body, the fulness of Him that filleth all in all.

And now unto Him that is able to do exceeding abundantly above all that we ask or think, according to the power that worketh in us, unto Him be glory in the Church by Christ Jesus, throughout all ages, world without end.

R. *Amen.*

The whole Congregation now rising, the Minister shall proceed:

The Lord be with you.

R. *And with thy spirit.*

Lift up your hearts.

R. *We lift them up unto the Lord.*

Let us give thanks unto the Lord our God.

R. *It is meet and right so to do.*

It is very meet, right, and our bounden duty, that we should at all times, and in all places, give thanks unto Thee, Lord God Almighty, Father, Son, and Holy Ghost.

Before the mountains were brought forth, or ever Thou hadst formed the earth and the world, even from everlasting to everlasting, Thou art God.

Thou didst in the beginning create all things for Thyself. By Thy word were the heavens made, and all the host of them by the breath of Thy mouth. The armies of the invisible world, angels and archangels, thrones, dominions, principalities, and powers; the glorious firmament on high, sun, moon, and stars; the earth <u>and the fulness thereof</u>; all are the work of Thy hands, and all are upheld by Thee continually in their being, as they stand by Thee, likewise, in their appointed order and course.

Thou also at the first didst make man in Thine own image, and after Thine own likeness, and didst set him over the works of Thy hands, endowing him with the excellent gift of righteousness, and forming him for immortality. And when afterwards, through the fraud and malice of Satan, he fell by transgression from that first estate, Thou didst not leave him still to perish utterly in his fall, but wast pleased to raise him up again and to restore him to the joyful hope of everlasting life, by the promise of redemption through Jesus Christ; who, being ⟨God of God, very God of very God⟩ dwelling in the bosom of the Father with unspeakable blessedness from all eternity, at last when the fulness of time was come, ⟨came down from heaven,⟩ and became / man, ⟨for us men and for our salvation⟩

For all Thy mercies and favors, known to us and unknown, we give Thee thanks. But most of all, we praise Thee, the Father everlasting, for the gift of Thine adorable, true, and only Son, <u>our Saviour Jesus Christ,</u> <u>who by His appearing hath abolished death and brought life</u> <u>and immortality to light through the gospel.</u> We bless Thee for His holy incarnation; for His life on earth; for His precious sufferings and death upon the cross; for His resurrection from the dead; and for His <u>glorious ascension</u> to Thy right hand. We bless Thee for the giving of the Holy Ghost; for the institution of the Church; for the means of grace; for the hope of everlasting life; and for / the glory which shall be brought unto us at the coming, and in the kingdom, of Thy dear Son.

Thee, mighty God, heavenly King, we magnify and praise. With patriarchs and prophets, apostles and martyrs; with the holy Church throughout all the world; with the heavenly Jerusalem, the joyful assembly and congregation of the first-born on high; with the innumerable company of angels round about Thy throne, the heaven of heavens, and all the powers therein; we worship and adore Thy glorious name, joining in the / song of the Cherubim and Seraphim, and with united voice, saying:

[Here let the people join aloud in the
Seraphic Hymn.]

Holy, Holy, Holy, Lord God of Sabaoth; heaven and earth are full of the majesty of Thy glory. Hosanna in the highest! Blessed is He that cometh in the name of the Lord. Hosanna in the highest!

Then the minister shall proceed:

OUR LORD JESUS CHRIST, THE SAME NIGHT IN WHICH HE WAS BETRAYED [*here he shall take some of the bread into his hands*], TOOK BREAD; AND WHEN HE HAD GIVEN THANKS, HE BRAKE IT [*here he shall break the bread*], AND SAID, TAKE, EAT, THIS IS MY BODY WHICH IS BROKEN FOR YOU; THIS DO IN REMEM-BRANCE OF ME.

AFTER THE SAME MANNER ALSO [*here he shall take the cup into his hands*], HE TOOK THE CUP, WHEN HE HAD SUPPED, SAYING, THIS CUP IS THE NEW TESTAMENT IN MY BLOOD; THIS DO YE AS OFTEN AS YE DRINK IT, IN REMEMBRANCE OF ME.

Let us pray.

ALMIGHTY GOD, our heavenly Father, send down, we beseech Thee, the powerful benediction of Thy Holy Spirit upon these elements of bread and wine, that being set apart now from a common to a sacred and mystical use, they may exhibit and represent to us with true effect the Body and Blood of Thy Son, Jesus Christ; so that in the use of them we may be made, through the power of the Holy Ghost, to partake really and truly of His blessed life, whereby only we can be saved from death, and raised to immortality at the last day.

R. *Amen.*

And be pleased now, O most merciful Father, graciously to receive at our hands this memorial of the blessed sacrifice of Thy Son, which we, Thy servants, thus bring before Thy divine Majesty, according to His own appointment and command; showing forth His passion and death; rejoicing in His glorious resurrection and ascension; and waiting for the blessed hope of His appearing and coming again. We are not worthy in ourselves to offer unto Thee any worship or service. Wherewith shall we, sinners of the dust, come before the Lord, or bow ourselves before the most high God? We bring unto Thee, O holy and righteous Father, the infinite merits of Jesus Christ, Thine adorable, true, and only Son, in whom Thou hast declared Thyself to be well pleased, and through the offering of whose body once for all, full satisfaction has been made for the sins of the world. Have respect unto this glorious sacrifice, we beseech Thee, in union with which we here offer and present unto Thee, at the same time, O Lord, the reasonable sacrifice of our own persons; consecrating ourselves, on the altar of the gospel, in soul and body, property and life, to Thy most blessed service and praise. Look upon us

through the mediation of our great High Priest. Make us
accepted in the Beloved; and let His name be as a pure and
holy incense, through which all our worship may come up
before Thee, as the odour of a sweet smell, a sacrifice
acceptable, well pleasing to God.

   R. *Amen.*

   Remember in mercy, we beseech Thee, Thy Church militant
throughout the whole earth. Let her ministers be clothed
with righteousness, and her priests with salvation. Build
up her desolations; restore her disorders; heal her divisions; and grant unto her prosperity, safety, unity and
peace.

   R. *Amen.*

   We commend unto Thee especially this particular church
and congregation, pastor, elders, deacons, and people, beseeching Thee to accept their piety and faith, and to increase towards them Thy heavenly grace, so that they may
come behind in no gift, waiting for the coming of our Lord
Jesus Christ.

   R. *Amen.*

   We pray for all estates of men in Christian lands; for /
kings, princes, and governors, and for the people committed
to their charge and care; especially for Thy servant, the
President of the United States, and for all the rulers of
this land and nation. Make us a righteous people, and give
us power to serve Thee in quietness and peace.

   R. *Amen.*

   Vouchsafe unto us, we beseech Thee, favorable weather,
that the fruits of the earth may ripen and be gathered in

for us in due season; and be pleased of Thy great goodness
to preserve us from war, pestilence, and famine.

R. *Amen.*

Send forth Thy light and Thy truth unto the ends of
the earth; cause the glorious Gospel of Thy grace to be proclaimed among all nations; and powerfully incline the hearts
of men everywhere, that they may hear and obey the joyful
sound.

R. *Amen.*

Regard in tender compassion those among Thy people, who
are called to suffer heavy affliction, or sore temptation and
trial of any kind; and be Thou graciously nigh unto them with
Thy divine help, according to all their need.

R. *Amen.*

Especially do we commend unto Thee those departing this
life; let the arms of Thy love be round about them in their
last hour; defend them against the assaults of the Devil;
enable them joyfully to commit their spirits into Thy hands;
and so receive them to Thy rest.

R. *Amen.*

O God, the Father of our Lord Jesus Christ, of whom the
whole family in heaven and earth is named; we rejoice before
Thee in the blessed communion of all Thy saints, wherein Thou
givest us also to have part. We praise Thee for the holy
fellowship of patriarchs and prophets, apostles and martyrs,
and the whole glorious company of the redeemed of all ages,
who have died in the Lord, and now live with Him for evermore.
We give thanks unto Thee for Thy great grace and many gifts
bestowed on those who have thus gone before us in the way of

salvation, and by whom we are now <u>compassed about,</u> in our
Christian course, as a <u>cloud of witnesses</u> looking down upon
us from the heavenly world. Enable us to follow their faith,
that we may enter at death into their joy; and so abide with
them in rest and peace, till both they and we shall reach
our common consummation of redemption and bliss in the /
glorious resurrection of the last day.

    R.   *Amen.*

       Here let the people join aloud in the
       Lord's Prayer.

Our Father who art in heaven, Hallowed be Thy name.
Thy kingdom come. Thy will be done in earth, as it is in
heaven. Give us this day our daily bread. And forgive us
our debts, as we forgive our debtors. And lead us not into
temptation. But deliver us from evil. For Thine is the
kingdom, and the power, and the glory, for ever and ever.
Amen.

       Then the Minister shall say:

    Almighty God, the Father everlasting, from whom all
blessing / and power proceed, shed down upon you abundantly
the riches / of His heavenly grace.

    The Lord Jesus Christ, the Head of His body the Church,
who holdeth the seven stars in His right hand, and walketh
in the midst of the seven golden candlesticks, send forth
His light and His truth, and guide you in the way of eternal
salvation.

    The Holy Ghost, the Comforter, the Spirit of the Father
and of the Son, come down upon you in His glory, and take up

R. *Amen.*

The peace of our Lord Jesus Christ be with you all.
Amen.

> Here the *Holy Communion* shall take place.
> While a suitable sacramental hymn is sung,*
> the people shall come forward for the pur-
> pose in successive companies, and take their
> position in front of the altar, all rever-
> ently and devoutly standing. The proper
> order requires, that the officiating Minis-
> ter should first receive the Communion in
> both kinds himself, and administer the
> same to his assistants; and that he should
> then proceed with their help to administer
> it, first to the elders and deacons, and
> afterwards to the people; distributing
> first the bread and then the cup.
>
> The bread may be presented with the words:

The bread which we break, is the Communion of the Body
of Christ.

> The cup with the words:

The cup of blessing which we bless, is the Communion of
the Blood of Christ.

> Or, instead of these forms, if it be pre-
> ferred, the Minister may repeat the words
> of institution in full relating to each
> part; adding afterwards, any other suitable
> sentences which he may see proper to use,
> from the Holy Scriptures. It is not neces-
> sary, however, that he should continue
> speaking all the time he is distributing
> the elements; full silence at times may be
> better than any words.

Each company of Communicants, when its
turn of receiving is over, may be dismissed with one of the usual Benedictions, or with this form:

May the Holy Communion of the Body and Blood of our
Lord and Saviour Jesus Christ, keep and preserve you, each
one, in body, soul, and spirit, unto everlasting life. *Amen.*
Depart in peace.

When all have communicated, the Minister
shall offer a free *Prayer*, or the *Post-
Communion Prayer* may be said, as follows:

Almighty and everlasting God, we give Thee most hearty
thanks for the great goodness Thou hast shown toward us at
this time, in vouchsafing to feed us, through these holy
mysteries, with the spiritual food of the most precious body
and blood of Thy Son, our Saviour Jesus Christ; assuring us
thereby, that we are very members incorporate in the mystical
body of Thy Son, and heirs through hope of Thine everlasting
kingdom, by the merits of His most blessed death and passion.
And we most humbly beseech Thee, O heavenly Father, so to
assist us with Thy grace, that we may continue in that holy
fellowship, and do all such good works as Thou hast prepared for us to walk in; through Jesus Christ our Lord, to
whom with Thee and the Holy Ghost be all honor and glory,
world without end. *Amen.*

Then shall be sung or said the *Te Deum*,
unless it may have been used in the first
part of the service; in which case it will
be proper to use instead of it here, the
Gloria in Excelsis, or a part of the 103d
Psalm. After which the Minister shall

pronounce, in conclusion of the whole
service, this *Benediction*:

The peace of God, which passeth all understanding,
keep your hearts and minds in the knowledge and love of
God, and of His Son Jesus Christ, our Lord; and the blessing of God Almighty, the Father, the Son, and the Holy
Ghost, be amongst you and remain with you always.   *Amen.*

APPENDIX VI

Ordination of Ministers

The Ordination of Ministers from the Provisional Liturgy is
color-coded to show the sources of the various parts, as
these have been determined through a comparison with other
Liturgies Nevin primarily used. A solid line indicates that
all the words are found in the same prayer and in the same
sequence in the respective Liturgy. A broken line indicates
adaptation; while a slash (/) indicates an omission. The
code is as follows:

> GREEN: Original in the Provisional Liturgy
>
> RED: *Book of Common Prayer*
>
> ORANGE: Catholic Apostolic Liturgy
>
> BLUE: The Mayer Liturgy
>
> BLACK: Scripture.

Ordination of Ministers

At the time appointed, the Minister who is
to conduct the service shall commence with
the following *Collect*:

MEET US, O Lord, in all our doings, with Thy most
gracious favor, and further us with Thy continual help;
that in all our works begun, continued, and ended, in Thee,
we may glorify Thy holy name, and finally by Thy mercy attain
unto everlasting life: through Jesus Christ our Lord. *Amen.*

Here the Candidate for Ordination, his name
being distinctly announced, shall be requested to present himself before the
Altar; whereupon the presiding Minister
shall address the Congregation as follows:

DEARLY BELOVED IN THE LORD: Almighty God, whom it
hath pleased by His Spirit and Word to gather and preserve
to Himself continually, out of the whole human race, a Church
chosen to everlasting life, hath given to all the members of
the same, both ministers and people, a common interest in its
welfare. For this reason it hath ever been the practice,
that in the ordination of those who have been called to the
office of the holy ministry, the people also should have an
opportunity to express their voice. Now, therefore, in order
that we may be assisted in the case before us by your knowledge and past observation of him who is here present for admission to this office, we call upon you to the end that if
you know any just cause or impediment, because of which he
ought not to be ordained to the Christian Ministry, you do
come forward in God's name and make it known.

If there be no objection, then, after a
sufficient pause, he shall address the
Candidate:

DEARLY BELOVED BROTHER: It is now our part, solemnly
and for the last time, before proceeding to lay upon you
irrevocably the burden and responsibility of the Ministry,
to remind you how great is the dignity of the office, and
how weighty and momentous also are the duties which it involves.

The office is of divine origin and of truly supernatural character and force; flowing directly from the Lord
Jesus Christ Himself, as the fruit of His resurrection and
triumphant ascension into heaven, and being designed by Him
to carry forward the purposes of His grace upon the earth,
in the salvation of men by the Church, to the end of time.

"All power," we hear Him saying after He had risen from
the dead, "is given unto Me in heaven and in earth. Go ye,
therefore, and teach all nations, baptizing them in the name
of the Father, and of the Son, and of the Holy Ghost; teaching them to observe all things whatsoever I have commanded
you: and lo, I am with you alway, even unto the end of the
world."

To this answers in full what is written also by St.
Paul: "Wherefore He saith, When He ascended up on high,
He led captivity captive, and gave gifts unto men. Now
that He ascended, what is it but that He also descended
first into the lower parts of the earth? He that descended
is the same also that ascended up far above all heavens,
that He might fill all things. And He gave some, apostles;
and some, prophets; and some, evangelists; and some, pastors and teachers; for the perfecting of the saints, for the
work of the ministry, for the edifying of the body of Christ:

till we all come in the unity of the faith, and of the Son
of God, unto a perfect man, unto the measure of the stature
of the fulness of Christ. That we henceforth be no more
children, tossed to and fro, and carried about with every
wind of doctrine, by the sleight of men, and cunning crafti-
ness, whereby they lie in wait to deceive; but, speaking the
truth in love, may grow up into Him in all things, which is
the head, even Christ; from whom the whole body fitly joined
together and compacted by that which every joint supplieth,
according to the effectual working in the measure of every
part, maketh increase of the body unto the edifying of itself in love."

Consider well, dear brother in Christ, how much all
this means, as declaring and setting forth the true nature
and significance of the holy office. The first Ministers
were the Apostles, who were called and commissioned immediately by Jesus Christ Himself. They in turn ordained and
set apart other suitable men, as pastors and teachers over
the churches which they had gathered and established in
different places; and these again in the same way appointed
and sent forth others to carry onward and forward still the
true succession of their office; which, being regularly
transmitted in this way from age to age in the Christian
Church, has come down finally to our time. The solemnity
of ordination, through which as a channel this transmission
flows, is not merely an impressive ceremony, by which the
right of such as are called of God to the Ministry is owned
and confessed by the Church; but it is to be considered
rather as their actual investiture with the very power of
the office itself, the sacramental seal of their heavenly
commission, and a symbolical assurance from on high that
their consecration to the service of Christ is accepted,

and that the Holy Ghost will most certainly be with them in the faithful discharge of their official duties.

These duties are of the same order with the high origin of the office and its glorious design. The Ministers of Christ are set in the world to be at once the representatives of His authority and the ambassadors of His grace. As My Father hath sent Me, He says, even so send I you. He that heareth you, heareth Me; and he that despiseth you, despiseth Me; and he that despiseth Me, despiseth Him that sent Me. Let a man so account of us, says St. Paul, as of the ministers of Christ and stewards of the mysteries of God. Again: We are ambassadors for Christ, as though God did beseech you by us. It is their business to baptize, to preach the word, to administer at fit times the holy sacrament of the Lord's Supper. They are appointed to wait upon and serve the Church, which is the spouse of Jesus Christ, His body mystical; to offer before Him the prayers and supplications of His people; to feed, to instruct, to watch over and guide the sheep and lambs of His flock, whom He hath purchased with His own blood. They are charged also with the government of the Church, and with the proper use of its discipline, in the way both of censure and absolution, according to that awfully mysterious word: I will give unto thee the keys of the kingdom of heaven; and whatsoever thou shalt bind on earth, shall be bound in heaven; and whatsoever thou shalt loose on earth, shall be loosed in heaven.

Such being the character of the office to which you are now called, beloved brother in the Lord, and such the high and arduous nature of its duties, it is easy to see with what seriousness and godly fear, with what solemn forethought, with what holy caution, you should approach unto it, as you are now doing, in the present transaction; and

with how great care and study also you ought to apply yourself, that you may appear hereafter to have been worthy of
being put into the Christian Ministry, by being found faithful to its mighty trust. Know, at the same time, that for
this you are by no means sufficient of yourself. All proper
sufficiency here is from God alone; to whom therefore you
should pray earnestly, through the mediation of our only
Saviour Jesus Christ, for the heavenly assistance of the
Holy Ghost; that giving yourself wholly to this office, with
daily meditation and study of the Scriptures, you may be
able to make full proof of your ministry, being nourished
up in the words of faith and good doctrine, and showing thyself a pattern to others in piety and godly living. In
doing this, thou shalt both save thyself and them that hear
thee. And when the Chief Shepherd shall appear, you shall
receive a crown of glory that fadeth not away.

And now, that this / congregation of Christ may also
understand your view and will in these things, and that
you may yourself also the more feel the binding force of
what you thus publicly profess and promise, we call upon
you to make answer plainly to these following questions
which we shall propose to you in the name of God and of
His Church:

Do you receive the Holy Scriptures as being the true
and proper word of God, the ultimate rule and measure of
the whole Christian faith?

Ans. *I do*.

Do you believe in one God the Father; and in one Lord
Jesus Christ, the only begotten Son of the Father; and in
one Holy Ghost, proceeding from the Father and the Son, and
with the Father and the Son one God Almighty? And do you

believe in one holy Catholic Church, in which is given one
true Baptism for the remission of sins? And do you consent
unto the system of Faith set forth in the three Creeds,
commonly called the Apostles' Creed, the Nicene Creed, and
the Athanasian Creed?

Ans. *I do.*

Do you receive the doctrines of the Heidelberg Catechism as flowing from the Bible, and answering to the proper
sense of the ancient Christian Creeds?

Ans. *I do.*

Are you truly persuaded in your heart, that you are
called of God to the office of the Holy Ministry, and do
you desire and expect to receive, through the laying on of
our hands, the gift and grace of the Holy Ghost, which shall
enable you to fulfil this heavenly commission and trust?

Ans. *Such is my persuasion, and such my desire and hope.*

Do you acknowledge the rightful authority of this Church,
from which you are now to receive ordination, as being a true
part in the succession of the Church Catholic; and do you
promise to exercise your ministry in the same with faithful
diligence, showing all proper regard for its laws and ordinances, and all suitable obedience to its lawful government
in the Lord?

Ans. *So I confess, and so I promise.*

> Here the Candidate shall be directed to
> kneel; the Ministers shall lay their hands
> severally upon his head, and the presiding
> Minister shall say:

464

In the name of the Lord Jesus Christ, the Chief Shepherd
and Bishop of the Church, and trusting in the power of His
grace, we ordain, consecrate, and appoint you to the Ministry
of reconciliation, to proclaim His gospel, to dispense His
holy sacraments, to administer Christian discipline in His
church, and to be wholly set apart as an instrument to His
use in the salvation of our fallen race: and to this end
may the blessing of God Almighty, the Father, the Son, and
the Holy Ghost, rest upon and abide with you always. *Amen.*

> The Brother shall then rise, when each of
> the Ministers in turn shall give him the
> right hand of fellowship, saying:

We give you the right hand of fellowship, to take part
with us in this Ministry.

> Or this:

Our fellowship is with the Father, and with the Son,
and with the Holy Ghost.

> Or this:

The grace of our Lord Jesus Christ, the love of God
the Father, and the fellowship of the Holy Ghost, be with
you always.

> When the new Minister is to be installed at
> the same time as Pastor of the Charge in
> which he is ordained, the Installation
> services shall now go forward according to
> the Form provided for that purpose. If
> there be no installation, the presiding
> Minister shall here say:

Let us pray, beloved brethren, to God the Father Almighty, that He may be pleased to multiply His heavenly gifts upon this His servant, whom He hath called to the office of the holy Ministry: through Jesus Christ our Lord. *Amen.*

Then kneeling down:

Let us pray:

Almighty God, most merciful Father, who of Thine infinite / goodness ❙ hast given ❙ Thine only ❙ Son Jesus Christ be our Redeemer and the Author of everlasting life; who after that He had made perfect our redemption by His death, and was ascended into heaven, poured down His gifts abundantly upon men, making some apostles, some prophets, some evangelists, some pastors and teachers, for the edifying and perfecting of the Church; send down, we beseech Thee, the anointing of the Holy Ghost upon the head of this Thy servant, who has now been set apart in Thy name, through the solemn act of ordination, to the office of teacher and ruler in Christ's Church. Grant unto him, O most merciful Father, such fulness of Thy grace, that he may be a faithful and wise steward whom Thou settest over Thy household, using the authority Thou givest him, not unto destruction, but unto salvation; that he may be an able minister of the New Testament, knowing how he ought to behave himself in the house of God, a workman that needeth not to be ashamed, rightly dividing the word of truth; that he may be a true preacher of righteousness; a faithful leader of the blind, and of them that are out of the way; a light unto those who are in darkness; a watchful guardian over Thy fold, and a follower of the true Shepherd who giveth His life for the sheep. Make his feet beautiful to publish the gospel of peace, and to bring glad tidings of good things. Give him power to preach not himself, but Christ Jesus the Lord, and himself the servant of all for Jesus' sake. May he be an example of the believers, in word, in conversation, in charity, in spirit, in faith, in purity. So may he in all things fulfil his ministry unblamably and unreprovably in Thy sight, that he may be prepared to stand without shame before the judgment seat of Christ, and thus, finishing his course with joy, be received unto glory and immortality in Thine eternal kingdom, where they that turn many to righteousness shall shine as the stars for ever and ever. Hear us for the sake of Jesus Christ Thy Son our Lord, who liveth and reigneth with Thee and the Holy Ghost, ever one God, world without end. *Amen.*

> The Congregation shall then rise and join
> in singing a *Doxology* or *Hymn*; after which
> the whole service shall be concluded with
> this *Benediction:*

The God of peace who brought again from the dead our Lord Jesus Christ, the great Shepherd of the sheep through the blood of the everlasting covenant, make you perfect in every good work to do His will, working in you that which is well pleasing in His sight, through Jesus Christ: to whom be glory for ever and ever. *Amen.*

APPENDIX VII

Comparison of the Tables of Contents

PROVISIONAL LITURGY	ORDER OF WORSHIP
Christian Worship	
I. Primitive Forms	
	I. The Church Festivals
	II. A Table of Scripture Lessons
II. The Church Year	
III. The Lord's Day	III. The Regular Service on the Lord's Day
	IV. The Evening Service
	V. The Litany
	VI. Prayers and Thanksgivings for Special Occasions
	VII. The Gospels, Epistles, and Collects
IV. The Festival Seasons	
V. The Holy Communion	VIII. The Holy Communion
VI. Holy Baptism	IX. Holy Baptism
VII. Confirmation	X. Confirmation
VIII. Marriage	XI. Marriage
	XII. Ordination and Installation
	XIII. Excommunication and Restoration
IX. Visitation of the Sick	XIV. The Visitation and Communion of the Sick
X. Ordination and Installation	

468

BIBLIOGRAPHY

PRIMARY SOURCES

I. *Books and Pamphlets*

Bomberger, J. H. A. *Reformed, Not Ritualistic*. Philadelphia: Jas. B. Rodgers, 1867.

_____. *The Revised Liturgy: A History and Criticism of the Ritualistic Movement in the German Reformed Church*. Philadelphia: Jas. B. Rodgers, 1867.

Harbaugh, Henry. *The Golden Censer; or, Devotions for Young Christians*. Philadelphia: The Publication and Sunday School Board of the Reformed Church in the U.S., 1860.

_____, ed. *Hymns and Chants: with Offices of Devotion. For Use in Sunday-Schools, Parochial and Week-Day Schools, Seminaries and Colleges. Arranged According to the Church Year*. Philadelphia: Reformed Church Publication Board, 1861.

Nevin, John W. *The Anxious Bench*. Chambersburg, Pa.: Office of the "Weekly Messenger," 1843.

_____. *The History and Genius of the Heidelberg Catechism*. Chambersburg, Pa.: Publication Office of the German Reformed Church, 1847.

_____. *The Liturgical Question with Reference to the Provisional Liturgy of the German Reformed Church*. Philadelphia: Lindsay & Blakiston, 1862.

_____. *My Own Life: The Earlier Years*. Papers of the Eastern Chapter, Historical Society of the Evangelical and Reformed Church, No. 1. Lancaster, Pa.: 1964.

_____. *The Mystical Presence: A Vindication of the Reformed or Calvinistic Doctrine of the Holy Eucharist*. Philadelphia: J. B. Lippincott & Co., 1846.

469

_____. *Vindication of the Revised Liturgy.* Philadelphia: Jas. B. Rodgers, 1867.

Proceedings of the Convention of Ministers and Laymen belonging to the German Reformed Church, held at Myerstown, Lebanon County, Pa., September 24th and 25th, 1867. Lancaster: Pearson & Geist, 1867.

Schaff, Philip. *The Principle of Protestantism as Related to the Present State of the Church.* Translated by John W. Nevin. Chambersburg, Pa.: "Publication office" of the German Reformed Church, 1845.

Steiner, Lewis H. and Schwing, Henry. *Cantate Domino: A Collection of Chants, Hymns and Tunes, Adapted to Church Service.* Boston: Oliver Ditson & Co., 1859.

Tercentenary Monument in Commemoration of the Three Hundredth Anniversary of the Heidelberg Catechism. Chambersburg, Pa.: M. Kieffer & Co., 1863.

II. *Articles*

Apple, T. G. "The General Synod." *Mercersburg Review,* XVII (1870), 156-162.

_____. "The Late General Synod." *Mercersburg Review,* XXV (1878), 329-351.

_____. "The Western Liturgy." *Mercersburg Review,* XVIII (1871), 92-114.

Bomberger, J. H. A. "The Church and Charitable Institutions." *Mercersburg Review,* XII (1860), 64-85.

_____. "Dr. Nevin and His Antagonists." *Mercersburg Review,* V (1853), 89-124.

_____. "The Old Palatinate Liturgy of 1563." *Mercersburg Review,* II (1850), 81-96, 265-287.

Dorner, J. A. "The Liturgical Conflict in the Reformed Church of North America, with Special Reference to Fundamental Evangelical Doctrines." *The Reformed Church Monthly*, I (1868), 327-381.

Foulk, J. S. "Forms of Prayer." *Mercersburg Review*, XV (1868), 125-157.

Gerhart, E. V. "The German Reformed Church in America: Faith--Government--Worship." *Mercersburg Review*, XIV (1867), 249-277.

Harbaugh, Henry. "Reverence in Worship." *Mercersburg Review*, I (1849), 424-443.

Hodge, Charles. Review of *Eutaxia*. *The Biblical Repertory and Princeton Review*, XXVII (1855), 445-467.

_____. Review of *The Mystical Presence*. *The Biblical Repertory and Princeton Review*, XX (1848), 227-278.

_____. Review of *A Liturgy: or, Order of Christian Worship*. *The Biblical Repertory and Princeton Review*, XXX (1858), 182-183.

Krauth, Charles P. "The Liturgical Movement in the Presbyterian and Reformed Churches." *Mercersburg Review*.

Nevin, John W. "Anglican Crisis." *Mercersburg Review*, III (1851), 259-297.

_____. "The Apostles' Creed." *Mercersburg Review*, I (1849), 105-126, 201-221, 313-346.

_____. "Catholic Unity." Printed as an Appendix to Philip Schaff, *The Principle of Protestantism*.

_____. "The Christian Ministry." *Mercersburg Review*, VII (1855), 68-93.

_____. "The Church Year." *Mercersburg Review*, VIII (1856), 456-478.

_____. "Cyprian." *Mercersburg Review*, IV (1852), 259-277, 335-387, 417-452, 513-563.

_____. "Dr. Berg's Last Words." *Mercersburg Review*, IV (1852), 283-304.

_____. "Doctrine of the Reformed Church on the Lord's Supper." *Mercersburg Review*, II (1850), 421-549.

_____. "The Dutch Crusade." *Mercersburg Review*, VI (1854), 67-117.

_____. "Early Christianity." *Mercersburg Review*, III (1851), 461-489, 513-562; IV (1852), 1-54.

_____. "The Liturgical Movement." *Mercersburg Review*, I (1849), 608-612.

_____. "The New Creation in Christ." *Mercersburg Review*, II (1850), 1-11.

_____. "The Old Doctrine of Baptism." *Mercersburg Review*, XII (1860), 190-215.

_____. Review of Noel's "Essay on Christian Baptism," *Mercersburg Review*, II (1850), 231-264.

_____. "Theology of the New Liturgy." *Mercersburg Review*, XIV (1867), 23-67.

_____. "Thoughts on the Church." *Mercersburg Review*, X (1858), 169-198, 383-426.

_____. "True and False Protestantism." *Mercersburg Review*, I (1849), 83-104.

Schaff, Philip. "German Hymnology." Translated by T. C. Porter. *Mercersburg Review*, XII (1860), 228-250.

_____. "The New Liturgy." *Mercersburg Review*, X (1858), 199-228.

_____. Review of Baird's *Presbyterian Liturgies*. *Mercersburg Review*, VIII (1857), 324-326.

_____. Review of *A Liturgy: or Order of Christian Worship*. *Mercersburg Review*, X (1858), 165.

_____. "The Synod at Frederick." *Mercersburg Review*, XI (1859), 1-47.

Staley, George Lewis. "Preaching." *Mercersburg Review*, XVI (1869), 290-312.

Wolff, B. C. "Public Worship." *Mercersburg Review*, II
(1850), 296-307, 383-393.

III. *Liturgies*

Catholic Apostolic Church

The Liturgy and Other Divine Offices of the Church. Montreal:
Louell & Gibson, n.d.

The Liturgy and Other Divine Offices of the Church. New
York: J. R. M'Gown, 1851.

The Liturgy and Other Divine Offices of the Church. London:
Thomas Bosworth, 1880.

*The Order for the Daily Services of the Church and for Ad-
ministration of the Sacraments*. London: Printed by
Moyes and Barclay, n.d.

Dutch Reformed Church

*Church Book: Containing the Sacramental Offices of the
Reformed Dutch Church; Together with Other Offices
for Christian Service*. New York: Chas. Scribner &
Co., 1866.

The Liturgy of the Reformed Church in America. New York:
Board of Publication of the Reformed Church in America,
1873.

The Liturgy of the Reformed Church in America. New York:
Board of Publication of the Reformed Church in America,
[1882]

The Liturgy of the Reformed Dutch Church in North America.
New York: John A. Gray, Printer & Stereotyper, 1855.

*The Liturgy of the Reformed Protestant Dutch Church in
North America*. New York: Board of Publication of
the Reformed Protestant Dutch Church, [1857]

Dutch Reformed Church (cont.)

*The Psalms of David, with the Ten Commandments, Creed, Lord's
    Prayer, etc. in Metre. Also, the Catechism, Confession
    of Faith, Liturgy, etc.* Translated from the Dutch. For
    the Use of the Reformed Protestant Dutch Church of the
    City of New York. New York: Printed by James Parker,
    1767.

Episcopal Church

*The Book of Common Prayer and Administration of the Sacra-
    ments and Other Rites and Ceremonies of the Church
    According to the Use of the Church of England.* Oxford:
    Printed at the University Press, n.d.

*The Book of Common Prayer and Administration of the Sacra-
    ments and Other Rites and Ceremonies of the Church
    According to the Use of the Protestant Episcopal Church
    in the United States of America.* Greenwich, Conn.:
    The Seabury Press, 1953.

German Reformed Church

*The Book of Worship for the Reformed Church in the United
    States.* Philadelphia: The Publication and Sunday
    School Board of the Reformed Church in the United
    States, 1923.

*The Directory of Worship for the Reformed Church in the
    United States.* Reading, Pa.: Daniel Miller, Pub-
    lisher, 1884.

*Liturgy for the Use of the Congregations of the German Re-
    formed Church in the United States of North America.*
    Chambersburg, Pa.: Printed at the Publication Office
    of the German Reformed Church, 1841.

A Liturgy: or, Order of Christian Worship. Philadelphia:
    Lindsay & Blakiston, 1859.

A Liturgy, or Order of Worship for the Reformed Church.
    Cincinnati: T. P. Bucher, Publisher, 1869.

German Reformed Church (cont.)

An Order of Worship for the Reformed Church. Philadelphia:
S. R. Fisher & Co., Publishers, 1867.

Thompson, Bard, trans. "The Palatinate Liturgy." *Theology
and Life,* VI (1963), 49-67.

Presbyterian and Church of Scotland

Baird, Charles. *A Book of Public Prayer Compiled from the
Authorized Formularies of Worship of the Presbyterian
Church as Prepared by the Reformers Calvin, Knox, Bucer,
and Others; with Supplementary Forms.* New York:
Charles Scribner, 1857.

Bonar, Andrew A. *Presbyterian Liturgies with Specimens of
Forms of Prayer for Worship as Used in the Continental
Reformed, and American Churches; with the Directory for
the Public Worship of God agreed upon by the Assembly
of Divines at Westminster; and Forms of Prayer for
Ordinary and Communion Sabbaths, and for other Services
of the Church.* Edinburgh: Myles MacPhail, 1858.

The Book of Common Worship. Philadelphia: Presbyterian
Board of Publication and Sabbath-School Work, 1905.

The Church Book of St. Peter's Church, Rochester. Rochester:
Lee, Mann, & Co., 1855.

Comegys, B. B., ed. *Euchologion: The First Part and
Portions of the Second Part of a Book of Common Order:
Forms of Prayer Issued by the Church Service Society
of the Church of Scotland.* 2nd ed. Philadelphia:
Sherman & Co., 1898.

Hodge, Archibald Alexander. *Manual of Forms for Baptism,
Administration of the Lord's Supper, Marriage, and
Funerals. Conformed to the Doctrine and Discipline
of the Presbyterian Church.* Philadelphia: Presbyterian Board of Publication, 1877.

_____. *Manual of Forms for Baptism, Admission to the Com-
munion, Administration of the Lord's Supper, Marriage
and Funerals, Ordination of Elders and Deacons, etc.*
Philadelphia: Presbyterian Board of Publication, 1882.

Presbyterian and Church of Scotland (cont.)

Sprott, George W., ed. *Euchologion. A Book of Common Order: Being Forms of Prayer and Administration of the Sacraments, and Other Ordinances of the Church.* Edinburgh: William Blackwood and Sons, 1905.

Shields, Charles W. *The Book of Common Prayer and Administration of the Sacraments and Other Rites and Ceremonies of the Church as Amended by the Presbyterian Divines in the Royal Commission of 1661 and in Agreement with the Directory for Public Worship of the Presbyterian Church in the United States.* New York: Charles Scribner's Sons, 1864.

Compilations

Ebrard, A., ed. *Reformirtes Kirchenbuch.* Zurich: n.p., 1847.

Niesel, Wilhelm, ed. *Bekenntnisschriften und Kirchenordnungen der nach Gottes Wort reformierten Kirche.* Zurich: Evangelischer Verlag, 1938.

Thompson, Bard, ed. *Liturgies of the Western Church.* Cleveland: The World Publishing Company, [1961].

IV. *Synod Minutes and Constitutions*

Acts and Proceedings of the [Eastern] Synod of the German Reformed Church in the United States. Especially the following:
_____. Norristown, Pennsylvania, 1849.
_____. Martinsburg, [West] Virginia, 1850.
_____. Lancaster, Pennsylvania, 1851.
_____. Baltimore, Maryland, 1852.
_____. Allentown, Pennsylvania, 1857.
_____. Frederick City, Maryland, 1858.
_____. Chambersburg, Pennsylvania, 1862.
_____. Carlisle, Pennsylvania, 1863.
_____. Lancaster, Pennsylvania, 1864.

*Acts and Proceedings of the [Eastern] Synod of the German
Reformed Church in the United States.* (cont.)
_____. York, Pennsylvania, 1866.
_____. Baltimore, Maryland, 1867.
_____. Hagerstown, Maryland, 1868.
_____. Danville, Virginia, 1869.

*Acts and Proceedings of the General Synod of the German
Reformed Church in the United States.* Especially the
following:
_____. Pittsburgh, Pennsylvania, 1863.
_____. Dayton, Ohio, 1866.
_____. Philadelphia, Pennsylvania, 1869.
_____. Fort Wayne, Indiana, 1875.
_____. Lancaster, Pennsylvania, 1878.
_____. Tiffin, Ohio, 1881.
_____. Baltimore, Maryland, 1884.

*Acts and Proceedings of the General Synod of the Reformed
Protestant Dutch Church in North America.* Especially
the following:
_____. Philadelphia, Pennsylvania, 1853.
_____. Hudson, New York, 1854.
_____. New Brunswick, New Jersey, 1855.
_____. (Special Session.) New York, New York, 1855.
_____. Utica, New York, 1856.
_____. Ithica, New York, 1857.
_____. Newark, New Jersey, 1858.
_____. Hudson, New York, 1868.
_____. Newark, New Jersey, 1870.
_____. Albany, New York, 1871.
_____. Poughkeepsie, New York, 1874.
_____. Jersey City, New Jersey, 1875.
_____. Utica, New York, 1878.
_____. Schnectady, New York, 1882.
_____. Syracuse, New York, 1885.
_____. Catskill, New York, 1888.

*Constitution of the German Reformed Church in the United
States of North America.* Chambersburg, Pa.: M.
Kieffer & Co., 1850.

*Constitution of the Reformed Dutch Church in the United
States of America.* New York: Wm. Durell, 1793.

V. *Manuscripts*

Harbaugh, Henry. The Diary of Rev. Henry Harbaugh, D.D.
Copied from the original manuscript now in possession
of the Historical Society of the Evangelical and Reformed Church, located in the Philip Schaff Library
of the Lancaster Theological Seminary, Lancaster,
Pennsylvania.

Liturgical Discussion. A typed manuscript purporting to
be a record of the liturgical discussion at Chambersburg, Pennsylvania, October 1862. Historical Society
of the Evangelical and Reformed Church.

Minutes of the Liturgical Committee from March 13, 1856 to
October 17, 1866. Historical Society of the Evangelical and Reformed Church.

Original Manuscripts of *A Liturgy: or, Order of Christian
Worship* and *The Order of Worship*. Historical Society
of the Evangelical and Reformed Church.

SECONDARY SOURCES

I. *Books and Pamphlets*

Allmen, J.-J. von. *Worship: Its Theology and Practice.* New York: Oxford University Press, 1965.

Appel, Theodore. *The Life and Work of John Williamson Nevin.* Philadelphia: Reformed Church Publishing House, 1889.

_____. *Recollections of College Life at Marshall College, Mercersburg, Pennsylvania, from 1839-1845.* Reading, Pa.: Daniel Miller, Printer and Publisher, 1886.

[Baird, C. W.] *Eutaxia, or the Presbyterian Liturgies: Historical Sketches.* New York: M. W. Dodd, Publisher, 1855.

Binkley, Luther J. *The Mercersburg Theology.* Manheim, Pa.: Sentinel Printing House, 1953.

Bomberger, John H. A., Good, J. I., *et al. The Reverend John H. A. Bomberger, Centenary Volume.* Philadelphia: Publication and Sunday School Board of the Reformed Church in the United States, 1917.

Bready, Guy P. *History of Maryland Classis.* n.p.: By the Author, 1938.

Brenner, Scott F. *A Handbook on Worship: An Interpretation of the Book of Worship of the Evangelical and Reformed Church.* Philadelphia: The Heidelberg Press, 1941.

Brilioth, Yngve. *Eucharistic Faith and Practice: Evangelical and Catholic.* Translated by A. G. Herbert. London: Society for Promoting Christian Knowledge, 1930.

[Cardale, John Bate.] *Readings Upon the Liturgy and Other Divine Offices of the Church: On the Eucharist, and Daily Offices Connected Therewith.* London: Printed by George Barclay, 1851.

Corwin, E. T., Dubbs, J. H., and Hamilton, J. T. *A History of the Reformed Church, German, and the Moravian Church in the United States*. New York: The Christian Literature Co., 1895.

Cowley, Patrick. *The Eucharistic Church*. London: The Faith Press, Ltd., 1953.

Davies, J. G. *Worship and Mission*. New York: Association Press, 1967.

Demarest, David D. *The Reformed Church in America*. New York: Board of Publication of the Reformed Church in America, 1889.

Dubbs, Joseph Henry. *Historical Manual of the Reformed Church in the United States*. Lancaster: Inquirer Printing Co., 1885.

_____. *The Reformed Church in Pennsylvania*. Lancaster: The New Era Printing Co., 1902.

Good, James I. *History of the Reformed Church in the United States in the Nineteenth Century*. New York: The Board of Publication of the Reformed Church in America, 1911.

Hageman, Howard G. *Lily Among the Thorns*. Teaneck, N.J.: The Half Moon Press, 1961.

_____. *Pulpit and Table*. Richmond: John Knox Press, 1962.

Harbaugh, Linn. *Life of the Rev. Henry Harbaugh, D.D.* Philadelphia: Reformed Church Publication Board, 1900.

Hinkle, Gerald Hahn. "The Theology of the Ursinus Movement: Its Origins and Influence in the German Reformed Church." Unpublished Ph.D. dissertation, Yale University, 1964.

Janeway, J. J. *Antidote to the Poison of Popery in the Writings and Conduct of Professors Nevin and Schaff*. New Brunswick, N.J.: Press of J. Terhune, 1856.

Johnson, Robert Clyde, ed. *The Church and Its Changing Ministry*. Philadelphia: Office of the General Assembly of the United Presbyterian Church in the United States of America, [1961]

Kieffer, Elizabeth Clarke. *Henry Harbaugh, Pennsylvania Dutchman, 1817-1867*. Norristown, Pa.: Norristown Herald, Inc., 1945.

Klein, H. M. J. *The History of the Eastern Synod of the Reformed Church in the United States*. Lancaster, Pa.: Published by the Eastern Synod, 1943.

Kremer, A. R. *A Biographical Sketch of John Williamson Nevin*. Reading, Pa.: Daniel Miller, 1890.

Kuhns, Benjamine and Kelker, Rudolph R. *The Liturgical Conflict and the Peace Movement of the Reformed Church in the United States as Exhibited by the Official Records of the General Synod*. Dayton, Ohio: Press of the United Brethren Publishing House, 1896.

McNeill, John T. *The History and Character of Calvinism*. New York: Oxford University Press, 1962.

Martin, Samuel A., ed. *Thomas Conrad Porter, Essays, Verses, Translations*. Chambersburg, Pa.: Henderson and Mong, n.d.

Maxwell, W. D. *A History of Worship in the Church of Scotland*. London: Oxford University Press, 1955.

Melton, Julius. *Presbyterian Worship in America: Changing Patterns Since 1787*. Richmond: John Knox Press, 1967.

Miller, Edward. *The History and Doctrines of Irvingism*. 2 vols. London: C. Kegan Paul & Co., 1878.

Nichols, James Hastings. *Corporate Worship in the Reformed Tradition*. Philadelphia: Westminster Press, 1968.

_____. *History of Christianity, 1650-1950*. New York: The Ronald Press Company, 1956.

_____, ed. *The Mercersburg Theology*. New York: Oxford University Press, 1966.

_____. *Romanticism in American Theology*. Chicago: The University of Chicago Press, 1961.

Penzel, Klaus. "Church History and the Ecumenical Quest. A Study of the German Background and Thought of Philip Schaff." Unpublished Th.D. dissertation, Union Theological Seminary in the City of New York, 1962.

Richards, George W. *History of the Theological Seminary of the Reformed Church in the United States, 1825-1934, Evangelical and Reformed Church, 1934-1952.* Lancaster, Pa.: Rudisill & Co., Inc., 1952.

Routley, Eric. *Church Music and Theology.* London: SCM Press, Ltd., 1959.

Schaeffer, Charles E. *History of the Classis of Philadelphia of the Reformed Church in the United States.* Philadelphia: Published by the Classis of Philadelphia, 1944.

_____. *A Repairer of the Breach: The Memoirs of Bernard C. Wolff.* Lancaster, Pa.: The Historical Society of the Evangelical and Reformed Church, 1949.

Schaff, David S. *The Life of Philip Schaff.* New York: Charles Scribner's Sons, 1897.

Schaff, Philip. *Deutsches Gesangbuch.* Philadelphia: Lindsay und Blakiston, 1859.

Schneck, Benjamine Shroder. *Mercersburg Theology: Inconsistent with Protestant and Reformed Doctrine.* Philadelphia: Lippincott, 1874.

Seldomridge, Amos L. "A Study of the Office of Holy Communion from the Provisional Liturgy." Unpublished paper, Lancaster Theological Seminary, 1947.

Shaw, P. E. *The Catholic Apostolic Church.* Morningside Heights: King's Crown Press, 1946.

Shepherd, Massey Hamilton, Jr. *The Oxford American Prayer Book Commentary.* New York: Oxford University Press, [1950]

Sprott, George W. *The Worship and Offices of the Church of Scotland.* Edinburgh: William Blackwood and Sons, 1882.

Taylor, Michael J. *The Protestant Liturgical Renewal: A Catholic Viewpoint.* Westminster, Md.: The Newman Press, 1963.

Thompson, Bard, *et al. Essays on the Heidelberg Catechism.* Philadelphia: United Church Press, [1963].

Thompson, Bard. "Reformed Liturgies: An Historical and Doctrinal Interpretation of the Palatinate Liturgy of 1563, Mercersburg Provisional Liturgy of 1858, Evangelical and Reformed Order of 1944, and their Sources." Unpublished B.D. thesis, Union Theological Seminary in the City of New York, 1949.

Visher, Lukas, ed. *A Documentary History of the Faith and Order Movement, 1927-1963.* St. Louis: The Bethany Press, 1963.

White, James F. *The Worldliness of Worship.* New York: Oxford University Press, 1967.

Whitley, H. C. *Blinded Eagle.* Chicago: Alec R. Allenson, Inc., 1955.

II. *Articles*

Apple, Thomas G. "The Internal History of the Seminary." *Mercersburg Review*, XXIII (1876), 59-87.

Brenner, Scott F. "Nevin and the Mercersburg Theology." *Theology Today*, XII (1955), 43-56.

_____. "Philip Schaff the Liturgist." *Christendom*, XI (1946), 443-456.

Carlough, William L. "A Case Study in Protestant Sacramentalism." *Theology and Life*, VII (1964), 310-318.

Clemmer, Robert. "The Present Significance of the Mercersburg Theology." *Bulletin of the Theological Seminary of the Evangelical and Reformed Church*, XXI (1950), 11-23.

Davies, Horton. "Reshaping the Worship of the United Church of Christ." *Worship*, XLI (1967), 542-551.

Gerrish, B. A. "The Lord's Supper in the Reformed Confessions." *Theology Today*, XXIII (1966), 224-243.

Hageman, Howard G. "The Coming-of-Age of the Liturgical Movement." *Studia Liturgica*, II (1963), 256-265.

_____. Unpublished lectures on the History of the Liturgy of the Reformed Church in America, I, II, III.

Jansen, John Frederick. "Calvin on a Fixed Form of Worship. A Note in Textual Criticism." *Scottish Journal of Theology*, XV (1962), 282-287.

Nichols, James Hastings. "Is the New 'Service' Reformed?" *Theology Today*, XXI (1964), 361-370.

_____. "The Liturgical Tradition of the Reformed Churches." *Theology Today*, XI (1954), 210-224.

Niesel, Wilhelm. "The Order of Public Worship in the Reformed Churches." *Scottish Journal of Theology*, II (1949), 381-390.

Richards, George W. "The Mercersburg Theology--Its Purpose and Principles." *Church History*, XX (1951), 42-55.

Slifer, Franklin D. "The Traditions of Worship in the Evangelical and Reformed Church." Unpublished paper in the Archives of the Philip Schaff Library, Lancaster Theological Seminary, Lancaster, Pennsylvania.

Slifer, Morris D. "The Liturgical Tradition of the Reformed Church in the U.S.A." *Studia Liturgica*, I (1962), 228-240.

Wentz, Richard. "The World of Mercersburg Theology." In John W. Nevin, *The Mystical Presence*. Hamden, Conn.: Archon Books, 1963.

BIBLIOGRAPHICAL NOTE

Because manuscripts and denominational newspapers have been used so extensively in this research on the nineteenth-century German Reformed Liturgies, a Bibliographical Note is in order. Fortunately, it can be brief and pointed, since James Hastings Nichols has already covered the broader field of the Mercersburg movement in a corresponding "Note" in his volume, *Romanticism in American Theology*. [See pp. 313-316.]

Concerning the liturgical material *per se*, the library of the Historical Society of the Evangelical and Reformed Church, housed in the Philip Schaff Library of the Lancaster Theological Seminary, possesses the largest collection of manuscripts. Here are the minutes of the liturgical committee which produced the Provisional Liturgy, the *Order of Worship* and the *Directory of Worship*. Published copies of the Provisional Liturgy owned by Wolff, Fisher, and Gerhart are available, as are the dairies of Harbaugh, Theodore Appel, and Philip Schaff. A fascinating collection of Harbaugh's effects is to be found in "Harbaugh's Altar". Several boxes of correspondence complete the manuscripts most pertinent to the liturgical question.

The *Weekly Messenger* (Chambersburg) and the *Mercersburg Review* are imperative to any research on the German Reformed Church in the nineteenth century. The *Review* was first published in 1849 and contains the lengthier articles by the Mercersburg principals. This journal can be found in a number of libraries. Prior to 1849 the *Messenger* bore the weight of the Mercersburg controversy, and after 1849 it continued to carry most of the material pertaining to the liturgical debate. During the more heated years, rarely was a weekly issue printed which did not contain several exchanges concerning liturgical matters. Unfortunately the correspondents often used pseudonyms. As noted by Nichols, a useful, although incomplete Index to the *Messenger* has been compiled by Guy P..Bready and is available, along with the *Messenger*, in the Philip Schaff Library.

The *Christian Intelligencer* (New York), Reformed Dutch counterpart of the *Weekly Messenger*, contains the largest amount of anti-Mercersburg writing. Like the *Messenger*, the *Intelligencer* is not readily accessible; however, a complete set is to be found in the Library of the New Brunswick Theological Seminary. Also there one will find editions of the several provisional Liturgies of the Dutch Church.

Liturgical material pertaining to the Catholic Apostolic Church is rare in this country. Speer Library of the Princeton Theological Seminary has what this writer believes to be the first edition of the Liturgy (1842). Copies of the 1880 edition are to be found at the Lancaster Theological Seminary and the Union Theological Seminary in the City of New York. By far the largest collection of Catholic Apostolic Liturgies is located in the Library of the General Theological Seminary in New York City.

The Library of Ursinus College has catalogued the remnants of John H. A. Bomberger's personal library. This collection is interesting, but not particularly helpful to one pursuing the liturgical question, primarily because so many of Bomberger's volumes are no longer extant. His correspondence--what few letters have been preserved--is to be found in the Historical Society of the Evangelical and Reformed Church.